CANADIAN EVANGELICALISM IN THE TWENTIETH CENTURY

Canadians usually associate evangelical Protestantism with television evangelists and the new religious right in American politics. In this first portrait of Canadian evangelicalism in the twentieth century, John Stackhouse argues that Canadian evangelicalism is far from being either an echo of an American phenomenon or a residue of the British heritage, but instead is distinctly Canadian. He also points out that Canadian evangelicalism has become a powerful force in contemporary Canadian religion.

Stackhouse disputes the church-sect typology of previous studies and also challenges the accepted wisdom that flamboyant preachers like the fundamentalist T.T. Shields and preacher-turned-politician William Aberhart represent evangelicalism in Canada. On the contrary, he says, the true character of the tradition is more accurately found in Bible schools like the internationally known Prairie Bible Institute and the Ontario Bible College, seminaries such as Regent College and Ontario Theological Seminary, liberal arts institutions like Trinity Western University, student ministries such as the Inter-Varsity Christian Fellowship, and cooperative organizations typified by the Evangelical Fellowship of Canada.

This book complements current studies of Canadian evangelicalism in earlier periods and is informed by recent scholarship in Canadian, American, and British religion. It brings fresh insights to a field that is drawing increasing interest.

JOHN G. STACKHOUSE, JR, is an associate professor in the Department of Religion, University of Manitoba.

Canadian Evangelicalism in the Twentieth Century

An Introduction to Its Character

John G. Stackhouse, Jr

UNIVERSITY OF TORONTO PRESS
Toronto Buffalo London

Toronto Buffalo London
Printed in Canada

ISBN 0-8020-0509-8 (cloth)
ISBN 0-8020-7468-5 (paper)

Printed on acid-free paper

Canadian Cataloguing in Publication Data

Stackhouse, John G.
Canadian evangelicalism in the twentieth century

Includes bibliographical references and index.
ISBN 0-8020-0509-8 (bound) ISBN 0-8020-7468-5 (pbk.)

1. Evangelicalism – Canada – History – 20th century.
2. Canada – Church history – 20th century.
I. Title.

BR1642.C3S83 1993 270.8'2 C93-093888-7

This book has been published with the help of a grant from the Canadian Federation for the Humanities, using funds provided by the Social Sciences and Humanities Research Council of Canada.

To Kari
again
of course

Contents

Preface

In these postmodern times, a historian ought to declare his or her stance from the outset. One of the ways one can do this is to make substantive statements. So I shall say that I write about Canadian evangelicalism as an insider, as one raised in this tradition and still personally involved in it. Yet I undertook much of the research for this book while studying in the United States under American supervision, so that on research trips I encountered Canada as something of a foreign country, and examined Canadian evangelicalism as a network of which I was not, at the time, a part. The revision of the original doctoral dissertation towards the present form then took place first while I taught European history at Northwestern College in Iowa, another experience that provided some appropriate personal distancing from the subject. The book came to final form after I returned to Canada in 1990. And my subsequent contacts with Canadian evangelicalism, both scholarly and personal, provided new material and insights towards this end. The result, then, bears some of the marks of a 'family history,' for good and for ill, while my personal peregrinations have provided more than a simple 'insider' angle of vision on the matter.

Another way to make one's authorial position more clear, though, is to acknowledge the debts one has accumulated during the project. And this is by far the more pleasant path of the two. It was a conversation with George Rawlyk on his back porch one summer afternoon that convinced me that there might be something in twentieth-century Canadian evangelicalism worth my studying. George has offered his characteristically incisive advice at key points since. Ian Rennie put his extraordinary mental database and personal library at my disposal several times. And conversations with a number of other friends greatly improved the shaping of this study, particularly those with Doug Anderson, Bob Burkinshaw, Matthew Floding, Bryan Hillis, Larry Hurtado, Brian McKenzie, Rebecca Nelson, and Ron Sawatsky.

More than a dozen librarians provided guidance and materials, often well beyond the call of their already high duty. The staffs of the following libraries provided notable help: the Joseph Regenstein Library of the University of Chicago, the National Library of Canada, the J. William Horsey Library of Ontario Bible College and Ontario Theological Seminary, the Prairie Bible Institute Library, the Regent College Library, the Vernon Strombeck Library of Trinity Western University, and the Billy Graham Center Library and Archives at Wheaton College. Extraordinary help, especially in obtaining a quantity of interlibrary loan materials, was given cheerfully by the staffs of the J.O. Buswell Memorial Library of Wheaton College, the Ramaker Library of Northwestern College, and the Elizabeth Dafoe Library of the University of Manitoba.

Robert Wright and the late Keith Clifford contributed copies of their wide-ranging bibliographies on Canadian religion at key points in my research. Leaders and staffs of the seven institutions studied provided a broad range of help, including the opportunity to examine historic documents of their institutions. The following individuals in particular deserve mention: President William J. MacRae of Ontario Bible College and Ontario Theological Seminary, President Ted S. Rendall of Prairie Bible Institute, General Director James E. Berney of Inter-Varsity Christian Fellowship, President R. Neil Snider and Executive Assistant Jackson McAllister of Trinity Western University, Principal Carl E. Armerding of Regent College, and Executive Director Brian C. Stiller of the Evangelical Fellowship of Canada. It is most encouraging to note that at least some of these institutions have begun to catalogue and store such materials in archives for future researchers.

Pursuing such a study over a country as vast as Canada required many weeks away from home. For companionship and accommodation, I thank the proprietors of the following worthy establishments: the Annan-Cuthbertson Arms, the Barnard Barn, Enns' Inn, the Hillis Hilton, the Humbervale Hideaway, the Lunau Lodge, and Randy's Rest. Upon return, a lot of sorting, filing, data entry, and retrieval of still more material had to be done, and I have enjoyed the services of several excellent research assistants: Michael Haverdink, Crystal Dykstra, Jena Dukes, Gordon Richardson, Mary Massel, and Jacqueline Klassen.

The Canadian Studies Program of the Canadian Embassy to the United States funded a large part of the initial research. Further assistance was provided generously by the Institute for the Study of American Evangelicals and the Social Sciences and Humanities Research Council of Canada.

Anatole France once pronounced, 'All the historical books which contain no lies are extremely tedious.' The fewness of lies in this study can be traced to the careful reading of some portions of the book by the following colleagues: Ian S. Rennie of Ontario Theological Seminary; James E. Berney and Melvin V. Donald of Inter-Varsity Christian Fellowship; Keith A. Price of 'Sermons from Science' and the Evangelical Fellowship of Canada; Kenneth R. Davis of Trinity Western University; Carl E. Armerding of Regent College; Brian C. Stiller of the Evangelical Fellowship of Canada; and George M. Marsden of the University of Notre Dame. Jerald Brauer and Langdon Gilkey of the University of Chicago evaluated the original dissertation with exemplary care. Later drafts of the book were improved by the comments of several anonymous reviewers associated with the University of Toronto Press and the Canadian Federation for the Humanities. And editors Ron Schoeffel, Anne Forte, and John St James of the University of Toronto Press refined the manuscript still further. The blame for the lies that remain in this study, therefore, as well as for the tediousness thereof, must be placed upon whom it belongs, and not on these helpful souls.

It is a privilege to gain a mentor, and a rare privilege to gain two. Mark A. Noll and Martin E. Marty have been instructing, prodding, provoking, consoling, and inspiring me now for more than a decade. And they have done so with wisdom, humour, firmness, and (a favourite word of Marty's) *disponibilité*. 'The lif so short, the craft so long to lerne,' Chaucer observed, and I look forward to walking farther down the road they have marked out.

Family members contributed much-needed sums of babysitting time, prayer, and financial assistance: thanks to Jayne and David Gaddy, Cindra and Daniel Stackhouse Taetzsch, and Colleen and Jerry Sleeth. My parents Yvonne and John Stackhouse, who introduced me (in)to Canadian evangelicalism, have provided extraordinary encouragement in this regard. From their adopted home of

Abilene, Texas, they have whimsically appeared in the acknowledgments of previous publications as (at last it can be told) the 'Abilene Foundation,' and no foundation was ever more supportive of its client.

Our two sons, Trevor and Joshua, at ages six and four have passed the stage in which they literally followed Lord Bacon's dictum that 'some books are to be tasted, others to be swallowed, and some few to be chewed and digested.' It is a measure of their mother's stewardship of husband and home that, unlike many authors, I have few apologies to render to my family for evenings and weekends spent on this project: the boys, happily, have no idea that this book even exists. For that stewardship – strong, sweet, constant, and necessary – I am gratefully delighted to dedicate this book.

JGS
February 1993

Some material in this book has been adapted from the following articles by the author and is used by permission: 'The Emergence of a Fellowship: Canadian Evangelicalism in the Twentieth Century,' *Church History* 60 (June 1991); 'The Protestant Experience in Canada since 1945,' in *The Canadian Protestant Experience 1760–1990*, ed. George A. Rawlyk (Burlington, Ont.: Welch 1990); 'Respectfully Submitted for American Consideration: Canadian Options in Christian Higher Education,' *Faculty Dialogue* no. 17 (1992); 'William Aberhart' and 'Thomas Todhunter Shields,' in *Twentieth-Century Shapers of American Popular Religion*, ed. Charles H. Lippy (© 1989 by Charles H. Lippy; Greenwood Press 1989; an imprint of Greenwood Publishing Group, Inc., Westport, Ct.; reprinted with permission).

CANADIAN EVANGELICALISM IN THE TWENTIETH CENTURY

Introduction

In the 1980s, evangelical Protestantism emerged as a prominent new force in Canada. While political campaigns and sexual scandals among American evangelicals attracted attention north of the border as well, Canadian evangelicals were quietly establishing a network of individuals and institutions that reflected their distinctive concerns. While the United, Anglican, and Presbyterian churches continued to enjoy 'mainline Protestant' status in Canadian culture, more Canadians who actually practised Christianity in measurable ways could be counted among the evangelicals than among these dominant Protestant denominations. And while most Canadians – including experts in religious studies – continued to think of Canadian Christianity in traditional denominational terms, 'evangelicalism' was coming into focus as a category essential to understanding this new pattern of allegiance and activity.

The increasing prominence of evangelicalism in the 1980s and 1990s was manifest in a number of ways. For instance, in the mid-1980s, the United Church of Canada, the nation's largest Protestant denomination, sponsored Canada's third-largest theological seminary, Emmanuel College at the University of Toronto. Canada's largest two seminaries in the late 1980s and early 1990s, however, had been founded by evangelicals only a decade or so before: Regent College in Vancouver (begun as a full-time school in 1970) and Ontario Theological Seminary in metropolitan Toronto (begun in 1976).[1] Furthermore, thousands more students enrolled for theological education in Bible institutes and colleges, numbers that dwarfed enrolment in similar lay-training schools outside evangelicalism.[2]

To select a second criterion, evangelicals sent out far more missionaries than did the traditionally dominant Protestant churches of Canada – the United, Anglican, and Presbyterian churches. Three tiny evangelical denominations, for instance, the Associated Gospel Churches, the Christian and Missionary Alliance, and the Christian (or 'Plymouth') Brethren, each comprised no more than about one-tenth of one per cent of the Canadian population at this time. But each supported more missionaries to other countries than did all of the much larger three churches together.[3] To be sure, the relatively low numbers of staff sent out by the larger churches reflected an explicit policy of supporting through various other means the indigenous churches of other nations rather than continuing the traditional model of sending Canadian personnel. This shift in the understanding of 'mission,' therefore, helps to qualify this comparison.[4] Evangelicals themselves, however, would not have been persuaded of this policy, seeing it as abandoning a still-necessary form of missionary activity, and so they continued to hold high the traditional missionary ideal of personal sacrifice on behalf of those in other countries, and did so in considerable numbers.

Third, the mainline denominations in Canada through the years sponsored a number of clubs and organizations for young people on up to college age, like the Canadian Girls in Training or the Student Christian Movement.[5] Both of these, however, were largely in eclipse by this period, while the ministry of the Inter-Varsity Christian Fellowship was blossoming. And if one adds to this total the work of other transdenominational evangelical groups like Youth for Christ, the Navigators, Young Life, Campus Crusade for Christ, Child Evangelism Fellowship, Awana Clubs, and Pioneer Clubs – much less the denominational and congregational fellowships for young people unassociated with these groups – it is clear that evangelicals led the way in working with youth.

Fourth, it is a commonplace that evangelicals have long dominated religious broadcasting in Canada, especially at the local level. Religious programming on the national networks was rare (CBC's 'Man Alive' was perhaps the best example) and was scarcely favourable to evangelicalism, much less representative of it. None the less, popular radio pioneers like William Aberhart of Alberta gave way to television preachers like Terry Winter of British Columbia and David Mainse of Ontario (several of whom amassed significant audiences in the United States and Canada), and no one has yet counted what must have been hundreds of radio and television stations in Canada that, each week, carried evangelical programs.[6]

Among the most telling data, however, were those amassed by Dennis M. Oliver. In a paper delivered to the Canadian Society of Church History in 1979, Oliver developed statistics that measured the 'active constituencies' of Canada's churches,[7] rather than mere nominal 'adherence' to the churches. Oliver concluded that the total of the 'active constituencies' of the so-called 'believers' churches' (for instance, Baptist, Mennonite, Christian and Missionary Alliance) was greater than the total of those of the paedo-baptist churches (for example, United Church, Anglican, Reformed). More important for our purposes is his conclusion that those denominations that would happily have accepted the designation 'evangelical' or 'conservative evangelical' (including most Baptist churches, all Pentecostal churches, some Mennonites, and a number of independent traditions and churches) had a total Sunday morning attendance greater than that of the United Church of Canada. The final step was to consider that if one added the total attendance of these avowedly evangelical denominations to the numbers of those in pluralistic churches who would consider themselves evangelicals (such as those in the renewal fellowships of the United and Presbyterian churches and evangelical Anglicans), the balance tilted entirely to the evangelical side as representing, in Oliver's phrase, 'the strongest orientation within Canadian Protestantism.'[8]

Almost a decade later, sociologist Reginald Bibby sustained this basic pattern in his widely read study, *Fragmented Gods: The Poverty and Potential of Religion in Canada* (1987).[9] He found that 60 per cent of the Protestants he called 'Conservative' attended church weekly as compared with only 13 per cent of those in the United Church. Given that the 'Conservative' churches (which Bibby identified with 'believers' churches,' thus excluding those of evangelical convictions in the 'paedo-baptist' denominations) together included a little under 10 per cent of Canadians while the United Church served a little less than 20 per cent, the statistics here (and others regarding religious belief and practice) bore out Oliver's thesis that the religious commitment of evangelicals was significantly higher than that of persons in the large, mainline Protestant denominations. And all of this pointed to a significant orientation – if not in fact the *dominant* orientation – in Canadian Protestantism.

This characterization of evangelicalism in Canada, however, would have come as news (if not necessarily 'good news'!) to many Canadians of the time. A popular tract written by a United Church official in the early 1980s, for instance, characterized Canadian evangelicalism as, at best, a diluted version of the worst excesses of right-wing American evangelicalism.[10] A profile of Canadian Christianity in a thoughtful journal by the noted author Robertson Davies suggested that the 'soul of Canada' was best represented by the Roman Catholic, United, Anglican, Presbyterian, Lutheran, and Orthodox churches. Davies portrayed evangelicalism only as fundamentalism and as a pursuit of the few.[11] Even in scholarly treatments of Canadian Christianity published at this time, one looks in vain for an adequate characterization of Canadian evangelicalism in the twentieth century and for an estimate of its influence in Canadian life.[12]

Several scholars have begun the latter of these two tasks, notably Oliver and Bibby.[13] Much remains to be done, however, in assessing evangelicalism's place in and contribution to Canadian culture in general and to the cultures of Canada's particular regions and peoples.[14] The former task, that of *characterizing* evangelicalism in Canada – its constituents, concerns, and institutional expressions – has not yet been attempted in any full way. That is the burden of this study.

A definition of the key term 'evangelicalism' is here overdue. Initially it should be distinguished from the words 'evangelism' and 'evangelistic' that, although sometimes used as synonyms for 'evangelicalism' and 'evangelical,' in fact have to do with proselytizing per se, with the action of declaring the Christian message to others. 'Evangelicalism' and 'evangelical,' on the other hand, denote the broader categories that follow.

'Evangelical' has several designations. It can mean, especially in German- and Spanish-speaking areas, simply 'Protestant' – those churches that stand in the tradition of Martin Luther's articulation of the gospel (from Latin *evangelium*, Greek *euaggelion*, or 'good news'). In Germany and Switzerland, somewhat confusingly, the term has also been used to distinguish the particular Lutheran Protestants from those Protestants who followed Ulrich Zwingli and John Calvin, known as 'Reformed.' A third common use of 'evangelical' (and, as in the preceding cases, usually spelled with an upper-case 'E') is to identify a particular party of the Church of England that arose in the eighteenth century to reinvigorate the church by emphasizing personal conversion, salvation by faith in the atonement of Christ, the unique authority of the Bible, the importance of preaching (with a relative minimizing of liturgical worship), and the imminence of Christ's second coming.[15]

A fourth definition of 'evangelical,' however, has to do with the noun 'evangelicalism' described in this study. 'Evangelicalism' here refers to a group of movements in church history with both shared concerns and actual links. That is, this group looks back to the Protestant Reformation for its emphasis upon the unique authority of Scripture and salvation through faith alone in Christ. It adds to these convictions concern for warm piety in the context of a disciplined life and for the evangelism of all people. And this group holds these convictions as so important that members of it join with Christians – often of other denominations – in order to further these concerns, even if these others hold different views of important but less crucial matters. Those people described thereby are 'evangelicals' (and not 'evangelists,' a term that usually denotes people engaged vocationally in the activity of 'evangelism'). And examples of them are the Puritans of England and America, the Pietists of Germany, Methodists, Baptists, 'nineteenth-century restorationists, revivalists, black Christians, holiness groups, Pentecostals, and others.'[16] Timothy L. Smith outlines their common concerns: 'An evangelical ... is one who, since the time of John and Charles Wesley, George Whitefield, Jonathan Edwards, and August Francke, has believed that his or her religious life should rest fully upon the Hebrew and Christian Scriptures; that the center of those Scriptures is the promise of moral and spiritual rebirth through faith in Jesus Christ and the gift of God's Holy Spirit; and that, on both these accounts, believers should be devoted to evangelism, that is, to persuading lost persons to trust in Christ, and in that faith be born again.'[17] The word 'evangelical,' to be sure, sometimes is used as a pure and normative 'type.' In this case, a set of convictions such as these is set out in the abstract and then used as a canon to measure which groups or individuals are or are not 'evangelical.'[18] There is always, therefore, something of a 'chicken-or-egg' problem here: does the abstract definition come out of study of indubitably evangelical groups, or does the identification of those groups depend in the first place upon some abstract definition? This study leans heavily towards the first alternative: 'evangelicalism' is defined by the character of those Christians who belong to the broad historic stream that flows out of the sixteenth-century Protestant Reformation, down through the Puritan and Pietist channels, and into the so-called evangelical revivals of the eighteenth century. Those who (a) descend from these sources *without departing from the central convictions that defined them in the first place,* or who (b) later join up with the mainstream, are likewise identified as 'evangelical.'

Throughout Canadian history, from the eighteenth-century New Light revivals in the Maritimes and the Methodist incursions into that region and Upper Canada, there were a number of important individuals and organizations that maintained those concerns usually identified with 'evangelicalism.' Indeed, by the nineteenth century the Baptists and Methodists formed the dominant culture in the Anglophone Maritimes even as some of their revivalistic ardor cooled. George Rawlyk has asserted, 'By the late nineteenth century, ... one in four New Brunswickers was a Baptist, and one in five Nova Scotians, but only one in twenty Islanders; about one in ten persons was a Methodist in New Brunswick and Nova Scotia combined and one in eight on Prince Edward Island.' This dominance, Rawlyk goes on, had considerable effect: 'The political culture of the region ... had congealed by the 1850s into something "fundamentally conservative" and traditional and this process of congealment owed a great deal to the power of Evangelical religion in this region.'[19]

In Ontario, the situation was somewhat more complex. The growth of Methodism came in the teeth of resistance from the Anglican bishop and government officials. Throughout the first third or so of the nineteenth century the Methodists responded by questioning the assumed privileges of the Church of England. Indeed, under the leadership of Egerton Ryerson (1803–82), the Methodists joined with others to challenge government support of the Church of England, especially through the Clergy Reserves, and by mid-century the Church of England was effectively disestablished.

This levelling of denominations, however, had an ironic result. Methodism rose to rival the Anglicans in numbers even as it helped to reduce the Anglican church to the level of one-among-many, but simultaneously Ontarian culture became significantly more secular. Increasingly, the churches began to feel the threat of marginalization – just when some former sects, like the Methodists, thought they had come into the centre – and the churches began to adopt similar strategies for influencing the new country after 1867. William Westfall has shown this trend graphically by demonstrating the proliferation of a general style of 'Ontario gothic' in church architecture during the latter half of the nineteenth century. Methodists, no less than Anglicans or Presbyterians, erected medieval buildings to symbolize their determination to assert a Christian moral order in a society increasingly preoccupied with material gain.[20]

In many respects this Christian consensus – an evangelical consensus – won important victories, whether in Lord's Day legislation, poor relief, temperance, and so on. The Methodist, Presbyterian, and Baptist colleges, forerunners of some of Canada's most important universities, educated society's leaders in the 'evangelical creed.'[21] The evangelicalism of the outsiders became more and more the evangelicalism of the insiders. Rather than denouncing and prophesying to the culture from its margins, now evangelicals enjoyed status in the culture as they attempted to improve it. As John Webster Grant has put it, 'in those days ... the term "evangelical" denoted a belief in the transforming power of faith in Christ to which the great majority of Protestants would have laid claim.' Indeed, he continues, 'by 1867 church and world were virtually identical in composition.'[22]

A number of evangelical institutions, furthermore, represented a commitment to these basic evangelical concerns that transcended denominational distinctives and led to cooperation with others in matters of joint concern. Indeed, typical of such organizations and the evangelicals they represented was the belief that these common convictions were more important, more fundamental, than the beliefs that separated them from each other in denominations. Few of these Christians, to be sure, advocated abandoning denominational distinctives entirely, but they clearly saw this commonality as a kind of ecumenism and were committed to this transdenominational identity and cooperation per se. That is, these Christians were committed to 'transdenominational evangelicalism,' the belief that the evangelical 'basics' are most important in Christianity and that transdenominational cooperative action should be undertaken on this basis. Voluntary societies thus sprung up in Canada to deal with a variety of issues. Sunday schools, YMCAs and YWCAs, temperance and missionary societies, publishing houses, and evangelistic enterprises all brought differently-denominated Christians together for worthy causes.[23]

So as the twentieth century dawned, evangelicalism in Canada had established a variegated heritage. Within it was a prophetic, spiritual, 'outsider' tradition reaching back to Henry Alline in eighteenth-century Nova Scotia but continuing among the Millerites, Plymouth Brethren, and Salvation Army in the nineteenth. Within it also, however, was a pastoral, socially conscious, 'insider' tradition reaching back to Egerton Ryerson and coming to dominate Anglophone culture – albeit with regional differences – in both the Maritimes and Ontario. Both types of this complex heritage would become manifest among evangelicals in the twentieth century as well, as this narrative will demonstrate.

At the risk of obfuscating an already complicated semantical problem, one might see the Canadian Christians who cooperated across denominational lines as at least implicitly committed to the *idea* or even *ideology* of 'evangelical*ism*.' Thus they might be termed 'evangelical*ists*.' There were others, by contrast,who were not so committed, those who saw other issues as primary also or instead, and so would not have joined up with such a coalition. In particular, those denominations of strong denominational*ism*, who tended to see everything about the denomination as important, would have had trouble compromising *anything* in order to cooperate. These non-joiners, then, who would none the less have shared those basic evangelical doctrines and concerns with others, would be seen as generic 'evangelicals' per se, members of the set one might call (with apologies to C.S. Lewis) 'mere evangelicality.'

Making thus a distinction between the more generic 'evangelicalism' ('mere evangelicality') and the particular conviction of 'transdenominational evangelicalism' ('evangelical*ism*') might be valid enough, but there is no obvious nomenclature to distinguish persons belonging to the one group from those in the other. One could use the standard term 'evangelical' for the former, inclusive group and 'transdenominational evangelical' for those identified with 'evangelicalism' in this special sense, but the latter term might inaccurately misrepresent evangelicals who none the less maintained denominational identities. Indeed, the term 'nondenominational' should be reserved for instances in which denominational differences are eroded or even explicitly resisted and the term 'interdenominational' reserved for instances of official cooperation among denominations.[24] One could resort instead to a neologism, 'evangelicalist,' for this more narrowly defined group, but its unfamiliarity might engender its own confusions. In this book, then, 'evangelical' as both noun and adjective will denote particularly the transdenominational sort of evangelicalism at the focus of this study, with the hope that context will make clear the particular instances when the larger sense of 'evangelical' is meant.

It is important in this context also to be clear about the several definitions of the term 'fundamentalist' and its relationship to 'evangelical.' While in the 1980s 'fundamentalism' became a generic term used for any sort of militantly anti-modernist religion, with the Shi'ite Islam of Iran particularly in view, its definition as such derives from the American scene.[25] Originally it was a positive term, coined by magazine editor Curtis Lee Laws in 1920 for those who maintained the essential 'fundamentals of the faith' against modern attacks from liberal or modernist theology (following the publication between 1910 and 1915 of the booklet series known as *The Fundamentals*). In this positive sense the term was used in America, and in Canada and Britain as well, at least into the 1950s.[26] The controversies of the 1920s, however, brought out its chief characteristic of militancy, of a crusading spirit against what it saw to be modern threats to the faith. Following the *débâcle* of the Scopes 'monkey trial' over evolution in 1925, fundamentalism became stereotyped as Southern, rural, and anti-intellectual. In fact, fundamentalism was more typically led by Northern, urban, educated men who industriously set about building a network of institutions that would substitute for the colleges, seminaries, missionary societies, and so on that they had lost to their enemies. Out of this network after the Second World War emerged the so-called new evangelicals, those typically associated with the National Association of Evangelicals, Wheaton College, Fuller Theological Seminary, and *Christianity Today* magazine.[27] These 'evangelicals' retained the doctrinal orthodoxy of their fundamentalist forebears, but denounced the insularity of this community, its fear of modern learning, and its abandonment of social responsibility. 'Fundamentalism,' then, especially after 1960, became the more marked by separatism and, in particular, by the distinctive practice of 'second-degree separation': separation not only from those who compromise the faith ('first-degree separation'), but also from those, admittedly fully orthodox, who none the less do not themselves separate from the unorthodox.[28] (The most conspicuous *bête noire* here was Billy Graham who, while indubitably conservative in theology, yet included liberals and Roman Catholics in his crusades.) It is a paradox that certain fundamentalists engaged wholeheartedly in politics in the 1980s, having avoided that arena for generations (almost literally since William Jennings Bryan's humiliation over the Scopes trial), with the hopes that a 'Moral Majority' could bring America back to a kind of generic 'Judeo-Christian' righteousness. With the embarrassments and disappointments of the later Reagan and Bush years, however, this project seemed to run out of steam at the national level (although some saw it relocating to grass-roots politics instead). And many fundamentalists typically went back to their gospel-preaching enclaves.[29]

In arriving at a Canadian definition, then, to distinguish 'fundamentalist Protestantism' from the larger category of 'evangelicalism' that includes it as a constituent, we can provisionally appropriate the leading characteristics of American fundamentalism: militant opposition to modernity – especially modern ideas (liberal theology, biblical criticism, and evolution chief among them) – and separation from all who are not wholly pure in their convictions and associations. This study will demonstrate that there was a Canadian fundamentalism *of this sort* in the twentieth century (exemplified by T.T. Shields and discussed in part 1, chapter 1), but that it was not in fact central to Canadian evangelicalism.[30]

To trace out, then, the characteristics of evangelicalism (*transdenominational* evangelicalism), this study examines important institutions that evangelicals came together to support. Rather than examining denominational institutions that manifested indubitable evangelical characteristics, that is, but yet could also manifest denominational peculiarities, this book focuses on institutions that all were self-consciously transdenominational.[31] Careful examination of several such institutions, then, ought to make clear those things that have characterized Canadian evangelicalism in the twentieth century and even indicate important differences within this orientation.

It is important to be clear about what is and what is not being attempted here. This is not a comprehensive history of all Canadian individuals, movements, institutions, and so on that could be called 'evangelical' in the broad sense. It is not even a history of all those that would fit into the 'transdenominational evangelical' category – which explains why important individuals like R.V. Bingham, Oswald J. Smith, and David Mainse are not discussed at length, nor are institutions like Briercrest Bible College, the Sudan Interior Mission, or Child Evangelism Fellowship. It is, instead, an initial character sketch of the fellowship as a whole drawn largely from profiles of a few key institutions, an outline that further research should fill in and modify.

In Canada, scholarly treatment of evangelicalism in the twentieth century has been limited almost entirely to a 'church-sect' typology, in which the mainline denominations (the Roman Catholic, United, Anglican, and Presbyerian – and, for some, the groups making up the Canadian Baptist Federation) are 'churches' and groups like the Salvation Army and Pentecostals are 'sects.'[32] The original meanings of these terms, as formulated by Max Weber (1864–1920) and Ernst Troeltsch (1865–1923) in a Europe of state churches, do not apply exactly to the Canadian situation in which there are no established churches and dissenting sects. By derivation, however, the terms have come to denote something like the following. A 'church' is a denomination that enjoys status in the culture, participates in the culture, and indeed manifests something of a proprietorial interest in the culture. It includes many whose allegiance is only nominal and typically comprises a variety of views and practices (remnant of the 'territorial church' idea) as part of its stature as a broadly 'accepted' and 'accepting' denomination. The 'sect,' by contrast, enjoys no status in the culture but rather consciously separates itself from it. It is made up only of 'believers,' only of those who consciously join it and who maintain its intellectual and behavioural discipline. The understanding of Canadian Christianity governed by this typology, then, has led to some important conclusions, but conclusions that need serious qualification or even revision in the light of the present study.[33]

First, the 'church-sect' model correctly identifies centres of Canadian evangelicalism in Toronto and the Alberta prairie (although it tends to ignore the Atlantic Provinces, home to strong Baptist and Presbyterian evangelical traditions in the Maritimes and Salvationist and Pentecostal traditions in Newfoundland[34]). It does so, however, generally by identifying these places with the careers of two prominent individuals, T.T. Shields, the Baptist fundamentalist, and William Aberhart, the Baptist preacher-turned-politician. Yet this characterization is not correct. Part 1 of this study demonstrates that Shields and Aberhart did play important roles in the history of Canadian evangelicalism, but also that their influence was limited.[35] The first two chapters in part 2 go on to show instead that the best representatives of evangelicalism in Toronto and Alberta – indeed, of two different *types* of evangelicalism apparent elsewhere in Canada as well – were not in fact these flamboyant individuals but relatively prosaic institutions: Toronto Bible College and Prairie Bible Institute.

A second theme in the 'church-sect' model is that evangelicalism, as a 'sectarian' movement, played the role of 'outsider,' estranged from the larger culture, and attracted especially individuals who saw themselves at the margins of society.[36] In this, the model is correct to some extent. First, it is true that Canadian evangelicalism for much of the twentieth century was engaged with the larger culture only in narrowly 'religious' terms: religious education, direct relief (for instance, to alcoholics or the poor), and evangelism above all. Questions of public policy generally were left alone: evangelicals either agreed with the general direction of social change or believed themselves separated enough from the mainstream of society as to have no role in its decision making (attitudes, of course, that are not mutually exclusive). Part 2 traces out this attitude of alienation from society and its institutions in the history of two key institutions: Prairie Bible Institute, which trained youth for evangelism and church leadership with no interest in broader cultural influence, and the Inter-Varsity Christian Fellowship (IVCF), which stood over against the student organization sponsored by the mainline denominations and approved by the universities, the Student Christian Movement. To be sure, a third representative institution, Toronto Bible College, did not demonstrate this pattern of alienation as clearly until mid-century. Up to that point, it worked in concert with the mainline churches as well as the smaller evangelical denominations, and drew back from the former only as they themselves increasingly departed from evangelical emphases. In this respect Toronto Bible College manifests significant continuity with its nineteenth-century Ontarian roots, and the discussion below will show that IVCF itself was not so 'sectarian' as it appears in this brief characterization.

From the 1960s on, though, evangelicals founded a number of new institutions or modified existing ones more expressly as alternatives to those of the mainline churches or of society-at-large, as part 3 details. Symbolic of the former was evangelicals' refusal to endorse the ecumenical Christian pavilion at Expo '67 and the erection of their own, 'Sermons from Science.' Prairie Bible Institute maintained its separatist stance, while Toronto Bible College, which merged with another school in 1968 to form Ontario Bible College, not only began to offer pastoral degrees at the undergraduate level but went head-to-head with the denominational theological colleges when it established Ontario Theological Seminary in 1976. Inter-Varsity Christian Fellowship continued to grow, greatly surpassing the declining Student Christian Movement in this era. South of the Vancouver area, evangelicals with links to the prairie Bible schools established an alternative to the secular universities in Trinity Western University. Vancouver evangelicals themselves began Regent College, a school of Christian graduate studies that trained not only pastors but also laypeople in an evangelical view of contemporary culture. And evangelicals from across the country banded together to support an organization that represented their concerns to government, an alternative to the Canadian Council of Churches, the Evangelical Fellowship of Canada.[37]

While the history of these alternative institutions demonstrates a continuing estrangement from the direction and leadership of the mainline denominations and much of the larger society, however, it also shows that evangelicals since the 1960s increasingly sought to re-engage the culture at a number of levels. The seminaries offered courses for laypeople that helped them understand and practise their callings in a Christian way – rather than merely training them in Bible study and evangelism. Regent College, in fact, established this as its central task. Trinity Western University, despite its general isolation from the secular university world, sought to train leaders for the whole community, not just the church per se. And the Evangelical Fellowship of Canada not only helped evangelicals preach, study, pray, and witness better through its publications and seminars, but increasingly took on the role of representing (and shaping) evangelical opinions on a variety of social issues to local, provincial, and national governments. In all of this, evangelicalism belied the 'sectarian' label.

The 'church-sect' model implies, third, that evangelicals belonged to small, homogeneous denominations. Analysis of the denominational support for and leadership of the evangelical institutions here described indicates instead that while the smaller groups did exert a great influence in Canadian evangelicalism, significant representation in and support for evangelical institutions and especially those in urban centres came from the Presbyterian, Anglican, and Federation Baptists. Given the heritage of evangelical influence on Anglophone Canadian culture sketched above, this link with 'mainline' denominations is scarcely surprising, and demonstrates as much as anything else the inappropriateness of characterizing evangelicalism narrowly in terms of 'sectarianism.' Furthermore, a related point in the model is that evangelical movements or denominations were largely separate from each other, sharing some similar beliefs and attitudes yet mostly isolated by geography and distinctive convictions. It is indeed true that evangelicals shared similar beliefs and attitudes, and this study of several institutions that evangelicals erected together across denominational lines indicates these commonalities. The existence, however, of these transdenominational institutions indicates, in the first place, that evangelicals of different theological, ethnic, and denominational stripes did in fact cooperate. Evangelicals also supported institutions, in the second place, that existed largely for the purpose of joining them together: Inter-Varsity Christian Fellowship and the Evangelical Fellowship of Canada are the most important examples of this version of ecumenical interest. Evangelicals, in the third place, sponsored special projects together, with the 'Sermons from Science' pavilion at Expo '67 being the first one of national significance in this century. And finally, all of these institutions interlocked by formal and especially informal connections of people, denominations, and joint projects to form something of a network.

To be sure, some Christians across Canada, especially those isolated by strong ethnic, regional, or denominational identities, doubtless shared some or even all of the concerns of this movement (that is, they were truly 'evangelical' in the general sense) and yet did not support the institutions described here. Even more to the point, the evangelicals who *did* support these institutions did not constitute a full-fledged, organized religious movement. Without leaders, schools, mass media, or other institutions of sufficient influence to draw them all together into a coherent, national whole, they were separated by the vast geography of Canada, by the influence of and allegiance to regionally dominant leaders and institutions, or by different dispositions towards even concerns common to all evangelicals into definite subgroups only loosely linked to make up the larger evangelical fellowship. Indeed, the very word 'fellowship,' which was used by Canadian evangelicals to describe the two institutions that did the most to bring them together, namely, Inter-Varsity Christian Fellowship and the Evangelical Fellowship of Canada, in fact denotes such a relationship of distinct elements united by limited, if crucial, common concerns and engaging in limited common activity.

Canadian evangelicalism, therefore, cannot be described adequately by the traditional denominational or 'church-sect' typologies of Canadian church history or as a direct parallel of movements like the so-called 'ecumenical movement' among the mainline churches or the social gospel movement. It was instead something in between: a largely informal network of Christians united in their central concerns but pursuing them with only limited cooperation.

It appears, in fact, that two different dispositions, two *menta-*

lités, were evident within this fellowship. One involved itself more with the culture at large and tended to embrace a wider diversity of Christians: this I will refer to as the 'churchish' type of evangelical, employing this neologism (with a historian's squeamishness about such things) to indicate its resemblance to but also important difference from the Weberian/Troeltschean adjective 'churchly.' The other type separated itself from the culture and tended to include a smaller and more clearly delineated spectrum of constituents: this I will refer to as the 'sectish' type of evangelical, again with hopes that readers will understand that this denotes especially a mind-set, rather than the Weberian/Troeltschean 'sect' per se.[38] These differences characterized various Canadian evangelicals in the past, as we have seen. Yet in the twentieth century these two streams drew closer together into a definable evangelical mainstream. Furthermore, by the last quarter of the twentieth century, this confluence had both expanded and coalesced to rival the mainline movements as a powerful force in Canadian Protestantism.

This book, then, intends to introduce twentieth-century Canadian evangelicalism to several audiences. First, it should begin to fill a gap in the accounting of religion in Canada, and encourage scholars of Canadian history and religion to take more seriously this aspect of recent Canadian Protestantism – even inspiring, one might hope, studies that will go beyond and improve upon this one. Second, it should help journalists, other observers of contemporary Canadian life, and religious believers of other persuasions to understand better this kind of Christianity so typically identified only with its extreme manifestations. Finally, it should acquaint Canadian evangelicals themselves with something of their recent heritage in the hope that they might make the best of it and eliminate the worst of it as they face challenges ahead.

Part One

The Eccentrics: Shields and Aberhart

Introduction

Thomas Todhunter Shields and William Aberhart naturally have attracted the attention of historians of evangelicalism in Canada. Both were well-known and popular preachers in their day, but they have engaged scholars largely because of the controversies in which they participated. Shields led fundamentalists out of the Baptist Convention of Ontario and Quebec in the 1920s. Aberhart led the province of Alberta into a new kind of politics, Social Credit, during the Depression. These incidents, then, brought lasting national attention to these pastors so that they have become the most prominent representatives of Canadian evangelicalism.[1]

To be sure, Shields and Aberhart shared basic convictions with other evangelicals. They maintained the basic doctrinal beliefs common among evangelicals, and in particular defended the unique authority and inspiration of the Bible. Indeed, their lengthy and thorough expositional sermons abundantly manifest these commitments. Shields and Aberhart encouraged spiritual discipline and vitality among their flocks. And both men were evangelists who drew especial pleasure from conversions under their preaching.

T.T. Shields and William Aberhart, however, do not stand at the centre of Canadian evangelicalism. Many Canadian evangelicals have respected Shields for his concern for orthodoxy as well as for his eloquent preaching, but Shields was militant in all that he did, and his contentiousness ultimately cost him the support of most evangelicals. At the end of his career he presided over a tiny denomination and had little influence beyond it. T.T. Shields, then, marks out the fundamentalist limit of Canadian evangelicalism.

William Aberhart, for his part, introduced Alberta evangelicals to the possibilities of radio through his pioneering religious broadcasts. But his insistence on unorthodox doctrines, on his personal authority in his church, and especially on Christian involvement in politics cost him the support of many evangelicals who preferred traditional doctrines, strong but not overbearing pastoral authority, and distance from the 'worldly' practice of politics. His own church fragmented, and no greater proportion of evangelicals supported his political campaigns than did that of any other group. William Aberhart, therefore, moved beyond mainstream evangelicalism, even beyond fundamentalism, and out of evangelical leadership.

Even the following brief sketches illustrate something of the intriguing nature of the careers of these two individuals. These portraits also indicate, however, that other candidates must be sought to represent Canadian evangelicalism than T.T. Shields, the 'battling Baptist,' and William 'Bible Bill' Aberhart.[2]

— 1 —
T.T. Shields: The Fundamentalist Extreme

> As far as I am concerned, I will have no compromise with the enemy. I have declared again and again that I have resigned from the diplomatic corps; I am a soldier in the field, and as God gives me strength, everywhere, as long as I live, in the name of the Lord, I will smite [modernism], and I will make it as hard as I possibly can for any liberal professor to hold his position; and it will not be my fault if he does not get out of a job.[1]

Church historians may debate definitions of fundamentalism, but standing squarely in the middle of anyone's definition is Canada's best-known and most influential fundamentalist, Thomas Todhunter Shields, DD (1873–1955). T.T. Shields had a remarkable career, one noted by the Canadian edition of *Who's Who*.[2] He pastored one of Canada's largest churches for forty-five years; edited a newspaper that reached thirty thousand subscribers in sixty different countries;[3] served on the board of managers of McMaster University, from which he received the honorary degree of Doctor of Divinity; was the major force in the split of three denominations; founded the Toronto Baptist Seminary and the Canadian Protestant League; presided over Des Moines University and its parent organization, the Baptist Bible Union; wrote the doctrinal statement of the International Council of Christian Churches; and continues to fascinate historians of Canadian religion and culture. Despite this prominence and his indubitable evangelical commitments, however, T.T. Shields was not and is not the symbol for the mainstream of Canadian, Ontarian, or even Baptist evangelicalism. He marks out instead the fundamentalist limit of the fellowship of evangelicals.[4]

Shields was born in Bristol, England, in 1873, the fifth of eight children. His father, formerly an Anglican priest and later a Primitive Methodist, was a Baptist preacher when he moved the family to Canada in 1888 to pastor a church in southwestern Ontario. Under his father's tutelage and example, T.T. Shields grew up with the ambition to become the Canadian equivalent of Charles H. Spurgeon, the most prominent English Baptist preacher of the nineteenth century. Indeed, Shields aspired to preach at Spurgeon's own London Tabernacle and to pastor the pre-eminent church of the Baptist Convention of Ontario and Quebec, Jarvis Street, Toronto.[5]

Shields was to realize these ambitions after a pastoral career in several southwestern Ontario towns. Following his father's advice to write his sermons longhand and in full, using simple, clear language and without relying on commentaries or 'the opinions of others,' he had prepared over 1100 sermons by the time he was called to the Jarvis Street pastorate in 1910.[6] This was the preparation for a career that would lead a prominent historian of preaching to comment: 'Although remembered for his controversial life, Shields was an excellent preacher with the pastor's heart and concern. A gifted speaker, a forceful personality, a decisive expositor, he preached sermons of substance.'[7]

Shields had come to the attention of the Jarvis Street congregation in at least two ways. First, word undoubtedly had reached Toronto from nearby London, Ontario, in which Shields had pastored the large Adelaide Street Church since 1904 and had led it in a revival. Second, Shields had taken on increasing responsibility within the administration of the denomination, serving in 1905 on the relatively unimportant Committee on Obituaries, but in 1908 as convention speaker on the program with the eminent E.Y. Mullins of Southern Baptist Seminary in Kentucky.

Nineteen ten marked a turning-point for Shields in another respect as well. The convention of that year heard the Baptist statesman Elmore Harris repeat charges he had raised in 1908 questioning the orthodoxy of a professor, I.G. Matthews, at the denomination's McMaster University in Hamilton, Ontario.[8] In response, the board of governors of the university presented the report of its theological faculty affirming the orthodox doctrinal statement in McMaster's trust deeds and Matthews's agreement with it. Harris and his friends yet pressed the matter. John J. Mc-

Neill, eminent pastor of Walmer Road Church in Toronto, responded by asking Shields to sponsor a motion to clear the air and cut off debate. Shields agreed, and the motion passed, putting the convention on record as approving the statement of the board and relying on it to ensure that McMaster's teaching was in accord with the doctrine of the trust deeds. No doubt Shields was swayed by the fact that the doctrinal statement in question was identical to that in the trust deed of his own Jarvis Street Church, of which Senator William McMaster himself had been a member. Shields believed that the university's apparently genuine affirmation of what was an obviously orthodox document would be the end of the matter.[9]

With the war came both a rest from theological controversy and several honours. Shields preached at Spurgeon's Tabernacle in 1915 and again in 1918. Back in Toronto, he received word in 1917 that Temple University would award him the Doctor of Divinity degree at its June convocation. Shields, a man who respected higher education even though he himself had not attended a college or university, expressed his reluctance to accept it since he thought that preachers often hid their true ability behind honorary degrees.[10] But his friend Russell H. Conwell, president of the school, surprised him while visiting Toronto with an impromptu presentation at an evening service. (McMaster needed no such subterfuge to award him its DD the next year.[11]) The war years encouraged Shields also as he saw the church increase by over a hundred people per year and the offerings average over $40,000 per year, up from just over $28,000 in the first year of his pastorate.[12]

One wartime issue did arouse Shields: conscription – especially justified, he thought, in the defence of his beloved England. He vehemently championed it and denounced the Roman Catholic church in Quebec for its reluctance to support the Allied cause. This conflict with Canadian Roman Catholics over politics would arise again with wider implications in Shields's future.

Following the war, however, the battle that Baptists in Ontario and Quebec have called 'the great controversy'[13] began in earnest. Since the 1910 convention Shields had heard reports of Matthews's unorthodoxy, but Matthews resigned in the spring of 1919 and that seemed to be the end of the matter. In the autumn of that year, however, two editorials appeared in the *Canadian Baptist* that defended liberal views of the Bible.[14] Addressing the annual convention in Ottawa less than a month later, Shields threatened that if the convention supported the views of the editorials, he and others would leave. He did believe, however, that the majority of the convention in fact disagreed with these views and that the *Canadian Baptist* should hew to the orthodox line of this majority. An amendment was proposed that set out a typical Baptist response to such a call for the delineation of orthodoxy: it affirmed the Bible as the Word of God, the right of the individual to private interpretation, and the evil of controversy arising from doctrinal precision. This apparently generic Baptist position was shouted down from the floor, however, and once Shields had concluded his hour-and-a-half-long speech, the convention voted with him and rapped the knuckles of the *Canadian Baptist.*[15]

Shields returned, flushed with his victory, to encounter dissension within his own ranks. He had asked the deacons of his church to support him in a dispute with the choir leader and organist – apparently Shields thought there were too many lengthy anthems during the service. The deacons did not comply with his request, and Shields submitted his resignation. In a special congregational meeting that he had called, the church rejected his resignation and placed all control over the services in his hands.

There were hints, however, that the problem was hardly a matter of music alone.[16] Following Shields's well-publicized sermon in February 1921 denouncing 'Worldly Amusements,'[17] some of the deacons and other church leaders took offence at what they saw to be Shields's arrogance and love of controversy, if not a direct, though veiled, rebuke to them.[18] A committee of members of the church drafted a letter, published in a Toronto newspaper, that asked the deacons to take action towards Shields's resignation. The letter explicitly denied any theological difference with Shields: 'it is the man in whom the fault lies.' Shields, they said, 'has assumed the position of a dictator, and a self-appointed Bishop of the Baptist Church of Ontario and Quebec.'[19]

Shields again resorted to the ultimatum, calling a church meeting and polling the church as to whether they wanted to keep him or not. He agreed with his opponents that he would submit his resignation should less than two-thirds of the vote be cast in his favour. At the meeting itself, however, the congregation repealed the 'two-thirds' agreement (it is not clear how the congregation saw itself as the authority to repeal such an apparently private agreement) and voted to retain Shields. It did so, though, by a 284–199 count, or a 58 per cent majority. Shields did not resign. The next regular business meeting in June called for him to resign by a count of 204–176. Shields replied that he had no intention of resigning for the sake of a 28-vote majority and both sides looked to the final showdown in September.

Coincidentally, perhaps, Shields had invited John Roach Straton of New York to conduct an evangelistic campaign in the intervening summer months. The September business meeting sustained Shields by a 351–310 count, significantly with the votes of 46 members who had been added to the church rolls that summer as converts from the campaign but without the customary membership interviews by the deacons.[20] The aroused congregational majority (but, one must notice, still not the 'two-thirds' originally agreed upon) voted to discipline the leaders of the minority, and the disaffected group responded ultimately by leaving the church with 341 members to found Park Road Baptist Church.[21] It is this schism, rather than Shields's success at the Ottawa convention, that marks the pattern for the results of Shields's subsequent efforts to lead pure, orthodox institutions.

Things got a little better, however, before they got worse. In August 1924 Shields hosted his friend J. Frank Norris, the American fundamentalist, as Norris preached an evangelistic campaign at Massey Hall, Toronto. Shields's biographer reports that over fifty thousand people attended sometime during the month-long campaign.[22] With this kind of verification of the rightness of his cause,[23] Shields protested when McMaster awarded an honorary degree to W.H.P. Faunce, president of Brown University in Rhode Island and defender of the renowned liberal preacher Harry Emerson Fosdick. His alliance with Fosdick damning him enough in conservative eyes, Faunce had also published several books that placed him 'squarely in the liberal camp.'[24] McMaster's board, of which Shields himself had been a member appointed by the convention a few years before, denounced Shields as a meddler with whom they could no longer work.[25] The 1924 convention, however, agreed with Shields and instructed McMaster to award degrees in future only to those whose views were in accord with evangelical principles.

McMaster, though, had had enough of Shields and his friends. After the sudden death of J.L. Gilmour, professor of practical theology, late in 1924, McMaster appointed L.H. Marshall of Coventry, England, to replace him. At least two students of the attending controversy have seen evidence that Marshall held liberal views, as did the new chancellor, H.P. Whidden, himself,[26] but Marshall at the time made no obviously liberal pronouncements and seemed basically sound, as the university claimed he was. A pastor in Liverpool, England, however, who apparently himself had no direct contact with Marshall, accused him of modernism in two letters to Shields. Shields asked the board to hold back on the appointment until the charges could be investigated. The board, understandably anxious to fill the vacancy, if a little cavalier about how Shields and others of his views might respond to their decision, went ahead with the appointment. The 1925 convention upheld the appointment by the necessary two-thirds majority but only after an eight-hour debate.[27] This was the shape of things to come.

Shields refused to yield. Over and over in the pages of his house organ, the *Gospel Witness*,[28] Shields denounced the man whom, he believed, doubted the verbal inerrancy of the Scriptures, the vicarious atonement and bodily resurrection of Jesus, and the total depravity of human beings.[29] At the 1926 convention he repeated his charges.

Marshall would not roll over either. Stung by Shields's accusations of dissembling, Marshall replied: 'Calmly and deliberately, and without malice [!], I take all those suggestions and thrust them down Dr. Shields's throat, and I say to him, 'Thou liest.' The phial of poison of which you have heard so much is not in my hands, it is in his. And I commend Dr. Shields to this text – I know that it deals with the most elementary morality – 'Thou shalt not bear false witness against thy neighbour.'[30]

Shields defended his charges, but the convention was tired of controversy and particularly, it seems, of Shields. It offered Shields the opportunity to apologize to the convention or to resign from McMaster's board of governors and to be barred from future conventions. Shields characteristically declared that he counted it an honour to be opposed by such a spirit, and left the hall. Shields left, in fact, to set up the Regular Baptist Missionary and Education Society of Canada early in 1927, a channel for missionary funds that were to be diverted from the normal giving to the Baptist Convention of Ontario and Quebec. The convention responded by securing the power to expel any member churches who, it deemed, were out of harmony with the convention. Shields, seeing the crisis coming, fought this action, but in the end fell victim to its success. Jarvis Street Church and other like-minded participants in the Regular Baptist society were read out of the convention in 1927.

These churches and some others (thirty in all) formed a new denomination, the Union of Regular Baptist Churches of Ontario and Quebec, and elected Shields as its first president.[31] Shields's church formed a Bible college, Toronto Baptist Seminary, which served as the denomination's training school.[32] His own church's membership had increased to 2219, almost twice that of the church before the 1921 split.[33] Surely a new era was at hand. Shields saw hope, in fact, in other projects too. Having formed the Baptist Bible Union with like-minded American fundamentalists in 1923 (of which Shields was elected president also), Shields became chairman of the board and acting president of the Baptist Bible Union's newly purchased Des Moines University in 1927. With this new role, however, Shields's fortunes began to reverse.

The faculty in the departments of chemistry, biology, physics, and mathematics left almost immediately. They objected to the Baptist Bible Union's statement of faith, which all faculty members were required to sign, since it included a highly articulated clause on creation that stipulated belief in the direct creation, not only of human, but also of vegetable and animal life.[34] By the end of the first year, perhaps for other reasons, seven more faculty had left.

Shields brought in a new president, Harry Clifford Wayman, from a Southern Baptist school, William Jewell College, to take over in the summer of 1928. Shields left on campus his personal deputy, the secretary of the Baptist Bible Union, Edith Rebman. He also maintained contact with students who shared his strong convictions about the fundamentalist direction in which he wished to steer the school. Rebman and these students told Shields during the academic year 1928–9 that Wayman was not living up to their expectations: he had, for instance, been seen in a theatre, as had his son and daughter (just how these reporters knew that the Waymans had been there is not recorded). Shields wrote to the trustees questioning Wayman's fitness for the job. The school's deans responded by asking the trustees to remove Shields and Rebman from the school's administration.

The confrontation came on campus early in May 1929. The board first heard and dismissed charges that Shields and Rebman were conducting an improper relationship. After sixteen hours of meetings the first day, however, Shields pressed on the next morning to have the board declare all university positions vacant and to have applications for those positions submitted through Rebman. Only by appealing to unity was Shields able to get this passed.

The students, however, made their own feelings known. Already irritated by Shields's Anglophilia (he had insisted that the students, most of them American, sing 'God Save the King' at assemblies), angered by his suspension of fraternities and sororities, and insulted by his questioning of their faculty and president, the students met Shields upon adjournment of the board meeting with angry words and a few bad eggs. A planned convocation to discuss the board's work with the students was cancelled.

The students were not finished, however. As the board met that evening, the students threw more eggs through the windows of the boardroom and called for Shields and Rebman. Impatient, they broke into the building and attacked a few reporters who had heard of the ruckus and come to investigate. The football coach, evidently a man of some presence, broke them up, but could not prevent them from laying waste to the administration building. When the police arrived, they found Shields, Rebman, and five other trustees hiding in a storeroom. The police took the frightened fugitives to their station, the only place in which the police would guarantee their safety, and closed the school. Shields returned to a cheering crowd of supporters in Toronto.

Further political machinations by both sides, the board and President Wayman, ended on commencement weekend as Wayman awarded graduates their diplomas with a sheriff and two deputies standing watch while Shields, Rebman, and a second, male, colleague of Shields – all of whom had returned from Toronto perhaps to interrupt the proceedings – hid under assumed names in a motel nearby. Shortly thereafter, on 7 August 1929, the school was closed for good.

As one observer unkindly put it, 'the two-year history of Des Moines University is a history of the blunders of Shields.'[35] But Shields soon encountered further trouble. He held to a quasi-amillennial view of eschatology (the doctrine of 'last things') – a subject of doctrine unimportant to many Christians but very important to fundamentalists.[36] This placed Shields in the minority among fundamentalists, who were usually premillennialists. Allowances were made within the Baptist Bible Union and other fundamentalist groups for Shields,[37] but within his own Union of Regular Baptists he encountered militant premillennialists of the dispensational sort. This was difficult enough, but when Shields attempted to bring under control of the Union two independent fellowships – one for women and the other for youth – a number of these premillennialists resisted. These incorrigible 'Scofieldites' (so named after their adherence to the ideas of C.I. Scofield, one of the founders of Dallas Theological Seminary and writer of the widely popular *Scofield Reference Bible*) Shields expelled in 1931. In 1933, those expelled formed the Fellowship of Independent Baptist Churches of Canada.[38]

Shields weathered the rest of the 1930s, enjoying preaching in London at the celebration of the centenary of Spurgeon's birth in 1934, enduring a heart attack in 1937, and seeing Jarvis Street Church burn in 1938, after which it was rebuilt. When war came, Shields once again enthusiastically represented England's cause and once again attacked the Roman Catholic hierarchy in Quebec for its opposition to conscription.

In 1941, however, several incidents coincided to prompt Shields to take more than verbal action against Catholicism.[39] With traditional Baptist antipathy towards linkage of church and state, Shields opposed the saying of a Roman Catholic mass for peace on Parliament Hill in September 1941. He also heard with alarm of a Toronto Protestant book store that had had its mail service suspended because it was judged to have distributed anti-Catholic literature – a charge apparently unfounded. A meeting of disaffected Toronto clergymen founded the Canadian Protestant League and elected Shields as president.

This League, which included several prominent evangelical laypeople and clergy of Baptist, Anglican, Presbyterian, United, and Salvationist churches,[40] had a threefold object: to defend 'the traditional, civil, and religious liberties of British subjects,' to believe in and propagate 'the great doctrines and principles of the Protestant Reformation' (orthodox doctrines of the Trinity, Christology, soteriology, and Scripture were spelled out), and to resist the religious authority of Rome and its 'political methods of propagating its tenets, and of extending and exercising this illegitimate authority.'[41] By December 1941 the League had over eighteen hundred members, and this number more than tripled following Shields's tour of the West.[42] Support came in from across the country, although national membership rarely exceeded six thousand,[43] but most activity centred in Toronto. The League held mass rallies, distributed anti-Catholic literature,[44] and supported political candidates favourable to its cause. In 1945 a 'Protestant Party' was formed to oppose Ontario Premier Drew's proposal to introduce religious education into the schools and to increase support for Catholic separate schools: three candidates ran and were all badly defeated.[45]

The League attracted the attention of members of Parliament, who denounced Shields and the *Gospel Witness* (as of October 1942 renamed the *Gospel Witness and Protestant Advocate*) on the floor of the Commons. In 1943 a resolution to muzzle Shields was actually debated, with the measure failing only when Prime Minister W.L.M. King opposed it on the high ground that he wanted to avoid religious controversy in wartime and on the somewhat less high ground that he wanted to avoid making a martyr of a man for whom he had nothing but 'utter contempt.'[46]

Prominent Canadian historians have lent credence to the League's fears that King's wartime policies threatened the unity of Canada and the freedom of Canadians.[47] And the League's publications were joined by the United Church *Observer* and the *Presbyterian Record* in expressing concern over Roman Catholic doctrine and political influence.[48] What is not clear, however, is what difference, if any, the League made in Canadian politics. And some Protestant missionaries in Quebec denounced the League as making 'all Gospel activity [seem] anti-Catholic.'[49] With the declaration of peace came the waning of interest in perpetuating quarrels that seemed more important in wartime and the waxing of interest in reuniting the country. The League protested the official welcome afforded Cardinal McGuigan by the City of Toronto and the Province of Ontario in 1946, the Marian Congress in Ottawa in 1947, and the arrest of Protestant street preachers in Rouyn, Quebec, in 1947. But the League faded: by 1949 there were just over two thousand members. With Shields out of the country during much of 1948 and 1949, and then with his ouster from the presidency of the Union of Regular Baptists in 1949, the League lost much of the impetus it had owed to his leadership. Shields resigned the presidency in 1950, and the League carried on only in drastically attenuated form.

As the next-to-last sentence indicates, Shields not only lost influence in Canadian cultural and political life with the ebb of the Protestant League, he also lost influence within his own denomination. Having forced a large number out in 1931, he himself was forced out of the presidency in 1949. After he had fired W. Gordon Brown from the deanship of Toronto Baptist Seminary, Brown promptly led the disaffected students and faculty (and chef!) to form Central Baptist Seminary. The Union, out of patience with Shields's autocratic manner, removed him from the presidency. Shields promptly withdrew his church with several others following suit to form a new, tiny denomination that would later be known as the Association of Regular Baptist Churches of Canada.[50]

By 1950, Shields had isolated himself from all but a few Baptists and fundamentalists of other denominations. He had joined with American fundamentalist Carl McIntire to form the International Council of Christian Churches in 1948 as a counterpart to the World Council of Churches and was head of its little Canadian chapter. Besides the circulation of the *Gospel Witness* and the enrolment in his dwindling seminary,[51] Shields enjoyed no other links, no other fellowship, no other influence. He died in 1955, deeply loved by his church and honoured by other fundamentalists,[52] but well outside the mainstream of Canadian evangelicalism.[53]

Shields had once said, 'I find myself referred to in the press as "the militant Pastor of Jarvis Street Church." I should like to enquire, what other sort of Pastor is of any use to anyone?'[54] It is clear that many Baptists in Ontario and Quebec found Shields's combination of principle and pugnacity of significant value in the struggles over theological pluralism in the denomination during the 1920s that resulted in the most significant of very few and otherwise minor schisms of this sort in Canada.[55] So did other Protestants in the reaction to Roman Catholicism in Canada during the Second World War. It is also clear, however, that most evangelicals viewed his militancy as dogmatism, if not sheer arrogance, in the years that followed, and he enjoyed prominence for only a short while. The militancy that brought him to the attention of the nation as he provoked the most important of the schisms on the Canadian side of the fundamentalist-modernist controversy also prevented him from forming lasting alliances that would give him enduring influence upon Canadian religion. Most of the organizations he headed, with the conspicuous exception of Jarvis Street Church itself, enjoyed at best only modest support, if widespread notoriety, and then faded into insignificance. It is finally clear, therefore, that most Canadian evangelicals sooner or later decided to separate themselves from the most prominent ecclesiastical separatist in Canada. If one searches for the mainstream of Canadian evangelicalism, one must look elsewhere than to the 'battling Baptist,' T.T. Shields.[56]

— 2 —
William Aberhart: Beyond Fundamentalism

> There are to be found in all communities erratic people who get hold of an idea and, without stopping to get all the bearings of the case, jump at conclusions and then make everything bend to their opinions. In some cases these men are men of influence and personal magnetism and therefore they soon gain a following.[1]

William Aberhart (1878–1943) has received a great deal of scrutiny from historians, sociologists, economists, and political scientists because he founded a political party during the Depression and led it to dominance in the legislature of the province of Alberta. Indeed, it maintained this success for a generation after his death and dominated British Columbian politics for decades after that.[2] Because of this and because of his religious activities before and during his term as provincial premier, he has been given a place of prominence in Canadian religious history as well.[3] W.E. Mann, in his widely read study *Sect, Cult, and Church in Alberta*, credits William Aberhart with indirectly helping to weld Alberta evangelicalism together into a unified movement through his personal influence and that of the Social Credit movement he founded.[4] John Webster Grant writes that 'fundamentalist Albertans readily extended to Aberhart's economic theories the authority they were accustomed to accord to his expositions of the Book of Revelation.'[5]

Other scholars, however, have challenged this idea, noting that the proportion of 'sectarians' (meaning here members of non-mainline churches and especially evangelical ones) among supporters of Aberhart's Social Credit party was not unusually high[6] and that Aberhart in fact was losing most of his influence on Albertan

Christianity by the time he became involved in politics.[7] These data begin to indicate that Aberhart's undoubtedly deserved prominence in the history of Canadian politics does not justify the same prominence he has been given in the history of Christianity in Canada, nor even that of evangelicalism in Alberta. Instead, William Aberhart is important in the history of Canadian evangelicalism for his successful pioneering of radio ministry and his few years of large Bible classes in Calgary in the days before his involvement with Social Credit. At the same time, his 'radical sectarianism,'[8] as D.A. Goertz puts it, and also his unorthodox theology, egocentricity, and political career separated him from the mainstream of Canadian evangelicalism.

William Aberhart was born on 30 December 1878 in southwestern Ontario, the son of a German father and an English mother. He studied to become a schoolteacher and principal, graduating from programs in several schools in geometry, drawing, and business. With difficulty he graduated in 1911 from Queen's University in Kingston, Ontario, through a correspondence course.[9] As a child he had walked to the Presbyterian Sunday School nearby and now, as a school principal, became active in the Presbyterian church.

Somewhere in the course of his studies, Aberhart encountered the higher criticism of the Bible, the application of historical and literary interpretive techniques in the study of Scripture. Higher criticism deeply challenged Aberhart's faith, and he rejoiced to find answers in a correspondence course written by C.I. Scofield, author of the well-known study Bible. These lessons moved Aberhart from his previously held Reformed theology to dispensationalism, the idea that human history is divided into various epochs, or dispensations, that will culminate in the millennial reign of Christ on earth.[10] He began to teach, while still a Presbyterian elder, that the true church could not produce a Christian society but rather was to add converts and wait for the rapture – a central feature in dispensationalist thought.

Aberhart approached the Presbyterian church for sponsorship to help him attend Knox College in Toronto to prepare for pastoral ministry. According to one source, he was turned down on the ground the denomination could not afford to support married men with children – Aberhart had two children by this time, having married in 1902 and having had two daughters shortly thereafter.[11]

Aberhart received an offer in 1910 to preside over a secondary school in Calgary. Over the next several years he served a number of schools and churches in Calgary before ending up in 1915 teaching at Crescent Heights High School[12] and preaching at Westbourne Baptist Church. This move to a Baptist church (by way of time in both a Presbyterian and a Methodist congregation) does not seem to have resulted from any deep theological difficulties with Presbyterianism.[13] Rather, he seems to have sought a place in which he could preach regularly, and Westbourne furnished him this opportunity. Westbourne did so because it was a poor, struggling church with large debts – a mission, really, shored up by its denomination, the Baptist Union of Western Canada. Aberhart filled in as pastor without pay, and with an increase of numbers and funds under his leadership the church retired its debt a year and a half later.

In the custom of many churches at the time, Aberhart had held a Bible class on Sunday afternoons in the two previous churches and continued the custom at Westbourne. Under the charismatic leadership of the tall, heavy man with piercing blue eyes, the classes had drawn so many that by late 1917 Aberhart had begun a Thursday evening class as well. This class, open to all Christians, had attracted members of several denominations, and once it moved to Westbourne it continued to attract many non-Baptists, including some from his earlier Presbyterian and Methodist classes.

Aberhart attracted people particularly by his preaching of this unusual theology, dispensationalism, and especially its explanations of the 'end times' or 'last days' before the second coming of Christ – which coming Aberhart thought to be quite near. From this emphasis the class received the name Prophetic Bible Conference. Aberhart, however, like many dispensational preachers, did not focus on the interpretation of prophecy as mere prediction of the future and eschewed the practice of setting dates for the Second Coming. Rather, he constantly emphasized the imminence of the Lord's return so as to prompt soul-searching, repentance, and conversion.[14]

Westbourne, having made good on its debts, petitioned the Home Mission Board of the Baptist Union of Western Canada for funds to hire a full-time pastor. The Union told them to remove Aberhart and his class first. This opposition to Aberhart, never explicitly justified, may have arisen out of concern over his being an influential teacher who was not formally a Baptist and not ordained. It may also have arisen out of concern over some of Aberhart's theological emphases – whether dispensationalism itself or some of his increasingly eccentric ideas, like the use of Matthew 5:18 to support the inerrancy of the King James Version of the Bible.[15] And one cannot discount the possibility of simple envy and jealousy over the success of a man teaching members of other pastors' churches. Westbourne did not care what the reason was: they countered by making Aberhart unofficial pastor instead, letting him retain his secondary-school principalship.

Aberhart continued to enjoy success in his Bible classes, ultimately having to move them to the Grand Theatre to accommodate the crowd.[16] Here he used a dispensational chart he had painted on a piece of cloth measuring six by twenty-one feet.[17] He welcomed audience response, and would take questions at the end of his lectures, the answers to which he would prepare while the audience sang a hymn. Well known for his ability to remember people's names, he also could identify chapter and verse references for most passages of Scripture and would preface his answers with the authoritative phrase, 'The Bible says ...'[18]

Aberhart adopted other media for his message as well. October 1924 saw the first issue of *The Prophetic Voice,* the official organ of the Calgary Prophetic Bible Conference of which Aberhart was the editor and to which he made almost all of the contributions.[19] It took a stand squarely in the fundamentalist camp, its subtitle declaring it to be 'A Monthly Journal for the Cause of Evangelical Christianity and the Faith Once for All Delivered unto the Saints.' 'We are fundamentalists in the actual sense of the word,' Aberhart declared. 'We believe that the final court of appeal is the infallible verbally inspired Word of God. We believe it all, and knowing that the original manuscripts have long ago been lost, we have no confidence in those individuals, here and there, who claim such superior wisdom in the Greek and Hebrew that they attempt to correct what the Lord Jesus pronounced infallible and adamantine.'[20]

In the autumn of 1925 Aberhart began a somewhat more formal sort of Bible instruction, an evening school known as the Calgary Prophetic Bible Institute. Once graduated from this school, Aberhart hoped, the students would be placed in empty rural pulpits and would withstand the menace of the brand new United Church of Canada (founded that year), which he saw to be the very incarnation of extreme liberal theology, or 'modernism.'[21]

Aberhart also began the Radio Sunday School correspondence course in 1926. At first American lessons were used, but Aberhart later prepared the lessons himself. Question sheets were attached and successful students were awarded prizes. The lessons were provided free, and adults were encouraged to sponsor a student for fifty cents a year. The peak year of 1938–9 saw over nine thousand students enrolled.[22] Members not only of uniformly evangelical denominations but of the United Church and other mainline groups enrolled in these radio classes and in the Bible Institute.

Aberhart continued to use the radio, in 1929 broadcasting the popular Prophetic Bible Conference from the Grand Theatre over Calgary station CFCN. By 1935 Aberhart was broadcasting five hours every Sunday over several Alberta stations, with a radio audience estimated at 350,000.[23]

The Bible Institute too had continued to grow, and Aberhart raised money for a permanent structure for it by encouraging supporters to purchase 'sods' (units of the lot) for one hundred dollars, bricks for two, and rafters and mortar for other prices.[24] Subscribers received the added bonus of having their names read over the radio – a bonus not to be despised among rural folk whose contact with the larger world came largely through the radio. An 'Institute Club' was also established with six levels of membership determined according to the amount of the contribution, all the way up to 'Super-Institute Membership' – which itself was graded according to the number of hundreds of dollars donated: 'A' membership for $200, 'D' membership for $500, and so on.[25] These schemes paid off, and William Bell Riley, well-known American fundamentalist, preached at the grand opening of the building in October 1927.[26]

The 1920s, which saw so much apparent success for Aberhart, however, saw also the emergence of several characteristics of his ministry that would alienate him from the general evangelical community. First, in this period Aberhart began to teach things well beyond the usual range of evangelical theology. Perhaps the least unusual teaching was Aberhart's defence of the inerrancy of the Authorized, or King James, Version (KJV) of the Bible.[27] True to the mentality of one trained in geometry and business, Aberhart looked for and found in the Bible straightforward truth. With the dispensational scheme to 'rightly divide the Word of truth,'[28] Aberhart had found the key and needed no study of the languages behind his infallible translation. He buttressed this idea with the contention that the Textus Receptus, on which the KJV was based, had been preserved by God in the Swiss Alps, free from Roman Catholic contamination.[29] Although Aberhart never claimed as much, it would be easy to trace the implicit logic of an infallible interpretation of an infallible translation of an infallible text to the idea that Aberhart's teachings were therefore, well, *infallible*.

Second, early in this decade he made friends with a 'Jesus Only' Pentecostal pastor, Harvey McAlister, of the new (1920) 'People's Church' in north-east Calgary. Under McAlister's influence, in 1922 Aberhart began to teach that believer's baptism not only declared one's faith in Christ and introduced one formally into the church – as believers' churches of most sorts assert – but it also was the occasion in which the believer received the Holy Spirit. Moreover, Aberhart taught, it should be performed in the name of Jesus only (hence the name of the Pentecostal group), presumably following Acts 8:14–17 and 19:1–6. With these ideas came emphasis upon each believer using his or her spiritual gifts in the life of the congregation, although Aberhart encouraged the church to value prophecy, faith, teaching, and exhortation above other gifts normally emphasized in Pentecostal gatherings, specifically those of tongues and healing. These teachings would have been enough to separate Aberhart from most evangelicals of the time, who would not have had fellowship with Pentecostals of any stripe, and even from most Canadian Pentecostals, who would have seen the 'Jesus Only' baptism as but a step removed from the 'Jesus Only' unitarian tendencies current in some Pentecostal circles.[30]

Aberhart's new theology embraced more than ordinance and worship, however. Westbourne had hired a new pastor at last, Ernest Hansell, but Aberhart retained both his job as school principal and his role as leader of the church. He had used the title 'moderator' before Hansell's arrival. But later, as part of his unusual interpretation of the New Testament's teaching regarding the church, he assumed the title 'apostle' – while sharing it, to be sure, with Hansell – on the grounds that spiritual gifts could be received, he said, only directly as by the original apostles at Pentecost or by the laying on of an apostle's hands subsequent to baptism.[31]

With these unorthodox teachings came an increased sectarianism. Aberhart originally had intended the Prophetic Bible Conference to bring Christians of many denominations together. But by 1922 he forced members of other churches to break with him or their own group and brought control of the Conference directly under Westbourne. In 1926 Hansell resigned. Some acquainted with the situation cited several reasons: Hansell had difficulty defining his pastoral role vis-à-vis Aberhart's 'apostleship'; Hansell could not accept several of Aberhart's teachings; Hansell had personal troubles of his own, culminating in a divorce; and, according to at least one well-placed source, Hansell had discovered Aberhart at a typewriter composing letters to himself to read over the air.[32] Hansell left in October and took a number of members with him.

Perhaps with this incident in mind, Aberhart and the deacons of the church acted to secure control of the new building. They placed the building funds in the name of the Institute, and then obtained tax-free status by forming the Calgary Prophetic Bible Institute Church, which consisted only of the deacons and those they appointed. Westbourne, then, would rent the facilities of this 'church.'

Aberhart, by mid-decade, began to denounce other Canadian denominations. He referred to the United Church as Sardis and to the Baptists as Ephesus of Revelation 2 and 3,[33] and in 1927 he pulled Westbourne out of the Baptist Union of Western Canada over alleged heresy at its college in Brandon, Manitoba, and formed an independent church.[34] Aberhart began advertising the church as 'extreme fundamentalists.'[35] He drew up a new creed for the church that distinguished between 'general' members (those who had been converted and baptized) and 'active' members (those who had been baptized by the Holy Spirit and possessed spiritual gifts). Most Christian theology, of course, has not made this distinction, seeing those truly converted and baptized as necessarily possessing the Spirit and spiritual gifts. More unusually, the creed also lifted Aberhart to an even higher ecclesiastical eminence as it set out only two church offices: apostle and deacon. Pastors, who in a creed written by Aberhart in 1923 were to be ordained by other Baptist clergy, were no longer even mentioned, and the ordinances of the church were now to be administered by the apostle. The strain of these innovations soon cost Aberhart a majority of his congregation. Having moved into the new Institute buildings, more than half of the congregation withdrew in 1929 to return to Westbourne. And this congregation subsequently rejoined the mainstream of Canadian evangelicalism, first employing L.E. Maxwell and his colleagues from the Prairie Bible Institute as interim preachers, and then under Morley Hall joining Regular Baptists who would eventually help constitute the Fellowship of Evangelical Baptist Churches in 1953.[36]

Aberhart had already lost much of his support among evangelicals because of his unusual doctrine, sectarianism, and personal arrogance. His subsequent foray into politics would cost him most of the rest. The story has been told at considerable length elsewhere of Aberhart's discovery of the Douglas system of economics during the early years of the Great Depression.[37] It is hard for those born since those awful times to sympathize fully with the plight of whole provinces of destitute farmers, victims of financial powers in Ottawa, Toronto, Washington, and New York they could neither understand nor influence, and victims of drought and pestilence the solution to which would have taxed the compassion and wisdom of the best of governments. William Aberhart had a pastor's concern for his people, and he was thrilled to find the solution to everyone's problems in a little book outlining Douglas's ideas, Maurice Colbourne's *Unemployment or War*.[38]

In 1932 Aberhart began a series of lectures on 'the Bible and modern economics' at the Calgary Prophetic Bible Institute. In 1933 he wrote his first secular book, a little outline of *The Douglas System of Economics*.[39] He used radio time increasingly to teach his version of Social Credit ideas – that a relatively few financial powers in the big cities were squeezing the farmers and that with governmental rearrangement of the credit system plus a monthly dividend of $25 paid to each citizen of the province to prime the pump of the economy things would improve dramatically.[40] Apparently preposterous in their simple answers to complex problems, at least one later critic none the less suggested that Douglas's ideas bore an important resemblance to the economics of John Maynard Keynes, whose theories influenced later policies of both Franklin D. Roosevelt in the United States and W.L.M. King in Canada.[41]

The governing party, the United Farmers of Alberta, refused to listen to Aberhart's ideas. When sexual scandals emerged involving leaders of the party, however, and when the socialist Cooperative Commonwealth Federation appeared on the political horizon, Aberhart formed a new political party to contest the 1935 election. His party would sing 'O God, Our Help in Ages Past' as its anthem and would set forth Social Credit as 'an economic movement from God himself.'[42]

Aberhart's party won the election with 57 of 63 seats and 54 per cent of the popular vote, thereby making Aberhart premier.[43] They won again in 1940, although by a much smaller margin.[44] The Supreme Court of Canada declared most of his distinctive Social Credit legislation ultra vires, but Aberhart did accomplish considerable good for the province, including a reform of the educational system and the protection of at least some farms from foreclosure through debt legislation.[45] He died in office in 1943, but his Social Credit party, under the leadership of a graduate of the Bible Institute's first class, E.C. Manning, went on to dominate Alberta politics for a generation.[46]

Aberhart's political success, however, came at considerable religious cost. His church went through several pastors in the 1930s, pastors who had been hired to take some of the load off Aberhart so that he could promote Social Credit. The last one, Ralph C. Crouse, was so incensed when church leaders wouldn't listen to his complaints that he took his concerns in 1939 to the *Calgary Herald*. The newspaper then ran a three-week series of articles charging Aberhart with lending money at high interest while denouncing banks for doing the same and with running the institutions surrounding the Institute like a dictator – a term that had considerable force in that year. About 130 members left with Crouse to form a new church.

Aberhart lost friends in the wider fellowship of evangelicalism as well. A small battle was fought in letters and over the radio between Aberhart and leaders of the Prairie Bible Institute in rural Three Hills, Alberta, over Aberhart's espousal of political solutions to the Depression. Like most evangelicals, the Prairie people believed the Depression to be a divine judgment on a civilization that had rejected God. They thought that Christians should vote intelligently and prayerfully, to be sure, but also that Christians had no business trying directly to bring about social reform. The real problem was personal sinfulness, and the real solution was evangelism.[47] Aberhart's proposed solution, by contrast, smacked of 'materialism, lawlessness, and communism' (Aberhart, no Communist, had drawn liberally from the *Communist Manifesto* for his first tract and for many ideas afterwards).[48]

Aberhart was also guilty by association. He himself had recognized affinity between himself and others working for social justice, the others being no friends of evangelicals, like the Pope himself and American Roman Catholic priest Charles E. Coughlin.

United Church pastors and even Mormons were running as Social Credit candidates. And Aberhart had the notorious Hewlett Johnson, Dean of Canterbury, to speak at the Institute – the socialist who became known as the 'Red Dean.'

Aberhart came on the air to declare his critics 'bad sinners' for defaming one who 'went to eat with the sinners.'[49] The differences were clear: Aberhart would welcome to his cause people of any religious persuasion because the cause was, at least immediately, political – even as he would justify it in his own religious terms to himself and his congregation. Most evangelicals, however, believed with Maxwell that Aberhart offered nothing distinctly Christian and that he compromised for the sake of vain politics the supreme evangelical commitment to evangelism (which was, it is worth pointing out again, the basic evangelical solution to the temporal as well as the spiritual problems of humankind, since temporal evils arise as a result of spiritual evils). Far from leading an evangelical political crusade, therefore, Aberhart gained support among identifiable evangelicals only in the same proportion as he did among voters at large in the province.[50]

The career of William Aberhart, known to many as 'Bible Bill,' has proved perennially fascinating to Canadians, whether provoking decades of academic study or scrutiny by several generations of journalists and playwrights.[51] His experiment with Social Credit was unique in the western world in the political success of its combination of unusual ideas with evangelical fervour, thus rightly attracting the interest of scholars in political science, sociology, and history. His pioneering of religious broadcasting set the pace for a number who would follow in Alberta and throughout Canada. His Bible lectures gave many people their first exposure to disciplined methods of Bible study and to dispensational theology in particular – a theology that became popular in many evangelical circles in the twentieth century. He also, like others, articulated an alternative to the social gospel and United Church brand of ecumenism prominent in that region at the time. In these latter, religious, instances, Aberhart's career deserves the study of historians of Canadian religion as well.

As important a religious figure as he was on the Canadian and northwestern American prairies in the 1920s and early 1930s, however, it remains that William Aberhart's major impact on Canadian life came from his 'baptized' political experiment with

Social Credit. Indeed, it was just as he made that impact that he moved away from the common pattern of evangelicalism in this and other respects.[52] As 'Apostle' and 'Premier' Aberhart grew in prominence, therefore, 'Bible Bill' lost his influence in Canadian popular religion.[53] As in the case of T.T. Shields, then, students of the history of Canadian evangelicalism have focused far too long on the career of a flamboyant individual at the expense of studying the broader community for more typical representatives.[54] The best symbols for the evangelical mainstream, in fact, were not individuals at all, but the institutions that evangelicals together founded, incarnations of their concerns.

Part Two

The Mainstream of Canadian Evangelicalism to the 1960s

Introduction

From the turn of the century to the 1960s, Canadian society became much larger, much richer, much more diverse, much more independent – and much less traditionally Protestant. Historians of Canada have mapped out elsewhere the expansion of Canada from a few small provinces along the St Lawrence River and Atlantic coast to a continent-spanning giant. They have traced its economic maturation from a colonial supplier of raw materials to an industrialized and urbanized nation. They have followed the immigration patterns that turned Anglo- and Franco-Canada into a bewildering 'salad bowl' of nationalities. And they have chronicled the increasing distance between Canada and Britain, both culturally and officially, even as these moves away from Britain sometimes seemed simply like moves towards the United States.[1]

Canadian religion underwent less obvious, but still important, changes over this period of dramatic evolution. The traditionally dominant Protestant denominations – Anglican, Methodist, Presbyterian, and Baptist – all experienced a decline in their proportional hold on the Canadian people. Religious depression characterized the 1920s and 1930s especially, and the apparent revival after the Second World War did not make up this lost ground. In fact, the numerical growth in the churches in the 1950s and early 1960s was buoyed by the Canadian 'baby boom' and the general postwar turn towards conservatism and therefore traditional institutions. The increases in membership and activity indeed disguised the shallowness of the rooting of this return to traditional religion (which later developments would expose) and the fact that the mainline Protestant churches none the less continued to decline in their proportional representation in the Canadian population.

This half-century-long decline in numbers was accompanied by fragmentation in the traditional focuses of these Protestant churches. The First World War damaged badly the optimism of nineteenth-century liberal theology and the social gospel in many circles, leaving some to pursue yet more radical political options (including the Cooperative Commonwealth Federation and Social Credit parties, founded in the 1930s). Others began to investigate the new theological options blowing over from Germany and Britain and up from the United States, especially those known collectively as 'dialectical' or 'neo-orthodox' theology and associated with such figures as Karl Barth and Reinhold Niebuhr. The formerly vigorous programs of foreign missions, intended to convert the 'heathen'[2] from their errors, increasingly lost support and, in some cases, began to soften the evangelistic edge with greater emphasis on inter-religious dialogue and the drive towards international brotherhood and peace.[3] And all of this was thrown into relief by the increasing strength of churches at other ends of the religious spectrum. Roman Catholics and Lutherans gained considerable numbers through immigration and maintained or increased their share of Canadian society throughout this period. The small, uniformly evangelical bodies and other small religious groups experienced remarkable growth as well, whether the Pentecostals and Salvation Army or the Mormons and Jehovah's Witnesses.[4]

The shift, then, from the broadly evangelical consensus dominating Anglophone Canada in the nineteenth century to the pluralism of the later twentieth would take until the 1960s to be noticed widely as such. As the particular changes along the way did take place, however, evangelicals paid attention and adjusted their commitments and activities according to their perceptions. The more 'churchish' evangelicals differed with much of the mainline Protestant agenda and therefore progressively parted with its institutions, but reluctantly and slowly. The more 'sectish' evangelicals, for their part, had no alliances to maintain with the traditionally dominant denominations in the first place, and so watched these developments without feeling the need to modify their own agendas much at all. As Canadian society in general, though, became less influenced by the old evangelicalism of the previous era, many of the evangelicals in the twentieth century, of both *mentalités*, began to draw together more than ever before, a coalescence that would only increase in the subsequent decades.

The three most important institutions that Canadian evangelicals founded in the first half of the twentieth century, other than foreign-mission societies, were two Bible schools and a student fellowship. The oldest of the three, Toronto Bible College, stood as a centre of evangelical life in that city and remained the largest Bible school east of the prairies throughout this era. As such, it represents much of the history and character of the mainstream, the common experience, of Canadian evangelicalism. It also represents especially a particular variety of Canadian evangelicalism, a 'churchish' sort common in metropolitan centres but present elsewhere as well.

The second of the three, Prairie Bible Institute, rapidly became the largest Bible school in Canada, a distinction it continued to hold until the 1980s. It stood as the central institution and representative of a 'sectish' sort of evangelicalism common especially outside urban areas but present in cities across Canada as well. None the less, it shared central characteristics and developments with Toronto Bible College and so its history also helps to indicate the nature of the emerging national fellowship.

The third group, Inter-Varsity Christian Fellowship, began as an alternative to the Student Christian Movement on university campuses. It grew to encompass chapters of students at secondary schools, of students at schools of nursing and education, of university graduate students, and of university faculty, as well as an extensive camping program, so that it became the largest student religious movement in the nation, represented in all Canadian provinces but especially in Ontario and Alberta into the 1970s. The story of Inter-Varsity Christian Fellowship demonstrates again the common concerns of Canadian evangelicals, even as tension within it speaks of regional and dispositional differences among them.

Canadian evangelicals, then, as seen in these three central institutions, were concerned to maintain orthodox doctrine, to develop personal spirituality, and to evangelize at home and abroad. As these concerns were neglected or replaced by other priorities on the agendas of the mainline Protestant denominations, some Canadian evangelicals maintained or took on a separatist stance, manifested by the growth of the newer, small, uniformly evangelical denominations in Canada. The evangelicals represented by Toronto Bible College and by the Toronto-based national leaders of Inter-Varsity Christian Fellowship, however, generally represented a broader spectrum of denominations and an increasingly broad view of the nature of the church's mission than did their counterparts on the prairie. And these differences, among others, would mark the two kinds of Canadian evangelicalism ('churchish' and 'sectish') throughout this century, even as the two kinds began to coalesce into a national fellowship.

— 3 —
Toronto Bible College: 1894–1968

In the autumn of 1946, a testimonial dinner was held in Toronto to celebrate the fortieth year in the career of a statesman in theological education. At the head table sat prominent leaders in the Canadian church: Colonel Layman of the Salvation Army; A.E. Armstrong, associate secretary of the Overseas Missions Board, United Church of Canada; E.A. Brownlee, secretary-treasurer for Canada, China Inland Mission; A.L. Fleming, Anglican Bishop of the Arctic; J.B. McLaurin, secretary of the Foreign Missions Board, the Baptist Federation of Canada; George C. Pidgeon, first moderator of the United Church of Canada; and the heads of the four Toronto theological colleges, Armitage of Wycliffe, Seeley of Trinity, Matheson of Emmanuel, and Bryden of Knox.[1] The prime minister of Canada, William Lyon Mackenzie King, sent a telegram to honour his old classmate: 'In our days at Toronto University no undergraduate stood higher in the esteem of his fellow students than [this man]. That regard for his attainments of character and scholarship has grown with the years and to-day is recognized throughout Canada and abroad.'[2] The speakers credited the guest of honour with several traits in particular: he was theologically orthodox without pursuing controversy; supportive of the whole church without compromising essential Christianity; courteous and kind without dissembling or equivocating; and strong under criticism without responding with bitterness. In short, they said, this man was both ecumenical and evangelical.

Combining in his person what are sometimes supposed to be incommensurable qualities was not the most important accomplishment of this man, however. For he, through forty years of leadership, had inculcated them in the institution he led. Of John McNicol and Toronto Bible College it could be said, at least in these respects, that 'l'école, c'était lui.' Under John McNicol, for the first half of the twentieth century, Toronto Bible College stood for theological orthodoxy, evangelism, and the practical training of laypeople in evangelism and spirituality so as to further the work of the church around the world. Furthermore, it did so in cooperation with a wide spectrum of Canadian Protestant denominations without seeking controversy. With these principles and guided by McNicol's example and leadership, Toronto Bible College stood in the mainstream of transdenominational evangelicalism. This basic character and mission TBC[3] maintained for succeeding decades, even as some of the original emphases were modified in response to new developments in the second half of the twentieth century.

Toronto Bible College arose out of the evangelicalism characteristic of Ontario in the late nineteenth century.[4] This broad alliance of Christians had invested in a number of projects to win souls to Christ and to reform an increasingly godless society. Ian S. Rennie concisely lists some of the activities of the Toronto evangelicals, many of whom would support TBC:

> Both men and women gave themselves to church planting. They started many home missions including Yonge Street Mission and Toronto City Mission. They led the work of the Upper Canada Bible Society, the Upper Canada Tract Society, and YMCA and YWCA, and the publishing firm known as the Willard Tract Depository. They manned the committees of the denominational missionary societies, as well as those of the recently-founded faith missions, the two most prominent of which were the China Inland Mission (now Overseas Missionary Fellowship) and the Sudan Interior Mission, the latter having its home base in Toronto ... They founded the Home for Incurables (now Queen Elizabeth Hospital), the Haven for Fallen Women, the Newsboys' Home, and had a major part in the formation of the Hospital for Sick Children. Politically, they were very much involved in the Toronto City Reform Movement, which saw that eminent evangelical, William H. Howland, assume the mayoralty.[5]

The furthering of these sorts of endeavours required a large force of biblically knowledgeable and practically skilled laypeople. To meet this need in Toronto, as others were doing elsewhere on the continent, evangelicals began the Toronto Bible Training School in 1894.

The first Bible school in North America was started in 1882 by the former Canadian A.B. Simpson of the Christian and Missionary Alliance at Nyack, New York. D.L. Moody soon afterward began a school in Chicago that later bore his name.[6] Several schools in Canada came and went in this first decade of Bible school development,[7] but the first one to stay was the one that would become Toronto Bible College.

TBC began as the Toronto Bible Training School under the leadership of Elmore Harris, scion of the prosperous farm-machinery family. Born in 1854 and graduated from the University of Toronto in the later 1870s,[8] Harris began working with the YMCA, but soon entered the Baptist pastorate. After successful charges in St Thomas, Ontario, and Toronto, he began Walmer Road Baptist Church in what was then west Toronto, a church whose building at the time was the largest Baptist edifice in Canada.[9]

These and other activities were not enough for Harris, however. In his last year at Walmer Road he began what he himself regarded as the most important project of his life.[10] Convening a meeting on 14 May 1894, Harris set out before a group of church leaders, clerical and lay, his vision for a Bible school that would train laypeople as 'Sunday School teachers, as Pastors' Assistants, and as City, Home and Foreign Missionaries. It is intended for those who believe that they have been called of God to Christian service, and who, from age or other reasons, cannot pursue a full collegiate or theological course of study.'[11]

This group was dominated by Baptists and Presbyterians (as would be TBC's subsequent history), but early leaders included Methodists, Anglicans, and others as well.[12] From the start the school would be avowedly 'interdenominational' and stress those things the evangelical churches had in common.[13]

The school was laid out on the British model of an administrative president (Harris was elected to this post) and an academic principal (Baptist pastor and educator William Stewart was named to this position). Pastors and teachers in the area would teach the courses in the first years of the school (Stewart was the only full-time employee at the start). Their lectures dealt mainly with doctrine or specific texts of the Bible. The course originally was two years long. Admission standards were academically low, if spiritually high: 'Candidates for admission to the full course of study must be recommended by their Pastors, Churches, or other responsible persons as possessing an approved Christian character, and giving promise of usefulness in the Lord's service. They must have a fair English education, although in special cases instruction will be provided for those who are deficient in the ordinary branches ... All students will be expected to spend a reasonable part of their time in preaching, conducting prayer meetings and Gospel services, visiting the sick, conversing with inquirers, and other kinds of systematic Christian work.'[14]

Theologically, the school set out a terse evangelical creed:

I. The divine inspiration and authority of the whole canonical Scriptures.
II. The doctrine of the Trinity.
III. The fall of man, and his consequent moral depravity and need of regeneration.
IV. The atonement, through the substitutionary death of Christ.
V. The doctrine of justification by faith.
VI. The resurrection of the body, both in the case of the just and of the unjust.
VII. The eternal life of the saved, and the eternal punishment of the lost.[15]

Four years later, the school added scripture texts for each clause and new clauses that affirmed belief in the regenerating work of the Holy Spirit, the doctrine of sanctification (left undefined), and the second coming of Christ.[16]

Elmore Harris himself was persuaded of the new theological scheme of dispensationalism and contributed to the *Scofield Reference Bible*. H.M. Parsons, a guest lecturer, apparently taught 'Dispensational Truth' to the first class of the school.[17] C.I. Scofield himself was invited to become the second principal of the school and, while he declined this offer, he did provide guest lectures several times.[18] Anglican scholar W.H. Griffith Thomas, who lectured frequently at the school, and A.B. Winchester, pastor of Knox Church and under whom John McNicol served for a while as an assistant, helped to found the dispensational Dallas Theological Seminary. For all of this, however, the school never advertised the teaching of dispensationalism, and after a period of John McNicol's leadership it faded entirely.[19]

Indeed, in these years before the fundamentalist-modernist controversies of the 1910s and 1920s, considerable doctrinal latitude is evident at TBC in its choice of instructors and examiners. Nathaniel Burwash of Victoria University, who had earlier been embroiled in a controversy over higher criticism, was invited to speak in a summer session in 1899. And S.D. Chown, a leader of the Methodist Church who was suspected of liberal theological tendencies, was an early examiner.[20] This indicates something of the widespread theological fluidity in North American Protestantism before the First World War, however, rather than any unorthodoxy on the part of TBC's leaders.[21]

Harris's church, Walmer Road, housed the first four years of classes. In 1898 the school, largely through Harris's financial assistance, purchased property in downtown Toronto and soon had its first building. 'The [three-story] School was planned in the architecture of the day, with curlicues, turrets and "gingerbread" motif for the roof; with the class rooms and auditorium austere and dark in contrast to the large, bright, functional rooms of today.'[22] The building would serve for thirty years, as enrolment grew from the initial ten to almost two hundred by the time a new building was obtained.[23] After the initial growth in numbers with the school's start-up, however, the enrolment levelled off at about seventy students by the end of the First World War. Harris himself died of smallpox while on a trip to India in 1911. A few months later Principal Stewart died as well. The generation of pioneers was passing, but the heritage already had been entrusted to the young John McNicol, who would fashion the school in his image for the next three decades.

McNicol (1869–1956) came to TBC in 1902 with a distinguished record as a young Presbyterian clergyman.[24] He had graduated in 1891 from the University of Toronto with honours in Classics and in 1895 from Presbyterian Knox College with first-class honours in Divinity, leading his Knox class throughout.[25] He had gone on first to pastor a church in his native Ottawa Valley. McNicol then taught at Toronto Bible College for four years until the school asked him in 1906 to take over as principal for a year while they looked for a permanent replacement for Stewart. Unsuccessful in wooing Scofield and others, they asked McNicol to stay on for another year. This he gamely did until the board recognized their man in their midst and made him principal in 1908, a post he held until 1946.

Under McNicol the school developed in a number of ways. Its basic program expanded from two to three years.[26] The enrolment grew to its peak of 380 in 1938–9, a figure lessened drastically by the war in McNicol's last years.[27] The school moved from its 110 College Street address to larger quarters in two buildings on Spadina Avenue, still close to downtown Toronto. The graduation exercises became occasions for the gathering of evangelicals from all over southern Ontario and outgrew not only available Toronto churches, but Massey Hall itself – an auditorium seating almost three thousand – eventually to occupy the University of Toronto's Varsity Arena, as in 1937 a peak crowd of nearly six thousand attended.

Beyond sheer growth, however, the school in these years deepened previous commitments and developed new ones. When John McNicol looked back on what he called 'those formative years' at TBC, he discerned four main characteristics of the school.[28] These traits his administration strengthened.

The first was prayer. This was not a mere nod in the direction of piety. This term not only referred to the spirituality of the college's founders and leaders, but also characterized the tone of spirituality throughout the school. Prayer began administrative meetings. Students held prayer meetings regularly, both for their own concerns and especially for missionaries. On several occasions the school experienced a widespread and unplanned revival in which classes or conference meetings were suspended and students and faculty enjoyed a day of prayer, public confession of sin, restoration of damaged relationships, and renewed spiritual zeal.[29] And this tone of spirituality was manifest among the students in that they were trusted to discipline their own behaviour through an honour system of self-government. TBC did not hand out a list of rules to regulate conduct, as did many other Bible schools in Canada and the United States.[30]

'Prayer' also can stand as an abbreviation for an extraordinary application of another, related, emphasis of McNicol's leadership. McNicol believed strongly in the presence of the Holy Spirit in the church. This idea had two ramifications for him, the second of which coincides with a theme discussed below. But the first ramification for him was a polity known as the 'corporate leadership of the Holy Spirit.'[31] Under McNicol, all the deliberative bodies in TBC's economy, from the board of governors to the students' social committees, would make decisions based only on unanimity. McNicol explained:

> We went back to the New Testament and tried to reproduce in the fellowship of the student body what we found in the fellowship of the early Church. In other words, we sought to bear witness to New Testament Christianity by practising the presence of the Holy Spirit in the corporate life of the College. In order to do this we introduced a plan of student self-government and inculcated the principle of seeking the mind of the Lord about any matter by waiting on Him in a fellowship of thought and prayer till we arrived at unanimity.
>
> We believed that if each of us made a personal surrender to the Lordship of Christ and was not moved by any selfish interest, then the same Holy Spirit who dwells in each of us would lead us all finally to be of one mind. This is the real secret of spiritual unanimity. It took some time to work out this principle, but the students of those days responded to it year by year, and at last they found by their own experience that the presence of the Holy Spirit in the Church of Christ is a deep and sacred reality.[32]

This was Toronto Bible College's singular manifestation of the spirituality common in Bible schools.

McNicol described a second characteristic, typical of all Bible colleges: TBC's concern to provide Bible instruction. The very term 'Bible College' attests to the centrality of the Bible in the curriculum of the school. TBC's crest was an open Bible surrounded by the school's motto in an ellipse: 'Holding Forth the Word of Life.'[33] The first clause in the statement of faith declared the school's allegiance to the most rigorous belief in the unique authority of the Bible. McNicol called the teaching of the Bible 'the guiding and regulating centre of the whole course. We believed that Christians ought to know the Bible better than any other book.'[34]

To give students this deep knowledge of the Bible, McNicol began every day with a one-hour lecture on some portion of it. Over the course of the three-year program, students would hear McNicol proceed through both Testaments. Along with most Bible schools, TBC emphasized that its study of the Bible was 'inductive,' dependent only upon a fair reading of the whole of Scripture so as to let it 'stand upon its own feet.'[35] This emphasis upon 'induction' was quite common among Canadian evangelicals, as among those elsewhere. Other models of Scriptural study, and especially more radical forms of higher criticism, were seen by evangelicals as being 'controlled' by unorthodox theological presuppositions and therefore they arrived at unorthodox conclusions. Evangelicals well into the twentieth century instead had an Enlightenment-style confidence that a straightforward, 'reasonable' reading of Scripture would yield reliable truth – and, indeed, would yield the truth of their own beliefs.[36]

Like other Bible schools as well, however, and like Canadian evangelicals of the previous century, TBC studied the Bible 'devotionally,' rather than 'critically.'[37] Important as was the intellectual discipline of inductive study, all effort would be wasted if the Bible's revelation did not change hearts and equip students for service. And most 'higher' or historical criticism of the Bible, if not all, was feared as tending to reduce the Bible to mere human reflections on the divine than to exalt it as revelation of God to human beings.[38]

These lectures by McNicol were set in the context of a curriculum that included 'all the subjects that are found in the curriculum of the average theological seminary.'[39] And these subjects were taught within the boundaries of the new doctrinal statement introduced when the school was reconstituted in 1916. The new statement built on the old, changing a few terms and adding new clauses to make explicit what perhaps could no longer be assumed because of the recent 'flood' of modernism in some churches: 'The Deity of our Lord Jesus Christ'; atonement not only through the death of Christ but also through his 'life ... and resurrection'; and justification by faith 'in our Lord Jesus Christ.'[40]

McNicol wrote that 'the course should stand the test of scholarship,'[41] and pointed out that the students received instruction from men who themselves had been educated in universities and theological colleges. This was no idle boast. Unlike the faculties of many Bible colleges whose academic credentials were slim, McNicol frequently recruited men of first-rate ability. Most had baccalaureate degrees from Canadian universities and graduate degrees in theology from established denominational divinity colleges. Several had earned doctorates or went on to earn them during or after their tenure at TBC.[42] And when new teaching faculty were introduced to the College community through the *Recorder* they frequently were credited with graduating with various honours.[43]

Instruction in theology, however, was not the only end of the course. McNicol pointed out a third characteristic of the school that balanced this intellectual emphasis: practical training. This training was not mere instruction. The students did indeed take courses in evangelistic methods, in preaching, in music (as a means of worship and especially as a medium of evangelism), in visitation of the sick, elderly, imprisoned, or otherwise suffering, and, for a time, in elements of missionary medicine. These courses, however, were matched with experience in each of these activities (except the last, presumably), at least inasmuch as metropolitan Toronto could furnish opportunities for the practice of these skills. Throughout McNicol's tenure his annual reports describe the many activities of the students as they attempted to practise their training.

The final emphasis to which McNicol referred in his reflections on TBC was its self-understanding as 'handmaid of the churches.' TBC believed, he said, that 'no Church has a monopoly of Divine grace, and that every denomination bears witness to some special aspect of the whole truth of God.' The implications of this conviction were clear to him: 'Therefore, each of us should be loyal to his own church, and should at the same time try to cultivate a sympathetic understanding of other churches.' Undergirding this transdenominational sympathy was McNicol's fundamental belief that 'what makes any church a true church is not the form of its organization or the method of its worship or even the creed it professes to believe, but something that is given to it from above, the presence of the Holy Spirit in its midst.'[44]

These are not the words of the stereotypical fundamentalist who certainly would emphasize doctrinal rectitude above all in discerning the authenticity of a church. They are, to be sure, the words of a theologian who did indeed prize orthodoxy and resisted what he called modernism, and of a man who did prefer Presbyterian polity, worship, and creed to the point that he did not join the United Church. But these are also the convictions of an evangelical whose warm heart testified to the irreducible criterion for discerning the true church, the presence of the Holy Spirit of God.

McNicol recognized this difference between himself and (what we should now call) 'fundamentalists'[45] of his day. He consciously avoided denominational controversy, believing it to be beyond the purview of a transdenominational institution. But he also believed that controversy itself blew a 'blighting breath' under which 'the very meaning of Christianity seems in danger of being lost.'[46] Indeed, a quarter-century after he wrote those words (1924), he testified that 'during the past generation the greatest peril to the cause of Christ in the universal Church came from Modernism. In the present generation it comes from Ultra-Fundamentalism ... Now these are the two perils of Fundamentalism: preaching a gospel without love, and developing a carnally-minded kind of Christianity – a Christianity that is self-centred and complacent, not the New Testament kind that is pervaded by brotherly love and the fragrance of the presence of Christ.'[47]

Indeed, as orthodox as the College was by most standards, the greatest challenge to its determination to serve all the denominations came not from the mainline churches but from the dispensationalists. Pressure to make TBC a dispensationalist school came in several ways. Some offered money and threatened to withhold it should their wish not be granted; others spoke against the school, applying to it the ludicrous epithet 'modernist' because of TBC's refusal to teach the dispensational pattern.

The most powerful indication of the strength of this opposition was McNicol's abandonment of his characteristic reserve and irenicism in the most popular and notorious article he ever wrote, 'Fundamental, but Not Dispensational: An Answer to Criticism.'[48] In this piece, McNicol levelled a painful charge at dispensationalism: it was just as bad as modernism, since it too had departed from the essential teaching of Christianity. Modernism had done so in its 'rationalistic theory of the Bible and its naturalistic evolution.' Dispensationalism had gone to the other extreme 'with its parenthetic theory of the Church and its fantastic apocalyptic program.' McNicol proceeded to outline his disagreements with dispensationalism under the following heads: 'Dispensationalism was not the prevailing belief of the early church which its advocates claim it was'; 'Dispensationalism denies the fundamental doctrine of Christianity that there is but one way of salvation and thus attacks the historic faith of the church'; 'Dispensationalism subverts the divine unity of the Bible and dislocates the Divine procedure of redemption which it records'; 'Dispensationalism displaces the Cross from its central position in the Divine scheme of redemption'; 'Dispensationalism discards the New Testament method of interpreting Old Testament prophecy, the method used by the inspired Apostles'; 'Dispensationalism departs from the analogy of Scripture in the way it deals with unfulfilled prophecy'; 'Dispensationalism misrepresents the significance of the blessed hope of the Church'; 'Dispensationalism has played into the hands of the Roman Papacy [whom Protestants have seen as Antichrist] with its theory of a future Antichrist.'

Bad as modernism was, McNicol asserted, the church in the past had weathered such storms as it represented and showed signs now of renewed strength after the declension of so many Protestant leaders in recent decades. But – with typical evangelical regard for the health and ministry of all churches rooted in the crucial concern for evangelism – McNicol concluded that dispensationalism posed a more potent threat to the church now trying to overcome the debility modernism imposed upon it. Yet it was not dispensationalism's theological aberrations per se that constituted this threat.

Perhaps the greatest disservice which Dispensationalism is doing to the cause of Christ is in propagating the idea that the professing Church is apostate. This has produced a process of disintegration among the denominations, which is spreading widely and has given rise to innumerable independent and unrelated groups of believers, who are quite powerless to make any impact upon their own local communities or help forward the general evangelization of the world. And this at a time when, more than in any other period of her history, the Christian Church should be presenting an unbroken front to a paganized world.[49]

And now [McNicol said finally], having explained the criticism to which the College has been subjected and answered our critics, we shall go on with our own proper work. We shall continue to help the denominations, so far as we can, with the task which the Lord gave His Church to accomplish in the world, believing that in this way alone will His Kingdom come.[50]

TBC's constituency approved the article overwhelmingly, as the subsequent letters to the school proved. And theological leaders from around the continent, from Principal W.W. Bryden of nearby Knox College to the young Bruce Metzger of Princeton Theological Seminary, expressed their appreciation for a school that held to such a course.[51]

But TBC's concern to be a handmaid of the churches took form in more than its theological centrism. It also took a role as the trainer of laypeople, a role that explicitly did not overlap or interfere with that of the denominational colleges. Using military imagery at the height of the Second World War, McNicol wrote: 'It is not difficult to see that if Christianity is to prosper in the future and if the Gospel is to make headway in the world, a much larger share of Christian work and witness must be undertaken by trained laymen and laywomen. The task that confronts the Church cannot be accomplished by ministers alone. Battles are not won by officers alone. The real fighting force in any war is the rank and file. The business which Toronto Bible College has taken upon itself is the training of the Christian rank and file.'[52]

To be sure, a number of TBC graduates did end up in pastoral work in Canada: the newer denominations in particular were happy to get pastors with even the three years of theological education TBC offered. But the bulk of the graduates ended up either in foreign missions or in secular jobs and involved in Sunday School teaching, church administration, and other 'part-time' service.

Virginia Lieson Brereton has suggested that since the cost of founding liberal-arts colleges in the United States was high, evangelicals in North America founded Bible schools instead.[53] The question of cost, however, never appears in the records of Toronto Bible College as a reason for founding it or continuing it as a Bible school rather than transforming it into a liberal-arts college. (The same is true of Prairie Bible Institute, to be discussed in the next chapter.) Two different reasons determined this choice. In the first place, twentieth-century provincial governments across Canada made it difficult to begin any new school that would grant arts degrees, whether religious or secular. Most such schools were secularized by early in the century and therefore were under the control of these governments. The governments' proper concern for educational quality combined with their vested interest in the established schools meant that the few private schools that tried to win the right to grant university-type degrees fought long, difficult battles. (Trinity Western University, as we shall see, is a case in point.) Knowing this, evangelicals might well have hesitated to invest their resources in a project that likely would founder on governmental intransigence.

Much more important, though, was the second reason. Evangelicals, whether in Toronto or elsewhere, chose to establish a Bible school because *a Bible school is what they wanted.* This kind of institution, not a liberal-arts college, would provide the kind of instruction for certain lay Christians previously untrained for and insufficiently mobilized in the great works of evangelism and Christian education. Professionals could go to university; the Bible school unapologetically offered a different kind of training.

TBC had stressed foreign missions since its earliest years, and the general course of study was soon adapted for the particular training of missionaries.[54] Harris reported in 1895 that 'of the students of the first year five have gone to the Mission Field in China and six others have been accepted as missionaries for the foreign field. Two have been pursuing their studies as medical missionaries, and nine have been employed during the summer months as home missionaries in different parts of Ontario.'[55]

This missionary emphasis continued under McNicol, who himself was a charter council member for the China Inland Mission and the Sudan Interior Mission in Canada and was elected a lifetime governor of the British and Foreign Bible Society.[56] Early in his tenure a Toronto newspaper awarded the school the sobriquet, 'Hotbed of Missions.'[57] In 1943 McNicol reported that about three hundred of TBC's two thousand graduates of the day or evening courses had entered the pastorate in Canada, the United States, and England. One-quarter of the graduates, however, had entered foreign-missionary service with denominational or transdenominational mission boards.[58] Ten years later the school happily reported 950 graduates 'today in various forms of Christian service.'[59]

Thus under John McNicol the 'Great Design' of Toronto Bible College was worked out. On the occasion of the Jubilee Graduation Service in 1944, H.J. Cody, president of the University of Toronto, spoke of TBC's ideals: 'Interdenominational – loyalty to the Church of his choice is taught the student; Evangelical – it proclaims the glorious news of God's love to men and His desire to save them from their sins that they may serve Him and others; Ecumenical – it recognizes the fact that it is part of that great Church throughout all the world; Missionary – to the fingertips, because into the lands of the world it has sent missionaries to proclaim the glorious gospel; Co-educational – in order to live the highest life both men and women, young and old, have the high prerogative of entering into fellowship with the great Creator.'[60] In the twenty-two years between McNicol's retirement in 1946 and the merging of the school with London College of Bible and Missions to form

Ontario Bible College in 1968, the school maintained this pattern for the most part. But as Canadian Christianity changed, and as evangelicals themselves changed, so did TBC modify the 'Great Design.'

The school appointed the brilliant J.B. Rhodes to the principal's office upon the retirement of McNicol.[61] The Presbyterian Rhodes had taught full-time at the school since 1939 and a bright future was forecast for the school as it attempted to recover from the difficult wartime experience. Rhodes was soon diagnosed as having cancer, however, and Anglican pastor E.L. 'Ted' Simmonds took over in 1954. The ambitious Simmonds responded to the request from mission boards and TBC alumni for a degree-granting program. These friends of TBC informed the school that there was increasing pressure placed by foreign governments upon missionaries to present actual degrees. Moreover, more and more evangelical denominations without their own seminaries or without a history of formal pastoral education looked to the Bible schools, bastions of orthodoxy, to provide the more educated pastors they now wanted.[62] So TBC joined with other Bible schools across the continent as it won the right to grant degrees, first the Bachelor of Theology (1956) and later the Bachelor of Religious Education (1963).[63] In 1966 it finally received full accreditation with the Accrediting (now 'American') Association of Bible Colleges. (The ability to grant degrees, however, prompted TBC to re-examine its policy of admitting students who had not graduated from high school. This problem was solved by dividing the school into Bible School and Bible College divisions in 1961.[64]) Simmonds, throughout all this, maintained a teaching schedule at the school, fulfilled numerous speaking engagements, and began doctoral studies at the University of Toronto.[65] In 1961 this load proved too much for him, and he relinquished all but his teaching duties at the school.[66] R.A. Killen took the reins as executive vice-president for two years, but left in the spring of 1963.

The coming of Stewart L. Boehmer as president in 1963 would mark not only a new episode in TBC's history – the road to merger with London College of Bible and Missions to produce Ontario Bible College in 1968 (and so a part of the story dealt with in a subsequent chapter) – but also a change in the administrative arrangements at TBC. The offices of principal and president were rearranged on the more common model of an administrative president and an academic dean. Wheels set in motion under Simmonds turned in that same year to bring TBC accreditation with the American Association of Bible Colleges.

The enrolment through this period ending with Simmonds' principalship was the lowest in TBC's history. When McNicol left, Rhodes inherited a class for the 1946–7 year of 217. When Simmonds took over in 1954, TBC enrolled its smallest class since McNicol's earliest days, 108. This nadir was followed by modest gains, significantly rising in 1956–7, when the B.Th. program was introduced, to 167. As the school developed more specialized programs, including concentrations in pastoral, missionary, and Christian educational work (1953), and its ability to grant degrees became more widely known, the enrolment climbed slowly, with only two classes being smaller than their predecessors, until TBC's last class before the merger in 1968 numbered 246.

Some have seen in these years a betrayal of TBC's original vision of training laypeople, believing that it introduced pastoral programs only to save itself from disappearing in the mid-1950s.[67] There is enough substance in this interpretation to warrant a hearing. TBC's original vision, carried on by McNicol, did not entail training pastors except by 'accident.' The 'Great Design' assumed that pastors would go the normal route of university and divinity-college education. And it seems more than coincidental that TBC's perilously declining enrollment reversed itself for the better when these programs were introduced.

Several other things, however, must be taken into account. In the first place, evangelicals who were interested in formal pastoral education had had a couple of generations of disillusionment with the mainline theological colleges by the time they began asking for pastoral education from faithful TBC.[68] Second, many evangelicals belonged to new denominations (that is, founded in the nineteenth or twentieth centuries) that were just now awakening to the need for formal pastoral training – partly at least, one might suppose, because of the general rise in educational expectations among Canadians as part of the postwar rise in standard of living.[69] Members of these groups naturally would look to the Bible colleges for this training. Indeed, as these denominations continued to require more and more training for their pastors, Bible colleges across Canada and the United States would respond by developing theological seminaries (as Part 3 of this study demonstrates). Third, TBC itself reported letters from mission boards and missionary alumni who requested that TBC begin such a program to meet the increased educational requirements placed on missionaries. And fourth, TBC had trained a number of pastors throughout its history, and it had gloried in that fact. There was perhaps a little double-mindedness all along that was simply recognized and positively dealt with in these explicitly pastoral programs in the 1950s.

The entry into competition with the mainline seminaries in fact marks a realignment of TBC with the non-mainline evangelical denominations while it yet attempted to maintain ties with the mainline groups, especially to evangelical Baptists and Presbyterians. A few statistics show this point clearly. In the first full year after the First World War, out of a daytime class of 66, the only denominations in double figures were the Baptists with 28 and the Presbyterians with 13.[70] At the height of the controversial 1920s, McNicol reported these as the largest denominational contingents among the students: Baptist, 89; United Church, 18; Presbyterian, 17; Anglican, 11 (all others in single digits).[71] In 1939 McNicol reported that 'the great majority of [our] students, 230 of them [of a total of 380], belong to the four major denominations in Canada, the Anglican, Baptist, Presbyterian and United churches.'[72] In the last report McNicol gave in which he indicated denominational representation, there was a significant change: 'The great majority, about three-fourths of them, belong to the major denominations. The largest groups come from the Baptist, Mennonite, Presbyterian, and United Churches. The Anglican Church, the Evangelical Church, and the Associated Gospel Churches are well represented.'[73] This coincides with a decline in evangelicalism in Canadian Anglicanism at mid-century and with the increasing interest of Mennonites in mainstream evangelical institutions – an interest that would grow dramatically in the 1950s and 1960s. No further denominational breakdown is available, unfortunately, until the 1960s. But by then the shift to the 'non-mainline' churches is accomplished. The 1967 class, the last before merger, had the following denominations represented in double digits: Baptist, 69; Associated Gospel Churches, 43; Presbyterian, 23; Non-denominational (which might include some Christian Brethren), 22; Christian Brethren Assemblies, 17; Christian and Missionary Alliance, 11. The United Church, by contrast, sent 8 and the Anglicans 7.[74]

This realignment is the more important move away from TBC's original identity. Further, it is the engine behind the move to granting pastoral degrees. The original 'Great Design' reflected the attitude of the mainline denominations who expected their pastors to have university and divinity-college educations. TBC's later offering of an undergraduate 'pastor's course' and B.Th. implicitly endorsed the view of the non-mainline churches who did not expect such qualifications.[75]

Why, however, did TBC realign itself increasingly with these other denominations? The answer can be seen not only positively, in the growth of the newer denominations themselves and their subsequent desire and need for pastoral training, but also negatively, in the changes taking place within the larger churches whom TBC previously had served, changes seen in the theological complexion of the denominational seminaries but of much broader extent. Among the denominations that would constitute the United Church of Canada in 1925, evangelical emphases had begun to shift and fade already by the turn of the century.[76] This trend continued, a trend towards pluralism in ministry and theology with pre-eminence given to the Social Gospel and liberal theology.[77] The Presbyterian Church in Canada, always a stronger supporter of TBC than the United Church, weakened through this period to the point that its most distinguished historian later described it as a 'smouldering bush.'[78] Evangelicalism within Canadian Anglicanism, of the sort once identified with W.H. Griffith Thomas and Dyson Hague, largely disappeared from the life of TBC, as it did generally in Canadian church life, after the first quarter of the century, only to reappear in small numbers in the 1960s. The Baptists, who often have been considered 'mainline' even though they have constituted a relatively small number of Canadian Protestants, continued to support TBC, with both the Baptist Convention and the separated Fellowship churches sending the largest contingents of students to Toronto Bible College throughout the century, earning it the unwanted identity of a 'Baptist school.' Given the generally evangelical theology and emphases of Ontario Baptists of both types, such support for the college was to be expected.[79] So the shift at mid-century from TBC's identity as 'handmaid to the churches' – meaning a broad spectrum of denominations, mainline and non-mainline – to primarily a servant of *evangelical* denominations[80] signals a change in TBC's character only in response to the change in the character of the various Canadian churches.

This character, then, had much in common with other North American Bible schools: transdenominational, Bible-centred, missions-oriented, spiritually vital, and fundamentally practical in its training. Yet in its emphasis upon faculty who had strong academic qualifications, its concomitant appreciation for university education, its relations with a broad range of denominations, and its eschewing of dispensationalism, Toronto Bible College stood apart from most of these Bible schools.[81] And as it represents the mainstream of 'churchish' evangelicalism in these respects, so it differs from a representative of 'sectish' evangelicalism, the internationally recognized Prairie Bible Institute.

— 4 —
Prairie Bible Institute: 1922–1977

Six o'clock on a January morning is cool and dark most places in North America, but it is cold and black eighty miles north-east of Calgary, Alberta, in the little town of Three Hills. A student at Prairie Bible Institute reaches over to shut off her rattling alarm clock. Paula bids good morning to her room-mate as they shiver, wash up, and reach for their clothes: dresses, of course, with sleeves past the elbow, hems below the knee (even when the wearer sits), and necklines that truly line the neck. By 6:30 they are both ready for the next of the day's activities: private morning devotions.

Paula and her friend open their Bibles and read silently. Paula's room-mate has a copy of 'Daily Bread,' the pamphlet that many students use which suggests Scripture readings for each day and provides brief lessons and poems to go with them. Paula herself simply reads for fifteen minutes – every day over her four years at Prairie and she easily will read the Bible through. She reaches under her bed for a notebook and records a summary of what she has read, chews on the pen for a moment, and then writes down how she intends to apply what she has read to her own life.

Paula then kneels beside her bed to spend the next fifteen minutes in prayer. The notebook also serves as a prayer list, and Paula carefully notes both requests and answers in parallel columns. By now, early in the second semester of her second year at Prairie, she has filled dozens of pages of such requests and can look over a wide variety of answers. Following such a list is as liturgical as the young women's prayers will get, since Paula comes from a Baptist church and her friend from an 'interdenominational' one. Indeed, they don't really know what 'liturgical' means, except Paula knows it has something to do with Roman Catholicism and is therefore wrong. Paula prays especially about missions. She prays for specific missionaries – those her home church supports and those she has heard about or met at Prairie. Like a majority of students here, she wants to be a missionary herself and prays for God's leading in her life: in preparing her for service, in directing her to the right 'field,' and, if at all possible, in selecting the right mate to go with her – Philip Judson might be nice, Lord, she suggests – and then blushes.

Seven o'clock comes and the women leave their dormitory room to join their schoolmates for the walk to the dining hall. Some of the women are girls fresh out of high school; others are seasoned missionaries back from the field to take further training. Paula herself is of average age, in her early twenties. The women step outside into the darkness to be pleasantly surprised by the warm chinook blowing in off the mountains, some hundred or so miles to the west. Paula chats with her friends as they traverse the centre of the hundred-plus-acre campus, most of the buildings of which, fortunately, are close together, and they enter the huge dining hall through the women's door. Some of her friends have been up since five preparing food for the day brought in from Prairie's farm, which provides most of the supplies for the students and staff. Paula did this herself last year as her 'gratis work,' the traditional ten-and-a-half hours of labour per week each student donates to the school to keep costs down. Paula fills her tray and proceeds to her table in the area reserved for women – the men sit on the other side of the hall. When the table is full, the table leader prays and then they begin.

Just before eight, Paula and her friends leave for class in the academic building. Most of Prairie's buildings are wooden frame structures, although some of the newer ones are made of more permanent materials. Paula's first two classes are Bible II (part of the Bible survey she will receive over the four-year program) and Voice II. Paula has a good, strong soprano voice and rehearses with one of the Prairie musical groups. They look forward to both the annual music night at the Jubilee Auditorium in Calgary and the summer's work publicizing Prairie with a member of the faculty – in her case, touring the American Northwest, Washington, Oregon, and Idaho.

In the Bible class, Paula sits on the women's side of the classroom and takes out her answers to the 'search questions' of last night's homework. The class is beginning the study of Paul's letter to the Philippians. As in every Bible course, the teacher has provided the students with questions meant to guide their independent, inductive study of the Bible. The school catalogue explains: 'These questions are especially select and are designed to enable the student to sound the depths of God's Word as an organic body of revelation. The teacher refrains from coming between the student and his subject. The student, by personal first-hand research, but under careful guidance, is pushed into rich original findings. The result is that the Bible is not mediumized to the student, but the student has his own revelation and his own message of the truth.'[1]

Paula's assignment last night was to answer several questions, including the following: 'Discuss the unique presentation of the divine-human character of our Lord given by Paul in 2:1–11, and explain his practical object,' and 'Explain Paul's reason for the different uses of our Lord's Names, "Christ" and "Jesus," in this passage.'[2] The class now reviews their answers with the teacher, himself a graduate of Prairie and well versed in this method. The teacher makes sure that the students grasp not only the meaning of the text but also its application to their own development as Christians and especially to the furtherance of the chief work of the church, evangelism.

Bible and voice classes over, Paula joins the rest of the students for the daily chapel service in the 'Tab,' or 'Tabernacle.' This structure easily accommodates the hundreds of students and staff who attend, having hosted many more for Prairie's well-known fall conference and spring missions conference. President Maxwell rises from his seat on stage and moves to the microphone. Welcoming the students, he invites them to sing the first of several songs. The singing and announcements over, Mr Maxwell begins his sermon – a rare treat for the students, since Maxwell's Sunday preaching responsibilities at the Tabernacle church keep him from speaking often in chapel.

L.E. Maxwell is a short, strongly built man with a firm jaw and bright eyes behind his spectacles. The men like to tell each other how one magazine referred to his build as that of a middle-weight fighter,[3] and those men who have worked with Maxwell in the fields of Prairie's farm or who have heard of his energy on one of his annual elk-hunting trips in the Rockies tell their stories with proud enthusiasm. His presence looms large over everything at Prairie – he was the founding principal, he set up the distinctive Bible-study method here, he edits the school's magazine, he runs the show.

Maxwell's sermon begins with a reference to Prairie's crest: a simple cross and the reference to Galatians 2:20: 'I have been crucified with Christ; and it is no longer I who live, but Christ lives in me; and the life which I now live in the flesh I live by faith in the Son of God, who loved me, and delivered himself up for me.' The sermon sounds familiar themes: the glory of Christ, the need of the world for salvation, the Great Commission, the necessity of self-discipline (he usually says 'self-denial'), and the pre-eminence of missionary work among all other vocations. The students have heard these themes before. They will hear them dozens of times over their years at Prairie and from every direction: not only in the daily chapel services, but in Friday night youth meetings, annual missionary biography nights, missionary portraits and mottoes on building walls, daily missionary prayer meetings, nightly dormitory-floor prayer meetings, and in Prairie's magazine, the *Prairie Overcomer*. President Maxwell concludes the half-hour meeting with prayer, and Paula heads to the library for an hour of study before lunch at noon.

After the 'big meal of the day,' following farm-country tradition, Paula feels a little sleepy. Her English II class wakes her up, though, since the textbook to be discussed that day is a biography of her personal heroine, Mary Slessor.[4] Paula later moves on to a fascinating class, 'False Cults,' in which a variety of exotic aberrations receive critical attention. The teacher exposes the errors of Jehovah's Witnesses, Mormons, Seventh-Day Adventists, and Modernists in the light of the clear testimony of the Bible.[5]

Paula finishes classes at four PM and heads over to the music building for rehearsal with her mixed quartet. The sun already is low in the south-west sky, the shadows from the trees planted by Prairie's pioneers now long on the walks. Paula spies Philip Judson approaching. She smiles and calls out. Philip responds warmly, and as they meet they pause for a moment to remark on the pleasant weather. Then the conversation stops, before it has really begun, since both remember the words of the *Student Handbook*: 'There are to be no exclusive conversations anywhere on campus between students of the opposite sex except by permission and arrangement of the Dean. *It is to be clearly understood that a conversation will not be regarded as casual if there are only two people of opposite sex involved. Therefore, no couple ... is to stand or walk and talk together.*'[6]

Paula gets in half an hour's homework between rehearsal and supper at 5:30. She returns to the library for more homework until 9:30, at which time she hurries back to the dorm, late for the 9:30 curfew. Gladly she gets out of the dress and the mandatory hose and into her pajamas and robe for the floor prayer meeting. Like everyone else on her floor, Paula brings out a chair from her room and sets it up along the hallway – no one room can accommodate all thirty women. At ten, the women go back into their rooms for a half-hour of private devotions, and then at ten-thirty the lights are turned out for all.

Paula slips into bed, a little worried about the Church History test tomorrow, but happy after another day of clear thinking, vital prayer, inspiring preaching, hard study, and beautiful gospel music. She drifts off ... to Africa, with Philip.[7]

All Bible schools shared the same basic qualities: concern for correct doctrine, a Bible-centered curriculum, and practical training – especially in evangelism. But Toronto Bible College and Prairie Bible Institute yet differed in important respects. Toronto Bible College represented the 'churchish' form of Canadian evangelicalism and therefore the 'Bible College' type of school in its emphases upon university and divinity-college training for its teachers, its accreditation and offering of degrees, and its greater willingness to offer liberal-arts courses. It also had a history of serving the mainline churches as well as the uniformly evangelical denominations. Prairie Bible Institute, by contrast, represented the 'sectish' form of Canadian evangelicalism and therefore the 'Bible Institute' type of school with its homegrown teachers, its independence from accrediting institutions,[8] and its greater concentration upon Bible instruction.[9] And it served almost solely uniformly evangelical churches from its beginning. None the less, what the schools – and the types of Christianity they represented – shared in common was more basic than their differences. Both stood together for evangelical concerns: classical Protestant orthodoxy, the unique authority of Scripture, the importance of vital spiritual experience, and the centrality of evangelism in the church's mission.

In 1921, several Presbyterian farming families in the Three Hills area, led by Fergus Kirk, a recent immigrant from Ontario, decided they needed better theological education for their children and themselves than they could provide. Fergus Kirk's sister Hattie had attended Bible school in Nyack, New York, and had been taught by W.C. 'Daddy' Stevens. She had given Kirk a set of Bible study questions composed by Stevens and these had helped him a great deal in his own Bible-study and teaching. After teaching a few others these questions, Kirk realized the district needed someone better trained than himself to carry on the instruction. He sat down and wrote a letter to the author of the questions, who had by this time moved to Kansas and begun his own school, Midland Bible Institute.

Stevens was delighted to hear of the opportunity for one of his students. Four would be finished their studies in another year, and the Three Hills people were content to wait. The one man among the four, a young Kansan named Leslie Earl Maxwell, consented to go, overcoming considerable reluctance to head up to farm country, of which he had grown tired – and duller, colder country at that!

L.E. Maxwell (1895–1984) stepped off the train in Three Hills in September 1922 to be met by a friendly Kirk, who embarrassedly told him how little they had to offer Maxwell. The harvest was poor that year, and the families had never known wealth even in the best of times. Maxwell no doubt looked around at the brown and gold fields and the three bumps on the horizon from which the town got its name and wondered how long he would stay – he had agreed to come for only a year or two.

Classes started just over a week later, on 9 October 1922, in an abandoned farmhouse that had been purchased for the school. Maxwell had endeared himself to the farmers by pitching in with the work in the intervening days. His abilities and interest in both education and manual labour pleased Prairie's constituency for years and characterized the life of the school he led. The first class were local students, eight teenagers and two 'bald-headed' men.[10] No record survives of the course of instruction for that year, but Maxwell composed a prospectus for the school's second year, a year that saw the enrolment double.

In the first paragraph of this three-page, handwritten document, Maxwell lays out principles that would guide the school throughout the fifty-five years of his presidency: its doctrinal orthodoxy, its transdenominational character, its concern to develop men and women of deep and disciplined personal spirituality who would devote themselves to spreading the gospel, and its financial policy of relying on gifts of the church for maintenance and expansion of the school without incurring debt: 'The School stands for every whit of the "Fundamentals"; it is of an interdenominational spirit and character, and has as its motto: "To know Christ and make Him known." Believing that God will supply all the needs for His own work, the School is established on a faith basis throughout.'[11] (In fact, Maxwell extended the ideas of depending directly on God for financial support, of self-denial, and of fellowship in the Lord's service by refusing to take a salary after his first year and by having the rest of Prairie's staff equally divide with him whatever income was available for their use, rather than devising a pay scale.)

The original curriculum also served as a template for all the curricular expansion to follow. Most courses in either the two-year introductory course or the three-year 'graduate' course were Bible courses, history and literature were taught 'in Bible light,' and special courses discussed missions and church music. These classes were supplemented by practical training in evangelism: 'The outstanding feature of this branch is the evangelistic effort being put forth by the faculty and student body to care for at least eight untouched school districts each Lord's day. This proves a great success.'[12] The curriculum expanded rapidly: the original two- and three-year options became by 1929 a four-year course. This four-year program, whose contours simply followed those of the original program, would remain the norm throughout Prairie's history.[13]

Throughout its history until 1990, in fact, Prairie refused to seek accreditation from the American Association of Bible Colleges (which, despite its name, was the recognized accrediting agency for Bible schools on both sides of the border). It did so, among other reasons, because it would have had to require of its students a greater proportion of liberal-arts courses than it did. Prairie maintained instead a preponderance of Bible courses even relative to many other Bible schools. (An early catalogue testifies to this concern: 'We believe that the continual temptation facing us as a Bible School is that of endlessly multiplying various subordinate and isolated studies, valuable as they may be, to the crowding out of the great objective of securing a first hand grasp of the whole Bible.'[14])

In this terse document Maxwell also set out the principles of the study of the Bible that would guide the school to the present. He too had admired and profited by 'Daddy' Stevens's 'search question' method of instruction and determined that Prairie Bible Institute (at this time known as the 'Three Hills Bible School') would use it.[15] 'The whole Bible is studied consecutively and constructively under the guidance of select questions given to each student. This method enables each student to produce his own original findings from the Scriptures thereby to secure the Book as *his own possession – his very own.* This is the culminating object of the school.'[16]

The next year's prospectus, now professionally printed, added the declaration that 'the aim of the School is to produce a Bible Teaching and Missionary Ministry under the unction of the Holy Spirit.'[17] These emphases upon missions and (implicitly) transdenominationalism were extended later in the same brochure: 'The School pushes missionary interest to the ends of the earth, and opens its doors to all true missionaries of the Cross, regardless of denominational affiliation.'[18] (By 1973, the school had sent out over sixteen hundred graduates to foreign missions.[19]) The school year concluded with a missionary convention, establishing a perennial tradition. And within the first four years of the school's opening, it had collected and distributed over $10,000 to foreign missions: all of it to 'Interdenominational Faith Missionary Societies.'[20] The school would provide to its constituency this service of distributing missionary donations ever after.[21]

Prairie's links with these societies reflected its constituency. Prairie claimed to be 'unsectarian,' and indeed its students came from a variety of churches. But not a wide variety: throughout its history Prairie's students came almost entirely from non-mainline, non-Pentecostal,[22] evangelical churches. In the early years Prairie drew students especially those from churches calling themselves 'interdenominational' or 'nondenominational' and later predominantly from Baptist churches.[23] It did not, however, seek to serve the mainline denominations at any time in its history. This marks it out as different from TBC, but typical of most Bible schools. As one historian has commented, the generic Bible-school claim to be nondenominational means that these schools 'are not hampered by the particular emphases of the various denominations and that they do not subscribe to certain views which they consider modernistic and which they associate with the churches. They are free to put forward a statement of doctrine of their own, and in addition to this they are also free to solicit funds from denominational people who otherwise might not give to them.'[24] Such churches especially could be expected to support the 'interdenominational faith missions' of the time, and the China Inland Mission (CIM) and Sudan Interior Mission (SIM) were favourites of the donors.[25]

The enrolment, now including students from outside the Three Hills area, required a new building, which was secured in 1924. This was the start of a building program that would culminate decades later in a 130-acre campus with a centrepiece auditorium seating four thousand.[26] Nineteen twenty-four also saw the school change its name to Prairie Bible Institute. And the prospectus for that year outlined Prairie's new statement of faith:

The Bible as the Very Word of God.
Salvation by faith through the substitutionary death of Jesus Christ.
Sanctification, victory and preservation through faith in and obedience to Jesus Christ under the Holy Spirit.
Prayer for the sick in accordance with the injunctions of God's Word.
The Second Premillennial Return of Christ.
The Church's sole business – with no worldly alliances, but looking for her Lord's return – to shed the light of the gospel continuously in all the earth.[27]

By 1926 the focus of the school had shifted slightly. To be sure, the main thrust yet was the training of students in the Scriptures especially so that they might convert and train others, and particularly on the mission field. As Ted S. Rendall, Maxwell's right-hand man and later president of the Institute, wrote in 1969: 'The Church must not allow itself to be distracted from its main mission in the world – the rescuing of men and women ... The early Church did not go into all the world preaching the Gospel of healing, or of education, or of rebellion. They preached the good news of Christ's death and resurrection and glorification ... But what of the twentieth-century Church? Is it not in too many cases involved in secondary ministries? The Church's supreme ministry is still the saving of that which is lost.'[28] And, unlike TBC, Prairie expected to train pastors as well as layworkers of various sorts.[29]

The spectre of 'modernism,' however, made its first appearance in the 1926–7 prospectus (the reference to Thomas Paine doubtless reflecting Maxwell's American evangelical heritage rather than that of the Canadian farmers who invited him): 'Furthermore, we believe that the best antidote for the wide-spread unbelief of Tom Paine and various other free thinkers – commonly posing under the guise and misnomer of 'Modernism' – is a program of aggressive personal evangelism and constructive Bible teaching.'[30]

Perhaps with modernism in mind, the school altered the first clause of its statement of faith to declare belief in 'the Plenary Inspiration of the Scriptures,' using terms made popular by those stalwart defenders of the Scriptures at Princeton of a generation or two before.[31] Withstanding modernism and its supposed ally, the ecumenical movement, would figure in Prairie's mission thereafter.[32]

The statement of faith was also expanded to include a clause regarding 'the distinctive gift of the Holy Spirit as Comforter for the child of God and the servant of the Lord.'[33] The statement as it now read would remain substantially unchanged until 1934, at which time clauses were added to bring the school more squarely into line with most other schools influenced by fundamentalism.[34] And in 1952 the statement was changed again, this time moving away from Maxwell's former belief in the Christian and Missionary Alliance emphasis upon prayer for the sick (this clause was dropped) and substituting a new clause regarding the ministry of the Holy Spirit: 'the infilling of the Holy Spirit for the child of God.'[35] This final form of the statement would guide Prairie for the remainder of Maxwell's term of leadership, and from first to last was a sample of generic evangelicalism in both Canada and the United States, from its emphasis upon the authority of the Scripture to its belief in a literal heaven and hell. Even its premillennial clause – the one thing that marks it off from Toronto Bible College – simply speaks for the majority of evangelicals.[36] TBC itself was led by premillennialists, and only its concern to serve a broader constituency than Prairie's kept it from articulating what in fact was its point of view on that subject.

Prairie was so satisfied with its own teaching (both its doctrine and its Bible-study method in particular) that it usually hired its own graduates as faculty. Often faculty members would have served as pastors or missionaries and then returned for a teaching career. Maxwell underscored both this high regard for Prairie's teaching and the constituency's suspicion of the established theological seminaries when he wrote the following. It came at the end of a letter from a Prairie graduate that bewailed the dead scholasticism and Biblical ignorance he said he had witnessed at 'one of the rather better seminaries': 'We are convinced that rarely does God ever lead an Institute graduate to continue his studies under such auspices. However, we are not laying down rules, much less passing judgment on these who have gone on to seminary, but simply to let our readers see first hand what our students are receiving from the Word of God and kindred studies in this Institute.' Indeed, in another of the magazine's rare references to theological seminaries, a sad story was told: 'Not long ago a theological student came up to us at the close of the meeting and said, "I have taken just one year here at the seminary, and ..." Well, he looked so sick. His very face looked as though his stomach was full of bile. His heart and mind had been poisoned and he felt sick-at-heart. If he keeps on at that particular school he will soon say what another graduate said after finishing his theological course, "I have finished my course, I have *lost* the faith." '[37]

Most faculty were men, but a few women followed the pattern of D.R. Miller, who exercised a teaching ministry at Prairie since 1928 and helped Maxwell edit the *Prairie Pastor*. Miller was unusual in several respects for a Prairie faculty member, having graduated from both Columbia and New York universities and served in Bible-school work for twenty years before coming to Prairie.[38] On only one occasion did she defend her role as Bible teacher in the *Prairie Pastor* to the many evangelicals who believed this to be contrary to Scripture, and Maxwell backed her up.[39] Women also frequently wrote for the school magazine.

Prairie manifested a rural attitude in one distinctive respect. Until the early 1960s, it required students to perform manual labour without pay. (By that time, with the increased mechanization at the school, there was not enough labour to go around. The school then hired students who needed to earn extra money.) This former practice reflected both the school leaders' decision to keep costs down as much as possible and also the general rural respect for physical work, as much as they valued formal education.

Another characteristic was typical not only of rural schools but of the Bible school movement in general: a strict approach to student life and responsibility. Toronto Bible College's entrustment of student behaviour at least initially to the hands of students themselves was exceptional. Normally Bible schools did what Prairie did: outline a set of regulations by which students were intended to abide.

One might see this as paternalistic, but the appropriate metaphor, at least in Prairie's case, is military. Prairie prepared students in a particular way because it understood world missions in a particular way. Maxwell again here stands for the school. Military imagery figured often in his description of the sort of Christianity Prairie stood for.[40] A collection of his radio broadcasts and journal articles was entitled *World Missions: Total War.*[41] On the left wall of the new Tabernacle was painted a heraldic shield with the motto, 'Disciplined Soldiers.' And Prairie's explanation of the rationale for the rules drew upon athletic and military analogies:

> When an athlete subjects himself to the rigourous discipline of regimented exercise, sleep, diet, instruction, teamwork, and obedience to orders, he does not consider this as punishment. He knows that these are the indispensable prerequisites to winning the game. Likewise the soldier is placed under strict authority and austerities, some of which appear to infringe on his individual and personal life. But the final objective and result of this military discipline is effectiveness in combat ...
>
> Now regimented discipline is not an end in itself; it is merely the prologue to godly self-control. If rightly accepted and appropriated, enforced regulation leads to a self-regulated life. This is the ultimate aim of the standards set down here at Prairie. They are high standards designed to produce high quality of Christian holiness, consecration, and dedication, by being incorporated into the individual's character and pattern of life.[42]

So Prairie's regulations are understood better as part of a missionary 'boot camp' experience than as an extreme attempt to ward off behaviour parents didn't like in their children.[43]

The pamphlet called *General Information* given to students for the 1947–8 school year (roughly the mid-point of Maxwell's tenure) can serve as a sample of Prairie's application of the principle of discipline. The manual began with a daily timetable by which all students were to abide. All were to rise at 6:00 AM and all were to turn lights out at 10:00 PM. In between were specific times for private and group devotions, meals, classes, chapel, and study.

Saturdays and Sundays had their timetables too. Almost a page of regulations followed for the correct use of study hours, then two pages of 'general regulations.' These miscellaneous rules, among other things, required students to secure permission to accept supper invitations in homes outside the Institute; to exercise forty-five minutes every day they were not in physical-education classes; to go 'downtown' only on the days prescribed for their sex (women on Tuesday, Thursday, and Saturday; men on Monday, Wednesday, and Friday); and to be careful in the use of precious water. Two pages of rules for mealtimes, including a page of guidelines for table etiquette, clearly were intended to help civilize the farm folk who attended – a judgment borne out by the following page of rules for 'everyday courtesies and considerations.' Sandwiched between rules for dormitory-room maintenance and the proper use of laundry facilities was a page of rules to help women students avoid bowing 'to the modern goddess, Fashion.'[44] (Later it must have become apparent that men needed guidance as well, although their problem was not idolizing 'Fashion' but emulating rock-and-roll stars and hippies by growing long hair, large mustaches, and beards – all of which were forbidden.[45]) The women were instructed: 'We do not approve of short skirts, low necks, short sleeves (three-quarter length sleeves are permitted), sheer material in waists or dresses, sheer or conspicuous stockings, or the use of cosmetics. We believe that Christians should dress scripturally, not conforming to the fashions of this world.'[46] Charts were provided on the facing page that detailed the appropriate skirt lengths for women of each height. Length of hair as well as of skirt and sleeve came under Prairie's guidance as well. Although haircutting was later allowed, at this time 'young women are requested not to cut their hair during their years of attendance at the Institute' since 1 Corinthians 11:15 spoke plainly that 'If a woman have long hair, it is a glory to her.'[47]

It was left to the Student Handbooks, however, to outline what to some was Prairie's most attractive and to others its most notorious feature of student life: its regulation of romantic relationships. Nowhere is Prairie's sense of commitment to disciplined Bible training, and especially missionary training, more obvious than in its elaborate code of behaviour for men and women. Throughout Maxwell's tenure, Prairie distinguished several levels of relationship, using such an ascending scale as 'acquaintance,' 'interest,' 'going steady,' 'understanding,' 'engagement,' and 'marriage.' Each level had to be approved by the school and carried with it a set of guidelines.

The school preceded these regulations, however, with a statement of its intent. The essence of it follows:

> The distinctive function of Prairie Bible Institute is to train young people for Christian service – approximately 50 per cent of our students have gone into missionary service overseas. Therefore, in order that our students may be unhindered in the serious business of studying the Word of God, of completing their training for the Lord's service, and of finding and fulfilling the will of God for their lives, social relations are carefully regulated between men and women during their years of attendance at Prairie.
>
> ... One of the most crucial tests which face Christian young people today is whether or not they will lay aside or control their interest in one another so that they may put God and His will first in their lives.
>
> Basically, then, our social standards are but a segment of the far greater principle of the Christian life – namely, the life of dynamic discipleship; the crucified life; the renunciation and denial of the self-life. Since many young people today do not possess the self-discipline required to keep their interests in proper perspective to their divine calling, these regulations are designed to assist them to seek first the kingdom of God and His righteousness.[48]

Maxwell himself had shown years of exemplary self-control in the courting of his wife – as had she – and so was disposed to steer students along the same path, especially since some of them could fairly be assumed to be less dedicated than he had been.[49]

Under Maxwell's leadership, the school grew dramatically, taking its place in the vanguard of the Bible-school movement across North America and establishing a reputation as Canada's best-known Bible school. Most of its students came from the Canadian and American west (from 1949–50 until 1975–6, in fact, more students came from the United States than from Canada[50]) and from points beyond – some each year came from overseas, whether missionaries' children or nationals of other countries who had come into contact with one of Prairie's many missionary alumni.[51] By 1940–1, Prairie's original enrolment of ten had swelled to five hundred (this figure included ninety-six in Prairie's young high school, founded in 1938).[52] Attendance hit its peak as Prairie enrolled servicemen returning from the Second World War in 1948–9 for an aggregate total of nine hundred, making Prairie the largest Bible school in Canada and one of the largest in the world.[53] This five-year, one-time boost from those who had delayed education during the war was followed by a relative decline in enrolment. Prairie's numbers dipped during the 1950s to a low of 560 in mid-decade, but rebounded to reach 671 by 1960–1 and over 800 by 1970–1. At the time of Maxwell's handing over of the reins to his son Paul in 1977, Prairie's attendance was still just over 800.

Prairie's growth and development reflects changes in Canadian or at least western Canadian society in these years. Its initial growth came from the recent immigrants to the West – whether American, eastern Canadian, or eastern European – who sought training for themselves and their youth to prepare them for the pastoral work at home that the frontier needed and for the mission fields beyond.[54] The Depression hardly slowed it down, as only one year saw fewer students than its predecessor. Even during the Second World War Prairie's numbers increased.

Some have seen evidence of a spiritual revival on the Canadian prairies in the 1930s and 1940s, exemplified in the founding of many Bible schools, which helps to explain the large numbers making their way to Prairie Bible Institute in the most desperate of times.[55] Prairie's numbers declined in the 1950s relative to the immediate postwar figures, yet the numbers were still significantly higher than the pre-war figures. This decade also marks the dramatic shift in the relative numbers of Canadian and American students at Prairie as the United States experienced a religious revival on many fronts, not least among evangelicals. And as evangelical churches continued to grow in the 1960s and 1970s, so Prairie continued to grow – a correlation that would not extend into the next decades.

L.E. Maxwell and other leaders at Prairie Bible Institute were alert to changes not only in Canadian society but also across the world. In the Institute magazine, Maxwell and his associate editors regularly commented on 'The World in the Light of the Word.' In this column the editors concentrated on the forces of evil they saw to be most dangerous to the health of the church and the spread of the gospel. The three most frequently mentioned foes were modernism (and its supposed offspring, the ecumenical movement[56]), communism,[57] and Roman Catholicism. As did other fundamentalists, Prairie's leaders often linked the three.[58] All opposed the gospel, all were militant, and all posed some threat to the church in some part of the world. Communism and Roman Catholicism especially were dangerous because of their commitments to world domination, and the Prairie editors were quick to spot attempts by either to extend its influence in Canada or the United States.[59] Modernism was an internal problem, a cancer in the church – although Prairie's leaders seem to have had little first-hand contact with it: most of their references are to newspaper articles and their most frequent target was the distant fundamentalists' favourite foil, liberal preacher Harry Emerson Fosdick of New York City.[60]

Indeed, as the years rolled on and Prairie continued to expand, there is little evidence of actual engagement with these foes, whether in debate, public protest, or political action. The enemies, even modernism, seem at one remove at least from Prairie and its constituency: dangers against which Prairie was a bulwark, but still distant dangers for most readers of its warnings. This apparent absence of contact is extraordinary when one considers the large presence of the United Church on the prairies, the church most evangelicals viewed with disaffection if not outright hostility, and Prairie's avowed identity as a militant opponent of modernism.[61] Unexpectedly rare, also, are references to evolution. Prairie clearly eschewed anything close to evolutionary science,[62] but this was not at all the animating issue it was in American fundamentalism. Indeed, in at least one five-year period, 1960–4, the *Prairie Overcomer* did not mention evolution at all. Prairie Bible Institute, then, seems a centre of a community only indirectly involved with these forces of evil, content to set out its alternative rather than contend with them directly. This lack of engagement makes sense, therefore, only if Prairie is not seen as essentially a 'fighting fundamentalist' school, but rather as an evangelical institution preoccupied with preparing missionaries.

The Prairie magazine did comment on politics from time to time, but in typical evangelical fashion its most direct judgment of political figures usually was occasioned by revelations about their personal lives. To be sure, the editors especially disliked policies of Pierre Trudeau that smelled to them of socialism, if not communism. But Trudeau's own private improper behaviour drew more of their fire,[63] as had W.L. Mackenzie King's personal practice of spiritualism before him.[64] Indeed, when Prairie was directly approached (at least twice) by politicians to support their fellow Christian, William Aberhart, in his campaign for Social Credit, Prairie refused even to let him use their auditorium, declaring that their facilities existed for the spreading of the gospel, not for the pursuit of politics.[65] This almost completely spiritual understanding of the gospel typified Prairie under Maxwell. In one article, for instance, Maxwell rebuked those who held a 'lifeboat ethic' regarding world hunger, but then concluded with – not an exhortation to work to end world hunger – but an exhortation to give people what they *really* need, the gospel: 'But hearken, O Church of Christ! Amos foretells a time of a still worse famine, a scarcity not of bread and water, but a much sorer judgment than that, even a *"famine of hearing the words of the Lord"* (Amos 8: 11, 12 [emphasis Maxwell's]). How shall the famine-stricken hear without a preacher? But how can they preach except they be sent? Is it not our one business as believers to send starving peoples the Bread of Life?'[66] Hints of a new, more inclusive point of view came only well after he had left the presidency.

This concern for evangelism, indeed, is at the heart of everything at Prairie Bible Institute and was at the heart of the magazine as well. To make much more of the Prairie magazine's comments on the larger world would be to misrepresent its general character through these fifty-plus years. It was decidedly not preoccupied with any of these matters as a typical fundamentalist magazine would be. Nor did it feature many articles on Biblical prophecy – as those used to seeing fundamentalists preoccupied with dispensationalism would expect.[67] Instead, the overwhelming majority of its full-length articles were Bible studies for the general information and edification of the readers,[68] excerpts from great evangelical authors of the recent past on devotional or theological subjects,[69] and above all, stories or exhortations regarding evangelism and foreign missions.[70] The usual fundamentalist targets of alcohol, dancing, television, and rock-and-roll do come in for frequent attack in these pages.[71] And the Institute's strong commitment to discipline surfaces often in the form of exhortations to parents to spank their children, as the magazine's editors saw the removal of corporal punishment from home and school to be the leading cause of the increasing juvenile delinquency in Western societies.[72] They also consistently enjoin the use of capital punishment along the same lines.[73] These latter concerns, however, simply reinforce the central thrust of Prairie Bible Institute: to train disciplined Christians to proclaim the gospel throughout the world.

Throughout these changes in numbers and facilities, then, Prairie's character did not change. It continued to emphasize basic Bible training; it maintained an environment in which students would develop patterns of personal holiness; and it put all its efforts into what it saw to be the central task of the church, the evangelism of the world. In this, rather than in its strict behavioural codes, its large American contingent of students, its rural flavour, its links with few mainline congregations, and its distance from the academy, it stands with Toronto Bible College as a centre of evangelicalism in Canada.

Those several and important characteristics that distinguish it from TBC, however, alert one to the fact that there were at least two kinds of evangelicalism in Canada. And the history of the Inter-Varsity Christian Fellowship through these years manifests both the unity and diversity of these two types, as IVCF provided an organization in which the two could meet and cooperate.

— 5 —
Inter-Varsity Christian Fellowship: 1929–1970

I landed at the University of Alberta in the fall of '34, I was seventeen years of age, and I was very pleased to find that there was a Christian organization on campus. I came out of a background where there was no university influence whatever, either in our family or in the families that were friends of our family in the small prairie town that I lived in. I didn't know anyone apart from my high school teachers who had ever gone to university. And I'd been led to believe that it was the playground of the devil, so to speak, that there wouldn't be anything positive there whatever. So I was delighted to find there was a Christian organization on campus.

I immediately joined it: it was the Student Christian Movement. And I started meeting weekly in what was called a Bible study group ... But the approach was very naturalistic and rationalistic, very negative, so by Christmas I realized that there was nothing positive in this SCM group, that they had no understanding of salvation or forgiveness, they had no sense of mission, they had no message to proclaim. They were just asking all kinds of questions, usually very skeptical questions ('Oh, you don't really believe that, do you?' 'You can see how, of course, this has been misunderstood ...'). So I was pretty dissatisfied.

And then in January of '35, a little notice appeared on the bulletin board of the Arts building saying, 'Anyone interested in Bible study and prayer meet in such-and-such a room.' So I went that week, and there were about ten of us: a couple of 'med' students, a pharmacy student, a geology student, a math student, and so on. I discovered students who really knew the Lord and had a desire to follow the Lord and be a witness and grow in Christ. And so that was the beginning of the VCF at the University of Alberta. We met every week, and it's been going on ever since, since January of '35.[1]

This testimony is typical of many students who participated in the Inter-Varsity Christian Fellowship (IVCF) in Canada. From small, closed, theologically conservative denominations, these students would find in the howling wilderness of the university a haven where the familiar verities were believed, familiar piety was practised, and familiar priorities (personal spiritual growth and evangelism) were taken for granted.

For many of these students as well, however, Inter-Varsity would be the first contact they would have with members of other churches, especially mainline churches, or even with new converts with little or no church background. These Christians, who used different words to speak of the Christian faith and who believed different things about many subjects, yet practised what their conservative friends had to agree was authentic Christianity and stood with the well-churched conservatives for the authority of the Scriptures, the necessity of vital spirituality, and the priority of evangelism in the mission of the church.[2]

So did the Inter-Varsity Christian Fellowship of Canada not only bring together students from different parts of Canada, but also from different religious backgrounds as well. To be sure, for all the variety of traditions it embraced, Inter-Varsity represented and promulgated one distinctive form of Christianity, evangelicalism. But it was also virtually the only link among evangelicals of various sorts across Canada until the 1960s. Moreover, its history over the first forty years shows development, diversity, and sometimes signs of stress within Canadian evangelicalism, especially during the turbulence of the 1960s. Still, the commonality was affirmed throughout, and the Inter-Varsity Christian Fellowship stands as a third important manifestation of the mainstream of Canadian evangelicalism.[3]

English antecedents for Inter-Varsity in Canada were fifty years old before the idea was transplanted across the Atlantic in 1928.[4] The first of the 'Christian Unions,' the Cambridge Inter-Collegiate Christian Union (CICCU) began to meet in 1877.[5] The next decade saw a number of Christian Unions begin on other British campuses and these groups joined together to constitute the British Colleges Christian Union. In 1905 they adopted the crisper name Student Christian Movement (SCM), uniting with student elements of the nascent 'ecumenical movement' spearheaded by American John R. Mott.

That same year the Oxford chapter of the SCM surprised the Cambridge group with the question of whether Unitarians could join their fellowship, a question naturally arising from the SCM's increasing inclusivism. This was the beginning of doctrinal disagreements within and between the groups. In 1910, two hundred members of the Cambridge Union were encouraged to leave by the SCM after long negotiation, believing their ethos to be so distinctly different from that of the SCM that Cambridge ought to have two student groups, not one. They also thus broke with the World Student Christian Federation, an arm of the 'ecumenical movement' that would receive so much impetus from the Edinburgh missionary conference of that very year. A London fellowship similar to the one in Cambridge was formed shortly thereafter, and like-minded students at Oxford resurrected the 'Oxford Inter-Collegiate Christian Union' (OICCU) name (dropped by the previous owners as they joined SCM) in 1919. Evangelical unions sprang up in the early 1920s in Aberdeen, Belfast, Bristol, Cardiff, Dublin, Edinburgh, and Liverpool.

Beginning in 1919, these groups held an annual 'Inter-Varsity Conference,' so named because the date of the first one coincided with the annual 'Inter Varsity' rugby game between Oxford and Cambridge. In April 1928 fourteen of the twenty-eight universities were represented at a conference that saw the birth of the Inter-Varsity Fellowship of Evangelical Unions, known more briefly as the Inter-Varsity Fellowship (IVF).[6] This conference, moreover, also saw the first glimmerings of the Canadian movement. Norman Grubb, Cambridge (and CICCU) graduate and missionary, had just returned from a tour of Canada and challenged the conference to send someone to begin a similar fellowship there. His sentiments were echoed by a Canadian evangelical leader present, Rowland V. Bingham, founder of the Sudan Interior Mission. A graduating London medical student, Howard Guinness, agreed to go, and the new Fellowship sent him off with a one-way ticket, with pocket money paid for in part by the sale of students' tennis racquets.

Guinness traveled to Montreal in the autumn of 1928 and then was met in Toronto by Noel Palmer, an OICCU graduate and at that time a pastor of the Christian and Missionary Alliance, who had just begun a Christian Union at the University of Toronto. Guinness began a year of travel across Canada that brought him into contact with several other evangelical student groups of various sorts – a few of which had been started out of disaffection for the increasing theological pluralism of the SCM – and Guinness reorganized some of these into Christian Unions.[7]

Before a national network was formed, however, Guinness realized the second of his two goals in coming to Canada. The British Christian Unions had supported Christian camps set up for youth around their country since late in the previous century. Guinness hoped to duplicate this ministry in Canada, and succeeded in mustering thirty campers and counsellors for the first session of Ontario Pioneer Camp on a lake in the Muskoka region of Ontario in 1929.[8]

Guinness brought together a handful of representatives of the Universities of Toronto, Western Ontario, and Manitoba at Kingston, Ontario, for a conference in September 1929. Arthur Hill, president of the group at Western and later to be a major figure among English-speaking evangelicals in Quebec, was elected the first president. A few months later, Guinness left to pioneer work in Australia. Hill's medical studies were ending, and Noel Palmer took over as general secretary[9] in the fall of 1930. Guinness returned in early December and with Palmer launched the high-school version of I-V, known as Inter-School Christian Fellowship (ISCF), in a Vancouver secondary school, and early in 1931 in southern Ontario.[10] This pioneering period also saw the establishment of two more branches of Inter-Varsity, among students of normal schools (as colleges of education were then called) and of nursing schools.

Noel Palmer left the Fellowship to become an Anglican rector in Toronto in 1933. Arthur Hill took over as general secretary for a year, and then a new chapter opened as C. Stacey Woods succeeded the young physician as general secretary in 1934. Woods would serve in this office for another eighteen years.

Stacey Woods had come from Australia by way of Dallas Theological Seminary and Wheaton College, whence he had earned degrees in theology and arts respectively. Woods intended originally to stay for only a year and then pursue plans to work with Howard Guinness in India for two years before seeking Anglican ordination in Australia.[11] Instead, he would not only establish Inter-Varsity in Canada, but would extend it into the United States and become general secretary of the International Fellowship of Evangelical Students (IFES).

Woods came to a movement that already had been consolidated to some extent. The camping work in Ontario was on firm footing, chapters were continuing to open in the different levels of schools, and in 1933 the Fellowship had adopted a Statement of Agreement. This document outlined the theology upon which all leaders of IVCF agreed:

1. The Divine inspiration, integrity, and authority of the Bible.
2. The Deity of our Lord Jesus Christ.
3. The necessity and efficacy of the vicarious death of Jesus Christ for the redemption of the world.
4. The presence and power of the Holy Spirit in the work of regeneration.
5. The consummation of the Kingdom in the 'glorious appearing of the great God and our Saviour, Jesus Christ.'[12]

Arthur Hill, present at the drafting of the statement, described its context. The Basis of Faith, as it was also known, was drawn up

> in the vestry of Knox Church in Toronto and Dr. [John G.] Inkster was the chairman ... I have the strong impression that our basis of faith was drawn pretty well from that of the China Inland Mission. The China Inland Mission had a very strong influence on the fellowship in the early days ... I believe that all of us present at the time were premillennial as far as our outlook on the last things [was] concerned. However, Dr. Inkster pointed out that it would not do to put a statement regarding the premillennial coming of the Lord into a basis of faith which must be acceptable to all evangelical Christians. I believe it was he who hit upon that verse in Titus which is quoted in full as our belief regarding the coming of the Lord ... We all felt this was a very happy solution to what might have been a thorny problem and the whole basis of faith actually passed quite rapidly.[13]

This statement was joined by a declaration of the purposes of Inter-Varsity drawn up by Stacey Woods, Arthur Hill, and Ted Simmonds (who would later become principal of Toronto Bible College): 'The purpose of the Fellowship shall be to establish and maintain in the schools and colleges of Canada groups of students whose object it shall be to (a) witness to the Lord Jesus Christ as Saviour and God Incarnate, and to seek to lead others to a personal faith in Him as Saviour; [and] (b) to deepen and strengthen the spiritual life of the members by the study of the Bible and by Prayer.[14]

With these two statements, Inter-Varsity identified itself with typical evangelical theology and typical evangelical concerns.[15] It did so, in addition, with a specific alternative in mind: the Student Christian Movement, which was well established in Canada. Noel Palmer had spoken to this point in 1931: 'With regard to the SCM we feel that we are trying to do a distinct work, namely to win students to Christ as their Saviour, Lord and God, which is frankly not the aim of some of the SCM groups. Our distinct function is therefore clear.' Yet Palmer recognized that some of the SCM groups still stood with Inter-Varsity for evangelical principles: 'But we are not to stand merely for an organization, nor must we hesitate to join freely with any in the SCM who show themselves genuinely determined upon the same goal.'[16] As the SCM in Canada continued to move away from these evangelical principles and into its subsequent history of shifting theological allegiances, however, the prospect for joint action became remote, and Inter-Varsity's identity as a distinct group of evangelical Christians became increasingly clear to schools and churches through Woods's tenure and beyond.[17]

Inter-Varsity Christian Fellowship also sought to serve evangelicals across denominational lines. A statement accepted by Inter-Varsity's board of directors in 1949 put on record a sentiment that dated back to the origins of the movement: 'The Board of Directors is pleased to reaffirm the essentially interdenominational character of the Inter-Varsity Christian Fellowship. As an organization, we desire to co-operate with any local church or religious organization which is loyal to Jesus Christ as God incarnate and which trusts in His atoning death as the only basis of acceptance with God. We seek to encourage students to obey the call of Christ. We do not discourage the loyalty of any student to his denomination or the leading of God in his life in the call to ministry, but rather seek always to be a constructive force in the cause of Christ universal.'[18] The last clause, 'We do not discourage the loyalty of any student to his denomination,' seems to have been a true portrayal of Inter-Varsity's transdenominational character. Evangelical Anglicans and Christian Brethren held leadership positions out of proportion to their numbers in Canadian Protestantism at large (a phenomenon paralleled in the British movement, although in

British evangelicalism generally the Anglicans and Brethren are prominent). Other mainline denominations as well as some uniformly evangelical denominations, though, were well represented among both staff and students.[19] (Only in the 1950s and 1960s, however, would the Fellowship begin to include significant numbers of Christians from other groups formerly isolated from Canadian Protestant life, as younger members of these groups entered the universities and older leaders entered ecumenical fellowships out of their respective enclaves, whether Holiness and Pentecostal churches or ethnic Protestant communities like those of Anabaptists and Dutch Reformed.)

Under Stacey Woods, Inter-Varsity moved well out beyond the relatively urbanized centres of southern Ontario and British Columbia. Within three years of his taking office, over one hundred groups of high-school students had been organized, the budget for administration had grown six-and-a-half times, and the full-time staff had increased to five. And, what to Woods was particularly encouraging, 'the majority of campers this year came from homes and churches that could not truthfully be called evangelical.'[20]

As the Second World War came, Woods shifted his attention to the nascent work in the United States, begun under the guidance of Charles Troutman, another Wheaton College graduate and a friend of Woods. Melvin V. Donald was appointed associate general secretary in 1941, and presented a report to the board of directors of IVCF of Canada in 1943 outlining the growth of the movement that had been hampered by the loss of all male staff save himself to the armed forces.

Donald's report is notable here for at least two reasons. On the one hand, it described a continuing increase in Inter-Varsity chapters in high schools, normal schools, nursing schools, and universities. But it also described an inverse correspondence of Inter-Varsity's success or failure with that of the Student Christian Movement – as well as giving one leader's perspective on that latter movement: 'Without taking time to produce the evidence, it would appear that the SCM in Canada is distinctly on the wane. It is also safe to say that on precisely those campuses where the SCM is quite obviously losing favour (i.e. among students), it seems that the VCF chapters are rapidly assuming the ascendency. This is not a fact over which to gloat – but it is, I believe, a distinct cause for praise, that in the short space of 15 years on Canadian campuses the only student voice calling itself Christian and in reality being liberal, idealistic and non-Christian should be supplanted to such a large degree by student groups standing as a witness to the Saviourhood and Lordship of Jesus Christ.'[21] Donald's pleasure at the growth of IVCF versus the SCM was tempered by the acknowledgment that in the Maritime provinces, which had small schools and received only sporadic staffing by Inter-Varsity (and that only since 1939), little had been accomplished in the face of the firm position of the SCM.[22]

The war years saw not only growth in numbers, however, but also the explicit recognition of a third purpose for the movement. At a joint conference of the staffs of Inter-Varsity in the United States and Canada in September 1942, a resolution was passed to encourage Inter-Varsity to 'make the call of the mission field central in all its thinking and planning. To this end, we, as staff members, will endeavour, by helping Christian students to understand the needs and claims of the unevangelized fields, to lead them to the place where they shall volunteer for service in whatsoever position the Lord may appoint.'[23] This resolution led to the addition in the Letters Patent of Incorporation (1944) of a third clause in Inter-Varsity's purposes. In addition to witnessing to Christ and deepening one's own spiritual life, student leaders and staff alike determined to 'emphasize the essential duty and privilege of every Christian to take a definite interest and share in world-wide missions – to give and pray and serve where God directs.'[24]

This missionary emphasis had always been a part – if only an implicit part – of the IVCF ethos, as the informal links with the China Inland Mission, for instance, demonstrate.[25] Missions took centre stage, though, in the first international missions conference sponsored by Inter-Varsity at the University of Toronto during the Christmas break of 1946–7. Among the speakers were Harold John Ockenga, prominent Boston pastor and leader of the soon-to-emerge 'new evangelicals' in the United States; Samuel Zwemer, pioneer missionary to the Muslim world; and L.E. Maxwell, president of the Prairie Bible Institute.[26] Attended by 550 students, 250 of which volunteered for foreign missions, this conference was relocated in Urbana, Illinois, and continued as a triennial missions conference attended by thousands.[27]

This missionary interest, however, was rightly placed third, as Inter-Varsity never succeeded in making this as central in its program as the other two. Its activities always were distinguished by emphasis either on the growth of the Christians within the group or on the evangelism of non-Christians without. For most students, that is, involvement with Inter-Varsity meant participation in one or more of the following activities. Almost all chapters arranged for small groups to gather weekly in dormitory rooms or common rooms for conversational study of the Bible. Students themselves normally led these meetings, often with training gained from a staff worker or a session of leadership camp. Prayer meetings were a staple, and were usually held early in the morning before classes or at noon – times that fit most student timetables. Individual problems, chapter projects, and foreign missionaries generally comprised the standard list of petitions, while prayers of praise and thanks, perhaps augmented with songs, framed the requests. More publicly, groups usually held large meetings from time to time (even week to week in more ambitious chapters), in which guest speakers would offer Bible lessons, tales of missionary experience, or apologetics lectures. Such meetings normally began with vigorous singing, accompanied by piano or guitars, as IVCF – especially under Stacey Woods – developed a strong tradition of song. Some chapters set up book tables in areas of high student 'traffic' like student unions and dormitories. These offered evangelical literature for sale or even for free, usually of a devotional or apologetic sort. And those who worked at the tables typically hoped for conversations with browsers that would lead to links with the group and, most excitingly, the conversion of the inquirer. Finally, the Canadians took over the British custom of holding periodic university missions, large-scale evangelistic campaigns on a campus conducted by a guest speaker over several days. Indeed, as the staff conference of May 1950 affirmed, 'The foremost purpose of the Fellowship is soul winning, and staff, students and sponsors should direct their efforts to this end.' This problem of integrating a foreign-missions emphasis into a movement directed originally toward the evangelization and nurture of students on school campuses – trying, in effect, to encourage one kind of missionary to consider a different sort of work after graduation while mostly helping and encouraging him or her to do what he or she was doing in the first place – would not be fully and articulately resolved in the Fellowship. Indeed, later leaders of IVCF would implicitly challenge this emphasis upon 'full-time missionary service' in terms of a broader understanding of Christian vocation.

By the late 1940s, Woods was overwhelmed by the work in overseeing the American and Canadian movements and the new IFES (begun in 1947). Thomas R. Maxwell was appointed to oversee the university work, but he soon left for the mission field[30] and was replaced by a young staff worker, H.W. 'Wilber' Sutherland, in September 1948. Sutherland took on more of the load by becoming Secretary also of the ISCF and Secretary to the board of directors in 1949. Woods, though, had asked to be relieved of all his duties in Canada as early as 1947.[31] By 1952 there were some two hundred ISCF groups across Canada.[32] Ontario Pioneer now had counterparts in Alberta and Manitoba. A summer camp in Ontario, known as Campus-in-the-Woods, had been organized successfully to train student leaders. The staff had grown to twenty-five: fifteen in Inter-Varsity, Inter-School, and Camp work, one in Nurses Christian Fellowship, one in Teachers Christian Fellowship, and eight in office work.[33] And chapters continued to develop across Canada in the schools of higher education. Moreover, Inter-Varsity's character had been well established: it was a movement of students, aided by full-time staff, that sought to evangelize other students, grow in personal discipleship, and consider the call of God to foreign missions while standing for traditional evangelical theology. It welcomed anyone who could join with it in its basic principles, whatever one's denomination. In 1952, then, the board decided, apparently with some reservation about his youth,[34] to appoint Sutherland to the post of general secretary. It was about six years before the movement faced its first controversial decision, the foretaste of more than twenty years of controversy that would cause the movement to reconsider often its identity and mission and that would end only in the term of General Director James E. Berney in the 1980s.

In the late 1950s the board confronted the question of appointing the first black person to the staff, Frederick Bernard Smith (known to subsequent generations of Inter-Varsity members as 'Bernie' Smith, the gifted song-leader at several Urbana conferences). The board met in September 1958, fully aware of the racial tensions growing in the southern United States at the time (the chairman alluded specifically to the forced integration at Little

Rock, Arkansas). Some of the board members clearly were concerned about elements in the Inter-Varsity constituency who might object to this move, but when the vote came the motion was carried with only two abstentions, and these 'expressed that they felt the idea was sufficiently new that they could not really express an opinion.'[35]

Neither too much nor too little should be made of this decision. On the one hand, while Canadians have struggled with racism as have all other human societies, the small number of blacks in Canada as well as the very different history of relations between white and black races in Canada has meant that a Canadian board could make a decision like this far more easily than could its counterpart in the United States.[36] On the other hand, the Canadian board recognized that (for reasons not recorded) some of its constituency would likely object to this appointment – although subsequent minutes do not record any negative reaction to it – and went ahead in the face of this concern. The precedent was now set to admit anyone of any colour to the staff.

Early in the 1960s the board had to decide whether anyone of any Christian religious experience would be welcome on the staff. Specifically, it was faced with the outbreak of 'glossolalia,' or the spiritual gift of speaking in 'tongues,' characteristic of Pentecostalism and the nascent charismatic renewal movement in mainline churches.[37] The issue surfaced in the early summer of 1965 when Board members became aware that Jo McCourt, director of the girls' camp in Ontario, had spoken in tongues. (That this would be an issue for the board's attention at all indicates the absence of Pentecostalism among these evangelicals at this time.) The Central Ontario regional executive had investigated and concluded, 'The Committee does not wish to judge or condemn Miss McCourt, nor does it want to restrict the ministry that God has given her. The Committee has confidence in her handling of her own ministry in situations both at camp and in her opportunities to speak as a representative of the Inter-Varsity Christian Fellowship in formal, public situations.'[38] This response apparently satisfied the Board for the moment, since no discussion was recorded.

That summer, however, glossolalia was evident again at the girls' camp – more evident than during the summer before, and Sutherland and the board agreed that the situation deserved more investigation.[39] In the autumn, the executive committee of the board drafted a new statement, later accepted by the board, which set out a more detailed position:

> Inasmuch as this is a Fellowship which has brought together believers in the Lord Jesus Christ with the common objective of witnessing to Him, we welcome the variety of spiritual experiences which each of us brings to our fellowship and seek to learn from one another; there is liberty for each one to share his particular convictions in personal conversation and discussion; we are open to whatever new work God may be wanting to do among us; nevertheless, since the Fellowship consistently has been inter-denominational in character without leaning to special themes which some hold dear for denominational or personal reasons, this Board reminds the staff, Councils, and Camp Committees that within the framework of this Fellowship we emphasize those subjects which we find central in Scripture and discourage an emphasis not found in Scripture on controversial issues such as speaking in tongues.
>
> This reminder is issued with the intention of strengthening our solidarity on the expressed PURPOSE of the Fellowship and with clear reaffirmation of our subscription ex animo to the DOCTRINAL BASIS each of us has signed.[40]

The board also decided to move McCourt from camp work among girls to university work among presumably less impressionable young adults.[41]

This policy and this move apparently did not resolve the issue. On 5 January 1967 the executive committee discussed at some length the continuing practice of glossolalia by several of the staff, and some committee members disagreed regarding the extent to which staff members were observing the policy set out by the board. The committee concluded, however, that 'the Board should be assured that the Executive were doing everything possible to ensure that the staff conformed to the stated policy and would continue to do so.'[42] This seems to have satisfied everyone, for Wilber Sutherland could write in the summer of 1968 that 'I would say that period [of controversy over glossolalia] seems to be over.'[43] Inter-Varsity's leaders had reaffirmed the basic principles of the movement: diversity was fine – even something as volatile as Pentecostal/charismatic diversity – as long as it did not threaten the unity of the central beliefs and purposes of the fellowship. The corollary to this viewpoint was the principle that anything that represented even a possible threat to this unity was suspect and therefore controlled.

At this same time, Inter-Varsity had to face an even tougher decision: whether the thinking and ministry of its own general director were threatening this unity. Inter-Varsity Christian Fellowship had grown remarkably in the 1950s and 1960s under Sutherland's leadership during a time of tremendous growth in Canadian education in general. In 1965 Sutherland could report on twenty-six university chapters involving three thousand students.[44] By 1968 the full-time staff had grown to more than fifty, and their numbers were buttressed by a half-dozen 'associate staff.'[45] Camping ministry had developed in Ontario, Manitoba, Alberta, and British Columbia – indeed, it was now the backbone of the Alberta program.[46] With the 'Quiet Revolution' in Quebec opening that culture to the larger world in new ways, work began among Francophones in Quebec for the first time.[47] Several staff members established an unusual form of ministry, known as The Cross Roads, in a house near the University of Toronto, meeting students informally in coffee shops, holding discussion groups, maintaining a reference library of Christian books, and seeking in other ways to penetrate university life.

To be sure, Inter-Varsity was not advancing on all fronts. The staff responsible for the high schools were overextended and the work suffered in some places: the number of chapters dwindled from a high of five hundred in the late 1950s to about three hundred by 1970.[48] With the evolution of normal schools into graduate departments of education at universities and the merging of nursing programs into colleges of applied arts and technology, the teachers' and nurses' fellowships declined.[49] And as the American IVCF developed its own regional campsites and leadership training centres, their sponsorship of Campus-in-the-Woods dropped off, and the facility was finally sold in 1970.

Inter-Varsity, though, had to face another kind of problem. Some of its constituency were, by mid-decade, questioning its fidelity to evangelical theology and priorities. These questions were put at least as early as 1963, compelling the board of directors to convene a special meeting. Two issues in particular were raised: was Inter-Varsity involved with 'worldly' activities (such activities, unfortunately, were not defined in the minutes of the meeting), and was it tainted by its association with the SCM and other similar organizations?[50] Sutherland responded with a reaffirmation of Inter-Varsity's evangelical character, allowing that some of its constituency might misunderstand its ministry to non-Christians, which might give the impression of being too involved in 'the world' (a charge that would return again later with greater force). Secondly, he said, IVCF's occasional work with individual SCM chapters, undertaken only after due consideration of possibly harmful compromise to IVCF's character, might be difficult for some to accept. The board agreed, however, that 'there was no reason to believe that the evangelical character of the movement had in fact altered.'[51]

A few years later a challenge was mounted from within the board itself. R.E. Robins, a member from British Columbia, sent a long letter to the Board detailing a lack of confidence in the leadership of Sutherland and of the board itself. The main burden of the letter was that the leaders of Inter-Varsity were failing to outline a clear vision of what the ministry especially in the universities and high schools should look like and of how this vision would fulfil the basic purposes of the Fellowship. In particular, he said, Sutherland spoke 'in generalities of exciting prospects for the future ... but nothing happens.' Indeed, the general director allegedly involved himself in 'activities which are non-essential to the neglect of essential duties,' these latter presumably including the outlining of a clear vision for the movement and a plan for staff recruitment. (Robins didn't mention financial leadership directly, but all the board members knew this was another area of difficulty.)[52] And finally, Robins concluded, IVCF's very doctrinal stand had been questioned by members of its constituency.

The board devoted two special meetings to discussing Robins's letter. It is not clear, however, what concrete changes emerged. The board made recommendations regarding staff personnel changes, improved communication in the hierarchy, and a new manual and program for the training of staff, among other things, but also reaffirmed its confidence in Sutherland's leadership.[53]

Sutherland stirred the pot again in 1967, however, with a statement of the 'Objectives and Philosophy of Inter-Varsity Christian Fellowship.' Written with a steering committee, the document yet has the marks of Sutherland as the main author and the response to it indicates that others saw him as such as well. The document, and its appendix written solely by Sutherland, set out a strong and self-consciously Reformed statement of the so-called 'creation mandate' of Genesis 1:26 and its implications for the mission of Inter-Varsity Christian Fellowship. Sutherland addressed bluntly the fear and rejection of the world characteristic of many evangelicals, and presented the different biblical words for 'world' to distinguish appropriate Christian rejection of the anti-Christian 'world-system' and appropriate Christian involvement in the 'world' of human culture. This theology, Sutherland believed, entailed a three-faceted ministry for Inter-Varsity: to foster personal spiritual growth among students, to present the gospel to those outside Christ, and to involve itself – and encourage individual involvement by students – in the life of the campus. Sutherland set out several implications of this thinking, reaffirming the traditional evangelical priority of evangelism, but also making room for a wider involvement in human affairs – involvement that itself could be part of a better, more direct kind of evangelism:

> (1) The IVCF as a movement should regard its immediate task as evangelism and direct its principal activities accordingly.
>
> (2) However, the prior claim of the first mandate [of 'stewarding' the earth, so Gen. 1:26–8] must also be recognized, and the Board, staff and student leadership be encouraged to a positive attitude towards involvement in the world in general ...
>
> (4) In fulfilling the task of evangelism, the IVCF must have as its objective that the Gospel actually be taken into the various social and academic structures of the academic world and the world of youth in general, not simply up to them. This must be with the prayerful intention that in each area Christians will develop a continuing witness to the truth and power of the Gospel and its relevance to the world.[54]

An anonymous group, identifying itself only as 'a group of people who has [sic] been closely connected with IVCF for years,' furiously responded to this brief with a twelve-page salvo. Drafted in May 1968, this protest essentially argued a point of view that would have been shared by many other evangelicals: the world is fallen and condemned – no matter what definition of 'world' one uses; the 'creation mandate' was for human beings *before* the Fall and the New Testament gives no indication that it is in effect for the church, redeemed *from* the Fall; indeed, Christians are often exhorted by the New Testament to avoid contact with the world for fear of contamination and compromise;[55] therefore the world should look after itself and Christians should concentrate their energies on the central task of the church, evangelism.[56]

The paper misread Sutherland in crucial spots and contained serious theological problems of its own (for example, in championing the New Testament over Sutherland's supposed preference for the Old, it scarcely dealt with the Old Testament at all). But it correctly perceived in Sutherland's writing a point of view different from its own.

The Inter-Varsity executive committee and then the whole board of directors dealt with the dispute in June 1968. Again the criticism of Inter-Varsity was couched not in terms of a mere difference in theology or emphasis but in extreme terms of 'whether or not IVCF was still evangelical in its commitment.'[57] After much discussion the executive committee recommended to the board a statement that was altered only slightly by the board and then passed. The statement expanded Inter-Varsity's purposes from three to five, inserting two new ones between the second and third:

> (a) To witness to the Lord Jesus Christ as God Incarnate and to seek to lead others to a personal faith in Him as Saviour and Lord; EVANGELISM IS A PRIME OBJECTIVE;
>
> (b) To deepen and strengthen the spiritual life of students and others by the study of the Bible, by fellowship and by prayer; THE SPIRITUAL DEVELOPMENT OF CHRISTIANS IS AN EQUALLY IMPORTANT OBJECTIVE;
>
> (IVCF views Christian growth as primarily the responsibility of the home and the local church, but since Christian students are often geographically and sometimes psychologically separated from these influences, IVCF recognizes the need to give them encouragement and guidance in their educational environment.)
>
> (c) To encourage Christians under the enablement of the Holy Spirit to demonstrate responsible Christian love; THE LOVE OF ONE'S NEIGHBOUR IS A COMMANDMENT OF THE LORD;
>
> (d) To assist Christian students and faculty to explore and assert to the educational community the relevance of the Christian faith to every issue of private life or public concern; ALL TRUTH IS IN CHRIST;

(e) To challenge Christian students and faculty with the privilege and obligation of participating in missionary outreach – to give and pray and serve in whatever area of life they are called by God; EVERY CHRISTIAN IS CALLED TO BE SENT.[58]

The board hereby clearly stood with Sutherland. The previous statement could be seen as defining a protective, separated fellowship of Christian students that would meet together for spiritual nurture, then 'go out' to evangelize the campus, and from time to time consider similar activity as a lifetime vocation on the foreign mission fields. This picture characterizes the outlook of the critics. While continuing to endorse the centrality of evangelism and personal growth, however, the board's new statement set these concerns in a new context, a context that would repudiate the 'holy huddle' conception of Christian fellowship and the 'foray' model of evangelism. The third and fourth clauses in the new statement picked up themes Sutherland had sounded about how Christians should approach the modern campus: they should involve themselves fully in the life of that society with love and intellectual vigour, rather than isolating themselves from it, in order to witness to and contribute the full range of Christianity's offerings to the world. And the fifth objective, formerly the third, was altered to reflect a growing recognition of the sacredness of all true vocations. To be sure, the statement cast this idea in traditional evangelical language about missions, articulating thereby not a full-fledged doctrine of vocation, since it reduced vocation to evangelism rather than seeing vocation as an end in itself. But it did move away from seeing 'full-time' missionary work as the only 'real' form of missionary work.[59]

Inter-Varsity none the less by this time had played a major role in directing students to consider full-time service in foreign missions. A survey taken in 1965 of over a thousand Canadian missionaries in a range of denominations indicated that one-fifth had 'received their Missionary Call' through IVCF, and this ratio approached one-half for the missionaries of the Canadian Baptists, Presbyterians, and Anglicans. But this interest in missions, traditional in (if not always at the forefront of) Inter-Varsity's consciousness and activity, suffered somewhat in these later years of Sutherland's administration. The steering committee's controversial paper about the objectives of Inter-Varsity, for instance, does not mention foreign missions at all.[61] And Sutherland later admitted that despite the huge size of the Urbana conference, 'there is an obvious confusion on the part of many staff and students as to the ways in which this objective [encouraging students to consider foreign missions] can be realistically and helpfully realized today.'[62] This confusion never was addressed programmatically at Inter-Varsity.

Otherwise, though, the board made a clear stand. It recognized Sutherland's point of view as legitimately evangelical and implicitly rejected the stark, separatistic spirituality of the critics. In doing so while reaffirming the two prime objectives of the movement, evangelism and personal growth, the Fellowship maintained a central and centrist place in Canadian evangelicalism even as it set out a broader vision for Canadian evangelicals.

Wilber Sutherland, however, continued to stretch the Board's idea of what evangelicalism properly could embrace. His wife had been involved for some time with a Christian drama group, called 'CREATION 2,' and this troupe had performed at the camp Inter-Varsity held for graduates in the summer of 1969.[63] The troupe performed a series of sketches, some of which troubled a number of those attending, including board members. The incidence of speaking in tongues during one of the sketches in particular distressed some of the members. The executive committee discussed the problem and agreed that identification of the group with the Fellowship was unfortunate. Some members went on to express concern that the confidence and financial support of the 'Christian public' might be jeopardized by this identification. Enough positive remarks were made about the drama both here and at the full board meeting two days later, however, that the board took no immediate action.[64]

As things quickly turned out, the board didn't need to take action. This particular interest of Sutherland's typified his growing interest in a variety of endeavours, especially among Toronto's artists, that drew him away from the traditional and central mission of Inter-Varsity. Indeed, in the day between the executive committee meeting and that of the full board during which CREATION 2 was discussed, Sutherland resigned. His letter of resignation was without bitterness. Instead, he stated simply that he felt called by God to a path Inter-Varsity probably would not take (although there seems a glimmer of hope, or perhaps mere wistfulness, that the Inter-Varsity leadership would join him, even if it meant losing support from other quarters). Sutherland also remarked that two recent events in his own family had provoked this decision. The first was indeed his wife's involvement with CREATION 2: 'This group is already a centre of controversy and will undoubtedly become more so in the future as it moves into major productions. Under present circumstances it would seem that our involvement would be a serious embarrassment to the Board.'[65] The second was another matter affecting a close relative, a matter which, because of the familial links with Sutherland, also would harm his ability to represent Inter-Varsity. The board had traversed a considerable distance with Sutherland over his tenure, but this time it agreed that the parting of the ways had come. It accepted Sutherland's resignation at a special meeting called to consider it early in October 1969, and reaffirmed that decision in November following discussion at the national corporation meeting in the intervening period.[66]

The acceptance of Sutherland's resignation has been seen by some associated with IVCF as the repudiation of the direction in which he had led the Fellowship.[67] Instead, his resignation must be seen as revolving around his unusual ministry among artists, rather than around the broader ideas of mission that he encouraged the Fellowship to consider and that were ultimately incorporated into the new statement of objectives by Inter-Varsity in 1968. At the end of Sutherland's tenure Inter-Varsity still stood squarely for the same theological platform of fundamental orthodoxy it always had, still proclaimed evangelism and the spiritual nurture of Christians its primary objectives. In this it stood in the mainstream of Canadian evangelicalism with both Toronto Bible College (as it became Ontario Bible College in 1968) and Prairie Bible Institute.

Largely because of Sutherland, however, and also because of a staff and board responsive to a larger vision than these few evangelical principles marked out, Inter-Varsity also affirmed the dignity of all true vocations and the importance of Christian penetration into all fields of human endeavour. By doing so, Inter-Varsity at the close of the 1960s disturbed many within Canadian evangelicalism, but also reflected developments in Canadian evangelicalism that would manifest themselves in a variety of institutions. Three of these can serve as conspicuous examples: a new liberal-arts college that would become Trinity Western University; a new experiment in higher education, a graduate school for study in the integration of theology and vocation for laypeople, Regent College; and a national fellowship of Christians that not only stood for traditional evangelical principles but also spoke to a wider variety of issues in Canadian society, the Evangelical Fellowship of Canada.

Part Three

The Mainstream Broadens and Coalesces: Canadian Evangelicalism to the Early 1990s

Introduction

The three decades from 1960 to 1990 were tumultuous years in Canadian life. Events that stick in many memories – a new Canadian flag, Expo '67, the October Crisis of 1970 involving terrorist Québécois separatists, the energy crisis, the landslide victories of Prime Ministers Trudeau and Mulroney – only dramatize the important changes taking place across Canada. In brief, over this period Canada became not only officially bilingual and bicultural, but in fact more multilingual and multicultural than ever before even as nationalism and regionalism waxed and waned. Industrialization and urbanization with concomitant changes to the economic and social orders continued apace. And widely accessible higher education and mass media brought Canadians into closer contact with the world than ever before.[1]

All of these developments posed considerable challenges particularly to churches accustomed to tradition, status, and widespread loyalty. Indeed, as John Webster Grant has put it, Canadians (and their churches) emerged late out of the Victorian era. It was in this time of upheaval that the traditional dominance of mainline Protestantism in Anglophone Canadian life and of Roman Catholicism in Quebec finally and obviously began to break up. The leadership of the mainline churches increasingly articulated a strong interest in certain secular matters of justice and equality both at home and abroad – to the virtual exclusion of spiritual and next-worldly matters, in the view of some. They emphasized dialogue with other faiths rather than preaching the gospel, according to many in their own constituencies. They espoused controversial changes in church life, whether hymn-book and prayer-book revisions, theologically suspect Sunday school curricula (most notably the United Church's curriculum of the early 1960s), and the ordination of women – and, in the United Church of the late 1980s and early 1990s, sexually active homosexuals. For all this energetic concern to relate Christianity to contemporary issues, however, the mainline churches steadily lost their grip on the imagination, thought, and life-patterns of Canadians. Traditional religious observance across the nation declined precipitously throughout this period, after a cresting of church membership for the mainline Protestant denominations in the mid-1960s. Whereas in 1946 two in three Canadians were in a house of worship (and almost always a Christian church) on a given weekend, by the early 1990s the proportion had dropped to just over two in *ten*. And dramatically more people identified themselves as having 'no religion' at all.[3]

Canadian culture continued to diversify. It seemed, for instance, that Canadians became somewhat more politically conservative in the early 1980s, electing successive Progressive Conservative majorities at the federal level. Yet they also supported a variety of parties at the provincial level – including several New Democratic governments by the early 1990s. A greater proportion of Canadians also seemed more religiously conservative in the 1980s as many evangelical churches and organizations prospered. At the same time, though, the mainstream churches slowed their decline and retained at least the ostensible allegiance of most Canadians, and the number of those claiming 'no religion' continued to increase.

Canadian society was opening up to new patterns of thought and life, and the major denominations apparently were moving leftward both theologically and politically. In this atmosphere of change and challenge, transdenominational evangelicalism began to develop institutional resources to take advantage of the new openness of society and the declining strength of the mainline churches. It was primarily concerned, however, to conserve what it saw to be the true faith and the proper mission of the church in the face of growing secularity in the larger society and the declension of the leadership of the major Protestant churches from evangelical Christianity. In the face of these challenges and opportunities, therefore, evangelicals who previously had little to do with each other joined together in a wide variety of projects.

Canadian evangelicalism in this era maintained its commitment to doctrinal orthodoxy, personal spiritual vitality, and the priority of evangelism in the church's mission. But it embraced a wider variety of traditions than it had before as it welcomed into the network significant numbers of Mennonites, Christian Reformed, and Pentecostals as they emerged from their enclaves. Evangelicals increasingly stressed the importance of the church as well as of the individual believer. And they began to recognize the importance of all vocations, not merely the pastoral and missionary.

These changes characterized not only a few innovative institutions: they were manifested in the leading institutions in Canadian evangelicalism. The forerunners, Toronto Bible College (which became Ontario Bible College in 1968), Prairie Bible Institute, and Inter-Varsity Christian Fellowship each demonstrated both commitment to the traditional concerns and the emergence of the new trends. But the founding of Trinity Western University was a dramatic and increasing response to these developments by 'sectish' evangelicalism, as was the founding of a quite different institution, Regent College, by 'churchish' evangelicals in Vancouver whose version of evangelicalism closely resembled that of the old Toronto Bible College. And the origin and growth of the Evangelical Fellowship of Canada both symbolized and was itself an important factor in evangelicals across the country not only manifesting similar concerns and changes, but also doing so increasingly as a national fellowship of Christians. Evangelicals were increasingly aware and generally supportive of each other's projects, even as differences between the two styles of evangelicalism remained.

Indeed, one such commonly supported project implicitly gave Canadians notice that evangelicalism was emerging as a self-conscious national alliance even as it explicitly presented a traditional evangelical message to the secular society of the 1960s: the 'Sermons from Science' pavilion at Expo '67.

— 6 —

'Sermons from Science' at Expo '67

Canadians showed themselves off to the world at the international exposition at Montreal in 1967. Canadian Christianity joined in, as it presented itself in strikingly symbolic fashion.[1] In the ecumenical spirit flourishing at the time (these were the heady days following Vatican II), Roman Catholic, Protestant, and Orthodox churches – that together represented the vast majority of Canadians – jointly sponsored a pavilion. In the experimental and critical spirit also flourishing at the time (this was also the era of Harvey Cox's *Secular City* and its ilk, which proposed 'secular' theologies, and of Pierre Berton's widely read critique of Canadian Christianity, *The Comfortable Pew*), the pavilion put forth some disturbing reflections upon the fair's theme, 'Man and His World.' A kaleidoscope of dramatic pictures and texts celebrated the possibilities of the 'secular city,' but also reminded visitors how badly so many men (and women and children) were faring in their world. The exhibit offered no traditional religious cure-alls, no explicit promise of divine salvation, no diversion of attention from this world to the next, no direct attempt to proselytize. Its final presentation was, in the words of historian John Webster Grant, 'a meditation room where quiet music, pastoral murals, and Scripture texts suggested but never argued the possibility of redemption.'[2] For many Christians in Canada as elsewhere, 'the sixties' was the era for dialogue, for questioning of tradition and authority, for exploring other options, for cooperation with seekers of any faith. The Christian Pavilion at Expo '67 graphically reflected these attitudes.

It by no means, however, reflected the attitudes of *all* Canadian

Christians. The sponsors of the Christian Pavilion conceived it as a venture that would present a united Canadian Christianity,[3] and no doubt were disappointed that it served instead as one-half of a pair of Christian pavilions, the other half of which demonstrated that at least some Canadian Christians had very different concerns and would take pains to express them publicly.

In June 1964, two members of an evangelical, transdenominational fellowship known as the Christian Business Men's Committee (CBMC) walked along a Montreal street wondering if Christians could participate as such in Expo.[4] Not formally connected with those Christian groups who would produce the other pavilion, these men brought their concern to their CBMC chapter and were commissioned to investigate possibilities.

The work of Irwin Moon quickly emerged as the pattern to follow. Moon had presented exhibits at American world's fairs since the 1939 Golden State Exposition in California. He used dramatic demonstrations of the wonders of nature and technology to illustrate spiritual truths and thereby to arouse interest in a more straightforward presentation of the gospel.

This approach needs to be distinguished from two others. The first is the sort associated in another era with apologist William Paley (1743–1805), the sort that explicitly argues for the truth of Christianity from the evidence of the natural world (for instance, the marvellous intricacy and interdependence of the parts of the human eye testify to the wisdom and power of a great Designer). 'Sermons from Science' did engage in this sort of apologetics to some extent, but not exclusively and rigorously. Nor did 'Sermons from Science' explicitly defend the view of the origins of the earth and of human beings in particular associated with the 'Creation Science' movement.

Instead, the pavilion was an odd blend of Enlightenment 'evidences' and the common medieval practice of seeing biblical truths 'played out' in the natural world – updated now to include the world of human construction. That is, it generally used science as a collection of subjects for allegorization. This approach, to be sure, does not necessarily contradict the others. Rather, with them it relies upon the typical evangelical view of the world as being in clear harmony with God's revelation in the Bible. Indeed, the exposition's guidebook describes the 'message' of the pavilion as 'scientific laws governing life show the existence of a Supreme Planner.'[5]

These 'Sermons from Science' were institutionalized at the Moody Bible Institute in Chicago as the 'Moody Institute of Science,' and had been presented more recently at the Seattle and New York City expositions in the early 1960s. Sixteen-millimetre films of the demonstrations made possible numerous showings without the expense of transporting and operating the equipment necessary to achieve some of the more spectacular effects. And Inter-Varsity Christian Fellowship, among other evangelical organizations, had used them in meetings for years.[6]

The CBMC chapter, having decided on its approach, appointed a nominating committee that in turn appointed a board in December 1964 of interested Christians from a number of denominations in Montreal. This board then took over the administration of the project. In January 1966, with much of the preparation well under way, the board named as general manager of the pavilion a young pharmaceutical salesman. Keith A. Price was selected because the board wanted someone who knew about both sermons and science. Price, a preacher with the Christian Brethren when he was not representing his company, had also a keen interest in the relationship of Christianity with modern science and had lectured to a number of Inter-Varsity Christian Fellowship chapters on the subject. This brought him to the attention of the board and he took a two-year leave from his firm to direct the exhibit – a leave that turned permanent as he soon went on to head up the entire operation for almost a decade.

In 1966 Price began a series of monthly newsletters to a mailing list that reached 35,000 at its peak. He and Stan Mackey, chairman of the board of the pavilion, alternated from month to month in addressing the cross-Canada constituency. Most of the money for the original cost of the building and its first summer of operation, almost three-quarters of a million dollars, came in five- and ten-dollar donations.[7] Southern Ontario, home to half of Canada's Protestants, not surprisingly contributed the largest share, about 25 per cent of the total cost. British Columbian Christians contributed about 15 per cent, and the Montreal area contributed 10–12 per cent. The rest came from across the country. The Christian Brethren, with whom Price was identified, were the denomination most supportive of the project. Indeed, since many Brethren assemblies typically did not bear the cost of paying a pastor's salary (since most church leaders had other employment), the Brethren were often freer than were other evangelicals to contribute money to transdenominational projects, and individuals among the Brethren ended up contributing 30–40 per cent of the cost of 'Sermons from Science.'

The money went to build and operate a three-part exhibit. The first and largest part was a 300-seat theatre in which the films were shown. Four times a day, furthermore, a live demonstration was substituted for the films. 'Sermons from Science' presented seventeen programs a day in seven languages, all of the programs different, since they had a library of a dozen different films to intersperse with half a dozen live demonstrations. These sessions lasted twenty-eight minutes, at which time viewers were bid adieu unless they wished to hear more about the gospel. Those who did wish to hear more were directed to the second part of the pavilion, a 75-seat auditorium in which they would hear – in their choice of French or English – an eight-minute film based on the Billy Graham Evangelistic Association's presentation of 'Steps to Peace with God.' (This latter presentation was similar to that of Campus Crusade for Christ's better-known tract, 'The Four Spiritual Laws.') Counsellors, who had been trained for this work by the hundreds, then introduced themselves to members of the audience and engaged them in conversation about what they had seen, seeking to encourage them along the life of faith.[8] (Price, by the way, was adamant that 'conversions' should not be the primary goal of the conversations but rather simply helping people to advance in faith. Conscious of some of the excesses in the revivalist tradition, Price was concerned about premature or superficial spiritual decisions. Indeed, the staff heard of conversions that followed these contacts only years later. But throughout the running of 'Sermons from Science,' Price refused to allow any figures regarding 'conversions' to be printed, a decision true to his principle of not playing the evangelistic 'numbers game.'[9]) By the time the next group was ready to enter from the main theatre, this auditorium had cleared, with conversations either ended or continued in one of the small rooms opening off the smaller theatre, these constituting the third part of the pavilion.

In all of this, these evangelicals were faithful to a long-standing heritage of Anglo-Canadian-American evangelicalism as they presented the 'old-time' gospel with the latest technologies. The powerful public presentation to large crowds with the 'after-meetings' and private counselling that followed had evolved from the eighteenth-century days of George Whitefield and John Wesley preaching in the open air of Britain and New England, through the 'protracted meetings' and other innovations of Charles Finney and D.L. Moody in the nineteenth century, to the mass rallies of Billy Sunday and Billy Graham in the twentieth. Evangelicals had always presented a simple message in a popular, dramatic, and often technically sophisticated way, and the Canadians who sponsored 'Sermons from Science' continued in this venerable heritage.[10]

A number of evangelical organizations participated in the work. Toronto Bible College, for instance, volunteered to supervise the 'follow-up' program to carry on the ministry of the on-site counsellors.[11] Prairie Bible Institute had no official part, but it featured articles on Expo in its magazine and some of its staff served as counsellors.[12] Inter-Varsity was the most involved of the three. It officially endorsed and raised money for the project, provided a bilingual staff member (Ed Conacher) as one of two head counsellors,[13] sent more than a dozen more staff as counsellors for a month each or more, and pledged to participate in the work of 'follow-up.' Inter-Varsity also engaged in its own evangelistic outreach through 'Operation Friendship,' which involved a variety of activities, notably 'Friendship House,' a home-base for the staff and part-time drop-in centre for the many youth visiting Montreal.[14] However piecemeal and ad hoc this participation was, then, the 'Sermons from Science' pavilion none the less marked the sort of national cooperation among evangelicals that would increasingly characterize the fellowship in the decades to follow.

At first, 'Sermons from Science' was one of the less-attended pavilions at the fair. But by early summer only the first and last programs failed to play for capacity audiences, making for a daily attendance of five thousand. At the end of the exposition in cold October audiences still were lining up for four to five hours to get in. In the six months of Expo '67 a total of 840,000 people viewed 'Sermons from Science,' making the pavilion one of the most popular in the whole fair – despite the widespread ignoring of it by the secular and mainline denominational presses in favour of the other Christian Pavilion.[15] With these crowds, the board of the pavilion decided to keep it open in subsequent summers while many of the other Expo pavilions did the same. In 1969 several changes were made. The live demonstrations were terminated and the schedule was cut back to three months per year from the former six. Other ministries filled the rest of the year for the staff now assigned permanently to the pavilion, such as visits to schools, Bible correspondence courses, and television broadcasts. Some at the Moody Bible Institute became concerned about the association of their name 'Sermons from Science' with a group now involved in a broader range of activities than formerly, some of which were connected with the Billy Graham Evangelistic Association (BGEA). By this time the Montreal people were serving as the BGEA's French-language arm, translating their films into French, answering letters addressed to the BGEA in French, and so on. And with the expansion of the ministry well beyond mere support of the pavilion it also made sense to change the name. So 'Sermons from Science' became known as 'Christian Direction.'[16]

The attendance at 'Man and His World' slowly tapered off as the presentations moved through nine summers, and attendance at 'Sermons from Science' reflected this decline. The annual cost of $50–70,000 was supported by a decreased number of contributors who yet increased the amount of their average donation to $25 or so. Christian Direction shut the doors of the pavilion in 1975, despite the City of Montreal's encouragement to keep it open, as attention shifted to the upcoming Olympics in Montreal in 1976. By this time two-and-a-half million people had seen the major presentations, one-half million had entered the second theatre, and 160,000 had engaged in conversation with a counsellor.

'Sermons from Science,' then, clearly offered visitors an alternative to the mainline Christian Pavilion in at least several respects. Most obviously, it differed from the other exhibit by concentrating not on 'Man and His World' but rather (as the evangelicals would have put it) on *God* and *his* world. This focus in turn reflected the more traditional nature of its appeal. While the mainline Christian Pavilion relied on implication ('Seeing all this, how shall we respond?'), the 'Sermons from Science' concluded with proclamation ('Seeing all this, ye must be born again'). But the two pavilions did more than represent two understandings of Christianity. They also manifested two different transdenominational alliances to a nation used to thinking of Christianity in denominational terms. One was the mainline 'ecumenical movement'; the other, also ecumenical in its own way,[17] was the fellowship of evangelicals.

Writing in the early 1970s, United Church historian John

Webster Grant doubted that either option would characterize the church in Canada in the decades to come. But the 'new point of equilibrium' he hoped for had not arrived by the 1980s, and the 'experimental and ecumenical' version of Christianity presented by the mainline pavilion faded steadily in Canadian church life. Indeed, twenty years or so later, 'Sermons from Science' looked less like an anomaly from the fringes of Canadian Christianity and more like the proverbial cloud on the horizon. The decades following Expo not only saw development and growth in the traditional institutional centres of Canadian evangelicalism, like Toronto Bible College, Prairie Bible Institute, and Inter-Varsity Christian Fellowship, but they also saw the development of new centres that joined with the others in an emerging network. And this evangelical network emerged as a significant new force in Canadian religion.

— 7 —

Ontario Bible College and Ontario Theological Seminary

The history of the Inter-Varsity Christian Fellowship to 1970 exemplifies a trend in Canadian evangelicalism since the 1960s: it maintained the core of its evangelical commitments while redefining or expanding those commitments to broaden its horizon of concern. The 'Sermons from Science' pavilion at Expo '67, for its part, declared the existence and growing self-consciousness of Canadian evangelicalism as a community whose understanding of Christianity contrasted with that of many in the mainline churches. This pair of characteristics, of continuity and change in the first place and of the emergent self-consciousness of evangelicalism in the second, manifests itself clearly in the history of Ontario Bible College and Ontario Theological Seminary.[1]

Ontario Bible College (OBC) was formed from the merger of Toronto Bible College (TBC) and the London College of Bible and Missions (LCBM) in 1968. The London College of Bible and Missions began in 1935 as evening classes conducted by J. Wilmot Mahood, a native of Ontario who had spent much of his career as a pastor and evangelist with the American Methodist Episcopal Church.[2] At the age of sixty-five he accepted a position at the Moody Bible Institute in Chicago as head of the extension program. A few years of vigorous service here were followed by retirement in California. The retirement, however, was short-lived. James M. Gray, president of Moody Bible Institute, had challenged Mahood to establish a Bible school to serve southwestern Ontario. Mahood took up this challenge by contacting like-minded folk in London, Ontario, and arrived in 1935 to begin the classes that would evolve the next year into a full-time day program.

Throughout its history the London school showed its founder's links with Moody Bible Institute and with American evangelicalism in general more than with its Toronto counterpart.[3] The faculty generally had less formal education than did the Toronto staff, although by the late 1950s several of the dozen full-time members had earned doctorates. Most of the faculty throughout the history of the school had earned at least one degree in the United States, and the vast majority of these came from one of two schools, either Wheaton College in Illinois or Dallas Theological Seminary in Texas. And LCBM went on record as endorsing premillennial eschatology, a hallmark of Moody, Wheaton, and Dallas, in the late 1940s – a step Toronto Bible College refused to take in order to serve those of different views.[4]

The school yet stood with TBC for the evangelical essentials: commitment to a high view of the inspiration and authority of Scripture; belief in the necessity of the 'new birth'; pursuit of vital spiritual experience worked out in personal holiness; and devotion to the central task of the church, evangelism.[5] Moreover, Toronto Bible College's own president at the time of the merger, Stewart L. Boehmer, was a graduate of the Moody Bible Institute. And with the improvement of transportation in Ontario, by the mid-1960s the schools found it difficult to justify their continuing separate existence. The 150 or so miles separating them became a negligible distance, which meant that they found themselves serving overlapping constituencies and competing for students and support.[6]

So at this time negotiations began between representatives of the two schools that culminated in the merger of 1968 and the creation of Ontario Bible College.[7] For the next two decades, the new school maintained the direction established by its predecessors. Theologically, it continued to stand for the same basic principles held in common by the two previous schools[8] – although in a key area of difference, eschatology, Ontario Bible College maintained the position of TBC and did not make premillennialism an explicit item in its statement of faith.[9] Vocationally, the school continued to seek to develop in its students a basic knowledge of the inerrant Scriptures and the foundations of strong spirituality so that they would go out to evangelize and disciple the world.[10] As one advertisement put it, 'Bible college is not "a piece of cake"! Neither is evangelism nor being a disciple. But quality training can help you to win souls and disciple them for

Jesus Christ more effectively. That's our commitment at Ontario Bible College.'[11]

The merger brought together at the site of Toronto Bible College two sets of faculty, staff, and students. But clearly the combination worked at first to increase the ministry of the school. In its first year the new college enrolled 340 students. Five years later the number climbed to 381, and the next year saw a high of 460. This increase in numbers compelled the school to seek larger accommodations, and in 1976 it relocated to a renovated former Jesuit seminary in Willowdale, in northern metropolitan Toronto.[12] After this, however, the school suffered an almost continual decline in numbers so that by the mid-1980s OBC's enrolment had plateaued at 300–350 students.[13]

Several explanations for this decline may be offered. The first is that other Bible schools in Ontario were also accredited by this time and of sufficient size to offer an experience similar to that of OBC with the feature, more attractive to some, of denominational homogeneity.[14] But the two other explanations have to do with the trend already noted in the history of TBC in which the school shifted its primary attention to serving the younger, uniformly evangelical denominations and away from the mainline churches.[15] The union with London if anything helped to further this trend, and it is clear from the denominational make-up of the first class at OBC. Three denominations make up two-thirds of the total of 340: Baptist (not here subdivided into 'Fellowship,' 'Convention,' and so on), 135; Associated Gospel Churches (AGC), 59; and Brethren, 26. By contrast, the Presbyterians sent 19, the Anglicans 12, and the United Church 7, together making up just over 10 per cent.[16] This trend too is exemplified in the hiring of two men from evangelical denominations as successors to President Stewart L. Boehmer. Boehmer himself was a member of the Associated Gospel Churches; Victor Adrian, who served as president from 1974 to 1983, came from the Mennonite Brethren;[17] and William J. MacRae, the president who followed Adrian, previously pastored Christian Brethren assemblies.[18]

OBC was not quick to affirm *all* evangelical denominations, however. Pentecostal supporters of OBC may have seen only its bare statement of faith, with which they easily could agree, and sent some of their youth there rather than to the Eastern Pentecostal School in Peterborough, Ontario. About a dozen such students consistently show up in OBC's survey of first-year students in the 1970s, a number that increased 50–100 per cent in the 1980s. Yet OBC maintained an unofficial but consistent interpretation of the doctrinal statement that ruled out Pentecostalism and the similar ideas of the charismatic movement regarding the Baptism of the Holy Spirit and its manifestation in glossolalia. Toronto Bible College already had made clear its difficulties with Pentecostalism (see part 2), and this continued in the life of OBC.[19]

This seems to be, though, the only obvious case of an unstated but established theological consensus that excluded certain members of OBC's constituency. And the increase of Pentecostal students at both OBC and its seminary in the 1980s indicates that this consensus had eroded. For instance, the 1986–7 calendar of Ontario Theological Seminary (OTS) says that 'Baptists, Presbyterians and Pentecostals represent the three largest groupings in the student body' (10). Moreover, by the late 1980s OTS was offering a course in 'The Pentecostal Heritage' to complement its offerings in the Baptist, Reformed, and Wesleyan heritages.

With this shift to the uniformly evangelical denominations, however, OBC may have set itself on a course with unforeseen difficulties ahead. In the 1980s the contingents from the Presbyterian, Anglican, and United churches remained constant, if relatively small, so the decrease in enrolment was among those from the uniformly evangelical churches. These enrolment trends have yet to be studied and explained thoroughly, but it may well be that they reflect two trends among contemporary evangelicals, trends that would cause OBC to lose students. The first is that many evangelical young people were no longer scared off from attending university as they had been before and so were going there rather than to the safety of the Bible school – this indeed coincided with the general increase in the proportion of high-school graduates attending universities or colleges of applied arts and technology in Ontario since the 1950s.[20] And perhaps the erosion of the fear of the university was only the negative side of the growing evangelical appreciation of the worthiness of all vocations, and thus of university education as part of this – a trend evident in the Inter-Varsity Christian Fellowship in the 1960s. (Indeed, the presence of IVCF itself on most campuses would have reassured many evangelicals about entering the university world.) This change too would lead many more to seek training other than that a Bible school would offer.

Indeed, Ontario Bible College showed signs of a diffusion, if not confusion, of purpose as it sought to diversify its programs in various directions.[21] In the late 1980s it not only set up programs with several area colleges to offer secretarial studies, early childhood education, and special education training, but at the same time sought to increase its attractiveness to university students by having its charter amended so as to offer still more liberal-arts courses (up to one-third of the new three-year Bachelor of Religious Studies degree) that would allow students to transfer up to two years of credit to universities. Further restructuring under new Dean Rod Wilson in the early 1990s helped to integrate the evening- and day-school programs to make them more attractive to OBC's increasing number of 'returning' or 'mature' students. By 1990, then, it was clear that OBC was determined to serve a wide variety of students preparing for a wide variety of occupations. What was not clear was how coherently and thoroughly such a small school could do so.

The second development among evangelicals, though, coincided not only with the decrease in enrollment among students at Ontario Bible College, but also with the expansion of the ministry of Ontario Bible College in the founding of Ontario Theological Seminary (OTS) in 1976. That is, as evangelicals required more formal training for their pastors, they sent fewer to Ontario Bible College and more to university and then to schools like Ontario Theological Seminary.

The establishment of a graduate school had been on the minds of TBC and LCBM leaders for a generation before 1976. The London school had even won approval from the provincial government to grant graduate degrees in theology as early as 1950, although it never saw a successful seminary program emerge. But several times in the fifteen years or so before the opening of Ontario Theological Seminary, evangelical educators and pastors convened at Toronto or Ontario Bible College to discuss the well-established pattern of Canadian evangelical students heading to the United States for their theological training.[22] This pattern disturbed the Canadian leaders because, in the first place, many of those who went south failed to return to Canada, and, in the second place, many who wished to go south to study in the 1960s faced increasing restrictions on employment opportunities to finance their education. (Only in the 1980s would evangelical schools generally begin to emphasize the distinctive nature of Canadian society as another reason to study 'at home.') To establish an evangelical seminary in Ontario, then, was the second major reason the Toronto and London Bible schools decided to merge. And in 1976, with the move of the campus to Willowdale, the facilities were available to open the doors of the new Ontario Theological Seminary to 105 students. The seminary grew, first under the leadership of Roy R. Matheson and then since 1981 under that of former Regent College professor Ian S. Rennie, to become a friendly rival to Regent College as the largest seminary of any kind in Canada.[23]

Ontario Theological Seminary stood foursquare for the evangelical essentials characteristic of its predecessors. But it also represented more graphically than any development in Ontario Bible College itself two changes in 'churchish' evangelicalism in Ontario, at least, since the days of Toronto Bible College under John McNicol. (Conclusions about evangelicalism in all of Canada cannot be drawn from the case of OBC alone, but only in concert with studies of other institutions. As in the case of Toronto Bible College, OBC consistently drew over 90 per cent of its students from Ontario.)

The first change was the recognition among evangelicals of an identity in important ways separate from, and even opposed to, that of the mainline denominations. In the first five decades of Toronto Bible College, evangelicals associated with the school assumed that the denominational theological colleges were appropriate places for pastoral training and that evangelical students would go to university and then to the colleges for their theological study. A peaceful coexistence could be maintained with the theological colleges since, McNicol always made clear, the Bible College had a different ministry from theirs, the training of laity. More than this, good relations with the denominations that sponsored those colleges could be maintained with this division of labour established. (The London school, for its part, never accepted this relationship and was proud of its record of training leaders for pastoral work in particular.) But as the denominational colleges themselves became less and less evangelical and as newer evangelical denominations emerged into prominence in the constituency of TBC and then OBC, the pattern of complementarity with the denominational schools began to break apart. The first obvious breach was the offering of a pastor's course at TBC in the 1950s.

Then, finally and most directly, came the establishment of a new seminary, OTS, that stood as a direct alternative to the denominational colleges. This shift is mirrored in the training of the OBC and OTS faculty themselves, who since the 1950s increasingly earned their degrees from the growing American evangelical seminaries and graduate schools[24] rather than from Canadian denominational theological colleges and universities.[25] Canadian evangelicals more and more turned to evangelical alternatives to mainline denominational education.

This shift should not be overemphasized, however. The school still described itself in transdenominational, rather than merely 'evangelical,' terms, reflecting thereby its continued appreciation for denominational distinctives and its recognition of evangelicals within pluralistic denominations.[26] And by the late 1980s and early 1990s, a number of the OBC and OTS faculty, especially the younger cohort, had graduated from Canadian universities and theological colleges, notably Toronto-area universities and the constituent colleges of the Toronto School of Theology. There is a shift here, then, but it is a modification, not a repudiation, of the TBC tradition and 'churchish' evangelicalism.

The second change in contemporary evangelicalism was the expansion of vision, an expansion with several dimensions. First, there was a growing appreciation of the legitimacy of a variety of callings. Ontario Theological Seminary introduced a two-year degree in 1978 both for those interested in parachurch ministries (staff for IVCF or Youth for Christ likely were in mind here) and for 'students who intend to enter professional careers, but who wish two years of biblical and theological training to serve Christ more effectively.'[27] It later offered a one-year certificate program for those who did not seek a degree but wanted some basic biblical study at the graduate level. OBC and OTS, and TBC before them, had recognized the desire among older students already involved with full-time employment to engage in formal Bible study and had offered a popular evening program. But in 1978 OBC offered students the option of pursuing the Bachelor of Religious Education degree through evening courses.[28] Now students could pursue studies towards a 'non-pastoral' degree, even on a part-time basis, at either the graduate (OTS) or undergraduate (OBC) level.

A small, but significant, step in this direction was taken in the spring semester of 1984 when OTS offered its first course in 'Christians in Business,' co-taught by an executive of Shell Oil of Canada, Raymond Binkley, and one of OTS's faculty, Douglas Webster.[29] This became a regular course in the curriculum for several years, sponsored by the short-lived OTS Centre for Christians and Business, which blossomed out into seminars in cities across Canada.[30] With the departure of both Binkley and Webster the course as such was dropped, although courses on urban ministry and Christianity and society helped to maintain some of this emphasis (as noted below). This admittedly modest start none the less symbolized a deepening appreciation among evangelicals for the importance of Christian thinking not only about standard 'theological' and 'spiritual' subjects (like doctrine, personal spirituality, and missions) but also about the broad range of vocations to which God calls Christians. To be sure, this was just a start. The majority of courses offered were yet from the standard theological/pastoral curriculum and it remained to be seen what sort of institutional support for this concern would continue at OTS. Moreover, the graduates of both schools still generally went into pastoral or missionary work. None the less, a growing proportion of graduates chose other vocations.[31]

The second dimension of breadth among evangelicals shown by OBC/OTS was an increasing recognition of social responsibility. Early in the 1980s, for instance, OTS began a semi-annual conference called 'Reach the City' in which strategies to minister to the wide needs of a rapidly urbanizing Canada were discussed. The *Evangelical Recorder* under the editing of Douglas C. Percy began in the 1960s to feature articles on a variety of social problems and especially those that commonly alarmed evangelicals, such as abortion, pornography, and the occult.[32] The September 1982 issue of the magazine featured an editorial by President Adrian holding up John Wesley as an example of proper commitment to both evangelism and 'social concern' and also an article by OTS Dean Rennie that surveyed the history of 'Evangelical Concern for Personal and Social Ethics.' In the spring semester of 1984, OTS welcomed visitor Paul Marshall, professor at the Institute for Christian Studies in Toronto, as he lectured on 'Public Concerns in Christian Perspective.'[33] And the OTS calendars began in the mid-1980s to list courses in urban ministry and Christianity and society.

Again, however, not too much should be made of this. The evangelical priority placed upon evangelism had yet to be challenged. One looks in vain, moreover, for significantly frequent occurrences of key words like 'justice,' 'liberation,' and 'peace' with anything other than purely spiritual meanings in the pages of the *Evangelical Recorder* or the calendars of OBC/OTS. Even as President Adrian exalted Wesley's concern for social ministry, he yet affirmed that 'we have made evangelism our priority.' Finally, an article by the next president, William J. MacRae, that outlined his 'dreams' for the school spoke of biblical knowledge, excellence in leadership, personal holiness, strong homes, church planting and development, evangelism, and worship.[34] It hardly needs pointing out that these are unexceptionable and traditional evangelical concerns, but also that there is nothing directly to do with social ministry among them. These evangelicals, that is, still struggled to embrace fully the social-action side of Christianity.

The third area in which Ontario Theological Seminary represented a broadening of Canadian evangelicalism was in its ministry to ethnic groups.[35] With hundreds of thousands of Asians in Canada by the 1980s, and the largest concentration of these in the Toronto area, OTS consciously sought to train the pastors needed to serve these people and began offering an M.Div. concentration particularly in Chinese studies in the late 1980s. Indeed, by 1984, 20 per cent of its full-time students came from the Chinese community, and another significant proportion was Korean.[36] OTS took notice also of the black communities in Canada, and in particular the 100–200,000 blacks (mostly of Caribbean descent) in the Toronto area. It devoted its 'Reach the City' seminar in February 1982 to hearing from black leaders on how to reach this group.[37] To be sure, the black community in Canada was yet seen as a target for missionary work: there were relatively few black evangelicals in Canada at this time, and scarcely any in leadership positions in the transdenominational network.[38] Ontario Theological Seminary did not do well in serving the Native Canadian population, but no Christian group had succeeded well among them since the nineteenth century. Signs of improvement in the relationships between aboriginals and whites in Canada appeared in the 1980s, however, and signs in particular of a resurgence of Christianity among the Native peoples were welcomed by OTS.[39] Indeed, two members of the OTS community, Dr and Mrs Daniel Kelly, worked extensively with Native Christians in Toronto in the mid-1980s. All of these developments touched only the edges of Canadian evangelicalism, however, which remained overwhelmingly Caucasian. As immigration continued, especially from the Indian subcontinent and the Pacific Rim, it remained to be seen how effectively Canadian evangelicals would reach their neighbours.

Finally, OBC and especially OTS were conspicuous in their treatment of women. Women had always constituted a great proportion, and frequently a majority, in many Bible schools. But they generally had been restricted from pastoral education per se given the refusal of most evangelical groups to ordain women to higher church offices. At OBC and OTS, though, they enrolled freely in the programs of their choice, and by the 1980s OTS offered specific courses in women and ministry that featured as guest lecturers prominent female academics and clergy in the Toronto area. In this, the schools ran ahead of most of their constituents, including some among their own faculty and student body. Even by the early 1990s, that is, most evangelical denominations and churches refused to place women in offices of elder or pastor. The 1990s, however, promised to be the decade in which evangelicals would have to face the question of gender directly as never before. OBC/OTS therefore was poised to make a significant contribution to that discussion.

As Ontario Bible College and Ontario Theological Seminary anticipated the centennial of the founding of Toronto Bible College in 1994, therefore, it could have seen in itself some new emphases and ministries, some of which arose at least partly out of the expansion of its constituency. It also would have had a sense of alienation from many of those Christians in the mainline denominations and especially from most of their leaders – a sense that would have been foreign to Toronto Bible College pioneer Elmore Harris and especially to his successor, John McNicol. Indeed, it was a feeling (somewhat ironically) more in keeping with the ethos of the London College of Bible and Missions. To be sure, this feeling had at least as much to do with the changes in the mainline denominations themselves as with the influence of this 'sectish' evangelicalism at Ontario Bible College. None the less, in its embracing of this spectrum of evangelical opinion and disposition, Ontario Bible College and Theological Seminary also could recognize that the heart of evangelicalism still beat strongly in the centre of its work, a heart directed by the authoritative Scriptures, renewed in personal conversion, warmed and disciplined by the Holy Spirit, and dedicated to preaching the gospel.

— 8 —
Prairie Bible Institute

L.E. Maxwell had more than fifty years in which to impress his ideals upon Prairie Bible Institute. Since 1977, when Maxwell left the presidency to take the specially created office of 'Founder,' his successors maintained the shape of the school.[1] But Prairie's history too reflects some of the changes in evangelicalism manifest in other Canadian institutions, even as it indicates that not all of those changes seen elsewhere were immediately welcome in this bastion of 'sectish' evangelicalism.

Ted S. Rendall, who succeeded L.E. Maxwell's son Paul as president, in fact preceded Paul in leadership at Prairie. Rendall had come to Prairie from his native Scotland in the mid-1950s to study. In his last school year, 1955–6, his 'gratis work' was to prepare eight pages per issue for young readers of the *Prairie Overcomer*. Following graduation, Rendall was asked to stay on as researcher for Maxwell and devoted himself to reading books and magazines, indicating those he thought would interest Maxwell. The friendship that emerged from this relationship with Maxwell continued until the older man's death. Rendall impressed Maxwell, and the president rapidly promoted his protégé: first to helping Maxwell edit the school magazine, then in 1960 to the newly created office of vice-principal (Rendall was twenty-seven), then to principal of the Bible School and editor of the *Prairie Overcomer*.[2] Maxwell, it seemed, had picked out his successor and groomed him for some time.

In the mid-1970s, however, others at Prairie saw Paul Maxwell, L.E. Maxwell's son, to be the more appropriate person to receive the mantle from the founder – perhaps mostly because of the power of the family name among Prairie's constituency, since the younger Maxwell had no administrative experience. Encouraged to return from the South American mission field in the early 1970s, the younger Maxwell taught at Prairie for a few years and then succeeded his father in 1977.[3]

Given Rendall's long term of influence previous to Paul Maxwell's entrance into PBI leadership and Rendall's continued responsibilities in the Bible school, it is impossible to apportion with confidence credit or blame between the two leaders for the direction of Prairie after 1977 until Paul Maxwell's resignation in 1986.[4] Neither man, though, showed interest in changing the fundamental character of the Institute.[5] The school continued to maintain its statement of faith essentially unchanged, differing from its 'churchish' counterparts in its straightforward defence of premillennialism and, implicitly, dispensationalism (as it used terms like 'rapture of the Church') and – even more unusually – in its articulation of direct creation of the world in six days.[6] Its primary vocation remained that of training lay workers for evangelism and church work, and of training missionaries above all. PBI still carefully regulated campus life, and the words 'Disciplined Soldiers' yet stood above the heads of all who attended services in the Prairie Tabernacle. Prairie still drew its teachers largely from the ranks of its graduates and maintained the fundamental shape of the curriculum, which revolved around a large core of basic biblical and practical studies. The *Prairie Overcomer*, which became *Servant* magazine in 1989, continued to feature articles that interpreted world events, with emphases similar to those of the previous era,[7] while yet focusing on edifying the reader's spiritual life[8] and stirring up interest in revival and foreign missions.[9] The school continued to draw its students from across the United States and Canada[10] and mostly from evangelical denominations or independent churches in the Midwest and West. Indeed, Prairie's physical plant itself scarcely changed, with the odd new or renovated building marking the only difference in a campus whose site had not changed in the midst of a town only slightly bigger than it was fifty years before. In all these respects and more, Prairie was easily recognizable as the school L.E. Maxwell had built, and as a bulwark of prairie evangelicalism.

Since the elder Maxwell stepped down in 1977, however, the Bible school's enrolment did not grow, and indeed declined since the 1980–1 school year. This pattern coincides with that at Ontario Bible College and can be attributed to the same trend: as the younger, evangelical denominations these schools primarily served required more training of their pastors and missionaries, so they sent fewer of them to Bible school.

This coincidence of patterns, however, does not stand alone to justify this explanation. Several other developments at Prairie demonstrate the PBI leaders' attempts to meet this concern for more, and more mainstream, education. Indeed, schools like Briercrest Bible College and Canadian Bible College in Saskatchewan were quicker to innovate and their enrolments grew to rival or surpass Prairie's by the late 1980s.

The first change was the introduction of degree programs in the 1980–1 school year. With authorization from the Alberta Legislative Assembly, the school's three- and four-year programs now led to bachelor's degrees in biblical studies, religious education, or theology.[11] With this change, prospective Prairie students could enrol with assurance that their training would receive greater recognition at home and abroad. This change did not affect enrolment trends as positively as the school's leaders had hoped, though, except for the one-year surge in 1980–1 as alumni took advantage of the school's offer to upgrade their diplomas to degrees with one semester's additional study.

Then in the late 1980s the school considered a move several other Bible schools took, the establishment of a graduate division.[12] In accord with the move towards graduate study, however, was a change in the Bible school's name. In 1986 the board of directors voted to change the name of the Bible School division to Bible *College* with a view towards establishing also a graduate-school division.[13] This change, Prairie's leaders felt, made clear that the school was a full-fledged, degree-granting institution of higher learning and distanced it from smaller, less reputable schools.[14]

Prairie, third, hired faculty with significantly more formal education than it had previously, with several possessing arts and theology degrees from universities or theological seminaries. By 1990 the thirty-two full-time faculty could boast a dozen or more MA's, M.Mus.'s, Ph.D.'s, and Th.D.'s. Other faculty already on staff were encouraged to seek more education: the president himself, Ted Rendall, began work towards a Master of Theology degree by special arrangement with Regent College, Vancouver.

And finally, in 1986 Prairie dropped a number of its 'soc regs,' the rules governing social life on campus. In a pamphlet sent to all on PBI's mailing list, President Rendall explained that Prairie's governance of social relationships was helping to hurry couples into the status of 'recognition' by the administration so as to enjoy meeting privileges denied to more casually related couples. This effect, of course, was opposite to that desired by Prairie's leaders, and in one stroke in the summer of 1986 the whole scheme of officially 'recognized interests' – a scheme almost as old as the school – was dropped. In its place, the school determined to continue to guide students so that they would proceed cautiously in this important area of discipleship, and appointed a residence dean specifically to counsel couples who developed a serious interest in each other. As Rendall wrote, 'Students now enjoy mixed seating in the Prairie dining hall, and can converse with each other naturally in the center area of campus. We seek to discourage prolonged private discussion between students in public on the grounds of the best use of time, the misunderstanding that such conversations can create, and the general principle of encouraging students to maintain the spirit and not merely the letter of social regulations.'[15] Rendall also implied in this newsletter that the reputation attributed to Prairie because of these regulations had hurt enrolment. He initially confronted the humorous caricature of Prairie as having 'pink and blue sidewalks,' but seriously closed his letter by enlisting the help of Prairie's friends: 'In explaining what Prairie is all about in the area of social regulations, communicate to inquiring young people what is really going on now, not what its was twenty or thirty years ago! ... There are hundreds of young people in our churches who would profit from training at Prairie. We are convinced of that, and we do not want some kept away by an image of us that is unfounded ... Some young people may not be considering Prairie simply because of the distorted picture of us that is sometimes communicated because of a misunderstanding of what is presently happening on campus.'[16]

More than a few remnants of the old code remained, to be sure. In the late 1980s students were still forbidden to attend movies or dances, to drink or to play cards. Hairstyles and dress were still regulated, with women to be in skirts or dresses and men in ties for all classes. Indeed, the student handbook for 1986–7 still contained one-and-a-half pages of rules, among which were the following:

2. Permission must be first obtained from the Resident Counselor before phoning a student of the opposite sex.

3. Letters, notes, gifts, pictures, rings, food, etc. are not to be passed to one another without the Resident Counselor's permission ...

5. Men and women students may not visit in a home at the same time except where social privileges have been granted. The other exception is where brother/sister and other close relatives are involved.

6. Unless etiquette befitting a gentleman warrants helping a lady, physical contact is not allowed. Improper conduct [such] as lying on the grass and sitting and walking too closely must be avoided ...

Engagements, formal or informal, or marriages are not to be contracted during the years of attendance at the Institute without the permission of the Bible School Student Life Committee.[17]

As the catalogue explained, Prairie continued to provide an environment in which Christian disciples could learn the self-control necessary to further the work of God's kingdom: 'Basically, then, our social standards are but a segment of the far greater principle of the Christian life – namely, the life of dynamic discipleship; the crucified life; the renunciation and denial of the self-life. Since many young people today do not possess the self-discipline required to keep their interests in proper perspective to their divine calling, these regulations are designed to assist them to seek first the Kingdom of God and His righteousness.'[18]

Alumni of previous generations, though, might well have been surprised to find the school catalogue allowing women to wear jewelry (as long as it was 'tastefully chosen') and make-up (to be 'worn in moderation, striving for a fresh, natural look') and men to wear mustaches or beards (that 'should be well groomed at all times'). They also would have looked in vain for the former detailed prescriptions regarding dating, and might have raised their eyebrows at 'tape recorders and record players' being matter-of-factly allowed in dormitory rooms.[19]

Despite these changes (one is tempted to say 'cosmetic changes'), Prairie maintained much of its original course. As late as 1986, for instance, the school yet decided not to seek accreditation in the American Association of Bible Colleges (AABC), the main accrediting body recognized in Canada as well as in the United States. Such a step would have required, among other things, an expansion of the library that Prairie could not yet afford and even more formal training of its faculty. This latter step Prairie did not wish to take, since even under the new president it expected to continue to hire from its own graduates without insisting that all receive further education elsewhere. The main reason, though, that Prairie did not seek accreditation with this body was that accreditation would require relatively more liberal-arts courses and relatively fewer Bible and missions courses in PBI's programs. This the school was not prepared to do: it chose to maintain the emphasis on biblical and missionary study that had characterized it from the beginning.[20]

Four years later, however, Prairie joined an increasing number of Canadian Bible schools as it decided to pursue AABC accreditation after all. Official statements were brief and general, with the focus upon the benefit to Prairie of the self-study and external examination required by the accrediting procedure. The move seemed much more significant than that, however, as it located Prairie even closer to the mainstream of Canadian evangelicalism with its manifest concern for more culturally respectable higher education, for greater breadth of interest in learning beyond the traditional theological and practical. Here was another important instance of the mainstream coalescing.[21]

Most basically of all, though, Prairie continued to concentrate its efforts on training missionaries and pastors.[22] Its programs betrayed no determination to train Christians for other vocations, even as the increased liberal-arts component to the curriculum mandated by the AABC meant more vocational options for Prairie's students. To be sure, President Rendall was more appreciative of other vocations than was President Maxwell. Rendall recognized the validity of Christian service in a variety of professions where Maxwell seemed to have trouble doing so.[23] But Rendall did it while stressing 'the priority of the missionary calling.'[24]

He stressed this priority for two reasons. The first was that he saw the need of foreign missions to be so great and yet the cost to the missionary and to his or her supporters also to be so great that emphasis needed to be placed on this difficult calling lest Christians settle for an easier ministry. The second reason was more implicit but no less basic: the primary mission of the church, Rendall believed, is evangelization. Everything else it does is secondary. Therefore, missions deserved emphasis not just to balance the lure of easier vocations – a concern with which many Christians would have sympathized – but also, and perhaps primarily, because it is indeed the highest calling, fulfilling most directly and effectively the Great Commission. Assumed in this discussion is the typical evangelical belief that the Great Commission is the key text setting out the church's work in the world, an assumption that tends to undercut any broad doctrine of vocation. And maintaining this assumption, Prairie therefore still found time only in passing to discuss vocations other than the missionary.

So in the decade-and-a-half since L.E. Maxwell retired from the presidency of Prairie Bible Institute, the school sought to meet some of the demands from its constituency for more formal training. It also relaxed some of the discipline of campus life. This would be part of the legacy of Ted Rendall, who retired from the presidency in 1992. But PBI remained largely unchanged in ethos and program, and stood somewhat apart from its evangelical relatives, like Ontario Bible College and Inter-Varsity Christian Fellowship, in concentrating almost exclusively on missionary and ecclesiastical vocations, even as it stood with them in the broad fellowship of Canadian evangelicalism.

— 9 —
Inter-Varsity Christian Fellowship

In the two decades that followed the departure of Wilber Sutherland, Inter-Varsity Christian Fellowship of Canada maintained the course set in the difficult 1960s. Some of the projects and initiatives of those years, to be sure, were set aside as less useful means than others of achieving the purposes of the Fellowship. Some of the basic commitments of Inter-Varsity were affirmed more directly than they were during Sutherland's term. And in at least one important instance, over the issue of the possibility of hiring Roman Catholic staff, the Fellowship maintained its traditional Protestant evangelical character. The chief legacy of the 1960s for IVCF, though, was a broadening of vision to include all Protestant denominations and all legitimate vocations (ideas that entailed a broadening of Inter-Varsity's understanding of its own vocation). And this continued to characterize the movement.

With Sutherland resigning so suddenly in the autumn of 1969, the board of directors moved quickly to find a replacement. By March 1970 they had invited Eugene Thomas, an experienced American staff worker and popular speaker, to take the position of general director, but Thomas after long deliberation decided not to do so. A national staff executive was appointed then from among the senior staff, and it set about reaffirming Inter-Varsity's commitment to Bible teaching, evangelism, Christian fellowship, and leadership training.[1]

This interim council was succeeded in 1972 by an unusual appointment to the office of general director. Samuel Escobar, a Peruvian working with the International Fellowship of Evangelical Students (the international version of IVCF) in Latin America, had come to the notice of North Americans especially by his rousing speech at Urbana '70.[2] The tensions in Canada raised during the last years of Sutherland's leadership needed calming, so the board thought, and IVCF needed re-establishment of its focus and zeal. So Escobar came as general director with the understanding that he would serve a three-year term. Escobar made many friends in Canada within and without the Fellowship. He helped to win back some of the support among Canadian evangelicals lost by Sutherland, and reaffirmed the Fellowship's need for leadership training and its commitment to foreign missions.

Many in leadership positions with Inter-Varsity, however, recognized at that time or later that Escobar, as a foreigner and as a short-term leader, could not resolve some of the problems still troubling the movement.[3] Regional tensions had been raised especially in the late 1960s as Inter-Varsity commissioned a study of its operations and revamped its organization. The strong Alberta Fellowship in particular protested some of the moves towards centralization: Marjorie Long, director of the work in Alberta, established an administrative base in Edmonton independent of the Toronto head office.[4] Escobar also could not or would not confront the differences among staff and board members as to the direction of the movement, differences stemming again from Sutherland's innovations.[5] So while Escobar's term brought some superficial peace to Inter-Varsity, it remained for the next general director to set the movement on the course it would maintain into the next decade.

A. Donald MacLeod came to Inter-Varsity with no direct experience in leading student ministry. He himself, however, had been a student of some distinction, having graduated from McGill University in 1959 (having participated in the IVCF chapter there) and having won a Woodrow Wilson Fellowship at Harvard from which he received a master's degree in history. While pursuing a Ph.D. at Harvard he felt called to pastoral ministry, and after theological studies served churches in Nova Scotia and then Ontario. He founded a vital Presbyterian church in northern Toronto and involved himself in denominational and transdenominational activity. This last involvement, and particularly his role as president of the Evangelical Fellowship of Canada in the early 1970s, brought him to the attention of the board of Inter-Varsity. In MacLeod they saw a man who stood forthrightly for traditional evangelical principles and demonstrated the strength of character and personality both to reorder the Fellowship accordingly and to reassure troubled parts of its constituency.

The MacLeod years, 1975–80, were difficult ones for him and for the Fellowship. Programs, initiatives, and personnel inherited from the Sutherland era were cut loose. The most prominent of these was The Cross Roads ministry at the University of Toronto. At least as early as 1970 some within the Fellowship were questioning the usefulness of this ministry, different as it was from the traditional 'quasi-chaplain' role of the staff worker. Some other critics felt it was a 'luxury' the Fellowship could not afford. Still others, especially from outside Ontario and from Alberta in particular, thought it was a luxury Ontario should support if it wanted to, but that other regions should not have to bear its expense since they saw no profit accruing to their ministries from it. Samuel Escobar had led an evaluation committee that had recommended its continued ministry in 1973.[6] But clearly sentiments were running largely against such an untraditional mode of service: staff workers needed to serve larger fields, and such fields less intensively, than did the staff of The Cross Roads. By 1976 it was given 'affiliate' status by the Board and in 1977 even this link was broken.[7]

Staff members too who had joined Inter-Varsity under Sutherland and who enjoyed the freer, less structured leadership under which they could pursue a variety of ministries with more individual authority found it hard to work under the strong direction of MacLeod. Many of these staff left the organization during MacLeod's tenure; others protested to the board; and by the end of MacLeod's five-year term or shortly thereafter, most of those involved in these disputes, including MacLeod himself, had left Inter-Varsity.[7]

Another decision made during MacLeod's term made explicit a characteristic of Inter-Varsity assumed by most but quietly challenged during Sutherland's tenure. In the spring of 1970, Sutherland approached the executive committee of the board of directors on behalf of some IVCF supporters in Prince Edward Island. These supporters were considering forming an area committee of volunteers to develop IVCF's work there, and had recommended that a Roman Catholic who could sign Inter-Varsity's Basis of Faith and agree with its purposes should be included on this committee.[9] The executive committee unanimously agreed that 'there was no basis for association with Inter-Varsity other than that of the Basis of Faith and the Statement of Purpose and that there was no way that such a person could or should be excluded.'[10] But nothing apparently came of this decision: there is no record of a Roman Catholic joining this committee.

The executive committee's unanimity on this question, however, was unlikely to have been reflected among the constituency of Inter-Varsity as a whole, an organization founded and by this time staffed for forty years by Protestants. In 1977, the matter came up again. When it did, because of an application from the Ottawa area for a staff internship for a Roman Catholic,[11] the whole board decided differently than had the executive committee years before. Rather than affirming the Basis of Faith and Statement of Purpose as the last word on the matter, the board in 1978 decided to make explicit what probably had been implicit all along: Roman Catholics were not welcome on the staff. Roman Catholic *students* were welcome in the chapters, and even could serve as leaders by affirming the Basis of Faith and Statement of Purpose. But the 1978 Board devised a new policy to make clear its commitment at the staff level: 'we consider the local church to have great significance, Biblically and in practical experience, in the life of any Christian. Staff members are expected to be involved in and warmly recommended by a local church which can care for their spiritual growth and welfare. Therefore, the IVCF would appoint to its staff persons involved in a church whose accepted doctrinal position is in harmony with the IVCF Statement of Faith.'[12]

It is difficult to take quite at face value this particular affirmation of the importance of the local church in the life of Inter-Varsity. To be sure, Inter-Varsity generally had set an example to other parachurch groups throughout most of its history in working with and through local churches. But the general position of this evangelical organization as with most others was that one's *individual* commitments were what mattered when membership in such an organization was at issue.[13] So this affirmation of the importance of the local church seems to have been a case of theological articulation prompted by circumstances – a very old tradition, to be sure, in creedal formulation. Put bluntly, IVCF probably had never wanted Roman Catholics (or any others who were not Protestant evangelicals) on staff, but it had never had to say so before, and this was a theologically defensible way to do it. (This interpretation is apparently confirmed by the title affixed in the board's minutes to this section: 'Appointment of Practising Roman Catholic to IVCF of Canada Staff.')

A further theological development began at almost this same time, and was connected with this concern over Roman Catholics on staff. The Groupes Bibliques Universitaires (GBU), the francophone arm of IVCF in Quebec, recognized that the traditional Basis of Faith was not detailed enough. In their work with Québécois raised in Roman Catholic homes and churches, they were encountering all the time the problem faced by the board regarding Roman Catholic staff: Inter-Varsity in fact had a larger set of theological commitments than these terse statements articulated, commitments that came out in discussion with Christians of quite different traditions.[14] In 1977 the GBU adopted therefore a more detailed statement of faith that made clear some of the evangelical movement's essential differences with Roman Catholic doctrine.[15] Throughout MacLeod's term the question of adopting the even more detailed statement of the International Fellowship of Evangelical Students for the national Fellowship was discussed. Finally, after James E. Berney had succeeded MacLeod, the Fellowship did so in 1981.[16]

In this discussion regarding the relationship of the Fellowship to Roman Catholicism and to Roman Catholics, therefore, the traditional Protestant evangelical character of IVCF was maintained at the staff level.[17] However, the leadership of IVCF at the same time officially opened up the student membership significantly. But MacLeod's term saw a number of developments that continued emphases affirmed by the Fellowship in the late 1960s.[18] Leadership training, formerly conducted at Campus-in-the-Woods, relocated to become Campus-in-the-City. Graduate camp and Graduate Christian Fellowship continued, and MacLeod expressed concern that more be done for this group.[19] The National Student Leaders Conference held annually brought students from across the country in contact with each other and with some of the staff leadership of the movement.

Perhaps most important of all, in the midst of MacLeod's sturdy evangelical and Presbyterian affirmation of the theological, spiritual, and evangelistic missions of Inter-Varsity,[20] stood the continued, even expanded, affirmation of the broad range of vocations open to the Christian and of the necessity of honouring Christ in all of life. To be sure, the life of most Inter-Varsity chapters in the 1970s and 1980s revolved around the evangelical basics as much as ever. Methods might change: small group Bible studies became even more popular; university-wide missions faded away for a while to resume by the late 1980s; large-scale worship services succeeded in some places; and International Student Ministries continued to grow in significance. But most groups devoted themselves still to spiritual growth and evangelism. None the less, in the MacLeod years the theme of vocation received fresh attention. MacLeod himself spoke to this subject by devoting to it a large portion of his reflections on Inter-Varsity at the end of its first fifty years in Canada. 'It seems that the Christian has been paralysed in his vocational thinking,' MacLeod wrote. 'We have classified the usefulness of Christian gifts and functions (missionary/minister/Christian worker in the upper echelon) and denigrated other forms of service.' Instead, he concluded, 'The totality of our commitment to Jesus Christ demands ... a total vocational approach: marriage, parenting, profession or business, public and private commitments.'[21]

This concern received the most attention, however, in a major conference held during the Christmas vacation of 1978. Directed by staff workers Norman Beers and Tony Tyndale, 'Pursuit '78' attracted more than four hundred students to four days of education and reflection on the subject of vocation.[22] Plenary speakers John R.W. Stott and Samuel Escobar discussed the biblical basis of vocation and the challenge of the world's needs respectively. More than forty workshop leaders addressed specific vocational areas: health care, education, law and government, social services, business and commerce, the church, science and technology, fine arts, and communication. With the success of the conference attested to by all involved, the organizers hoped to repeat it triennially in one of Urbana's 'off' years. The American IVCF's failed experiment of rescheduling Urbana on a biennial basis in the early 1980s disrupted the Canadians' immediate plans for another Pursuit, and one scheduled for the autumn of 1982 was cancelled by an overstretched Ontario staff. Similar, smaller conferences, however, were sponsored by IVCF in the 1980s in Canada (as were some in the United States attended by Canadians), some of them under the name 'Marketplace.'

The MacLeod years thus were years of re-establishment after the tumult of the 1960s. Some of this redirection MacLeod implemented forcibly, and the price of this was high: hard feelings between many staff and the general director reverberated beyond MacLeod's term and were finally pacified only under his successor, James Berney, former director of IVCF in the American south-west.[23] In particular, Berney was empowered by the board to rein in the Alberta organization, drawing all administrative lines to the head office in Toronto, and to make a quite different move in the Ontario division, giving it enough administrative distinction to develop its own identity and program, as it then did under Donald Posterski. Under Berney's direction, too, the Fellowship revised its fifth statement of purpose to make its understanding of vocation clearer than ever. It read: 'To affirm our vocations as full-time service to God: to pray, give and serve in the global mission of the church. EVERY CHRISTIAN IS CALLED TO BE SENT INTO THE WORLD.'[24] Since Berney came, the movement by all accounts continued on the course set in the later 1970s but with the frictions largely alleviated. Indeed, there were indications that the charismatic and Pentecostal movements were having a quiet and positive impact on a number of chapters.[25] By the mid-1980s IVCF had groups across Canada in approximately 50 universities, 40 community colleges, 300 high schools, and 40 nursing programs.[26] Staff – including office, camp, and InterVarsity Press staff – numbered close to 150, and salaries were increased significantly.[27] The annual income of the Fellowship doubled to well over $2 million in the first half of the decade.[28] Moreover, the constituency of the movement had changed slightly to include even some Roman Catholics.

Finally, the course set was one that represented both commitments which had always characterized the movement – spiritual growth and evangelism – and also those apparent in Inter-Varsity during the 1960s, especially the broader concern for vocation. The founding of three other important evangelical institutions in the 1960s, however, gave all of these concerns even more concrete expression.

— 10 —
Trinity Western University

The plot line of the history of Canadian evangelicalism so far has demonstrated at least three developments. First, as the century goes on, many of the constituent churches of Canadian evangelicalism become interested in more higher education, especially for their pastors and missionaries. Second, evangelicals manifest an increasing self-consciousness and a corresponding separateness from the mainline churches – seen particularly in the establishment of alternative institutions like Inter-Varsity Christian Fellowship versus the Student Christian Movement, 'Sermons from Science' versus the other Christian pavilion at Expo '67, and Ontario Theological Seminary versus the denominational schools, not to mention Prairie Bible Institute's distinctiveness from its very start. And third, evangelicals begin to expand their understanding of Christian vocation to include appreciation for all vocations.

The three-decade history of Trinity Western University, located in the lower Fraser River valley an hour's drive south-east of Vancouver, British Columbia, exemplifies all three of these trends and confirms that these trends are true of 'sectish' evangelicalism as well as of the 'churchish' sort. Indeed, it underscores a phenomenon noticed in the later history of Prairie Bible Institute, namely, the increasing 'churchliness' of the 'sectish' evangelicals so as to make for an even more homogeneous evangelicalism in Canada.

The story of Trinity Western's growth has been told several times elsewhere, notably by its first president, Calvin B. Hanson.[1] The university began as a two-year college of the Evangelical Free Church (at the time comprising what later would become separate American and Canadian denominations), which purchased a former dairy farm outside the town of Langley, BC. In a beautiful river valley lined with the dark trees of the Lower Mainland, the school opened the doors of its campus of long, low buildings to the first class of seventeen in the autumn of 1962.[2] The school's development was vigorous. Its enrolment curved steadily upward so that by the mid-1980s it welcomed more than eleven hundred students to campus – a majority from British Columbia and a total of more than 88 per cent from Canada as a whole. Ten years before, in January 1975, the school introduced two popular additions to the liberal-arts curriculum: a business program and an aviation program. The latter paralleled the larger program sponsored by the Moody Bible Institute in Chicago; the former would later attract a quarter of Trinity Western's students. In 1977, the school won the right from the province to expand to a four-year program, and in 1979 was authorized to grant degrees.[3] One study conducted in the later 1970s found that its students who had transferred to the nearby University of British Columbia consistently ranked above the average, and by 1979 over 125 colleges, universities, and professional schools had accepted its graduates.[4] Its faculty, in the earliest years possessing few degrees beyond the master's level, increasingly came with doctorates earned at universities in Canada and the United States. And in 1984 the last academic recognition was granted Trinity Western as it was welcomed into the Association of Universities and Colleges of Canada. To reflect its university-level training, the college changed its name from Trinity Western College to Trinity Western University in 1985.[5]

The Evangelical Free Church of Canada (EFCC), which maintained with its American counterpart official responsibility for the school (although by the mid-1980s less than a quarter of the students at TWU came from the two groups), was an unlikely sponsor indeed for such an enterprise. Calvin Hanson describes the EFCC at the time of Trinity Western's founding:

> At the time that Trinity Western College was launched there was only one pastor in the Free Church in British Columbia with a university degree and he left the Free Church, at least in part, because of his opposition to the college!
>
> Not only were ministers without the benefit of a university education, but in those days there were very few university trained people in the pews of the Free Churches.

Moreover, there was a general spirit of skepticism concerning the value of higher education as evidenced by flippant and disparaging remarks which made fun of college degrees. It was apparently felt by many that a university education was quite incompatible with a strong and warm commitment to Jesus Christ. Furthermore, because many of the university educated clergy were within the liberal church element a kind of cause and effect relationship was summarily assumed between one's training and one's doctrine.[6]

This attitude coincided with the fact that many of the EFCC's churches and leaders had close ties to Bible schools and to Prairie Bible Institute in particular – a relationship that paralleled the American denomination's connections with Moody Bible Institute.[7] Hanson writes that the Canadian group had had little connection with or interest in professional and university people: its 'orientation and ministry in Canada had been towards the lower socio-economic groups.'[8] And most of Trinity Western's original sponsoring churches were in the lower Fraser Valley, which, despite its proximity to cosmopolitan Vancouver, was populated largely from the prairies and retained the marks of that culture.[9]

That this church, Hanson continues, would be the one to sponsor Canada's largest evangelical liberal-arts college is 'an inscrutable enigma until you think in terms of miracle, divine guidance, and the initiative and support of the larger body of the Evangelical Free Church in the United States.'[10] Without gainsaying the importance of the first two explanations, the third one at least is easily verified in the record. The Evangelical Free Church denomination, rooted in the Scandinavian free-church tradition but for some time in the mainstream of North American evangelicalism, was relatively stronger in the United States than in Canada, and indeed even the idea of financially supporting a two-year college initially overwhelmed many in the Canadian church.[11] But the American Evangelical Free Church had in the previous decade converted its Bible college in Deerfield, Illinois, into a liberal-arts college, and so strongly backed those elements in Canada interested in a similar enterprise. The Americans provided most of the initial funds and leadership for the project:[12] the first team of administrators all were Americans, as were five of the seven charter faculty members.[13] American students outnumbered Canadians for the first decade of the school's life.

At least one crucial concept in Christian higher education also came largely from the American leaders who had experience in the American evangelical colleges: the idea that all disciplines can be and should be prosecuted with sensitivity to the role of presuppositions, and that Christian presuppositions and their implications should be worked out in each area of human learning. This kind of theory was foreign indeed to most of the intellectually unsophisticated evangelicals in western Canada, but was essential to making Trinity Western University truly a Christian liberal-arts school, rather than in effect a Bible school offering liberal-arts courses.

Indeed, it was not this kind of thinking that brought the Canadians slowly around to supporting the school. As much as the faculty and administration might have worked towards the so-called 'integration of faith and learning,' the school prudently appealed to other concerns among the Evangelical Free Church constituency in Canada, concerns that were shared by other small, conservative evangelical Canadian denominations. Since the 1950s, as the histories of Prairie Bible Institute and Ontario Bible College and Ontario Theological Seminary demonstrate, many of the smaller evangelical denominations had sought better training for their pastors and missionaries. Precisely this reason was advanced for the founding of Trinity Western College by the 'School for Canada Exploratory Committee' of the Evangelical Free Church of America (of which the British Columbia churches constituted a division at this time) in 1959: 'Just as Trinity Seminary and Bible College [in Deerfield, Illinois] has made a vital contribution to our total effort in the Evangelical Free Church, so also a Free Church college in Canada would contribute much toward unifying, stabilizing and enlarging the work of our churches and our district organizations in terms of both home and foreign missions ... Further, a school in Canada would be expected to provide candidates for enrollment in the Seminary and candidates for the Gospel ministry in our churches and for missionary work both at home and abroad.'[14]

This theme was picked up by Arnold Olson, sometime president of the denomination, who suggested that Trinity Western would train specialists for the mission field – 'technicians, teachers, medical workers, geologists, public health experts, etc.'[15] These themes, as would be expected, appealed to evangelicals well beyond the ranks of the Evangelical Free Church, and especially to those in the 'believers' church' tradition, particularly as Trinity Western maintained 'believers' church' principles of church membership and polity in its statement of faith. Throughout its history the school attracted the vast majority of its students from these churches, with the strongest representation from the Evangelical Free, Baptist, Mennonite, Pentecostal, and Christian and Missionary Alliance communions.[16]

Indeed, the main reasons for the erection of a college presented by denominational and school officials in the early years were not those that motivated many of the leaders at TWU, as well as other major supporters of evangelical higher education in Canada: a recognition of the validity of all vocations coupled with an appreciation that Christian thinking will affect the instruction in and practice of every discipline of human learning.[17] There was in Trinity Western's history virtually no explicit publication of a doctrine of vocation,[18] nor was there much discussion in its publications, with the exception of brief paragraphs in the academic catalogue, of the epistemological issues that others have seen to require the establishment of Christian colleges.[19] Instead, Trinity Western generally maintained before its constituency two different ideas, ideas that reflected its roots in the prairie, 'sectish' evangelicalism of the Evangelical Free Church.

The first idea was the largely unexamined assumption that vocations other than the pastoral or missionary were appropriate for Christians, an assumption upon which the need for the college was based. As Olson explained in 1960, most young people were not led by God to be pastors, missionaries, and church workers and yet needed Christian training so as to be effective in the workplace.[20] The crucial questions of what 'effective' meant and how 'Christian training' would make any difference to that effectiveness were nowhere spelled out, though, and it is difficult to avoid the impression that Olson meant that Christians need to be trained in these other vocations in a Christian school not only to be competent at their jobs but also to be good evangelists among their workmates. This provision for those seeking non-ecclesiastical jobs did not necessarily mean that the missionary and pastor had been displaced from their traditional positions at the top of the evangelical vocational hierarchy. Rather, this question of hierarchy simply was not addressed. Western Canada already had a number of Bible institutes, and Trinity Western itself would provide early training for these 'spiritual' vocations, but would also provide for the many who would not pursue these callings.

This thinking seems to lie behind a major addition to Trinity Western's curriculum, the business program of 1975. This program was not publicly presented as an implementation of some wide-ranging doctrine of vocation. Instead, the case seems more simply to have been that Trinity Western's constituency wanted their young people to be able to study business and also to enjoy the benefits of a Christian college setting, and since President R. Neil Snider quite clearly came out for 'market-oriented' programs at Trinity Western, this move to add a business program seemed an obvious step.[21]

This, however, should be expected, given the second idea behind Trinity Western, another idea which would have appealed to the smaller prairie evangelical denominations. Trinity Western University provided an alternative to the secular universities of British Columbia and of western North America in general. This alternative was not cast in terms of an epistemological difference, a difference between an overarching and undergirding Christian worldview which affects all disciplines and the pluralism and fragmentation of worldviews at the secular university – even, again, as the *faculty* demonstrated sensitivity to precisely this difference (as, for instance, the school's academic calendars show). Rather, Trinity Western College, in its two-year form, was presented as providing preparation for the onslaught of non-Christian ideas and other influences at the secular university,[22] and Trinity Western University in its four-year form as providing an alternative for those who would avoid a direct encounter with the secular university altogether.[23]

In celebrating Trinity Western's earning of the right to grant degrees in 1979, a special edition of its publication, *Trinity Western World*, set out the college's raison d'être:

> A recent study shows that many Christians who attend a secular college lose their faith by the time they've completed their third semester. When a leading newspaper admits on their editorial page that some of the staff at the public universities may be 'avowed atheists, Marxists, or anarchists,' one does not wonder why ...
>
> Trinity Western College was founded to provide students an alternative to public university education. Its purpose – to confirm and strengthen

students in the Christian faith. Founding chairman of the board Rev. David E. Enarson states, 'We wanted a college that would support, not tear down, those values taught at home ... a college where young people of all persuasions could come and learn about the God who loves and cares for them personally ... All of this, in the context of a traditional arts and science program. We wanted to be thoroughly 'Christian' and thoroughly 'college' at the same time.[24]

Indeed, President Snider spoke to the board of governors in 1980 about 'keeping the College true to its mission and spiritual commitment' in terms of two things: 'Doctrinal purity and pietistic lifestyle must be retained at all costs.'[25] Thus the school required commitment on the part of staff and students alike to the university's statement of faith (which, in typical 'sectish' fashion, included clauses about biblical inerrancy and premillennialism) and code of conduct (which, again typically, included the proscription of alcohol and social dancing, although – versus PBI – with allowances for movie attendance). And these commitments were also at the heart of the public controversy over Trinity Western's right to grant degrees and of the resistance to Trinity Western's joining the Association of Universities and Colleges of Canada. Many academics, journalists, politicians, and others could not see how these commitments were consistent with the academic and personal freedom expected in a university.[26] These then were the things that for many, both friend and foe, distinguished the school.

Note again that Snider did not here characterize Trinity Western's education in terms of a whole world-and-life-view that affected all the university teaches and offers students. He spoke instead of those things that characterized all evangelical institutions without making any connection to academic education per se. Snider's comments taken together with Enarson's quoted above imply the following understanding of what constitutes evangelical education: 'Traditional arts and sciences' are taught neutrally, once purged of un-Christian (and therefore necessarily false) perspectives and conclusions, and this takes place within the context of the distinctively evangelical qualities of doctrinal orthodoxy and 'pietistic' behavioural standards. In this, Trinity Western echoed precisely the 'evangelical creed' of Canadian and American colleges of the nineteenth century, with their Enlightenment-style epistemology and evangelical piety.[27]

To reiterate, this was avowedly not the way many at Trinity

Western in fact saw its educational philosophy, and the university refined its presentation of such to its constituency. The mission statement of the school under Snider eventually made its broader concerns clearer: 'The mission of Trinity Western, as an arm of the Church, is to develop *godly Christian leaders*: positive, goal-oriented university graduates with thoroughly Christian minds; growing disciples of Jesus Christ who glorify God through fulfilling The Great Commission, serving God and man in the various marketplaces of life.'[28] And Vice-President for Academic Affairs Donald M. Page wrote in the school calendar for 1990–1 that 'education is never neutral, or values-free. Our liberal arts and sciences curriculum and our student activities are designed to be *faith-affirming*. In our classrooms, laboratories, and physical education facilities your faith and disciplinary development are integrated – not compartmentalized.'[29]

Yet the earlier ways of presenting Trinity's task, echoes of which still could be heard from its leaders in the 1980s,[30] did do an end run around the problem Hanson noted of justifying 'Christian training' outside a Bible institute to a constituency that thought of 'Christian training' in terms of Bible schools alone.[31] This mentality was not challenged to encompass the new idea that all disciplines need to be thought through from a distinctly Christian perspective. Instead, those evangelical young people who wished university-level training, especially for 'secular' vocations, simply could get it at TWU without fear of anti-Christian teaching and in the nurturing environment of a Bible school. This is not to imply, moreover, any cynical manipulation of its constituency by the leadership at Trinity Western. Given the strong Bible-school background of many of the university's leaders through the years, these ideas doubtless came genuinely from these people themselves even as others had a broader and deeper Christian philosophy of education.

Trinity Western University, therefore, answered to the simple desire for more, and safe, higher education among many western Canadian evangelicals. Furthermore, with its genuine and growing understanding of and commitment to a fully Christian approach to higher education, Trinity Western also introduced its constituency gradually to a new way of thinking that could only make a broader doctrine of vocation stronger among them even as it also widened Trinity Western's appeal to evangelicals across Canada. Trinity

Western's character, therefore, as well as the substantial American support it received in the early years, resolves the enigma that puzzled Hanson: it is entirely understandable that such a denomination should found such a school.

So the history and success of Trinity Western University exemplifies the trends among evangelicals towards seeking and sponsoring higher education, towards increasing distinctness from the mainline churches – and even the culture at large – to the point of erecting alternative institutions, and towards supporting a broad range of vocations. And increasingly it supported the latter with the reflection and justification apparent in other evangelical institutions, such as Inter-Varsity Christian Fellowship and Ontario Theological Seminary. As it represents a stream of Canadian evangelicalism already seen in Prairie Bible Institute, the 'sectish' form, the history of Trinity Western University therefore shows that these trends were indeed true of this stream as well. But they were especially true also of a different stream, that which supported another school just up the road in Vancouver, Regent College.

— 11 —
Regent College

In the later 1980s, Canada's most secular city was home to one of Canada's largest theological seminaries. On the campus of one of Canada's premier secular universities was a major evangelical school. A denomination well-known for a strong streak of anti-intellectualism, the Christian Brethren, founded a graduate school, fully accredited by the Association of Theological Schools, with a faculty among the most distinguished in North American evangelicalism. And one of Canada's leading training centres for Protestant pastors pioneered the graduate theological training of laypeople, a project that inspired similar efforts in Berkeley, California, and London, England.

The paradoxes embodied in the history of Regent College are not exhausted by this list. But as a survey of Regent's history resolves these conundrums, so it also furthers the story of Canadian evangelicalism. It demonstrates again not only twentieth-century evangelicalism's central commitments to the authority of Scripture, the necessity of personal conversion and piety, and the importance of evangelism, but also the later trends among evangelicals towards more education for its spiritual leaders, towards distinction from the mainline churches and the culture at large, and towards a recognition of and training for a variety of vocations.[1]

The fellowship of Christians known as the Christian (or 'Plymouth') Brethren in their Canadian and American communions generally have not supported advanced education as have those in Britain.[2] But, as in the case of other small, evangelical denominations in Canada, some young men did seek formal theological training, especially in the 1950s and 1960s, with the encouragement of older Brethren leaders.

In Vancouver, British Columbia, one such leader was E. Marshall Sheppard.[3] Sheppard not only personally encouraged young students, he also helped to found in 1958 a quarterly periodical named *Calling*. This journal was sponsored by some Vancouver-area assemblies (as the Brethren usually call their congregations) with the special interest of developing young writers. But Sheppard went considerably further when, at an Easter conference in Vancouver, he broached the idea of a graduate school of theology in Vancouver that would train leaders for the assemblies. Other Brethren leaders had suggested something like this in the past,[4] but the timing of Sheppard's proposal seemed right. Two young American students from Fuller Theological Seminary who were speakers at the conference, W. Ward Gasque and Donald Tinder, already had discussed this very idea and were thus early on brought into the Vancouver planning (the former would become professor of New Testament at the new school). And in December of that year, at the Inter-Varsity Christian Fellowship's 'Urbana '64' convention, more than fifty Brethren students met to discuss the proposal. A formal committee was struck in Vancouver in 1965, with Sheppard presiding. Another young American graduate student, Carl E. Armerding, began to confer with the committee in June of that year – he would later become professor of Old Testament and sometime principal of the college. A number of American leaders lent support as well, and by late 1965 it was time to make the matter public.

Writing on behalf of the Vancouver group calling themselves the 'School of Theology Committee,' John Cochrane published an article in *Calling* in the fall of 1965 that introduced the area assemblies to the idea.[5] Drawing on statistics that indicated a huge increase in students attending colleges and universities since the mid-1950s, Cochrane suggested that the leaders of the assemblies would come increasingly from these students and that these same leaders needed to be able to minister to the increasing proportion of university graduates in the pews. He proposed then the establishment of a school that would train such leaders and that it be located in Vancouver, a centre of Brethren influence. The school would offer a two-track program in keeping with the Brethren conception of church leadership: that there is no distinction between clergy and laity, and that the elders, or pastors, of a church generally do not work full-time in church-related work, although some indeed do. The first track would be a one-year course for those who would go on to a 'secular' vocation. The second track would be a three-year course for those who would engage in church-related work full-time, whether at home or abroad. The school therefore would differ from Bible schools, Cochrane wrote, in that it would be primarily for university graduates. It would differ from theological seminaries, further, in that it would serve especially the Brethren assemblies, as no other school did, and in that it would emphasize the training of all Christians, regardless of occupation.[6] To be sure, Cochrane concluded, students of all denominations would be welcome, in keeping with the fundamental ecumenical spirit of the early Brethren movement. But the faculty and leadership would be Brethren. September 1969 was set out as the target date to begin the school. But other developments would entail changing not only the starting date, but something of the initial character of the school itself.

Independently of these developments, since 1961 an Oxford University professor of geography had been thinking about a graduate institute for Christian studies on the campus of a major university.[7] He wrote to Billy Graham, who had sponsored or would sponsor in his career a variety of parachurch organizations, in the hope that he and his organization could support the idea, but Graham's father-in-law, Nelson Bell, replied that Graham was too involved in evangelism at the time to take up the proposal. In 1965, this professor saw the article in *Calling* and wrote a response to it. He decided, though, not to send it, concerned that his support for the idea not be seen as putting himself forward and feeling that if the project was of God and he himself were to be involved with it, the links would form some other way.

James M. Houston's intuition was correct. In October of that year, Ward Gasque, graduated from Fuller Seminary and now studying with Brethren scholar F.F. Bruce at the University of Manchester, reported to the annual meeting of the Christian Brethren Research Fellowship in Britain the idea of the Vancouver school. Through the contacts made there, in 1966 Gasque met with Houston, also a member of the British assemblies,[8] and Gasque was so impressed with him that he reported back to the Vancouver committee that 'if [Houston] were willing to come, he would be the ideal man to head up the school.' This same judgment was rendered later that year by Bruce himself during a visit to Vancouver.[9]

In 1967 Houston, then visiting professor at the University of

Texas, came up to Vancouver on the invitation of the school committee to discuss their possible cooperation. The first meeting ran into difficulties as some Vancouver Brethren felt things were moving too fast and walked out. In the second meeting, Houston laid out what for him were three essential qualities of the school: that it be located on a university campus and affiliated with that university;[10] that it be at the graduate level; and that it be transdenominational in character. Only the second of the three proposals was directly in line with the original Vancouver idea for the school, but the other ideas had been discussed favourably among the Vancouver Brethren before Houston had come[11] and his preferences met with approval.[12] The Vancouver committee was pleased to bring on board someone who could give the project instant credibility in the eyes of the university and, for Houston's part, his original visions seemed to be on the way to realization.

In 1968 the Vancouver committee petitioned the provincial legislature for a charter for a school of theology that would serve the smaller denominations of western Canada that had no graduate theological school of their own.[13] The original petitioners were all from Vancouver and Victoria assemblies, but the eventual transdenominational character of the school already had been agreed upon and was explained to the government committee involved. In April 1968, the school was incorporated as Regent College, taking its name from the business of one of the committee members who used it with the understanding that all Christians are to act as regents, or stewards, of God's world under his authority.

The school stood squarely and self-consciously in the evangelical tradition. It adopted the doctrinal statement of the World Evangelical Fellowship (the international group that emerged from the American National Association of Evangelicals)[14] and refused to take a position on eschatology – at the risk of offending many strongly dispensational Brethren[15] – in the interest of attracting evangelicals from all traditions. Its programs were designed expressly for the needs of church leaders and missionaries. And the college's early documents emphasized spirituality as infusing the whole life of the school. As Houston put it in an early brief to the constituency:

All meaningful conceptions gained in Biblical study must be related to personal and social life. It is the formation of Christian character and conduct that is essential, not an academic factory that manufactures its products called degrees and diplomas.

... 'Let the Word of God dwell in you richly." Nothing is more vital than personal nurture in a living faith, so that the personal concern of our staff and board members in each individual student must have the highest priority ...

... To know is also to witness. We expect our students and staff to lead others to Christ, not within a rigid duty of talking about the faith, but from the joyous spontaneity of knowing God's Word and responding to it.[16]

Clearly, though, Regent College embraced other elements as well. It trained not only pastors and missionaries, but those in other jobs who yet would serve in churches and witness to the gospel. And more than this, Regent was concerned to train these others in a Christian world-view that would inform precisely their pursuit of these extra-ecclesiastical occupations.[17] It was this last element in particular that made Regent stand out on the educational map.

Summer-school sessions were held in 1969 and 1970 to test the waters and prepare the way.[18] Over fifty students attended the first session, and then about one hundred the second. The school opened for full-time study in the fall of 1970. Four students began, to be joined by two others in the new year, and several dozen part-time students swelled the ranks. Houston was installed as principal; W.J. Martin and S.M. Block served as vice-principals; and Armerding and Gasque were named assistant professors of Old and New Testament studies respectively. These full-time staff were augmented with two special lecturers in church history, Ian S. Rennie (later of Ontario Theological Seminary), a Presbyterian, and J.A. Toews, a Mennonite. And Samuel J. Mikolaski, a Baptist, came part-time as professor of theology. The school held its classes in the basement of the Union Theological College, which merged with the Anglican school to form the Vancouver School of Theology the next year. The libraries of these schools and of the University of British Columbia, on whose campus the schools were located, were open to Regent students.

The first program offered was a one-year Diploma in Christian Studies. This was expanded the next year so that students could go on to a two-year Master of Christian Studies (MCS), which, even as other degrees were offered later, became Regent's most popular degree program. Most of the courses were traditional items in the academic theological curriculum: biblical studies, theology, church history, and ethics. These were seen as the bases for a Christian world-view. But Regent made early attempts to fulfil its mission of explicitly integrating theology and non-ecclesiastical vocations. To this end it offered a 'cross-disciplinary studies' course that brought in visitors from a variety of professions to lecture and discuss with students the prosecution of their vocations as evangelicals. Full-time students in the first year then were encouraged to take on a cross-disciplinary project in the second semester; MCS students were encouraged to devote their theses to this sort of project.

The college grew. It added faculty to teach the growing numbers of students, sixty-three full-time by 1973. In keeping with the school's intention to relate fully to the larger academic world, in 1972 it affiliated with the Vancouver School of Theology[19] and that same year the Academic Senate of the University of British Columbia voted to grant affiliation to Regent College, a motion renewed again in 1973 and then again in 1977 for an indefinite period. By the mid-1970s Regent had outgrown its borrowed facilities. In 1974 it hired its first full-time professor of theology, Canadian Clark H. Pinnock, and Pinnock's wide reputation among evangelicals in the United States and Canada drew even more students to the school.[20] So in 1975 it moved into two converted fraternity buildings on the UBC campus, that with the addition of portable classroom buildings constituted what would become a very crowded home by the early 1980s. (Finally, in 1989 the college moved into a new, more spacious building across the street.)

The growth at the school meant an increasing administrative burden on the principal. Houston, renowned among the Regent constituency and elsewhere for his personal warmth and public charisma, had done a great deal to form the vision for the school and to draw needed attention to its program. But in the later 1970s, the board of governors judged that he needed some administrative help in order for him to concentrate on the things he did best. So Carl E. Armerding was appointed vice-principal in 1977.

Regent had seen by this point a pattern which brought to the surface tensions which went back to the initial differences of vision for the school in the 1960s. Despite the school's international reputation as a laity-oriented graduate school,[21] a large proportion of its students were coming with the intention of becoming pastors or missionaries and then would go on to theological colleges for the rest of their training. Regent, that is, was attractive for both its evangelical character and sound academic standards:[22] further training in the practical side of professional ministry and in denominational heritage would then be sought elsewhere.[23] And, in many cases, these latter two dimensions of pastoral education were not being sought at all by graduates: many entered the professional ministry directly upon graduation, since many of the evangelical denominations or parachurch organizations were quite satisfied with this training.[24]

Some at Regent saw this as reason to raise again the original concern to offer training for full-time church leaders.[25] But Houston had early moved away from this orientation, seeing Regent as a graduate institute, virtually a division of Christian studies of a university, rather than as a training centre for religious professionals.[26] He was intent, not on training the next generation of pastors and missionaries, but on training the next generation of Christians involved in a variety of vocations who approached all of life with a strong Christian consciousness and intelligence. Houston did not want Regent to contribute to what he saw as the over-professionalization of North American life in general and of the church in particular. Rather, he thought, Regent should produce more Christians like C.S. Lewis, a personal friend of Houston's: Christians who would be 'amateur theologians' in the best Oxonian (and Brethren) sense of the terms.[27]

Coincident with this difference in perspective was the growing feeling among the faculty and board that Houston's own gifts could be used best in a non-administrative capacity. In 1978 Armerding was named principal and Houston was appointed to the newly created position of chancellor, from which he could continue to write and speak as a distinguished representative of the school.[28] With this administrative move, however, the way was also made more clear to introduce a degree program directed towards the training of professional church leaders. Regent decided to introduce a Master of Divinity program in the fall of 1979 – which development, not surprisingly, meant the end of Regent's affiliation with the Vancouver School of Theology.[29] The next year it began to cooperate with the Baptist Union of Western Canada, whose student residence on campus, Carey Hall, had been intended originally to serve as a seminary. Carey Hall took the responsibility of providing missing 'pastoral' courses to complement Regent's strong academic emphasis, supplying professors in pastoral theology, Baptist studies, and field education. Regent itself later appointed a professor of evangelism, the well-known British Anglican E. Michael B. Green (who returned to England in the summer of 1992). The program developed to become a rival to the MCS as the most popular at Regent.

Regent sought and earned full accreditation from the Association of Theological Schools in 1985. By that time it was enrolling a full-time equivalent of over 250 students, made up of a total of over 300 male and over 125 female students. And it attracted hundreds each year to its internationally recognized summer school. The denominational profile of the students resembles those for this era of the other institutions discussed so far, and especially those of Ontario Bible College and Ontario Theological Seminary and Inter-Varsity Christian Fellowship: strong contingents of Baptists and those listed under the category of 'Other' by the Association of Theological Schools, notably Christian and Missionary Alliance, Brethren, Mennonite, and Pentecostal, as well as consistent representation by Presbyterians and – especially in the later years with well-known authors J.I. Packer and Michael Green on the faculty – Anglicans.[30] Regent thus served the whole spectrum of Christians of generally evangelical convictions, except for the strongly fundamentalist or denominational groups.

Indeed, Regent clearly served a constituency broader than Canadian evangelicalism. American students had constituted a significant presence since the founding of the school, and Regent consistently hired Americans on its staff. (Indeed, Walter C. Wright, Jr., succeeded Carl Armerding after the latter's ten years of office, thus continuing the college's tradition of hiring a non-Canadian for its highest office.) By the mid-1980s, moreover, Regent's service to the burgeoning Asian communities of the Pacific Rim was increasing. A Chinese Studies Program was initiated in 1985, with special courses, lecture series, and an annual conference dedicated to the issue of Christianity and Chinese culture. Thomas In-Sing Leung of Hong Kong joined the faculty in 1990 to direct the program. And by the early 1990s, Regent's connections with China, Korea, Hong Kong, Singapore, Australia, and other Pacific Rim regions had multiplied through alumni and supporters to the extent that it began to consider explicitly whether it ought to see that region as its frame of reference, rather than North America per se. Indeed, Regent's penchant for hiring prominent American or British faculty members caused some to grumble about its 'un-Canadian' character. With such a faculty mix, however, which included Canadians, Chinese, and others, Regent did in fact reflect the character of its immediate context, at least, metropolitan Vancouver.

The shape of Regent's program betrayed yet its roots in the original vision of the Vancouver Brethren. On the one hand, it continued to struggle with the applied-theology part of the program. In the mid-1980s Regent overhauled its M.Div. program to attempt a better way of training pastors both academically and professionally, but the priority it had given to theological and especially biblical studies reflected the typically evangelical and especially Brethren emphasis upon Bible knowledge and teaching as defining the role of church leaders. On the other hand, Regent continued to work towards doing full justice to its commitment to integrate theological studies with all vocations, rather than just to train church leaders, whatever their jobs, in that role per se. Houston himself, a geographer who yet wrote works on theology and spirituality, exemplified the model Regent was seeking in this regard: a professional skilled at his or her job with a solid and comprehensive understanding both of basic Christianity and of its dominion over one's whole life. Houston's own teaching and personal example helped others at Regent along this path. The workshops with professionals brought in from the community moved further in this direction, although there is evidence that in the early years many of these professionals themselves had made too little connection between a Christian world-view and their vocations, making the sessions with Regent students often disappointing.[31] These encounters improved a great deal thereafter, however, as more and more evangelicals in the next decade who had developed more sophisticated understanding of the relationship of faith and vocation were available to help in this way at the school – not least because of training received at Regent itself.[32] Visiting scholars from non-theological fields brought to Regent their perspectives on a full-year basis. The MCS theses were intended to encourage students to make these connections themselves, although again a large number were devoted to subjects within the common theological curriculum. And beginning in 1982, Regent sponsored annual seminars, called 'The Christian in the Marketplace,' for business and professional people in the community at large – conferences that later were held also in Seattle and Calgary.

Most crucial of all, as Regent's own principal pointed out (as did its self-study document of 1990), Regent made room for only one faculty position in addition to Houston himself in this area of integration. Moreover, it was established only in 1976 with the appointment of Michael Tymchak, was held a year later by Irving Hexham, and finally was held by Loren Wilkinson beginning in 1981.[33] Instead, teachers were hired mostly in the traditional disciplines of academic theological study. And while Regent wanted to keep this theological core strong, to be sure, the next stage was to decide whether to hire experts in the relationships between Christianity and business, Christianity and the healing arts, Christianity and public policy, and so on. Several professionals indicated to Regent, in fact, that they might retire early in order to come to the school in such a capacity. This was a perennial problem at Regent: whether to hire people out of the professions to become full-time teachers, which action would isolate them from their former world, or to continue to do as Regent had done, to bring them in as adjunct faculty.[34]

These problems, however, were on the way to satisfactory resolution by the later 1980s. And Regent's general character was well established.[35] In sum, Regent College demonstrated in a new way Canadian evangelicalism's increasing concern to educate its leaders.[36] It also stood with other educational institutions as a self-conscious alternative to those of the mainline churches, especially in its offering of the Master of Divinity degree. In 1989, the Regent board accepted a mission statement that set out these two 'streams' together as equals. As Regent's 1990 self-study document characterizes it, 'This statement deliberately avoids clergy-laity language in its expression of the College['s] educational mission and has greatly strengthened statements about the equipping goal of our pastoral training, the integrative orientation of the College, the spiritual formation of students and the critical role of research and publications.'[37]

Beyond these concerns, Regent's whole thrust was critical of contemporary Western culture as it sought to train Christians in developing an evangelical place to stand apart from that culture so as to devise a discerning approach and powerful ministry within and to it. And as Regent College and the other institutions so far discussed represented Canadian evangelicalism in the 1980s and early 1990s, it appears that this community was yet in the process of recognizing the breadth of God's call upon the church, while preserving the emphases that gave evangelicalism identity in the first place. The history of the Evangelical Fellowship of Canada, finally, illustrates these developments yet again.

— 12 —
The Evangelical Fellowship of Canada

Three themes that have emerged in the account so far show up clearly in the history of the Evangelical Fellowship of Canada. The first is the trend among evangelicals towards greater self-consciousness and cooperation while simultaneously distancing themselves from the direction and institutions of the mainline churches. Indeed, the Evangelical Fellowship of Canada also manifested and fostered the development of a network of such evangelicals, a mutually supportive fellowship of organizations and individuals. The second is the widening of this fellowship to include groups previously isolated in their respective enclaves, especially Pentecostals, Mennonites, and the Christian Reformed. The third is the growing breadth of evangelicals' understanding of their vocation. But, as the history of the Evangelical Fellowship of Canada shows, perhaps more clearly than that of any other institution, the first of these themes needs qualification, since many of the leading evangelical leaders came from mainline groups, as did a substantial number of supporters. And it shows too that the third theme is related to the first. That is, even as evangelicals supported institutions whose orientations differed from those of the mainline churches and in some ways were opposed to or at least critical of the culture at large, so evangelicals yet according to their broadening doctrine of vocation (as well as their loyalties to particular traditions) continued to work within these denominations and to engage the culture more directly than ever before since the First World War.

The history of the Evangelical Fellowship of Canada can be seen in two periods, the importance of which were inversely proportional to their length.[1] The first, longer period, stretched from the Fellowship's founding in Toronto in 1964 until the early 1980s when Brian C. Stiller became executive director. The second is the period since Stiller took over.

In the early 1960s, a series of meetings among evangelical leaders in the Toronto area resulted in the founding of a fellowship of pastors in 1964. The Evangelical Fellowship of Canada included clergymen in the Presbyterian and Anglican churches who sought fellowship with other evangelicals in the midst of their pluralistic denominations as well as church leaders in evangelical groups who sought fellowship beyond their small denominations. From the start, a number of the latter groups were represented in the membership,[2] nowhere more obviously than in the president's chair, held by J. Harry Faught, a pastor in the Pentecostal Assemblies of Canada who had spearheaded the founding of the group.[3] To be sure, Faught was an exceptional Pentecostal in that he had trained at the evangelically acceptable Dallas Theological Seminary, yet his role signalled the growing presence of Pentecostals in mainstream evangelicalism. And more traditional evangelical groups such as the Baptists, Associated Gospel Churches, Christian and Missionary Alliance, Mennonites, and Christian Brethren were represented as well.

None the less, three of the next four presidents who succeeded Faught were Presbyterian: William J. Fitch of the sturdy Knox Presbyterian Church in Toronto; Mariano DiGangi, later professor at Ontario Theological Seminary; and A. Donald MacLeod, who later would become general director of the Inter-Varsity Christian Fellowship.[4] Prominent also in the first decades were Anglican evangelicals Harry Robinson and Desmond C. Hunt.[5]

The pastors' meeting of 1964 and the follow-up meeting in Oswald J. Smith's Peoples Church in 1965 saw the birth of the group, and its constitution was ratified in 1966. The constitution that guided the Fellowship in this first period included three major statements: a preamble, a statement of purpose, and a statement of faith. The preamble made clear both evangelical distance from contemporary attitudes in the church and society that the Fellowship saw to be evil ('liberalism [presumably theological liberalism in this context], apostacy [sic], and spiritual nihilism') and evangelical commitment to unity so as to 'make their co-operative thrust more relevant and effective, particularly in the articulation of the great, historic truths of the Word of God.' The statement of purpose sounded traditional evangelical notes: affirmation of loyalty to the doctrines in the statement of faith, witness against apostasy, and 'fellowship ... defence ... [and] the furtherance of the gospel.' These latter phrases, drawn from Paul's letter to the Philippians, were given concreteness in the Fellowship's establishment of several commissions: Theology, Social Action, Inter-Church Relations, Foreign Missions, Christian Education, Public Relations, and, later, Evangelism and Spiritual Life Conventions. Here were a set of concerns more broad than merely defence of orthodoxy and evangelism, even as these latter yet seem primary in this document. The statement of faith was that of the World Evangelical Fellowship, of which the EFC became a member, a seven-point statement that affirmed the divine and unique authority of Scripture (without using the word 'inerrancy'), the triunity of God, the divinity and salvific work of Christ, justification by faith, regeneration and sanctification by the Holy Spirit, the unity of all true believers in the church, and the resurrection to salvation or judgment of all.[6]

The annual meeting of 1966 heard a report on the budget, which was just over $1000.[7] Five years later disbursements had increased to over $20,000, and by 1976 to over $30,000.[8] Beyond the cost of its own annual convention, which brought Canadian evangelicals of a broad range together to hear powerful speeches and enjoy workshops and worship together, most of this money went to sponsor several kinds of ministry. The first was the Fellowship's magazine, begun in 1968, called *Thrust.* Originally mailed free to a mailing list of over ten thousand, the magazine eventually relied mainly on advertising revenues and paid subscriptions. *Thrust* discussed common evangelical concerns: personal spirituality, biblical authority, church growth, relief work, and missions. It also brought news of developments in evangelicalism, the larger church scene, and Canadian society to its readers. In particular it served to acquaint Canadians with evangelical ministries beyond their own region or denomination. And it began to address larger social issues, whether the morality of government-sponsored lotteries or the treatment of women in Canadian society.[9] The EFC also sponsored leadership seminars, beginning in 1975 and running biennially, that brought some of the world's notable evangelicals to Canada for the instruction of Canadian leaders. American theologian Carl

F.H. Henry, expatriate Canadian evangelist Leighton Ford, and English preacher John R.W. Stott were among the most prominent. The EFC made good on its commitment to social ministries[10] as it took over the work of Share, Canada! from the Christian and Missionary Alliance in the late 1960s. This organization in 1982 became the Canadian arm of World Relief, affiliated with the American organization of the same name that constituted the social-action ministry of the National Association of Evangelicals.[11]

The Fellowship eventually recognized, however, that it could not realize its potential without full-time leadership: all the presidents were men busy with other, full-time positions. Funding an executive-director position proved difficult for some time,[12] but in the early 1980s, Brian C. Stiller moved from serving as vice-president to become executive director. Stiller was ordained in the Pentecostal Assemblies of Canada and a graduate of one of their Bible schools, but he had also obtained a university degree and completed his theological training at the evangelical Anglican Wycliffe College in Toronto. With this denominational broad-mindedness and his success as director of the transdenominational Youth for Christ work in Canada, Stiller seemed a man who could further the work of the Fellowship. That judgment by the EFC proved correct.

The first indication of a wider vision for the Fellowship in this era, which actually predated Stiller's term as executive director, was the revised constitution of the EFC, adopted in March 1981. This document distinguished itself from its predecessor in several respects. First, it did not set the EFC over against negative forces in the church: it spoke in positive tones, of the work of the EFC on its own terms. That is, the new constitution showed the Fellowship not reacting to particular external problems, but seeking generally to improve the life of the church. Second, it sought to improve the life of the church by emphasizing two things: the development of church leadership, and the fostering of unity even more extensively than the first constitution had outlined. The new constitution purposed to bring together leaders to consider common problems, whether leaders of various denominations or leaders of church and parachurch groups. The third indication of a broader vision was the declaration that this unity would be represented to government at local, provincial, and national levels. 'Such relationship with government will assist in practical ways; provide for liaison in united manner with government agencies; and be a means of influence to protect the rights and freedoms of individual Christians, of the Church, and Christian institutions.' More than this interest in defending persons and things Christian, this involvement with government would seek 'to bring moral direction in government decisions.'[13]

These things Stiller pursued with zeal. The Fellowship strengthened church leadership in several ways, among them the appointment of Keith A. Price (former head of 'Sermons from Science' and Christian Direction) as minister-at-large whose main calling was to model and instruct in expositional preaching, which he did more than four hundred times a year,[14] and the sponsorship of seminars around the country that acquainted church leaders with contemporary problems and set out plans of action to resolve them.

The EFC stepped up its ministry to evangelicals at large, especially through publications. *Thrust* was superseded by *Faith Today*, which combined discussion of contemporary issues with book reviews and news.[15] It discussed in particular broad social concerns like the nuclear arms race, poverty, prisons, and child abuse. Circulation of *Faith Today* by the mid-1980s grew to eighteen thousand and was expected by the EFC to continue to increase.[16] The EFC also published the *Sundial* for Fellowship members, a quarterly newsletter that presented the viewpoints and experience of the EFC's leaders and Stiller in particular on a variety of current topics. And *Understanding Our Times* was published quarterly for members of churches belonging to the EFC and brought news the knowledge of which was expected to help Canadian evangelicals respond better to their world. By the early 1990s as well, EFC had sponsored or was planning to sponsor (sometimes with other evangelical organizations) conferences on effective writing, religion and Canadian culture, and the nature of human life (in regard to issues like abortion and euthanasia), as well as on theology, gender and the church, and evangelism.[17]

The EFC under Stiller sponsored three commissions, one on the family, one on social action, and one on evangelism. These commissions not only informed the Fellowship's publications, but contributed to the increasingly visible work of the EFC in representing evangelicals to government. The EFC, for example, intervened with the Trudeau administration and helped to convince the government to include a phrase recognizing the sovereignty of God over Canada in the new constitution.[18] A decade later, its Task Force on Canada's Future represented an evangelical viewpoint to the Special Joint Committee on a Renewed Canada in Ottawa, and prepared study materials for its constituency on the constitutional questions of the time.[19] On another front, the Social Action Commission represented evangelical concerns over freedom of religion and the legitimation of homosexuality as a lifestyle to the Mulroney government. These concerns were sparked especially by the government report *Equality for All*, which recommended that no organization in Canada discriminate on the basis of religion (clearly a problem for most religious organizations!), and that no organization discriminate on the basis of sexual orientation (again, clearly a problem for the vast majority of evangelicals who saw homosexual intercourse as sin).[20] Other briefs were presented to the government outlining concerns over such issues as child care (the EFC wrote in favour of increasing maternity and paternity benefits to strengthen families), pornography, and a one-in-seven-days rest, whatever the day might be, for rest and worship (a brief prompted by the increasing number of provincial governments debating full retailing on Sundays).[21] And in the later 1980s, the EFC involved itself deeply in the national debate over abortion through conferences, publications, and representations to government. (Stiller began in 1989 to take some of these messages to a broader public, furthermore, as he hosted 'The Stiller Report,' a half-hour talk show on the new interfaith television network, VISION TV.)

EFC's understanding of Canada's multicultural society appears throughout its publications from this time. The writers of EFC documents firmly pressed what they understood to be evangelical views on particular issues, but only by force of reasonable persuasion in this pluralistic context. There was no call for a return to a 'Christian Canada,' no inappropriate appeal to special revelation per se, no threats of political revenge by evangelicals if their preferences were not obeyed. (All this was in marked contrast to many of their counterparts south of the border.) True, fund-raising materials did occasionally hit strident notes as they resonated with the fears of some evangelicals that Canadian Christianity was under attack from every side. 'Is God to become nothing more than a memory?' EFC asked. And it declared, 'We can do something about the battle for young minds in our public schools! ... Governments purge Christian faith from classroom.'[22] Furthermore, by the early 1990s the EFC had not yet formulated a clear and coherent philosophy of Christian engagement in the public sphere. At the heart of this ambiguity was the question of whether Christians ought to push politically to make Canada as Christian as possible, or instead ought to work with others towards some appropriate form of pluralism.[23] In their manner at least, however, Stiller and his colleagues played by the rules of Canadian public discourse. They generally argued their views with civility and cogency, holding makers of public policy and opinion to the standards of the Canadian public square.[24]

Stiller's initiative also showed up in increased membership numbers: by 1989 twenty-seven denominations had joined the EFC and the aggregate membership of denominations, individual churches, and individual persons (one could join the EFC on any of these bases) Stiller estimated as over one million. Support came also from leaders of transdenominational institutions. Carl E. Armerding, principal of Regent College, Henry Hildebrand, principal of Briercrest Bible College (heir to Prairie as the largest Bible school in Canada), and R. Neil Snider, President of Trinity Western University, all appeared in EFC promotional literature in the mid-1980s.[25] In addition, Ian S. Rennie, dean of Ontario Theological Seminary, was sometime vice-president of the Fellowship, and James E. Berney, general director of Inter-Varsity Christian Fellowship, sat on the General Council with William MacRae, president of OBC/OTS.[26] Memberships and magazine subscriptions in the 1980s were highest in Ontario by a good measure (about 40 per cent of the totals), but support stretched across the country, with British Columbia and Alberta ranking next (at 10–15 per cent each), Manitoba and Saskatchewan at the next tier (5–8 per cent), and Quebec and the Atlantic provinces at the bottom.[27] And finally, the EFC's income swelled from just over $60,000 in 1983 to over $1,200,000 in 1988, an increase of 2000 per cent in half a decade, and by 1990 it had increased by another 75 per cent to over $2,000,000.[28]

The traditional evangelical emphases remained, however. Stiller cautioned evangelicals that as they properly engaged the larger culture once again, they should not lose their former concerns: 'The emphasis on revivalism – life in the Spirit – and evangelism

– calling people to faith and repentance – must not be lost. The renewal of inner life and reaching out to others must remain on the top of our agendas. Now as we add another, redemptionism – the calling of our culture to obedience – let us not be trapped.'[29] And elsewhere Stiller wrote, 'Evangelism ... the Church must never lose sight of her primary task.'[30] Indeed, in the late 1980s the EFC's Task Force on Evangelism established 'Vision 2000 Canada,' a nationwide program to bring together denominational, congregational, and parachurch leaders in the interest of evangelizing all of Canada and thereby doubling the size of its evangelical population by the year 2000. Furthermore, while members of the mainline churches continued to support the EFC, the influence of the smaller, uniformly evangelical denominations dominated it in the 1980s.[31] For example, all of the presidents since Charles Seidenspinner in the mid-1970s were from such evangelical denominations.[32] And since a considerable proportion (although not a majority) of the membership of the general council was determined largely by denominational membership, and only uniformly evangelical denominations joined, they had a large share of the votes – quite apart from members of these churches who were council members on their own or because of their positions in evangelical organizations.

Even as the Evangelical Fellowship of Canada presented Christians with a parallel form of fellowship to that offered by the Canadian Council of Churches (although, unlike the National Association of Evangelicals in the United States, the EFC did not require its members to be dissociated from the mainline ecumenical group[33]), however, and even as it reaffirmed traditional evangelical emphases, it yet also demonstrated that evangelicals were moving back into involvement with Canadian cultural life, concerned not merely to separate from it but to influence it according to a broad sense of God's call to the church and to the world. In 1986 the general council of the Evangelical Fellowship of Canada approved a new logo for the association. Above the letters 'EFC' was a stylized open book, and above that a solid circle. The circle stood for Christ as the centre of the Fellowship's life and purpose. But together with the book the circle formed the image of a person standing behind an open Bible. Not many years before, this symbol would have been understood unequivocally by evangelicals: we believe the Bible and we stand to proclaim God's Word for conversion and spiritual nurture. Such emphases, of course, continued to characterize evangelicals. But the ministry of the EFC, at least, while not itself summing up the whole evangelical enterprise, represented yet a new part of this enterprise, and invested these symbols with a new meaning. For the explanation the EFC itself gave of the person standing behind the Bible was not that it represented evangelism or preaching per se, but that it 'represents our task of speaking forth the word of truth. We are called to action; we have a task – to represent evangelicals and our concerns to our nation.'[34] Evangelicals, as represented by the Evangelical Fellowship of Canada, thereby declared that the mainstream of Canadian evangelicalism, for all its conscious differences from the culture at large, intended now to flow into the mainstream of Canadian life.

Part Four

The Character of Canadian Evangelicalism in the Twentieth Century

— 13 —
The Character of Canadian Evangelicalism in the Twentieth Century

Between 1525 and 1529, dozens of European Protestants died at the hands of their fellow Protestants. Some were burned; some were beaten and left to die in prison; and some, with an awful irony, were drowned – drowned because they insisted on being baptized as adult believers, rather than as infant children of believers. Mortally deep, then, ran the differences between those Protestants whose reform was supported by political rulers, or magistrates (hence their reform was called the 'magisterial' reformation), and those who were driven out of the community, the 're-baptizers,' or Anabaptists.

In 1531, Ulrich Zwingli lay dead on a Swiss battlefield. Zwingli was chaplain to the troops of Zurich who had ridden out to meet their Catholic foes from neighbouring Swiss cantons. Zwingli and his compatriots were Protestants, but because he and Martin Luther had failed to agree on a precise definition of the nature of the Lord's Supper at the Colloquy of Marburg in 1529, German Protestants would not join with Swiss Protestants in battle. Without the Germans, the Zurichers were slaughtered. Thus the breach appeared in the magisterial reformation between German Lutherans and German-speaking Reformed.

In 1610, a Dutch blacksmith chased a man down the street with a hot poker because the man had not agreed with John Calvin's theology to the satisfaction of the scrupulous blacksmith. The blacksmith's theological leaders met at the city of Dordrecht and excommunicated all those whose opinions they deemed insufficiently Reformed – those who followed the dissenting opinions of Jacob Arminius. So began the often bitter fraternal debate about divine sovereignty and human freedom between 'Calvinists' and 'Arminians.'

After a long political and military battle to purify the Church of England from what they saw to be vestiges of Roman Catholicism after the sixteenth-century Reformation as well as to assert the rights of Parliament against the monarchy, the Puritans controlled the government of England in 1649. But the freedom victory brought also brought out into the open differences between Puritan groups. Oliver Cromwell, their military leader, tried to unite them, but the movement fragmented, largely over what form of church government or of baptism was most scriptural, into Presbyterians, Congregationalists, Baptists, Quakers, and other groups.[1]

David B. Barrett's *World Christian Encyclopedia* (1982) estimated that there would be more than 22,000 denominations in Christianity by 1985.[2] Most of these by far would identify with some sort of Protestantism. The plot-line of Protestantism, therefore, seems to be one of greater and greater fragmentation and emphasis upon differences rather than similarities.

The story has been told elsewhere and for some time of the attempts of the so-called 'modern ecumenical movement' to reverse this tendency.[3] But, especially since the 1950s, scholars and other observers have noted a different sort of alliance across denominational divisions: evangelicalism.[4] To come to our own story: In Canada, most historians interested in movements that bring Christians together have focused on the Canadian Council of Churches in general and upon the United Church of Canada in particular.[5] But a growing number have noticed a transdenominational movement of Christians who owed an allegiance to things they all saw as transcending the differences that divided and continued to divide their respective communions.

Canadian evangelicals, that is, like Christians in the sixteenth and seventeenth centuries, continued to disagree about baptism and the doctrine of the church, about the character of Christ's presence in the Lord's Supper, about predestination and human freedom, and about church polity. These, and other areas that have divided Christians, still divided evangelicals into denominations. But Canadian evangelicals in the twentieth century recognized areas of agreement that they saw together to be more crucial than the disagreements that had utterly divided Christians in the past. Maintaining faithfulness to the distinctives that denominated them, nevertheless these Christians joined together in faithfulness to shared beliefs and concerns. And this joining together produced the institutions examined here.

Reading back through the life and character of these institutions, then, we can see what drew Canadian evangelicals together, what commonalities they held so dear that they would cross denominational lines to support them. In the first place, Canadian evangelicals held to a common core of doctrine. Each of these institutions insisted that those involved with them – or at least those in leadership and in some cases everyone – agree on a set of beliefs that set out the essence of evangelical Christianity. And these various statements in fact agree with each other remarkably. Indeed, the statement of the World Evangelical Fellowship, adopted directly by two of the institutions described here, Regent College and the Evangelical Fellowship of Canada, serves as a 'generic' statement of Canadian evangelical belief:

1. The Holy Scriptures as originally given by God, divinely inspired, infallible, entirely trustworthy; and the only supreme authority in all matters of faith and conduct.
2. One God, eternally existent in three Persons, Father, Son and Holy Spirit.
3. Our Lord Jesus Christ, God manifest in the flesh, His virgin birth, His sinless human life, His divine miracles, His bodily resurrection, His ascension, His mediatorial work, and His personal return in power and glory.
4. The salvation of lost and sinful man through the shed blood of the Lord Jesus Christ by faith apart from works, and regeneration by the Holy Spirit.
5. The Holy Spirit by whose indwelling the believer is enabled to live a holy life to witness and work for the Lord Jesus Christ.
6. The unity in the Spirit of all true believers, the Church, the Body of Christ.
7. The resurrection of both the saved and the lost; they that are saved unto the resurrection of life, and they that are lost unto the resurrection of damnation.[6]

Evangelicals did not all precisely agree on this statement, as respective statements of faith of each of the institutions they support make clear. For instance, some preferred to use the word 'inerrancy' in articulating the doctrine of Scripture, seeing it as a bulwark against creeping liberalism; others preferred *not* to use it, seeing it as a shibboleth that served only to divide evangelicals from each other.[7] But the disagreement among Canadian evangelicals over this matter was slight indeed: all the institutions here described set out very 'high' doctrines of Scripture's inspiration and authority and all these statements could be contained by the phrases above, even as some would use different language.

The remaining clauses of the statement aroused little controversy among Canadian evangelicals. To be sure, dispensationalists disagreed with Christian Reformed believers over the nature of the millennium and therefore over the exact character of Christ's 'personal return in power and glory,' but all agreed on the statement as written.[8] Methodists differed with Pentecostals, and both groups disagreed with Presbyterians when they went beyond the language of the statement to describe more fully the nature of the work of the Holy Spirit as he 'indwells' believers, 'enabling' them to live holy lives, but again all agreed with what *was* said therein. And while the conceptions of church polity among Canadian evangelicals ran the gamut from episcopalian to congregational and qualifications for church membership from public profession of conversion to completion of a full catechetical program, all agreed that the essential characteristics of a member of the universal Church were true belief and unity in the Holy Spirit. Canadian evangelicals, then, continued to disagree about matters they saw to be important enough to justify the continuance of denominations. But it is crucial to see here again that evangelicals from each of these traditions were content to leave these disagreements for certain forums, certain times: in other contexts, they were glad to work together on this sort of doctrinal basis.

Why it was *this* set of beliefs that united Canadian evangelicals and not others, however, can be explained best in terms of other concerns these Christians held in common. The development of personal piety, of both vital worship and holy living, characterized Canadian evangelicalism as well. Every school here studied and Inter-Varsity Christian Fellowship as well all esteemed worship services as a vital part of their programs. All these institutions also held throughout their histories that the spiritual development of Christian students was among their highest priorities. And the magazines of Prairie Bible Institute, Toronto and Ontario Bible

Colleges, and the Evangelical Fellowship of Canada consistently published articles to encourage both worship and holiness.

As important as these concerns was Canadian evangelicals' commitment to evangelism. Most of the institutions they established in the twentieth century were either missions themselves (whether foreign-mission organizations like the Sudan Interior Mission, home-mission organizations like Inter-Varsity Christian Fellowship, or special projects like 'Sermons from Science') or organizations meant to train missionaries (most notably the Bible schools, and, with a less exclusive focus, Trinity Western University and Regent College).

These three concerns – doctrinal orthodoxy, personal piety, and evangelism – interwove in evangelical life. In the first place, as we have seen, evangelicals did not found schools only to foster these things but to foster them together. Not one school focused exclusively on teaching doctrine, or developing spirituality, or training for missions. In the second place, evangelical emphasis upon doctrine, spirituality, and evangelism entailed a deep regard for those vocations that most directly manifest these concerns: the pastoral and the missionary. In other Christian communions pastors struggled with lack of respect and missionaries were few and poorly funded – not so among most evangelicals. But, in the third place, these emphases somewhat paradoxically also led to an emphasis upon the responsibility and role of the laity in the life and mission of the church. All Christians were to study the Bible, and evangelicals commonly held group Bible studies together, whether as whole congregations, Sunday school classes, or home discussion groups. The founding of Bible schools demonstrated this regard for the ministry of the laity most obviously, but so too did the emphasis on cultivating Christian leaders in Inter-Varsity chapters, Regent College, and Trinity Western University. The 'rediscovery of the laity,' often credited to the account of the mainline ecumenical movement,[9] was hardly news to a community of Christians who trained and mobilized laypeople throughout the century.

The particular doctrines emphasized by transdenominational groups square with these concerns. If a group of Christians understand the nature of Christian identity as involving belief in a basic doctrine ('by faith alone through grace alone') and a heartfelt commitment to the person of Christ, if they emphasize increasing holiness in the life of faith, and if they see the task of the church as primarily to evangelize the unconverted, then they will emphasize those doctrines that have to do with the basic nature of God, the salvific work of Christ, the regenerating and sanctifying work of the Holy Spirit, and the reward or penalty attached to one's response to these things. And they will emphasize the foundation for these particular beliefs, which they believe is the Bible alone. These are the doctrines of the evangelical statements.[10] And they are a reiteration of the basic convictions of Canadian evangelicals from the eighteenth century forward.[11]

Another concern, however, underlay these statements of faith. Creeds, for such these are, emerge in response to particular, historical circumstances. The nature of evangelicalism's central concerns, just described, are one set of circumstances informing these statements of belief. But the rise and spread of new theologies in the Canadian church since the beginning of this century seems also to have influenced these statements, since virtually all the ideas they contain have been challenged or denied by one strand or another of modern theology. This interpretation also agrees with the fact that many of the institutions of Canadian evangelicalism were founded as alternatives to organizations that bore the title 'Christian' and in some instances began in fact as evangelical organizations but, in the view of the evangelicals, had been compromised and diverted by new theologies (usually categorized by evangelicals simply as 'liberal') in other directions. Denominational seminaries that no longer taught evangelical truth but presented or even advocated alternatives; student organizations that no longer sought to evangelize but rather sought only this-worldly justice; universities that no longer encouraged Christian belief but rather hired and defended its attackers; ecumenical organizations that paid lip-service to evangelical concerns while watering down the truth and neglecting missions: all these, as seen through evangelical eyes, demanded new schools, new student groups, new fellowships. And, to provide backbones to these new groups, statements of faith per se were seen to be necessary, and statements of these doctrines in particular, which would fortify these evangelical organizations against those ideas that had compromised the others.[12]

The third consideration that explains these statements is evangelical consciousness of Roman Catholicism. In Canada, which has areas of such strong Roman Catholic dominance, the distinctness of evangelicalism has lain not only in its commitment to orthodoxy, personal piety, and missions, and not only in its differences from new theologies, but also in its strong Protestantism.[13] Evangelical magazines, like *The Prairie Overcomer,* have spoken for many in their repudiation of Roman Catholicism. The Canadian Protestant League, founded by T.T. Shields, found supporters across the denominational and even theological spectrum and involved prominent evangelicals. Inter-Varsity Christian Fellowship, which contained elements quite favourable to Roman Catholicism, especially since the openness of Vatican II and the rise of the charismatic movement that shared many concerns with evangelicals, yet decided to adopt a statement of faith that made it more explicit than ever that it was a Protestant organization. And indeed most evangelical statements dealt with the matter directly, and usually right at the beginning, as they posited the singular authority of the Bible, which quite clearly implied evangelicalism's basic disagreement with the Roman Catholic understanding of the joint authority of Scripture, tradition, and teaching office.

These concerns together outline one dimension of the mainstream of evangelicalism as it flowed through the twentieth century. So, too, does the participation of evangelicals from a variety of denominations trace another. In the earlier years, 'churchish' evangelicalism, as seen in the founding and growth of Toronto Bible College, was led by Christians from a range of denominations. Many were from small, uniformly evangelical groups, with the Baptists and Christian Brethren dominant among these. But evangelicals from the large Anglican and especially Presbyterian communions figured just as importantly in the story as well. As the century progressed, 'churchish' evangelicalism continued to manifest this mix of Christians from mainline and wholly evangelical groups. The smaller groups did, however, emerge into greater prominence, and Mennonites and Pentecostals began to rival or surpass even the Anglicans, Presbyterians, and Brethren in numbers and influence. In this regard, Regent College drew from a similar constituency in Vancouver, which is scarcely surprising given the large English immigration to the area and the leadership of the school coming from Brethren, Baptists, Anglicans, and Presbyterians. Its enrolment and staff hiring, however, both demonstrate the increasing influence of Mennonites and Pentecostals in Canadian evangelicalism since the 1970s.

In the 'sectish' evangelicalism common on the prairies, the story revolves around the smaller evangelical groups seen in Ontario, but also some others that had a larger presence on the prairies than they had in central Canada because of a higher proportion of east European and American immigration – out of which came, for instance, Evangelical Free, Mennonite, and independent churches. So Prairie Bible Institute never attracted many Presbyterians or Anglicans, drawing its numbers primarily from Baptist or interdenominational/nondenominational churches. Mennonites did support it in significant numbers, but Prairie's long-time opposition to Pentecostal distinctives kept small the numbers from this latter group.[14] The same pattern was generally true of Trinity Western University, except that TWU put no brake on Pentecostal enrolment.

The national fellowships, Inter-Varsity Christian Fellowship and the Evangelical Fellowship of Canada, resembled more the pattern of the Toronto and Vancouver institutions, which probably reflects their roots in Anglo-Canadian southern Ontario. Originally led by evangelicals of both mainline groups and wholly evangelical ones, they maintained this combination but experienced a shift in weight towards the smaller groups and embraced increasing numbers of Mennonites and Pentecostals, especially since the 1970s.

It is not strictly true, then, that evangelicalism through the century increasingly withdrew from the mainline denominations per se, much less that evangelicalism was made up merely of 'sectarian' groups in the traditional sense of the term,[15] since Presbyterians, Anglicans, and 'mainline' Baptists continued to support the movement. But several related observations are in order. The first is that the United Church of Canada never was well represented among Canadian evangelicals, and certainly not in proportion to the numbers on its rolls. As several historians have detailed, however, this reflects the decline of evangelical concerns within this communion, a decline manifest earlier among the Methodists, Congregationalists, and Presbyterians who made it up and a decline increased since the 1960s.[16] There were evangelicals within this church, and a movement of them intent on renewal began to sound evangelical notes in the 1960s, but the general direction of the denomination throughout the century was away from those things that united evangelicals.

A different case is that of Canadian Lutherans. Many of these shared Canadian evangelicals' concern for orthodoxy, piety, and mission, even if the traditional evangelical imperative of *personal* evangelism was uncommon among them. But these Lutherans, notably those affiliated with the American Missouri Synod, like their American counterparts kept to themselves in ethnic and denominational enclaves and so did not join the larger movement.[17]

A somewhat similar situation obtained in the Atlantic provinces. The influence of evangelical Protestantism was strong in many parts of this region, seen in the relatively large numbers of Salvationists and Pentecostals in Newfoundland, Baptists in Nova Scotia and New Brunswick, and Scottish Presbyterians in northern Nova Scotia and elsewhere. But the cultural separation of this region from the rest of the country, well known in other contexts in Canada, shows up here again in the fewness of links with the transdenominational and transnational movement elsewhere.[18] And the denominational isolation typical of the region meant that evangelicals in this area did not start significant transdenominational movements of their own.

A final observation in this regard is that evangelicals indeed felt increasingly alienated from the *leadership* and *institutions* of all three of the mainline Protestant groups, whether United Church, Anglican, or Presbyterian. Evangelicals saw a prevalence of liberal or neo-orthodox theology and destructive biblical criticism in the seminaries, preoccupation with politics and ideology among denominational leaders, and neglect of evangelism both home and abroad. So the century witnessed evangelicals, including many from within these denominations, sponsoring alternative organizations that represented evangelical concerns.

With this developing sense of separateness from the leadership of the large denominations and the forming of these alternative institutions, evangelicals became conscious of themselves as a network of like-minded individuals and organizations. That all the institutions shared basic similarities – similar doctrine, similar concern for piety and evangelism – is quite clear. What remains is to delineate the historical connections between them. This task, however, is made difficult by two facts. In the first place, the formal links between the institutions were relatively few. The Toronto-based organizations sponsored only a few special events together, notably the summer conferences at Ontario Bible College and Ontario Theological Seminary sponsored with Inter-Varsity Christian Fellowship, and the writers' conference sponsored by OBC/OTS and the Evangelical Fellowship of Canada. (Later, this writers' conference would be sponsored by the EFC at Trinity Western University as well, among other western campuses.) And among the western institutions themselves, Trinity Western University professors, for example, served as external examiners for the Regent College extension program, and Trinity Western held annual 'Regent Days' on campus to acquaint its students with Regent's program.

There were informal links among the institutions, however, that increased to an overwhelming number through the century. Only representative examples can be presented here of the hundreds easily documented from the records. In the first half-century since the First World War, evangelical institutions had little contact with each other over distance. Inter-Varsity Christian Fellowship and Toronto Bible College naturally had interlocking boards of directors even then, for example, but they had little direct contact with Prairie Bible Institute, whose board was drawn from local supporters well into the late 1980s. They were yet connected, however, by several indirect links. In the first place, Christians of certain denominations, notably the Baptists and the Christian and Missionary Alliance, supported all three institutions. In the second place, evangelical leaders and organizations contributed to them. Rowland V. Bingham, for instance, sat on the board of Toronto Bible College and was an early supporter of Inter-Varsity Christian Fellowship. And his Sudan Interior Mission sent missionary speakers frequently to Prairie, in turn receiving for some decades the largest amounts of money given through Prairie each year for foreign missions. Moreover, L.E. Maxwell himself was invited to address Inter-Varsity groups in Ontario and to speak at IVCF's first triennial missions conference in Toronto. And third, American and British evangelical institutions and individuals linked Ontario with the West. Most important of the former were Moody Bible Institute, which served as a model both for Prairie Bible Institute and for Ontario Bible College's other predecessor, London College of Bible and Missions, and the China Inland Mission, whose missionaries inspired students and staff of all three institutions. Among influential individuals from the United States none was more important than Billy Graham, and the three organizations admired and supported him in their periodicals and during his few missions in Canada. British speakers were also significant, the Welsh preacher D. Martyn Lloyd-Jones perhaps being the most prominent of those who visited all three institutions. The reality remained, however, that the evangelicals on the prairie farms and those in Canada's cities lived in virtually different countries for all the contact they had with each other. United in central concerns, they yet pursued them in distinctly different ways and largely independently of each other.

With the improvement of transportation across Canada and the increasing urbanization and cosmopolitanism of the West, more links developed among evangelical organizations in the 1960s and afterwards. But again, these were largely informal. Denominational networks continued to interact with the evangelical network, the more so as Mennonites and Pentecostals plugged in. Individuals continued to support various organizations. J. William Horsey, for one example, sat on or chaired the boards of OBC, IVCF, and the EFC, and the foundation that bore his name was a charter supporter of Regent College. Ian S. Rennie served as dean of Ontario Theological Seminary in the 1980s, but previously served IVCF as a staff worker, Regent College as a professor, the EFC as vice-president, and even Trinity Western University as convocation speaker. Robert N. Thompson served, in various capacities, Ontario Bible College (corporation member), Trinity Western University (chairman of the board), and the Evangelical Fellowship of Canada (president), and spoke at Prairie Bible Institute. Projects like the 'Sermons from Science' pavilion at Expo '67 and the Evangelical Fellowship of Canada brought together evangelicals from across Canada.[19] And again, American and British evangelicalism provided resources to each of these institutions, whether by sending guest speakers (such as American Carl F.H. Henry, expatriate American Francis A. Schaeffer, and Englishman John R.W. Stott) or by educating many of their leaders (especially at Wheaton College, Trinity Evangelical Divinity School, Dallas Theological Seminary, and Fuller Theological Seminary).

Yet again, however, the relationships between evangelicals across regions and between institutions remained loose and informal for the most part. Subgroups of evangelicals generally continued to support their own institutions, even as they were grateful for the success of the projects of their fellow evangelicals. Canadian evangelicals also continued to disagree about political strategies (e.g., all-or-nothing versus piecemeal reform in the abortion struggle), about mission priorities (e.g., evangelistic projects versus academic consultations), about ecumenical relationships (e.g., links between charismatic Protestants and Roman Catholics), and about issues facing the whole church (e.g., the public ministry of women). Finally, the increasing size and prominence of Pentecostal churches in a network that included dispensationalists and certain kinds of Reformed whose theologies normally made no room for post-apostolic charismatic experience per se and of Asian, French-Canadian, and other ethnic churches in a network dominated by Anglo-Canadians challenged evangelicalism with more cultural plurality than it had ever experienced before.[20] By the late 1980s, that is, evangelicals in Canada had not been welded into a coherent movement by strong leadership, influential national institutions, or compelling issues. Instead, the vast geography of Canada, the influence of and allegiance to regionally dominant leaders and institutions, or different dispositions towards even concerns common to all evangelicals separated them into definite subgroups only loosely linked to make up the larger evangelical fellowship. Indeed, the very word 'fellowship,' used by Canadian evangelicals to describe the two institutions that did the most to bring them together, Inter-Varsity Christian Fellowship and the Evangelical Fellowship of Canada, perhaps best denotes this relationship of distinct elements united by limited, if crucial, common concerns and engaging in limited, but regular and substantial, common activity.

It is in this regard, in fact, that evangelicalism was *not* 'ecumenical' in an important sense. Evangelicals believed in cooperation, but not in formal union. They were glad to work together to accomplish common goals, but they had no commitment to organic union per se, as did leaders of the 'ecumenical movement.'[21] Indeed, the very strength of their primary commitments to evangelical essentials that encouraged them to work together usually had a parallel in the strength of their secondary commitments to denominational distinctives (since they would see the Bible as teaching both the transdenominational essentials and the denominational distinctives), and evangelicals saw no reason to compromise these secondary commitments for the reward of a single church organization. Evangelicals already resisted the 'one church' model of Roman Catholicism and were hardly eager to embrace a Protestant version of it, especially when it was espoused most often by those without commitment to typical evangelical concerns.

This attitude also suggests that transdenominational evangelicalism in Canada by the end of the twentieth century did not threaten to replace denominations, even as it did, in a sense, weaken denominational loyalties precisely by encouraging Christians to distinguish between evangelical 'essentials' and 'denominational distinctives.'[22] Too many questions face the life of an individual Christian and of a congregation, from baptism to burial, to be resolved by recourse only to the circumscribed evangelical consensus, and 'Bible-believing Christians' who took these matters seriously but who used a variety of theological methods to resolve them were not likely to come to agreement on them all. Of course, if evangelicals were to lose a keen interest in theology – always a threat in a tradition that valued experience and activity so highly – then the fine distinctions within certain groups of denominations might well fade into general categories like 'Baptist,' 'Presbyterian,' 'Pentecostal,' and so on. Indeed, the lack of concern for this sort of precision coupled with emphasis upon commonalities was important in most ecumenical unions in Canada in the last half of the nineteenth and the first half of the twentieth century. All of this is to say, in sum, that 'evangelicalism' was an important organizing principle and an important fellowship of individuals and institutions for these Christians, but not one to supplant the more fully articulated traditions and communities of the denominations.[23]

The second difficulty complicating the task of tracing connections among evangelicals is that differences remained between two distinct forms of Canadian evangelicalism. The first sort supported Ontario Bible College (and Toronto Bible College before it) and Regent College, dominated the central leadership of both Inter-Varsity Christian Fellowship and the Evangelical Fellowship of Canada, and provided most of the direction for 'Sermons from Science.' This first kind, then, which I have called 'churchish,' centred in urban southern Ontario, especially Toronto; in Vancouver; and in urban, English-speaking Quebec, especially Montreal.

The counterpart, the second sort of Canadian evangelicalism, which I have called 'sectish,' supported Prairie Bible Institute and Trinity Western University, and provided much of the support for the strong Alberta wing of Inter-Varsity Christian Fellowship. While present across Canada, it was most noticeable on the rural prairies and in their extension-by-emigration, the lower Fraser River valley, home to Trinity Western University in British Columbia.

The first kind drew support and leadership from evangelicals among the Presbyterians, the Anglicans, and the 'mainline' or Federation Baptists, as well as from smaller evangelical groups; the second drew from the smaller, wholly evangelical denominations almost exclusively, including sometimes the 'separatist' heirs of the Baptist fundamentalists, the Fellowship Baptists.[24] The first type was strongest in urban areas of long-standing British immigration, notably Toronto and Vancouver; the second was strongest in rural areas of more recent American and East European immigration. The first actively engaged contemporary culture and scholarship, including biblical and theological studies, and placed a premium upon leaders with education respected by society at large; the second manifested much more caution, and even suspicion of or outright hostility towards modern ideas, and sought leaders with training from 'safe' schools over those from 'prestigious' ones. The first declared its fundamental belief in the unique authority and divine inspiration of Scripture; the second insisted on the use of the word 'inerrancy' or its verbal equivalents in the same context and sometimes suspected the first of compromising or helping to compromise this doctrine.[25] The first refused to make anything more than a belief in Christ's literal second coming an article of common faith; the second preferred an articulated premillennialism. The first believed in the practice of personal holiness, but left its application up to the individual; the second was more comfortable with a clear code, and forbade particularly alcohol and dancing from the life of the Christian.

The differences in these two *mentalités* manifested themselves in terms particularly apposite to the institutions studied here, namely, in different attitudes towards liberal-arts education. The 'churchish' evangelicals until mid-century were happy enough with the universities to encourage some students, especially those interested in the pastorate, to attend them rather than a Bible college. So they at first saw no need for a distinctively evangelical liberal-arts education. And as the universities became increasingly secularized in outlook as well as funding, Toronto Bible College increased its own offering of courses in the liberal arts. Indeed, Ontario Bible College sought and won recognition from some Ontario universities as its students transferred from the college to these universities, thus making OBC a sort of religious 'junior college' as well as a Bible school. In the 1980s and 1990s, some evangelicals were watching the Christian Reformed Church's Redeemer College, just outside Hamilton, Ontario, campaign to win the right to grant arts degrees and so stand as a complete alternative to the secular schools. But the Ontario evangelicals yet seemed largely content with sending their youth to the secular universities, as few outside the Christian Reformed community directed support towards Redeemer, and the Christian Reformed church, for its part, maintained that the school would be a denominationally oriented institution.

By contrast, the 'sectish' evangelical constituency of Prairie Bible Institute originally was not especially interested in liberal arts. Mostly farmers, they wanted their youth to be trained in the basics of the Bible and Christian work – more education than most of them had as it was. Even as late as the 1980s Prairie resisted offering more than a minimal amount of liberal-arts courses, thus giving up accreditation with the American Association of Bible Colleges – until they finally sought it in the early 1990s.

Indeed, this last development indicates that in this respect as in others, Ontario Bible College and Prairie Bible Institute represented larger trends among Canadian evangelicals. As different as they were in ethos and emphasis, their increasing similarity pointed to the coalescence of the evangelical mainstream. By the 1980s and 1990s, a wide range of Bible schools across Canada were adding liberal-arts courses to their curricula, usually at the expense of the relatively large concentration in 'Bible' of years past. Accreditation with the American Association of Bible Colleges became increasingly important as students (and their parents) sought to keep open the possibilities of transfer of credit to the universities who would consider it and of graduate work in evangelical seminaries in Canada and the United States. Some even worked out cooperative and even affiliative arrangements with particular Canadian universities, as did some of the slowly growing number of Christian liberal-arts institutions.[26] 'High school plus Bible school' was no longer adequate for work with many evangelical churches and parachurch organizations.

This trend towards the 'universitizing' of Bible schools was widespread enough by the early 1990s, in fact, that several evangelical observers expressed public concern. They warned that Bible schools were in danger of abandoning their original intention to offer training for ministry that was not already available from other institutions. And the need, they suggested, still existed for institutions to train all Christians in the skills of Christian living – in theology, spirituality, mission, and so on – as well as to train some Christians in particular occupations, whether in parachurch work or, in some innovative programs that moved beyond Christian institutions, daycare and other public social services. The Bible schools clearly were attempting to adjust to the social realities in their constituencies, but by the early 1990s it was unclear how they would fare in the future. What is striking in this context is how *similarly* they were adjusting.[27]

These characterizations of 'churchish' and 'sectish' types, it should be noted, form two poles of a continuum along which Canadian evangelicals would have been individually located. Nevertheless, most would have been clustered at one end or the other, since the institutions they sponsored tended to manifest one type or the other. And the geographical-demographical referents in particular should not be pressed too far. The more important point is that there were in Canada two distinct kinds of evangelical dispositions, two *mentalités*, within this coalescing mainstream, rather than that they were dominant in these geographically and demographically distinct areas. Both dispositions were represented, albeit in various proportions, across Canada. Metropolitan areas especially, and Toronto and Vancouver in particular, were home to both types: Ontario Bible College, which resulted from the 1968 merger of Toronto Bible College and the more 'sectish' London College of Bible and Missions, provides one example of these two types within one institution.

Another important example, this time provided by Inter-Varsity Christian Fellowship, underscores this qualification. As we have seen, criticism of the direction of the Fellowship under Wilber Sutherland came from throughout IVCF's main areas of support, from Ontario to British Columbia, and not merely from the prairies. And even the Alberta division doesn't fit the pattern simply. Of its three pioneers, Cathie Nicoll, Joe Curry, and Marj Long, the first two were transplanted Ontarians, and the third, a westerner, herself needed some time to establish Inter-Varsity with wary prairie folk. With that time, to be sure, many of these evangelicals did support Inter-Varsity in that region. So the reaction even of the Alberta divisional leaders to the innovations in urban Ontario during Wilber Sutherland's tenure as general director represented not only the typical prairie evangelical response as characterized here, but also the feelings of many evangelicals of similar disposition elsewhere in Canada, including Ontario, as well.

None the less, the history and character of the major institutions of Canadian evangelicalism indicate that one pattern or the other tended to dominate cooperative evangelical activity in the various regions described. The continuing differences between these two kinds of evangelicalism are manifest in two episodes involving Trinity Western University and Regent College. In 1981, Trinity Western sought and received the resignation of a young New Testament professor because he taught his students that higher criticism was a neutral tool to be used with discrimination by evangelical scholars.[28] President R. Neil Snider, Academic Dean Kenneth R. Davis, and other members of the school's administration satisfied themselves that a major difference of opinion existed between the school and this professor, Raymond O. Bystrom.[29] And this difference of opinion was such that while the administration affirmed Bystrom's Christian testimony, his general orthodoxy, and even the fact that his position was one held by scholars elsewhere in the evangelical community,[30] it could not tolerate what it saw to be a serious diversion from its commitment to biblical inerrancy.[31] Davis set out 'Some Goals and Methodological Priorities and Parameters for Biblical Studies at TWC' which included the following position on Biblical criticism: '[Teachers should] develop by careful stages a full awareness of the secular/liberal critical methods (past and current). But also to *thoroughly* critique their presuppositions showing the basic invalidity and destructiveness of these techniques and their inappropriateness when applied to a uniquely divinely inspired and inerrant Scripture and showing the errors of most of their conclusions; recognizing at the same time that a few valuable contributions have been given to Biblical understanding which are consistent with inerrancy.'[32] Commitment to inerrancy, therefore, entailed eschewing virtually the entire higher-critical enterprise – a relationship many evangelicals elsewhere refused to accept.

Indeed, it was denied at Regent College. Bystrom was a graduate and former instructor of Greek at Regent College and, following his departure from Trinity Western for a Mennonite pastorate, sat on Regent's board, elected by the alumni. His views of the relationship of belief in the inerrancy of the Bible and the practice of higher criticism mirrored the views of his teachers at Regent.[33] So the judgment upon Bystrom's views by Trinity Western was an implicit judgment on the teaching at Regent College, and indicates that Trinity Western's leaders preferred a significantly different view of the doctrine and interpretation of Scripture.

The second episode consists of Trinity Western University's moves in the mid-1980s towards establishing a theological seminary on its campus, less than an hour's drive from Regent College.[34] In 1983 Trinity Western began to offer a graduate program in pastoral training, and looked toward cooperating with evangelical denominations in expanding this program into a seminary. The school's administration justified the need for a new evangelical seminary by characterizing it as standing for more narrow principles than had its alternatives in Canada, a reference that most obviously implied Regent College. The establishment of this school reflected deep concern among some at Trinity Western over Regent College's alleged 'softness' on inerrancy[35] and its allowance for individual and unregulated application of the common commitment to personal holiness. Trinity Western's leaders also were uncomfortable with the strong presence at Regent of many from the mainline churches, in particular the Reformed tradition behind both Presbyterianism and Anglicanism. And Regent was too academically oriented: apparently its development of 'applied' or 'practical' theology courses had been too small and slow for Trinity Western (a concern not without substantial justification, as the earlier discussion of Regent's development indicates). So the 1982 proposal to the board of governors of Trinity Western University says that the school would emphasize 'practical ministries combined with a strong internship element ... The program would be carefully designed to foster the fundamental commitments of a believer's church philosophy. These would include an emphasis on personal salvation as the criterion for church membership, a strong view of Biblical inerrancy, commitment to a pietistic lifestyle and to congregational autonomy.'[36] And, in an earlier discussion, it was agreed further that the school would be 'warm, theologically, toward the pretrib, premill interpretation of Scripture,' these abbreviations ('pretrib, premill') indicating a strong leaning towards dispensationalism.[37]

So the 'sectish' style of evangelicalism, as represented by Prairie Bible Institute and the administration of Trinity Western University, manifested some differences of conviction from the 'churchish' style. To be sure, the convictions of the former were a subset of those of the latter. By insisting on those more narrow convictions, however, the 'sectish' style maintained a different, less inclusive character.

This difference, real enough, should not be exaggerated, however. It certainly did not keep these two sorts of evangelicals from recognizing essential kinship in each other. They worked together in common projects, like the Evangelical Fellowship of Canada, but they also established direct links between leaders and between programs. For instance, Prairie Bible Institute's sometime president, Ted S. Rendall, engaged in part-time graduate studies at Regent College in the mid-1980s. Several professors of biblical studies at Trinity Western taught part-time at Regent College, while others held full-time positions at each school at different times.[38] Regent College professors of disciplines other than biblical studies lectured at Trinity Western on occasion, and there were other friendly and programmatic links between Regent and Trinity Western. More broadly yet, these two kinds of evangelicalism not only shared the qualities outlined above, but they also evolved in similar ways. Both increasingly articulated a broad understanding of Christian vocation. And both demonstrated a concern to affect society in a number of ways, not merely the evangelistic. They stood together even as fraternal differences remained. Finally, it perhaps should be underscored that differences among Canadian evangelicals over everything from gender roles in church and home to political philosophy could never be reduced to just two positions coordinate with these two mind-sets, since evangelicals characteristically held a variety of views on most subjects and those who might line up together on one issue might well disagree on another.[39]

The character of Canadian evangelicalism in the twentieth

century – indeed, the very propriety of using the term as if there were such a thing as a distinctly *Canadian* evangelicalism as opposed to a generic evangelicalism within Canadian society – can be thrown into relief by a brief comparison with evangelicalism in Britain and the United States, the two common reference points for Anglophone Canadian culture. In the first place, to be sure, the kind of transdenominational evangelicalism described here in Canada was present also in Britain and the United States.[40] A network of scholars, preachers, and writers spread across the Atlantic and on both sides of the Canada-U.S. border throughout this century, a network that shared the same basic commitments to biblical authority, theological orthodoxy, personal spirituality, and evangelism. Scholars have only begun to trace out these connections in a broad way,[41] but the references to British and American persons and institutions in this study are typical of studies of twentieth-century evangelicalism in Canada.[42]

In the second place, however, evangelicalism in Canada was not a matter simply of British colonial residues or American 'branch plants.' The institutions portrayed here as central in the life of Canadian evangelicalism in the twentieth century were, without exception, indigenous Canadian products. However much they benefited in typical Canadian style from British or American initiative (for instance, the British initiative in the drawing together of student groups into IVCF; the American model of Moody Bible Institute for PBI and the London College of Bible and Missions; the denominational support for Trinity Western University, especially in its early days) or from leaders from either place (for example, Americans L.E. Maxwell at PBI and Calvin Hanson at TWU; Englishman James Houston and Americans Carl Armerding and Ward Gasque at Regent), the institutions were founded and funded and staffed predominantly by Canadians. Moreover, they reflected the typically Canadian denominational representation in evangelicalism: stronger representation from pluralistic, mainstream churches (with the exception of the United Church) than was the case in the United States,[43] but also stronger representation from a wider mix of groups (like the Pentecostal, Mennonite, Holiness, and Dutch Reformed) than was the British pattern of dominance by Evangelical Anglicans and a relatively few Nonconformist denominations. In this regard, furthermore, Canadian evangelicalism was more varied than the British counterpart but less spectacularly varied than the

American: Canadian culture refused to produce the number and degree of colourful individual leaders, groups, and institutions that were all too typical of American evangelicalism.[44]

Instead, Canadian evangelicalism, like Canadian Anglophone culture in general, tended towards the norm, towards homogeneity, as this study has shown. Twentieth-century evangelicalism, furthermore, manifested this trait in a manner unparalleled in Canadian religious history. In previous centuries, both the sectish and churchish styles of evangelicalism had been evident, but in different movements (like the Salvation Army versus evangelical Anglicans) or in the same movement at different times (like Methodism in the eighteenth century versus Methodism in the late nineteenth). In the second half of the twentieth century, however, Canadian evangelicalism had broadened in its concerns but also coalesced into at least a loose network of institutions that incorporated moderate versions of both *mentalités.* In fact, the new fellowship of evangelicalism adopted a cultural stance moving beyond the former alternatives of 'outsider' and 'insider' towards that of an important group within a pluralized society, one 'participant' among many others in the shaping of Canadian culture.[45]

This remarkable confluence of Canadian evangelicalism took place as Canadian culture steadily became less influenced by traditional Christianity. Those evangelicals who once had been more comfortable in that larger culture (the 'churchish' evangelicals) began to set up alternative institutions to those they saw to have been compromised, and in this they began to resemble more their 'sectish' siblings. By contrast the 'sectish' evangelicals, perhaps owing to a rise in social and economic standing (although this has not been documented yet), perhaps because of the erosion of the 'mainline' alternative that had seemed to them the proprietor of contemporary culture, and perhaps through new sensitivity to the needs of Canadians in the post-Victorian religious situation, began to open up to a wider vision of ministry. This development led them to improve their educational institutions and join with the 'churchish' evangelicals in projects of cultural influence beyond the evangelistic. So Canadian evangelicalism became at once more unified and more prominent precisely as the old 'Christian Canada' fragmented.[46] Indeed, observers wondered if British Columbia was a bell-wether of Canadian society in this regard as it has been in others. By 1990 it not only included the largest proportion of those who claimed 'no religion' in all of Canada, but also included the largest and fastest-growing proportion of evangelical churches as well.[47] Canadian evangelicals, then, were reacting against certain modern trends and forces, to be sure, but they also were responding to those challenges in new ways and with some success.

It is important in this regard to note again that fundamentalism played quite a small part in Canadian evangelicalism, as it did in Britain, versus the importance of that impulse in American Christianity.[48] Canadians, like their British counterparts, became more and more concerned about the general drift of their cultures away from traditional Christianity and responded to that drift in various ways, but they did so generally without the militancy and sense of loss of cultural authority typical of much of American evangelicalism affected by the fundamentalist heritage.[49] Canadian and British evangelicals, that is, tended either to avoid the larger culture (the 'sectish' stance) or to seek to influence it as one viewpoint among many (the 'churchish' stance), rather than harking back to a golden age of 'Christian America' (although it could have been argued that Canada and Britain were, at certain times in their histories, as 'Christian' as America had ever been) in hopes of regaining cultural dominance.

Michael Gauvreau, at a different level, has suggested that there might be a significant 'relationship between a missing tradition of systematic theology [in nineteenth-century Canadian evangelicalism] and the failure of a militant fundamentalist movement to find a congenial home in Canada.'[50] Certainly Canadian evangelicals in the twentieth century were slow to institutionalize any substantial concern for advanced theology, as they founded such centres as Regent College and Ontario Theological Seminary or the Christian Reformed Institute for Christian Studies and Mennonite Conrad Grebel College only since the 1960s. And of these, only the Institute for Christian Studies was established with philosophical and theological scholarship primarily in mind.[51] The very nature of transdenominational evangelicalism, furthermore, militates against elaborate theological sophistication and precision, as it seeks only the minimal theological ground upon which to proclaim the gospel. Evangelicalism, that is, is concerned only for theological 'essentials' in its drive to evangelize the world and foster spiritual vitality. This spirit of pragmatic compromise is nicely in line with the Anglophone Canadian temper in general, then, so that it is not surprising to see fundamentalism much less important in Canadian evangelicalism than elsewhere.

In these respects, then, as well as in the basic convictions that marked the whole evangelical tradition, Canadian transdenominational evangelicalism manifested a 'mainstream' in the twentieth century: a more varied stream than the British, and yet a much more coherent, if also much smaller, fellowship than the American.

Several themes in this comparison between evangelicalism in Canada and its counterparts in the United States and Britain, finally, come together in a consideration of the temporal dimension. It has been a commonplace among Canadian pundits and scholars that Anglophone Canada has become steadily more American and correspondingly less British in the twentieth century. This examination of one aspect of Anglophone Canadian culture, however, should give one pause before that popular thesis is easily adopted. Evangelicalism itself in Canada has resembled the British in the ways outlined and in further respects as well. Perhaps most notably, the convergence of Canadian evangelicalism into a 'fellowship' or 'network' with an identity divergent from the leadership of the major Protestant denominations appeared institutionally in the 1960s, even as its roots went back further. This paralleled the British case, as the National Evangelical Anglican Congress at Keele, 'the chief landmark in a postwar Evangelical renaissance,' took place in 1967, exactly the same year as the opening of the 'Sermons from Science' pavilion in Montreal.[52] Unlike the stark polarization in the United States between the two world wars, that is, Canadian and British evangelicals did not coalesce into an alternative network until well after the Second World War and particularly only as their nations faced the turmoil of the 1960s. This *chronology*, then, underscores points made earlier about *character*.

With all these developments, however, Canadian evangelicalism experienced challenges that it had not met by the late 1980s. In the first place, while evidence supports the idea that Canadian evangelicalism indeed had become as strong as or stronger than mainline Protestantism, this was really only half of a perverse 'good news, bad news' joke. While evangelicals could rejoice in their newly won status, they confronted a society that had become only more secular as they had become more powerful. Their position relative to mainline Christianity, that is, had come from losses among the major denominations at least as much as from growth among evangelicals.

In this respect also, Canadian Anglophone culture resembled Britain more than the United States. The pattern of secularization in Canada looked more like the British model than the American – and more and more like it as the twentieth century continued. Rather than the American pattern of flourishing religion compartmentalized in the private sphere, Canadian Christianity eroded steadily along British lines.[53] While in 1990 nine in ten Canadians continued to identify with a religious group and the vast majority of them with Protestant or Catholic Christianity, only two in ten attended religious services regularly and only one-quarter read the Bible or other scriptures even once a month.[54] This pattern of crumbling Christianity in Canada, with a few churches dominating the landscape in a highly modernized culture, nicely fits the basic contours of David Martin's 'general theory of secularization.'[55] It also underscores one challenge that faced evangelicals in Canada as it did those in Britain. The gargantuan task of converting to evangelical Christianity a Canadian population mostly secular in orientation confronted evangelicals with the foolishness of any premature triumphalism,[56] especially as some students of evangelicalism were unimpressed with its ability to attract those without significant evangelical background.[57]

The second challenge confronting Canadian evangelicals was to reconsider their tradition of social ministry and engagement in the public square. Some Canadian historians and some evangelical leaders followed the historical paradigm about *American* evangelicalism in their interpretation of their own history in this regard. They taught that twentieth-century evangelicals in Canada abandoned their social ministry of the nineteenth century in some sort of 'Great Reversal' because the 'liberals' had taken it over in the name of the 'social gospel.'[58] Perhaps this line of interpretation does not hold completely for Canada, however, since there was no great split in Canada along the fundamentalist-modernist lines.[59] Perhaps instead twentieth-century evangelicals largely concentrated their energies elsewhere precisely because they apparently had accomplished their nineteenth-century goal of a generally Christian public policy of benevolence in certain issues, at least:

Sunday closings, child labour laws, poor relief, etc.[60] As a growing chorus of historians have argued, evangelicals in Canada as elsewhere in the nineteenth century were generally political conservatives and tended to concentrate their social action upon certain 'sins,' certain problems in society, rather than upon 'social structures' per se.[61] Once these specific problems were dealt with satisfactorily, then, as many of them had been dealt with by 1900 or so, perhaps the majority of evangelicals blithely left the driving of the social bus to the government. The Depression provoked some to action, as in Social Credit or the Cooperative Commonwealth Federation. But generally evangelicals *as such* did not act on the public stage until the 1960s when there could be no more illusion of a Christian consensus in Canadian life, and particularly as government at various levels more obviously and extensively intruded into the lives of all Canadians in ways not always congenial to evangelicals.[62] Since that time, then, evangelicals have had to consider taking up again and expanding upon their heritage of social ministry in an age of shrinking government budgets and their tradition of cultural engagement in a time of greater fragmentation of cultural consensus on matters of public policy.[63]

What remained an open question in the early 1990s, though, was just what political objective would guide this engagement. How much would evangelicals carry on the tradition of cultural transformation – that some would call 'domination' and even 'imperialism' – that they inherited from their forebears, particularly through the line descending from Calvin's Geneva through the Puritan commonwealths to the nineteenth-century evangelical voluntary societies for temperance, abolition, sabbath observance, and so forth? How much instead would they seek and work towards a genuine pluralism in which Christians had important voices, but by no means the only voices?[64] Canada itself, of course, struggled with similar questions, and it was a mark of growing evangelical awareness of and involvement in society that Canadian evangelicals recognized and wrestled with their own versions of such issues.

A third challenge was a perennial one. Despite the news reports from the United States in the 1970s and 1980s of vast financial empires dominated by television preachers or evangelical entrepreneurs, all these Canadian evangelical institutions perpetually had trouble raising money and staying within budget. Donations typically were small: Canadian evangelicalism produced few wealthy businesspersons and no large foundations to underwrite major projects, especially of a transdenominational sort. What this meant, then, is that if projects among these Christians were to survive, much less thrive, they had to appeal to a broad middle, rather than to the interests of a particular sector of evangelicalism. And this only confirmed the tendency of Canadian evangelical institutions to 'deviate towards the norm.' Whether or not bold ventures not typically supported by evangelicals in the past could fly, therefore, would depend on highly successful leadership among the grass roots, rather than upon the vision of a few well-heeled magnates.[65]

A fourth challenge marked a problem that had simmered among evangelicals for decades but only in the late 1980s and early 1990s began to boil over. The problem was gender roles in church and family, even as it was often, tellingly, called 'the women's issue.' The vast majority of evangelicals had espoused the principle of male leadership in both spheres, as had the Christian church and Western society generally for centuries. But a number of emphases within evangelicalism had always placed this principle under stress, and when Canadian society changed dramatically after the Second World War, and even more dramatically after the 1960s, the traditional evangelical understanding noticeably began to give way.

Evangelicals, as we have seen, characteristically expected laypeople to serve with vigour in 'religious' work at home and in 'the foreign fields' of missions. This meant that women often performed in leadership roles (like evangelism, Scripture teaching – at least to girls and other women – and administration) normally denied them in other churches and, indeed, in their own cultures. This dovetailed with the primary evangelical zeal for evangelism that pressed towards an attitude of 'all hands on deck.' That is, times of revival and missionary enthusiasm tended to blur – if not completely eradicate – the gender line in the interest of 'getting the job done.' So the training in Scripture and leadership that such women received for their work in the various kinds of evangelical schools and in the home and foreign-mission organizations themselves coupled with the later work they did provided resources of theology and experience upon which some such women could draw to reconsider the inherited notions of gender roles. Indeed, it was often women missionaries returning from abroad who most sharply questioned the gender patterns they encountered again at home. And men who had served with such women and had seen the fruit of their work were often the first to agree with such questioning. Finally, the opening up of evangelical scholarship to new ways of understanding the Bible and theology, especially after the 1960s, meant that evangelicals could maintain their traditional allegiance to the authority of the Bible while revising the interpretations and applications of that Bible to gender issues.

All these developments, of course, took place as Canadian society at large redefined women's roles progressively through each decade after the Second World War. As evangelicals engaged that society more and more, the incongruity of the roles of women outside their churches and families versus their roles inside added challenging currents to those already present within the tradition. The tradition was resilient: while the major Canadian Protestant denominations accepted the ordination of women in the 1960s and 1970s, evangelicals began to reconsider the issue in considerable numbers only in the subsequent decades. But in 1992, the Evangelical Fellowship of Canada sponsored its first national conference on the issue, and virtually all the advertised speakers held to an egalitarian view. The EFC in this case did not represent the views of the majority of its member denominations, to be sure. But this conference was a sign that evangelicals in at least some important positions and numbers were prepared at last to open up the issue directly for the broader national fellowship.[66]

The final challenge confronted Canadian evangelicals as it confronts any movement that moves from an 'outsider' or an 'insider' to a 'participant' status, from feeling estranged from or dominant over the culture to taking one's place with others in joint responsibility for the culture. The challenge was to maintain the evangelical commitment to orthodoxy, personal piety, and evangelism even as the mainstream of evangelicalism broadened to include a larger range of theologies, a commitment to social justice, and support of all vocations.[67] As wrong as it has been for Canadian historians and sociologists to see twentieth-century Canadian evangelicalism only in terms of particular sectarian movements or denominations, the basic character of the movement at mid-century was indeed classically sectarian in its growing sense of alienation from the new directions of the major denominations and the culture itself. As evangelicalism began to re-engage the culture in the 1960s, then – a new attitude for the 'sectish' style, a recovered, if altered, posture for the 'churchish' style – the second challenge remained: would evangelicals present Canadians with a new synthesis of evangelical convictions about orthodoxy, spiritual experience, and personal evangelism combined with convictions about theological sophistication, cultural responsibility, vocation, and social ministry? Or would 'theological sophistication' merely mask theological fuzziness, 'cultural responsibility' whitewash the selfishness of just another special interest, 'vocation' justify individual greed, and 'social ministry' serve as a more culturally acceptable alternative to proselytizing?

For all the apparent success, then, the significance and prospects of twentieth-century Canadian evangelicalism remained to be seen. Even those loyal to the evangelical community could see, for instance, that bigger churches, better schools, higher-tech mass media, and increased access to the corridors of power had all been enjoyed before by others – indeed, precisely by those mainline denominations suffering decline and with whom evangelicals sometimes favourably compared themselves. If evangelicals now had gained a measure of prominence, wealth, and respectability in modern Canadian society, did this indicate that they were influencing that society more than they had before, or that instead that society had in fact co-opted them?[68] Canadian evangelicals (and observers of them) might be pleased to find that, despite the extreme American stereotypes, they were not all that strange, not all that different from other Canadians. They might also find to their chagrin, however, that they were indeed not all that different.

By the early 1990s, therefore, it was not clear whether transdenominational evangelicalism represented an important new force that would continue to expand its influence in Canadian life, a network that had reached the limits of its support, or a last, brief flowering of an old-time Anglo-Canadian evangelical alliance now stretched too thin over a wide range of ethnic, political, intellectual, social, economic, and, yes, religious differences. What was clear for students of Canadian culture, though, was that this category of 'transdenominational evangelicalism' deserved notice in subsequent treatments of Canadian religion. And what was clear for all Canadians in the increasing pluralism of religious choices available to them was that this kind of Christianity should not be dismissed as some fringe group or some bizarre American export but, instead, deserved a serious look.

Notes

Introduction

1 The three schools reported the following Full-Time Equivalent (FTE) numbers to the Association of Theological Schools for the autumn of 1986: Regent College, 236; Ontario Theological Seminary, 220; and Emmanuel College, 195 (Regent College statistic sheet for ATS, records of the Registrar [photocopy]; telephone interview with Registrar's Office of Ontario Theological Seminary, 16 January 1987; telephone interview with Registrar's Office of Emmanuel College, 16 January 1987). By 1992, several seminaries had moved ahead of Emmanuel in terms of FTE student numbers, including Wycliffe College (Anglican), Canadian Theological Seminary (Christian and Missionary Alliance), and Providence Theological Seminary (nondenominational evangelical). Ontario Theological Seminary and Regent College remained virtually tied for first place in this respect (see '1992 Christian Higher Education Guide,' *Faith Today* 10 [January 1992]: 34).

2 H.H. Walsh remarked a generation before: 'None of the traditional church theological colleges can begin to match the achievement of the sectarian [i.e., "Bible"] colleges either in enthusiasm or in the number of their students' (*The Christian Church in Canada*, 322). More recently, the magazine of the Evangelical Fellowship of Canada (EFC) published a guide to evangelical higher education in Canada and listed 76 Bible schools with a combined enrolment (FTE) of 8300 (*Faith Alive* 3 [Nov. 1985]: 37). In 1992, EFC's (renamed) *Faith Today* updated those numbers to 74 schools with just over 7000 enrolled (FTE) ('1992 Guide,' 33–50).

3 David B. Barrett reports each of the three smaller groups' affiliated membership as about 20,000 as of 1980, compared with the Canadian population of more than 25 million (*World Christian Encyclopedia*, 215). Reginald W. Bibby cites slightly different statistics from the 1981 census in *Fragmented Gods*, 28. In telephone interviews conducted with representatives of the mission boards or their equivalents in each of the six denominations, the following foreign-missionary figures were reported: United Church of Canada, 129; Presbyterian Church in Canada, 43; Anglican Church of Canada, 9 (including 4 to start in 1987); Christian Brethren, 238; Christian and Missionary Alliance, 190; Associated Gospel Churches, 184 (January 1987). See similar statistics in Charles A. Tipp, 'Canadian Denominations and Overseas Missionaries,' June 1971; appended to Dennis Mackintosh Oliver, 'The New Canadian Religious Pluralism,' delivered to the Canadian Society of Church History, 1 June 1979, Saskatoon, Sask.

John Webster Grant makes a similar point with still-earlier statistics, establishing a pattern at least twenty years old. Referring to a study by K. MacMillan ('The Influence of the Church on the Life of the Canadian Nation,' four lectures given to the Northwest Mission Conference held in Salem, Oregon, August 1966), he writes: 'In 1966 there were said to be 5,100 Canadian missionaries abroad, of whom 1,700 were Roman Catholic, 700 were associated with churches belonging to the Canadian Council of Churches, and 2,700 represented conservative Protestant groups' (*The Church in the Canadian Era*, 181).

4 I am grateful to Elsa Tesfay-Musa of the Anglican Church of Canada, H. Glen Davis of the Presbyterian Church in Canada, and Fran Ota of the United Church of Canada for supplying valuable information and perspective on this issue.

5 For CGIT see Prang, '"The Girl God Would Have Me Be,"' 154–84. For the SCM see Kirkey, '"Building the City of God"'; and Beattie et al., *Brief History of the Student Christian Movement in Canada 1921–1974*.

6 See Stiller et al., 'Canadian Evangelicals: A Changing Face,' 10–17; and 'Huntley Street Covers the Continent,' 58.

7 Oliver mainly means weekly church attendance, although other figures, such as Sunday School attendance, were used to calculate the final totals.

8 Oliver, 10; see figures three and four.

9 See esp. pp. 106–8, comparing the church-attendance proportions with the membership and affiliate proportions described on pp. 14–15 and 113–16.

10 Rodney M. Booth, *The Winds of God,* 111–13. The book's jacket describes Booth as holding the post of Communications Director for the British Columbia Conference of the United Church of Canada.

11 The closest he comes to discussing evangelicalism is in a list of tiny, eccentric groups: 'If religion, in the sense of a binding creed and way of life, is to be found in Canada we must look to the Orthodox Jews, to the Doukhobors, to the Sikhs, and to the fundamentalist sects for examples' ('Keeping Faith,' 187).

12 John Webster Grant makes a commendable effort to be fair to evangelicals in his *The Church in the Canadian Era.* But for all of Grant's exemplary even-handedness, one still gains little idea of the shape and significance of evangelicalism in Canada from his book. Robert T. Handy does not even get this far, with few references to evangelical institutions in Canada and an index that lists references to 'liberal evangelicals' but none to their more conservative counterparts (*A History of the Churches in the United States and Canada*). And Hans Mol's more recent book is touted as including 'all the major components of religion in Canada' (back cover), but fails to take account of evangelicalism as being anything other than either 'sectarian' or 'Pentecostal' (*Faith and Fragility*). Reginald Bibby's work, especially *Fragmented Gods,* at least gives the 'believers' churches' their due under the rubric 'Conservative Protestants,' but the evangelicalism that unites such Christians with like-minded others in the mainline denominations escapes his analytical scheme.

13 For more instances of Bibby's work, see the bibliography to *Fragmented Gods*, 298–9.

14 To be sure, as the discussion that follows will indicate, some fine recent studies of evangelical Christianity in earlier periods of Canadian history contribute a great deal to this project. On this issue, see Gauvreau, 'Beyond the Half-Way House,' 158–77.

15 Cross and Livingstone, eds., *The Oxford Dictionary of the Christian Church*; s.v. 'Evangelicalism.'

16 George M. Marsden, 'The Evangelical Denomination,' xi

17 'A Shared Evangelical Heritage,' 10. Marsden sets out a similar outline: 'Evangelicals in this sense are Christians who typically emphasize (1) the Reformation doctrine of the final authority of Scripture; (2) the real, historical character of God's saving work recorded in

Scripture; (3) eternal salvation only through personal trust in Christ; (4) the importance of evangelism and missions; and (5) the importance of a spiritually transformed life' ('The Evangelical Denomination,' xi). English historian D.W. Bebbington articulates these same basic principles somewhat differently in *Evangelicalism in Modern Britain*, 2–17.

18 So Marsden, 'The Evangelical Dimension,'ix–x. For examples of this defining from different viewpoints, see the essays in Part 1 of Wells and Woodbridge, eds, *The Evangelicals.*

19 *Champions of the Truth*, 32–3. Rawlyk points out herein, however, that the legacy of Henry Alline was one also of cultural transformation, a legacy not maintained by Maritime Baptists in the later twentieth century. See Rawlyk's oeuvre for detailed studies of Maritime evangelicalism, including on this last point, 'The Champions of the Oppressed?,' 105–23. See also J.M. Bumsted, *Henry Alline 1748–1784* (Toronto: University of Toronto Press 1971); and Stewart and Rawlyk, *A People Highly Favoured of God.* And for concise accounts that prominently feature the evangelical impulse, see the relevant chapters of Rawlyk, ed., *The Canadian Protestant Experience 1760–1990.*

20 *Two Worlds: The Protestant Culture of Nineteenth-Century Ontario*

21 Gauvreau, *The Evangelical Century*; Masters, *Protestant Church Colleges in Canada*

22 *A Profusion of Spires*, ix, 167. In this Grant echoes the judgment made earlier in a pioneering essay by Goldwin French on British North America at the time of Confederation: 'one might argue that the dominant strand in Canadian Protestantism was evangelical' ('The Evangelical Creed in Canada,' 18. Cf. the definition of 'evangelicalism' provided in Gauvreau, 'Protestantism Transformed,' 50–7).

23 See Grant, *A Profusion of Spires*, 170–85. Cf. the brief description in Van Die, *An Evangelical Mind*, 9–10.

24 To be sure, this nomenclature is not universally accepted, but the distinctions yet seem worth observing (Brian A. McKenzie first raised this point with me, attributing it to his teacher, John Webster Grant).

25 Helpful articles in this regard can be found in Elwell, ed., *Evangelical Dictionary of Theology*; Ferguson et al., eds, *New Dictionary of Theology*; and Reid et al., eds, *Dictionary of Christianity in America.* On the more generic contemporary usage of 'fundamental-

ism,' see Marty and Appleby, 'The Fundamentalism Project vii–x. The definitive account of the origins of fundamentalism in America is George M. Marsden, *Fundamentalism and American Culture;* and see also his *Understanding Fundamentalism and Evangelicalism.*

26 An important example of the Canadian usage is the terminology used at Toronto Bible College, traced in part 2, chapter 3, below. For British usage, see Packer, *'Fundamentalism' and the Word of God*; and Hylson-Smith, *Evangelicals in the Church of England 1734-1984,* 297–302.

27 Joel A. Carpenter has published several accounts of these institutional developments. See, among others, ' "A Shelter in a Time of Storm," ' 62–75; 'From Fundamentalism to the New Evangelical Coalition,' 3–16; and 'The Fundamentalist Leaven and the Rise of an Evangelical United Front,' 257–88.

28 On this point see also Dollar, *A History of Fundamentalism in America.*

29 The journalistic literature on this episode is immense, but for guides see the following: Falwell et al., *The Fundamentalist Phenomenon;* Fowler, *A New Engagement*; Liebman and Wuthnow, eds, *The New Christian Right*; Neuhaus and Cromartie, eds, *Piety and Politics*; Neuhaus, ed., *The Bible, Politics, and Democracy*; and Bruce, *The Rise and Fall of the New Christian Right.* I am indebted to Mark A. Noll for some of these citations.

30 This terminological problem bedevils the otherwise clear and helpful discussion of Canadian evangelicalism in Wright, 'The Canadian Protestant Tradition 1914–1945,' 139–97. This essay at times confuses the various terms 'fundamentalist,' 'conservative evangelical,' 'evangelical,' and 'sectarian.'

31 Some of the limitations of focusing upon individual leaders, as another approach, are illustrated by the sensational and unsympathetic study by David R. Elliott, 'Studies of Eight Canadian Fundamentalists.' Elliott's own data (industriously gathered, to be sure) demonstrate that some of his generalizations from these flamboyant individual cases do not in fact hold for fundamentalism in general.

32 Important examples of this scholarship are the following: Clark, *Church and Sect in Canada* and *The Developing Canadian Community*; Walsh, *The Christian Church in Canada*; and Mol, *Faith and Fragility.*

33 Goldwin French challenged the appropriateness of these categories earlier in his 'Evangelical Creed in Canada,' 15–35.

34 This book apparently ignores Atlantic Canada as well, since all of the institutions studied are located elsewhere. Links between the transdenominational evangelicalism described herein and evangelicals in the Atlantic Provinces do appear throughout the following narratives, however, and the conclusion deals at greater length with this relationship.

35 Scholars will recognize that part 1 depends largely on secondary sources, which ought to suffice for this sort of historiographical 'slate-cleaning.' The remainder of the study depends mostly upon primary research.

36 This terminology has been used to considerable effect on the American scene in the recent study by R. Laurence Moore, *Religious Outsiders and the Making of Americans.*

37 Another sort of institution that might be studied here would be a major missionary organization. Inter-Varsity Christian Fellowship was a mission of sorts, to be sure: a mission to students. Yet one might miss study of a foreign mission per se in this profile, especially considering the major emphasis upon evangelism at the heart of Canadian evangelicalism. The most obvious subject for such a study would be the Sudan Interior Mission (SIM), once the largest transdenominational mission in the world and founded by evangelical statesman Rowland V. Bingham. But the lack of SIM in this story is not crucial for at least two reasons. First, its activities were by definition largely out of Canada and affected Canadians only indirectly. Second, SIM and Bingham himself show up often enough in the records of these other organizations to indicate that study of SIM would produce the same conclusions regarding the nature of Canadian evangelicalism. The story of the SIM yet is one that deserves to be told and added to the mosaics of Canadian, American, and African church history. (For Bingham himself, see McKenzie, 'Fundamentalism, Christian Unity, and Premillennialism in the Thought of Rowland Victor Bingham.')

38 This typology is advanced throughout what follows, and especially in the Conclusion.

Part One: Introduction

1 See, for example, Walsh, *The Christian Church in Canada*; and esp. Mann, *Sect, Cult, and Church in Alberta.*

2 Pathbreaking work on this interpretation was done in the follow-

ing studies: Elliott, 'The Dispensational Theology and Political Ideology of William Aberhart'; Goertz, 'The Development of a Bible Belt'; and McKenzie, 'A History of the Toronto Bible College (1894–1968).'

Chapter 1

1 T.T. Shields, in *Gospel Witness* 2 (31 May 1923); quoted without further reference in Tarr, *Shields of Canada,* 158
2 *Canadian Who's Who, 1952–54,* 964
3 Russell, 'Thomas Todhunter Shields,' 263
4 In addition to the sources cited below, see the following for Shields: Carder, 'Controversy in the Baptist Convention of Ontario and Quebec, 1908–1929' (thesis and article); Ellis, 'Social and Religious Factors in the Fundamentalist-Modernist Schisms'; Harrop, 'The Era of the "Great Preacher" among Canadian Baptists'; Hill, 'From Sect to Denomination in the Baptist Church in Canada.' For further bibliography on Shields, see Stackhouse, 'Thomas Todhunter Shields,' 400–2.
5 Tarr, *Shields of Canada,* 29, 32. George S. May provides the following, not altogether flattering, physical description of Shields at middle age: 'In 1927 Shields was fifty-four years old, six feet two inches in height, a broad-shouldered, somewhat paunchy but impressive figure. His most striking features were his huge head and his small, heavily lidded eyes which gave him a haughty, imperious look well suited to his general manner ... [T]o these imposing physical attributes was added a voice majestically ministerial' ('Des Moines University and Dr. T.T. Shields,' 194).
6 Tarr, *Shields of Canada,* 52: there is a misprint here which states that Shields took the Jarvis Street pulpit in 1912.
7 Ralph G. Turnbull, *A History of Preaching,* vol. 3 (Grand Rapids, Mich.: Baker Book House 1974), 329–30; quoted in Tarr, 'Another Perspective on T.T. Shields and Fundamentalism,' 221
8 John Moir suggests that George Cross was the real quarry. He, like Matthews, represented the growing influence of the University of Chicago on Canadian biblical studies, having graduated from there in 1899. Of the two, Clark Pinnock writes, he was 'probably the more deeply modernistic.' He had taught church history at McMaster since 1901 but had accepted a post at Chica-

go by 1909, leaving Matthews to bear the brunt of Harris's attack. See Moir, *A History of Biblical Studies in Canada*, 36–7; and Pinnock, 'The Modernist Impulse at McMaster University, 1887–1927,' 198. For contemporary struggles over higher criticism in Canada see Moir, 29–44; and Tom Sinclair-Faulkner, 'Theory Divided from Practice.'

9 This doctrinal statement constitutes appendix A in Tarr, *Shields of Canada*.

10 'I was very much distressed by this communication, for I had never set much store by honorary degrees, or ministerial titles of any kind. I had rather favoured the idea that it was well that ministers should be appraised, like furniture in the natural wood without any finish upon it, and before any sort of putty or paint had been applied to make a good joint of a bad one' (no source, quoted in Tarr, *Shields of Canada*, 60).

11 These were the only degrees Shields ever received. One needs more than this fact, however, to justify the psychohistorical judgment that Shields's 'criticism of professors at McMaster, the founding of his own seminary, and his takeover of Des Moines University probably were compensations for his own lack of higher education' (Russell, 277). Too many fundamentalist leaders (many of whom did have substantial formal education) also opposed what they saw to be hopelessly compromised schools and set up alternative institutions for this easy explanation to work without much more evidence (see Carpenter, '"A Shelter in a Time of Storm"'). J. Gresham Machen, one-time professor at Princeton Theological Seminary and founder of Westminster Theological Seminary in Philadelphia, is only one conspicuous example challenging Russell's supposition.

12 Tarr, *Shields of Canada*, 62

13 Trinier, *A Century of Service*, 138

14 The first and more important of the two is 'The Inspiration and Authority of Scripture,' *Canadian Baptist* (2 Oct. 1919).

15 See Tarr, *Shields of Canada*, 67–71 for a colourful account.

16 One account indicates that there was a salary dispute involved as well. J.D.E. Dozois writes that Shields was holding out for more than twice what the church initially offered him, ultimately accepting a larger raise ($4000) that was equivalent to the whole salary of the associate pastor (see Dozois, 'Dr. Thomas Todhunter Shields [1873–1955],' 71).

17 The full text of this sermon constitutes the last part of appendix C in Tarr, *Shields of Canada.*

18 Shields drew back the veil in his denunciatory sermon after the conflict, later published: *The Inside of the Cup.*

19 Tarr reprints the entire story (unfortunately without citing sources) in *Shields of Canada*, 79–80.

20 Russell, 268

21 Shields later presented his recollection of this episode in the tellingly titled *The Plot That Failed.*

22 Tarr, *Shields of Canada*, 87

23 Shields explicitly referred to the growth in his church, exemplified in this campaign, as evidence of God's blessing on his decision to withstand the elements that opposed him in 1921: 'For eleven years in this pulpit, I endured, I prayed night and day with tears, and sought by every means in my power to overcome the obstacles that were standing in the way of a great spiritual awakening and four years ago last Monday night that decision was taken [the confrontation with those who formed Park Road Baptist Church]; and God has been with us in power and blessing ever since. They may say what they like about revival by compromise; but I challenge the men of compromise to show me their revival. Where is it? Where are the fruits of it?' (*The Gospel Witness* 4 [1 Oct. 1925], quoted without further reference in Tarr, *Shields of Canada*, 90).

24 The phrase and judgment are Pinnock's; 'The Modernist Impulse,' 200

25 Tarr quotes from the resolution passed by the board, in *Shields of Canada*, 94

26 For Marshall, see Tarr, 'Another Perspective'; and Pinnock. See also the indications of something less than complete orthodoxy in Marshall's views in Russell's summary, 270. For Whidden, see Rawlyk, 'A.L. McCrimmon, H.P. Whidden, T.T. Shields, Christian Higher Education, and McMaster University,' 50–4.

27 Russell, 269

28 Founded in 1922

29 The list is Russell's, 269–70.

30 Proceedings of the Educational Session of the Baptist Convention of Ontario and Quebec, held in First Avenue Baptist Church, Toronto, 18 Oct. 1926, quoted (with minor grammatical changes) in Russell, 272.

31 For accounts of the similar schism in British Columbia over alleged heresy at Brandon College, Manitoba, see the following: Ellis, 'What the Times Demand'; Pousett, 'A History of the Convention of Baptist Churches of British Columbia' and 'The History of the Regular Baptists of British Columbia'; Richards, *Baptists in British Columbia*; Thompson, *The Baptist Story in Western Canada*.

32 David R. Elliott comments that 'his rationale for opening another Bible institute was that the existing ones, such as Toronto Bible College and Moody Bible Institute, were too superficial and non-Baptistic' (citing Shields in the *Gospel Witness*, 27 Aug. 1925, 10; in 'Studies of Eight Canadian Fundamentalists,' 149).

33 May, 195

34 Ibid., 201–2; May's account forms the basis for most of this section, but see also Russell, 274–6.

35 Bartlett, *A History of Baptist Separatism*, 17. Another unfriendly account of the affair was provided in Morrison, 'The Fundamentalist Fiasco.' Tarr, for his part, discreetly states, 'This Des Moines incident did not further the work of the [Baptist Bible] Union' (*Shields of Canada*, 106).

36 American fundamentalist historian George Dollar repeatedly uses premillennial eschatology as a hallmark of true fundamentalism, although he will allow for exceptions like Shields that prove the rule (*A History of Fundamentalism in America*). Ernest R. Sandeen sees 'millennialism' (a common synonym for 'premillennialism') to be one of two roots of American fundamentalism (*The Roots of Fundamentalism*). George M. Marsden sees more than two roots, but identifies millennialism yet as an important source (*Fundamentalism and American Culture*). On Canadian premillennialism, see Whan,'Premillennialism in Canadian Baptist History.'

37 It may well be that the absence of a premillennial clause in the doctrinal statement of the BBU is due to Shields's leadership.

38 Russell and Walter E. Ellis see the struggle in terms of eschatological differences. Dozois and Tarr, however, see it in terms of struggle over the independence of the fellowships. See Russell, 272; Ellis, 'Gilboa to Ichabod,' 123–24; Dozois, 92–3; and Tarr, *This Dominion His Dominion*, 96. For more on Shields's theology, see Parent, 'The Christology of T.T. Shields.'

39 This section relies on Wicks, 'T.T. Shields and the Canadian Protestant League, 1941–59.'

40 Of special interest to this study is that fact that Rowland V. Bingham, founder of the prominent evangelical Sudan Interior Mission, and his colleague at Evangelical Publishers, J.H. Hunter, were charter members (ibid., 43).

41 Ibid., 141

42 Ibid., 48, 60

43 Apparently many failed to renew their membership after one year (ibid., 74–5).

44 They produced their own, like Shields's *Three Addresses* (Toronto: Canadian Protestant League 1943), or reproduced tracts from earlier times, like Father Charles Chiniquy's sensational *The Priest, the Woman and the Confessional,* written in the mid-1800s (ibid., 73).

45 Ibid.

46 The phrase is from Hansard, quoted in ibid., 102.

47 Wicks (p. 58) refers to Mason Wade, C.P. Stacy, and A.R.M. Lower: the national plebiscite of 1942 is especially in view.

48 Ibid., 98–9

49 Wicks (p. 58) quotes Christian Brethren missionaries in this regard.

50 David Barrett estimates the 1980 membership of this denomination at 5000 (*World Christian Encyclopedia,* 215). An illustration of the (lack of) importance of this denomination can be seen in the fact that when commentators have remarked on the denominations emerging from the Baptist split in the 1920s, they invariably have referred to the Fellowship of Evangelical Baptist Churches of Canada (formed by the union of the Fellowship of Independent Baptist Churches and Union of Regular Baptists in 1953) – rather than to Shields's little Association of Regular Baptists. For examples see Ivison, 'Is There a Canadian Baptist Tradition?' 64–5; Bruce A. Woods, 'Theological Directions and Cooperation among Baptists in Canada'; and Zeman, 'Canada.'

51 Full-Time Equivalent enrolment was listed as five in 1985 ('101 Reasons to Prepare for Life and Ministry in Canada,' 39).

52 McIntire preached at his funeral (Tarr, *Shields of Canada,* 146). Ted S. Rendall, president of Prairie Bible Institute in the 1980s, once wrote: 'I will never forget the impact that sermon number

11, "For Jonathan's Sake," had on my heart when I heard it preached by Dr. Shields in Edinburgh in the late forties. It is one of the greatest sermons I ever listened to' (Ted S. Rendall, reviewing Shields's collection of sermons, *Christ in the Old Testament* [Toronto: Gospel Witness 1972], in his column 'With the New Books,' *Prairie Overcomer* 48 [February 1975]: 106).

53 In 1932 Shields heard the eminent Welsh preacher D. Martyn Lloyd-Jones when the latter preached over the radio during a visit to Toronto. Shields invited Lloyd-Jones to preach at his church, and when the latter declined, Shields arranged for them to meet. After a frank and spirited conversation about Shields's involvement in controversy, Lloyd-Jones, in his early thirties, finally made an appeal to the older preacher, now fifty-nine. In this appeal is the characteristic evangelical emphasis on evangelism and edification versus the prosecution of controversy that so marked Shields's career. 'Dr. Shields,' Lloyd-Jones said, 'you used to be known as the Canadian Spurgeon, and you were. You are an outstanding man, in intellect, in preaching gift, in every other respect, but over the McMaster University business in the early twenties you suddenly changed and became negatory and denunciatory. I feel it has ruined your ministry. Why don't you come back! Drop all this, preach the gospel to people positively and win them!' Lloyd-Jones's biographer writes that Shields responded with tears in his eyes, vowing to take Lloyd-Jones's advice to his board of deacons and to abide by their judgment as to which direction his ministry should take. The meeting took place and, according to this source, 'Shields's men told him not to listen to the advice he had received.' On account of this conversation is in Iain H. Murray, *David Martyn Lloyd-Jones*, 271–4.

54 'Contending for the Faith,' *Gospel Witness* 18 (22 June 1939): 5; quoted in Wicks, 81.

55 Some have seen the division of the Presbyterians over the United Church union in 1925 as being of the same order, but N. Keith Clifford has shown convincingly that there is much more to this story than some kind of Presbyterian fundamentalist-modernist division. See his *The Resistance to Church Union in Canada 1904–1939*.

56 The phrase is the title of an article on Shields by Gerald Anglin in *Maclean's*, 15 July 1949.

Chapter 2

1 William Aberhart, 'Second Coming of Christ,' sermon delivered in 1907, quoted in Elliott, 'The Dispensational Theology and Political Ideology of William Aberhart,' 186

2 See, for example, Barr, *The Dynasty*; Boudreau, *Alberta, Aberhart, and Social Credit*; Flanagan, 'Social Credit in Alberta'; Macpherson, *Democracy in Alberta*; Schultz, 'Portrait of a Premier: William Aberhart' and 'William Aberhart and the Social Credit Party.' For more bibliography on Aberhart, see Goertz, 'The Development of a Bible Belt'; Stackhouse, 'William Aberhart,' 8–9; Elliott and Miller, *Bible Bill*; and Elliott, 'Studies of Eight Canadian Fundamentalists.'

3 For example, Aberhart joins Shields and Prairie Bible Institute as the three foci of H.H. Walsh's discussion of evangelicalism in Canada in the twentieth century; see Walsh, *The Christian Church in Canada* 308–25.

4 *Sect, Cult, and Church in Alberta*, 156

5 *The Church in the Canadian Era*, 142–3

6 Bicha, 'Prairie Radicals,' 93. Bicha relies on Irving, *The Social Credit Movement in Alberta*, 197–248, 308, 340. Goertz lists two other sources: Mallish, 'A Socio-Historical Study of the Legislature of Alberta, 1905–1967,' 69; and Anderson, 'The Alberta Social Credit Party,' 215–19 (Goertz, 7).

7 These are themes in Goertz and in Elliott and Miller.

8 Goertz, iii

9 Schultz obtained his grades from the university registrar: Aberhart barely managed to pass, having failed Greek twice and political science (!) once ('William Aberhart and the Social Credit Party,' 9–10).

10 Brief descriptions of dispensationalism appear in the standard literature on American fundamentalism, notably Marsden, *Fundamentalism and American Culture*, esp. 51–4 and 62–6; Sandeen, *The Roots of Fundamentalism*, 62–70; and Weber, *Living in the Shadow of the Second Coming* (1983), 16–24 and 45–51. See also Bass, *Backgrounds to Dispensationalism*. Aberhart did not agree with everything Scofield taught, however. Elliott records several independent opinions of Aberhart ('Dispensational Theology,' 23–6).

11 Irving cites a 'less critical account, widely circulated by

[Aberhart's] disciples in Alberta,' but does not specify what it is (12–13). Cf. Elliott and Miller's well-researched biography that makes no mention of this question of financial support (18).

12 Schultz credits him with being a conscientious and popular principal with considerable physical attributes: 'Sitting behind his desk in the principal's office, weighing an eighth of a ton, with his penetrating blue eyes fastened on a student, or standing over six feet tall teaching his favorite subject, arithmetic, Aberhart was a formidable figure' ('William Aberhart and the Social Credit Party,' 15–16).

13 Goertz writes that Aberhart regarded himself as a Calvinist to his death (40–1), and David R. Elliott and Iris Miller record him as converting to Arminian theology as a young man (9). Schultz thinks theological differences were in fact involved in the move ('William Aberhart and the Social Credit Party,' 20). Aberhart's theological journey, however, would move him out of any standard definitions of either of these traditions.

14 Elliott, 'Dispensational Theology,' 59–61; Elliott and Miller, 40–1

15 Elliott points out that this was a convenient doctrine for a man who struggled with and usually failed at understanding Hebrew and Greek, as his university record shows ('Dispensational Theology,' 54–5).

16 Elliott and Miller state that the average attendance during the 1923–4 season was six hundred (67).

17 A photograph of this cloth appears in Elliott and Miller, 49.

18 Long before Billy Graham popularized this technique! Elliott and Miller credit Aberhart with possessing a 'photographic memory' (5).

19 Goertz, 65

20 *The Prophetic Voice* 1 (1924): 1; quoted in Goertz, 66

21 A full-length treatment of modernism in America, which story has some relevance here, is Hutchison, *The Modernist Impulse in American Protestantism*. A briefer treatment of similar developments in Canada is D.C. Masters, 'The Rise of Liberalism in Canadian Protestant Churches.' And see also Richard Allen, *The Social Passion*, passim.

22 See the enrolment chart in Elliott, 'Dispensational Theology,' 89.

23 Mann, 119. Ernest C. Manning, Aberhart's pastoral and political successor, testified at Aberhart's funeral that his finest service had been his religious ministry to 'thousands of homes across the

Canadian West' (*Edmonton Bulletin* [31 May 1943]: 16; quoted in Schultz, 'William Aberhart and the Social Credit Party,' 441). Schultz himself describes Aberhart's religious ministry as 'primarily a radio ministry' (442).

24 Elliott and Miller, 79

25 Elliott, 'Dispensational Theology,' 105. Elliott points out that the Institute executive deemed Aberhart's personal popularity so essential to the project that they insured his life for the amount of the ten-year mortgage (ibid.).

26 For the later history of the Institute, reorganized in 1948 as Berean Bible Institute, see *A Burning Bush in the West.*

27 Two well-known Canadian fundamentalist leaders, T.T. Shields and L.E. Maxwell (founder of Prairie Bible Institute), refused to defend the inerrancy of the KJV as part of their staunch defence of *biblical* inerrancy. Elliott says that Scofield himself, R.A. Torrey (founder of the Bible Institute of Los Angeles), and Riley all used the Revised Version of 1881 ('Dispensational Theology,' 55).

28 A key phrase from the King James Version's rendering of 2 Timothy 2:15 that was used by dispensationalists to justify their apportionment of salvation history into eras, or 'dispensations'; Marsden (p. 59) points out that C.I. Scofield wrote a presentation of his views entitled *Rightly Dividing the Word of Truth* (Westwood, NJ: Revell, n.d. [1896]).

29 'The Present Eastern Question in the Light of Prophecy of What the Bible Says about Turkey,' lecture 11 in *God's Great Prophecies* (Calgary, Alta.: Calgary Prophetic Bible Conference 1922), 7; quoted in Goertz, 58

30 On 'Jesus Only' or 'Oneness' Pentecostalism, see Burgess, McGee, and Alexander, eds, *Dictionary of Pentecostal and Charismatic Movements*; s.v. 'Jesus Christ' by W.G. MacDonald and 'Oneness Pentecostalism' by D.A. Reed.

31 Elliott and Miller, 64–6

32 The list of reasons is from Elliott, 'Dispensational Theology,' 97–8.

33 *Covenant, Confession of Faith and Duties of Members of Westbourne Baptist Church*, 1927; cited in Goertz, 134; see also Elliott and Miller, 70.

34 In this Aberhart evidently followed Shields's lead, but the extent of their relationship is hard to determine, although it seems not to have been great by anyone's estimation. Elliott and Goertz

assert that Aberhart supported Shields over McMaster (Elliott, 'Dispensational Theology,' 101; Goertz, 133 – who may simply be following Elliott). Walter E. Ellis, however, found an intriguing snippet in a letter from H.H. Bingham to McMaster's Chancellor Whidden regarding the visit of Shields to the Calgary Prophetic Bible Institute as he sought support in 1925: 'Personally, I do not think Dr. Shields after his arrival felt especially comfortable with Aberhart and the Prophetic Conference Crowd' (Letter of 13 Oct. 1925 in Whidden Papers, Canadian Baptist Archives, quoted in Ellis, 'Baptists and Radical Politics in Western Canada (1920–1950),' 181n.20).

It perhaps is telling enough that Westbourne remained independent, rather than seeking any affiliation with Shields's group or the British Columbia counterparts, until after it split with Aberhart (for Westbourne's role as the 'mother church' of the Fellowship of Evangelical Baptist Churches in Alberta, see Tarr, *This Dominion His Dominion*, 123–4). And Shields later would pronounce Aberhart's Social Credit ideas 'economic lunacy' and denounce his dispensationalism in the *Gospel Witness* ('Premier Aberhart,' 16 [2 Sept. 1937]: 9–10; and the lead article in the *Gospel Witness* of 7 July 1938, cited in Elliott and Miller, 361n.40).

Regarding the Brandon College controversy, see Ellis, 'What the Times Demand,' 63–87.

35 Elliott, 'Dispensational Theology,' 106
36 Elliott and Miller, 90
37 See note 2, Introduction to part 1, above.
38 The book (New York: Coward-McCann 1928) was Maurice Colbourne's popularization of Douglas's ideas. Aberhart's involvement in politics seems to some observers to contradict his basic dispensational theology. This is the burden, for instance, of Elliott's own work and of his book with Iris Miller, esp. pp. 34–42. Some explain the contradiction in cynical terms: as Aberhart's religious success waned, he turned to politics to rebuild support. So S.D. Clark: 'Increasing competition from rival radio evangelists led him to search for something new in his appeal, and he seized upon the message of Social Credit. Attacks upon his political teachings forced him into politics in their defense. What he did was to convert a religious crusade into a political crusade; political allegiances were forged to take the

place of weakening religious allegiances' (*The Developing Canadian Community*, 143). Elliott comes to a similar judgment: 'In order to widen his influence Aberhart had to enter another sphere of activity; he found it in politics' ('Dispensational Theology,' 122). Flanagan, by contrast sees strong formal similarities between Aberhart's premillennialism and Social Credit and sees no contradiction, therefore, to explain by resorting to ulterior motives ('Cargo Cult').

Perhaps only the difficult discipline of psychohistory can resolve this dispute. Timothy P. Weber, however, provides ammunition for those who oppose the judgment that premillennialism and a political program simply cannot mix (see his *Living in the Shadow of the Second Coming*, esp. 218–24 and 234–8). And Elliott and Miller themselves acknowledge at least some instances of fundamentalist involvement in politics (118–19).

39 (N.p., 1933)

40 Elliott and Miller detail the differences between Aberhart and Douglas, both personally and intellectually (see esp. pp. 133–46, 204–28).

41 Joseph A. Boudreau remarks, '[Douglas's] ideas regarding credit expansion, or "pump priming," were not all zany, but bear a relationship to the theories of Lord Keynes, the formal exposition of which was appearing in the thirties and the application of which can be seen in the New Deal of Franklin Roosevelt, and, by 1938, albeit reluctantly, by Prime Minister W.L. Mackenzie King in Canada' ('The Medium and Message of William Aberhart,' 19). Aberhart used so much time for Social Credit once that he ran out of time for the sermon (CFCN broadcast, 3 Feb. 1935, cited in Goertz, 164).

42 *Today and Tomorrow* (22 Oct. 1936): 1; quoted in Elliott, 'Dispensational Theology,' 170

43 Elliott, 'Dispensational Theology,' 162

44 John A. Irving reports that 'the issue was so close that a shift of only 1,000 votes, properly distributed in ten constituencies, would have led to Aberhart's fall. As it was, Social Crediters won thirty-six of the fifty-seven seats in the new legislature' (Irving, 'The Evolution of the Social Credit Movement,' 145).

45 Elliott and Miller set out some of these policies (235–7, 281–2).

46 And under its third premier in three decades, Bill Vander Zalm, it controlled the British Columbia legislature into the late 1980s.

47 L.E. Maxwell, 'Christians and World Reform,' *The Prairie Pastor* (May–June 1933): 1–2. And Goertz reports that the president of Prairie's sister school, Briercrest Bible Institute in Saskatchewan, also called on Aberhart to concentrate on evangelism rather than politics (Goertz, 184n36).

48 J. Fergus Kirk (one of the founders of Prairie Bible Institute), 'Social Credit and the Word of God' (Three Hills, Alta.: Prairie Bible Institute 1935), n.p. (mimeographed letter); quoted in Goertz, 166.

49 CFCN broadcast, 28 Apr. 1935; quoted in Goertz, 168

50 See the literature cited at the head of this chapter.

51 Aberhart has been the subject of at least two documentaries and two plays broadcast by the Canadian Broadcasting Corporation (CBC): 'Profiles in Politics: William Aberhart' (CBC Radio documentary, 4 October 1961); 'The Bible Belt: The Politics of the Second Coming' (CBC Television documentary, 1972); Frank Dabbs, 'William Aberhart and the Something for Nothing Gang' (CBC Radio play, 1973); and Jim Nichol, 'The Rapture of William Aberhart' (CBC Radio play, 1986).

52 Indeed, it should be underscored that Aberhart had removed himself from mainstream evangelicalism on purely religious grounds, quite apart from his political career. This point is exemplified in the fact that none of the graduates from the early years of his Bible institute became missionaries to foreign countries – contrary to the pattern of other evangelical Bible schools – and in the reason for that fact: Aberhart had written off the denominational missions as infected by modernism, and uniformly evangelical agencies (including fundamentalist ones) refused to accept Aberhart's graduates because of their peculiar doctrines (Elliott and Miller, 93).

53 David Elliott records that within five years of Aberhart's death, most of the staff and students of Calgary Prophetic Bible Institute left and formed Berean Bible College. The former soon closed, and Berean collapsed in 1986. Only a dozen churches remained associated with Aberhart's legacy in the late 1980s ('Studies,' 213).

54 Elliott and Miller come to a similar conclusion in their tendentious but well-researched biography: 'It is a mistake to see Aberhart's Social Credit movement as typical of religious fundamentalism. Aberhart's unique theology and his political ideology

brought him opposition from Pentecostals, Plymouth Brethren, Regular Baptists, Prairie Bible Institute, and even from within his own sect. Most of his political support seems not to have come from members of other religious sects, but from people who belonged to mainline churches or who had only marginal religious commitment' (319).

Part Two: Introduction

1 See the following: Bothwell, Drummond, and English, *Canada 1900–1945* and *Canada since 1945*; the relevant chapters of Brown, ed., *The Illustrated History of Canada*; and the relevant volumes of Cook and Morton, eds., *The Canadian Centenary Series.*
2 Indeed, one would not have put quotation marks around 'heathen' in this context in the former days!
3 One important recent study is Wright, *A World Mission.*
4 For accounts of Canadian religion in this period, see the following: John Webster Grant, *The Church in the Canadian Era*; Handy, *A History of the Churches in the United States and Canada*; and the relevant chapters in Rawlyk, ed., *The Canadian Protestant Experience 1760–1990.*

Chapter 3

1 This was not the first time the four major denominations had been represented at a Toronto Bible College occasion. They were represented also at the dedication of the new building in 1929 ('The Services of Dedication,' *Toronto Bible College Recorder* 36 [Dec. 1929]: 3) and at the Jubilee graduation service in 1943 ('The Jubilee Graduation Service,' *Toronto Bible College Recorder* 50 [June 1944]: 1–2). Toronto Bible College's publication was originally known as the *Toronto Bible Training School Recorder.* With the June 1965 issue, its title changed to *Evangelical Recorder.* As the volume numbers are consecutive throughout, the abbreviation *Recorder* will be used in the notes for all three publications. (All citations from Toronto Bible College documents are from those at Ontario Bible College and Theological Seminary, Willowdale, Ontario, unless otherwise noted.)
2 *Recorder* 52 (Dec. 1946): 1–2. The speakers' addresses are in the same place: pp. 3–9, 12–15.

3 The College name is often abbreviated to 'TBC' in its own literature, a practice followed here.
4 For a discussion of some of the leaders of this evangelicalism, see Sawatsky, '"Looking for that Blessed Hope."' For broader treatments of nineteenth-century religion in Ontario, see Grant, *A Profusion of Spires*; Westfall, *Two Worlds*; and Gauvreau, *The Evangelical Century*.
5 Ian S. Rennie, 'Gratitude for the Past,' *Recorder* 90 (Spring 1984): 6
6 On the history of the Bible school movement in Canada and the United States, see the following substantial studies: Boon 'The Development of the Bible College or Institute in the United States and Canada since 1880'; Brereton, 'The Bible Schools and Conservative Evangelical Higher Education, 1880–1940,' and 'Protestant Fundamentalist Bible Schools, 1882–1940'; Harder, 'The Bible Institute-College Movement in Canada'; O'Neil, 'A Survey of the Bible Schools in Canada'; Rennie, 'Theological Education in Canada' and 'The Western Prairie Revival in Canada'; Sawatsky, 'The Bible School/College Movement in Canada'; and Witmer, *The Bible College Story*.
7 See Sawatsky, '"Looking for that Blessed Hope,"' 259–63.
8 Rennie says 1876 (in 'Gratitude for the Past,' 7); Douglas C. Percy, writing a generation earlier, says 1877 ('There Were Giants in Those Days,' *Recorder* 60 [March 1954]: 3).
9 Rennie, 'Gratitude for the Past,' 8
10 According to Percy, p. 3
11 1894 Prospectus (which Harris had drafted and set out before the meeting), n.p. Brian A. McKenzie says this was approved with only one alteration – apparently a minor one since McKenzie does not list it ('A History of the Toronto Bible College (1894–1968),' 2; McKenzie's is a valuable study to which this section is indebted).
12 Rennie, 'Gratitude for the Past,' 8. For profiles of many of these leaders, see Sawatsky.
13 The 1894 Prospectus reads: 'The Council, officers and lecturers of the School represent the different leading evangelical bodies, and it is, therefore, inter-denominational in character ... Members of evangelical churches who have a real desire for Christian work will be welcome to all the classes' (3). The first class, at the beginning of the year only ten students, themselves represented eight different denominations, although unfortunately *which* denominations is not recorded (*Recorder* 59 [Dec. 1953]: 11).

14 1894 Prospectus, n.p.

15 McKenzie records this statement in appendix 2: 60, with the note: 'This statement follows the 7 February 1895 meeting's minutes in the minute book of the Executive Council.'

16 See 1899 Prospectus, n.p. Sawatsky notes that this change made the statement identical to that of the China Inland Mission (' "Looking for That Blessed Hope," ' 285).

17 He is listed as being scheduled to do so in the 1894 Prospectus, n.p.

18 Percy, 'Giants,' 6

19 The fact that the Second Coming of Christ was not part of the original statement of faith and the fact that dispensationalism was never a hallmark of the school – and was later disowned entirely – seems to militate against the central thesis of Sawatsky's generally useful dissertation (' "Looking for That Blessed Hope" '). In this study Sawatsky asserts that this late-nineteenth- and early-twentieth-century movement of evangelicals (whom Sawatsky unhelpfully calls 'proto-fundamentalists') was 'theologically grounded in a firm and optimistic belief in "that blessed hope," the imminent second coming of Christ' (ii). Or, as he concludes, 'the main link in the chain for the group was the peculiar or special emphasis it placed on "that blessed hope" ' (335).

To be sure, the Second Coming was important to these men: it appears in the revised TBC statement of faith of 1899 and the Niagara Prophetic Conferences did draw a number of them together, as Sawatsky shows. Still, Toronto Bible College does not provide much support for Sawatsky's placement of belief in the Second Coming – still less a particular, dispensationalist belief in it – at the centre of this network. Furthermore, Sawatsky's use of the term 'proto-fundamentalists' seems unhelpful since he does not connect them with the one indubitable Toronto fundamentalist, T.T. Shields, and instead holds up as a prime example of their work Toronto Bible College, which never had links with Shields and indeed avoided almost entirely all controversy that would mark it as fundamentalistic in the usual, militant sense of the term. Instead, Sawatsky's people should be seen simply as late nineteenth-century evangelicals, since what marks them most importantly are the traditional evangelical emphases: orthodox doctrine, personal conversion and piety, Biblical authority, social responsibility, and evangelism.

20 Sawatsky describes the theological stances of Burwash and other speakers in that summer session (' "Looking for That Blessed

Hope,'' 279–84). Chown is listed as an examiner in the 1899 Prospectus, n.p. For more on Burwash, see Van Die, *An Evangelical Mind*. For a defence of Chown's evangelicalism, see Gauvreau, *Evangelical Century*, 250–4 and passim.

21 This is Sawatsky's conclusion as well (ibid., 283). As we have seen in the section on T.T. Shields, Elmore Harris himself led the charge on I.G. Matthews of McMaster University in 1910.

22 Douglas C. Percy, 'Except the Lord Build the House ...,' *Recorder* 60 (June 1954): 6

23 All enrolment statistics, unless otherwise noted, come from the registrar's records, Ontario Bible College. Enrolment figures throughout this discussion are for full-time day students. From the beginning, TBC ran a program of evening classes for those unable to undertake the full course of study. These were consistently well attended. At least as early as 1918, however, John McNicol was complaining about the lack of space. 'No special effort is being made to draw students to the College ... The reason is that we have not adequate accommodation in our building for all the students who are now coming to us' ('Principal's Report,' *Recorder* 24 [June 1918]: 5). McNicol reiterated this concern throughout the 1920s in his annual reports until TBC moved into the new building in 1929.

24 Warren Charlton has uncovered several possible ways in which McNicol could have been known to the TBC staff; see 'Dr. John McNicol and Toronto Bible College,' 3–4.

25 Speech by F.G. Vesey on the presentation of the degree of Doctor of Divinity by Knox to McNicol, reprinted in *Recorder* 41 (June 1935): 8. Charlton records that A.L. Farris, archivist of Knox College, remarked to him that McNicol won the gold medal for his work in Hebrew while a student at Knox ('Dr. John McNicol,' n. 7). McNicol was awarded the Doctor of Divinity degree by Knox College in 1935 ('Our Beloved Principal Honoured by His Alma Mater,' *Recorder* 41 [June 1935]: 8).

26 McNicol had pushed for this change as early as the 1910s but saw it realized only in 1923.

27 Only 197 students were enrolled in 1944–5, although the school would see smaller classes still in the 1950s. McKenzie includes data to indicate that for much of McNicol's tenure TBC's enrolment grew at a higher rate than the general population in the college-age group (see McKenzie, 4–6, and appendix 3: 62). Throughout TBC's history, the great majority of the students came from Ontario, with

a few from elsewhere in Canada, the United States, and foreign countries.

28 In an address given on Founders' Day, 8 Nov. 1949, reprinted as 'Those Formative Years,' *Recorder* 55 (Dec. 1949): 1–4.

29 See, for example, 'Revival in the College,' *Recorder* 38 (Dec. 1932): 2–3; Douglas C. Percy, 'God Did Something Different!' *Recorder* 63 (March 1957): 6–7; Martin O. Wedge, 'The Missionary Conference That Became a Revival,' *Recorder* 71 (March 1965): 3. Brereton speaks of this as an occurrence common in Bible schools ('Bible Schools and Conservative Evangelical Higher Education,' 22–3).

30 John McNicol, 'The Soul of the Toronto Bible College,' *Recorder* 49 (March 1943): 1–2

31 This polity is discussed at some length in McKenzie, 48–58.

32 McNicol, 'Those Formative Years,' 3

33 A quotation from Philippians 2:16

34 McNicol, 'Those Formative Years,' 3

35 McNicol, 'Principal's Report,' *Recorder* 48 (June 1942): 4. And like many Bible schools, TBC claimed that this emphasis was something 'unique.' Perhaps the three-year cycle of lectures by the principal was unique, but this method of reading large tracts of Scripture, especially whole books of the Bible, and studying them inductively, was widespread in the Bible college movement (as Brereton shows, 'Bible Schools and Conservative Evangelical Higher Education,' 10–13, and n. 28; we shall see Prairie Bible Institute making a similar claim to a 'unique' method of inductive study below).

36 Study of the 'cognitive style' of Canadian evangelicalism is just beginning (see especially Gauvreau, Van Die, and Westfall), but on similar patterns in Britain and the United States see the following: Bebbington, *Evangelicalism in Modern Britain*, 50–60; Steve Bruce, *Firm in the Faith*, 186–93; Boone, *The Bible Tells Them So*; Marsden, 'Everyone One's Own Interpreter?' and *Fundamentalism and American Culture*; Weber, 'The Two-Edged Sword,' and Noll, *Between Faith and Criticism*.

37 This distinction is made explicitly and often; see, for example, John McNicol, 'Principal's Report,' *Recorder* 26 (June 1920): 4.

38 McKenzie and Charlton discuss McNicol's acceptance of some findings of higher criticism; see McKenzie, 37–8, and Charlton, 7–8. And these, again, are important themes especially in Gauvreau's and Van Die's treatments of nineteenth-century evangelical theologians and educators.

39 'Principal's Report,' *Recorder* 26 (June 1920): 4
40 McNicol spoke of these changes as arising from the perception that 'modernism was coming in like a flood and was undermining the spiritual life of the Church' (McNicol, 'Those Formative Years,' 1). McKenzie provides a helpful comparison of the three statements of 1894, 1898, and 1916 in appendix 2: 60–1.
41 'Principal's Report,' *Recorder* 26 (June 1920): 4
42 For example, J.B. Rhodes graduated at the head of his class at Knox and later received the Th.D. from Emmanuel College, Toronto, in 1949 ('He Served His Generation by the Will of God,' *Recorder* 59 [Sept. 1953]: 2); Thomas R. Maxwell left the faculty in 1961 to pursue his doctorate in sociology at Toronto ('A Parting Word,' *Recorder* 67 [Sept. 1961]: 21–2); and James Hughes joined the faculty as church historian in 1962 with a doctorate from Glasgow (albeit in Hebrew!; *Recorder* 68 [Dec. 1962]: 1).
43 For example, Andrew McBeath, who joined the faculty in 1950, graduated with honours in classics from Edinburgh University, winning the second prize in moral philosophy, and he graduated second in his class in divinity at New College, Edinburgh (J.B. Rhodes, 'Welcome to T.B.C.!' *Recorder* 56 [Sept. 1950]: 2); E.L. Simmonds, later principal at TBC, graduated with first class honours in Hebrew and ancient history at University College, University of Toronto (*Recorder* 59 [Dec. 1953]: 4); Thomas R. Maxwell came in 1953, having earned first-class honours in sociology at Toronto (ibid., 5); Horace K. Braden came in 1959, having stood in the top ten of a class of 350 at Victoria College, University of Toronto (*Recorder* [June 1959]: 9); and R.B. Strimple joined the faculty in 1961, having graduated first in his class and Phi Beta Kappa at the University of Delaware (*Recorder* 67 [Dec. 1961]: 1).
44 'Those Formative Years,' 3
45 The nomenclature ('fundamentalist,' 'ultra-fundamentalist,' 'evangelical,' 'orthodox,' etc.) continues to be confusing in this period until, perhaps under the influence of the American 'neo-evangelical' movement of the later 1940s and 1950s, Canadians begin to agree on a distinction between 'evangelical' and 'fundamentalist.' Context and usage are the only guides until then. TBC begins using the term 'evangelical' in the *Recorder* consistently to describe itself only as late as 1958 (see masthead for vol. 64 [Dec. 1958]: 2).
46 'Principal's Report,' *Recorder* 30 (June 1924): 5. McNicol outlined the rationale behind the response of TBC to what he called the 'four

Church controversies' in Canada during his tenure in his 'Founders' Day Address, October 28, 1947,' *Recorder* 54 (Sept. 1948): 2–3.

47 'The Perils of Ultra-Fundamentalism,' *Recorder* 55 (March 1949): 1–2. This is the heart of McNicol's refusal to engage modernism directly. McKenzie notes this concern, but attributes McNicol's eschewing of controversy particularly to his Reformed doctrine of the self-authenticating power of Scripture (36–40). McKenzie is correct that McNicol did sometimes speak this way: for example, 'We were convinced that the Bible could stand upon its own feet when it was interpreted in its own light and allowed to speak for itself. It did not need the defence of the Fundamentalists and we did not join the Fundamentalist movement' ('Those Formative Years,' 3). Aside from the point made earlier, though, that this sort of language could also be used in the Enlightenment, 'common sense' tradition of evangelical understanding of the Bible, many Reformed theologians who have held to this doctrine of the 'self-authentication of Scripture' none the less have engaged in direct controversy with heresy of various sorts and, later, modernism in particular. John Calvin himself, for instance, withstood a variety of foes, whether unitarian Michael Servetus or the whole Roman Catholic tradition. The American theologian Jonathan Edwards refuted the unitarian and Pelagian 'Arminianism' of his time, the eighteenth century. The Princeton theologians of the nineteenth century (notably Charles Hodge and B.B. Warfield) criticized most of the theological options of their day. And J. Gresham Machen, contemporary of Elmore Harris, broke away from the American Northern Presbyterian church over doctrine, having withstood modernism in it as long as he could.

The problem here, it seems, is one of confusing typical Reformed doubts about the efficacy of apologetics with a supposed Reformed avoidance of controversy because of a belief that the Bible can 'stand on its own.' To be sure, McNicol may truly have thought that the one implied the other, although it is even questionable just how much weight McNicol would put on the 'self-authentication of Scripture' since TBC offered courses on 'evidences' from its earliest days and continued to do so under McNicol's tenure. But whatever he thought about the latter issue, many Reformed theologians have disagreed with the view that this doctrine forbids contending with error. So it is scarcely evident that, as McKenzie puts it, 'the Reformed doctrine of scripture allowed McNicol to set aside the task of defending scripture from modernism' (40). Instead, the mainspring of McNicol's refusal to link up with the Fundamentalists was his concern to serve all the churches and his fear of controversy as a threat to that role and to the mission of the church.

48 *Recorder* 52 (March 1946): 1–11. McNicol had anticipated this article, for those who had ears to hear, in his discussion of 'Prophecy in War Time,' *Recorder* 45 (June 1940): 1–3. And he followed up 'Fundamental, but Not Dispensational' with 'What Is the New Testament Hope?' *Recorder* 52 (Sept. 1946): 5, and 'How Should We Interpret Prophecy,' *Recorder* 53 (Sept. 1947): 1–6.

49 'Fundamental, but Not Dispensational,' 10.

50 Ibid., 11

51 Clarence Bouma of Calvin Theological Seminary in Grand Rapids, Michigan, wrote: 'It is refreshing to know there are a few Bible Schools that see the error of Dispensationalism. If you will send me 50 – or even 100 – copies of your leaflet, I will take care that they will be put to good use.' Princeton's Bruce M. Metzger wrote at the same time, saying: 'Principal McNicol's article is excellent. Our book store manager would be interested in copies of this [article], should they be available in quantities. We could use at least 200 copies.' (These testimonies appear in J.B. Rhodes, 'The Reaction to Our Answer,' *Recorder* 52 [Sept. 1946]: 3.) Principal Bryden of Knox College, the 'Canadian Barth,' affirmed, 'Have you read the article that he wrote in the March *Recorder* – "Fundamental but Not Dispensational?" I give it as my humble opinion that you have in that article as fine a theological insight for this present time, as accurate knowledge and interpretation of history, and as exceptional exegetical scholarship as can be found in any kind of article' (*Recorder* 52 [Dec. 1946]: 7).

Philip E. Howard, Jr, notified TBC in a letter (4 June 1946), however, that the *Sunday School Times* would no longer carry its advertisement because of McNicol's article. In a three-page letter, Principal J.B. Rhodes successfully mollified Howard so that he changed his mind (letter of 27 Sept. 1949). Rhodes's argument is typical of TBC's ethos. It appeals to 'character witnesses,' citing Henry W. Frost of the China Inland Mission and R.V. Bingham of the Sudan Interior Mission as former members of the TBC council. It assures Howard that all of the faculty at TBC are in fact premillennialist. It goes on to say, however, that dispensationalism per se is a 'modern' innovation, and not held by any of the faculty. It concludes in classic style: 'There is no fundamental doctrine in which there is more marked division of view than the Doctrine of the Second Coming. Our position at Toronto Bible College is that we constantly stress the supreme fact of Christ's Return and do not magnify details on which equally good and godly men differ. We are therefore ready to extend fellowship to all who look for our Lord's Return in sincerity, whether they are pre-, post-, or a-millennial; pre- or post- tribulationist; Darbyite, Dispensationalist, or known by other classification. In His Name we will love and fellowship with them all as we will do fully in that glad day of His return and we dwell together forever' (15 Sept. 1949). All correspondence in the Ontario Bible College and Ontario Theological Seminary archives: file FB-HI-TBC-1.

52 'Principal's Report,' *Recorder* 49 (June 1943): 6. McNicol's metaphors sometimes indicated an estimation of the worth of pastoral training and ministry perhaps higher than one might expect. Following the glowing speeches at the banquet in 1946, McNicol replied: 'I count it a special honour to have sitting with me at this table the heads of the four Theological Colleges – not only the Principals of Wycliffe and Knox who have spoken, but also the Provost of Trinity and the Dean of Emmanuel. The Bible College is not in the same class with the Theological Colleges, for they are on the great highway of church life and work and we are only on the sidelines. It is a very gracious thing that they have done in honouring us with their presence and I appreciate that more than I can tell them' ('Dr. John McNicol's Reply,' *Recorder* 52 [Dec. 1946]: 13). This comment might reflect some personal sense of inferiority or of not living up to expectations on the part of a successful student of university and divinity college who ended up presiding over a Bible school. It at least as likely reflects, however, the general evangelical ambivalence that promoted the work of the layperson while giving most glory to the professional minister, whether pastor or, especially, missionary. This attitude receives further discussion below.

53 'The Bible Schools and Conservative Evangelical Higher Education, 1880–1940,' 113

54 Douglas C. Percy credits Henry W. Frost of the China Inland Mission with urging the school to take this step ('Giants,' 5; see n. 8 above). As Rennie and Sawatsky note, the pioneers at TBC were part of a network of evangelicals who supported foreign missions, both

those of their denominations and of the new 'faith missions,' especially the China Inland Mission and Sudan Interior Mission. Indeed, the cover of the 1905 Prospectus for the first time describes the Toronto Bible Training School as 'An Interdenominational and Missionary College.' This description was amplified on the cover of the 1912–13 Prospectus to read, 'Interdenominational, Biblical, Missionary.'

55 1895 Prospectus, n.p.

56 Douglas C. Percy, '"There Was a Man Sent from God Whose Name Was John ... "' *Recorder* 62 (Dec. 1956): 15–16. Once again McNicol represents the school. E.A. Brownlee of the China Inland Mission testified in 1946: 'We are glad to note that something over 500 of the graduates of this institution through these years have entered foreign missionary service. Of this number about 150, I am told, have entered foreign service with the various denominational mission boards. Something over 350 of them have gone out in connection with various inter-denominational mission societies. Of that number about a quarter, roughly speaking, from 80 to 90, have gone to Africa in connection with the Sudan Interior Mission; about an equal number have taken up foreign missionary service in China in connection with the China Inland Mission' (*Recorder* 52 [Dec. 1946]: 5. This pattern of sending a majority of missionaries to the transdenominational boards dates back to TBC's earliest days: see 'The Bible College and Missions,' *Recorder* 30 [March 1924]: 1).

57 As noted in the *Recorder* 15 (March 1909); cited in 'Seventy Years of Recorder News,' *Recorder* 69 (Sept. 1963): 14

58 McNicol, 'The Bible College Alumni,' *Recorder* 49 (Dec. 1943): 1

59 Douglas J. Paterson, 'The 59th Graduation Exercises,' *Recorder* 59 (June 1953): 2. This paragraph illustrates the typical evangelical 'hierarchy of vocations': 'missionary' is best, presumably since 'full-time' in 'spiritual work' (especially evangelism) and at great personal cost; 'pastor' is next, since 'full-time' in 'spiritual work,' even if clearly not requiring as much sacrifice as the 'missionary' vocation; other kinds of 'full-time service' come afterwards; and finally come the great mass of folk who give most of their energies to 'secular' jobs and a relatively little time to 'spiritual work.' Among Canadian evangelicals, full institutional recognition of and training in a Magisterial Reformation concept of 'vocation' that included 'secular' work would wait until the founding of Regent College in the late 1960s, even if other evangelical leaders, notably some in Inter-Varsity

Christian Fellowship, were already coming to this understanding in that decade (as detailed in the respective chapters on these institutions).

60 'Canon Cody's Address,' *Recorder* 50 (June 1944): 3

61 W.W. Bryden testified, 'We have had many students at Knox College, but we have not had any better than J.B. Rhodes' (*Recorder* 52 [Dec. 1946]: 6).

62 Simmonds, 'Why Degree Courses at Toronto Bible College?' *Recorder* 62 (March 1956): 1–5, and 'Our New Degree Course,' *Recorder* 62 (June 1956): 1. For accounts of this development, see Gasque, 'Christian Higher Education in Canada'; Rennie, 'Theological Education in Canada'; Davis, 'New Directions in Bible College Education'; and Boda, 'Theological Education in Canada.'

63 In 1963 the B.Th. course was lengthened to four years and the BRE was provided in its place as a three-year course.

64 Simmonds, 'New Department at T.B.C.,' *Recorder* 66 (Sept. 1960): 11. The Bible School Department was for those students with up to Grade 11 standing; the Bible College Department was for high-school graduates who had completed Grade 12 and for those who had completed the Ontario honours year, Grade 13. Graduation from Grade 13, however, was required for B.Th. students.

65 McKenzie, 'History,' 11

66 *Recorder* 69 (March 1963): 3

67 McKenzie, for instance, attributes the development of this additional program to a concern to arrest declining enrolment and preserve the institution: 'In the 1950s TBC was like an animal whose food supply was dwindling due to environmental changes. It had the choice to lay down and die or to transform itself and live' (22–3).

68 D.C. Masters speaks of the generally liberal tone at the theological colleges by mid-century (*Protestant Church Colleges in Canada*, 133–211).

69 There has been yet no study of the social, economic, and cultural changes among Canadian evangelicals at large in this century (as opposed to some studies of Mennonites and a few other specific groups), so this supposition must remain tentative.

70 Similar ratios obtain in the evening class of 198 (McNicol, 'Principal's Report,' *Recorder* 25 [June 1919]: 3).

71 'Principal's Report,' *Recorder* 32 (June 1926): 2

72 'Principal's Report,' *Recorder* 45 (June 1939): 3

73 'Principal's Report,' *Recorder* 49 (June 1943): 4

74 'We Are Interdenominational,' *Recorder* 73 (Dec. 1967): 4

75 This is not to say that TBC now endorsed only this view. Discussion at TBC in the early 1960s would run its course as the Toronto and London schools joined together in order, among other things, to support a full-fledged evangelical seminary in Canada. Here would be the most direct alternative to the mainline theological seminaries, even as it reflected the original view of TBC and mainline churches alike that pastors needed university and graduate theological education. There is not so much contradiction here as the representation of and provision for the views of different sorts of evangelicals regarding pastoral education. Part 3 presents a fuller interpretation of these developments.

76 Twila F. Buttimer writes: 'In the national [Methodist] church, the social gospel contributed to the decline of evangelicalism and was adopted in its wake. Acceptance of the social gospel was largely responsible for the favorable attitude to church union. In the Maritimes, the social gospel was not a factor in the decline of evangelicalism. Rather the evangelical traditions were waning and the social gospel was deliberately adopted in the belief that a more strict application of the ideals of Jesus Christ to everyday life would lead people back to God' ('"Great Expectations."' See also Semple, 'The Decline of Revival in Nineteenth Century, Central-Canadian Methodism'; Manning, 'Changes in Evangelism within the Methodist Church in Canada'; Van Die, *An Evangelical Mind*; Gauvreau, *Evangelical Century*; and Airhart, *Serving the Present Age*.

77 See Chalmers and Grant, 'The United Church of Canada'; Grant, 'The United Church and Its Heritage in Evangelism'; Clifford, 'The United Church of Canada and Doctrinal Confession'; Gauvreau, 'History and Faith' and 'War, Culture, and the Problem of Religious Certainty.'

78 Moir, 'The Smouldering Bush.' See also Rennie, 'Conservatism in the Presbyterian Church in Canada in 1925 and Beyond'; and the work of Gauvreau, noted above.

79 See Beverley, 'National Survey of Baptist Ministers.'

80 Not all denominations recognized as 'evangelical' were equally welcome at TBC. In 1963 the board of governors met to consider the appointment to the faculty of J.H. Faught, a Pentecostal pastor in Toronto (and soon to be founder of the Evangelical Fellowship of Canada). The minutes of the meeting record President Boehmer asking the Board, 'Would our alumni and friends react favourably or

otherwise to such an appointment? Would this denominational affiliation be harmful to the welfare of the College?' Boehmer spoke highly of Faught, to be sure, and was concerned specifically about the official link of Pentecostalism to TBC. One board member, T.G. McCormack, suggested that the College 'follow the most conservative course possible, in view of its history.' This latter enigmatic phrase perhaps confirms the absence of Pentecostalism from the leadership and identity of the school. The board went on record as agreeing with this suggestion, and affiliation with Pentecostalism would await the era after the merger with London (Minutes of the TBC Board of Governors, 10 July 1963).

81 Leonard F. O'Neil speaks of Toronto Bible College as exceptional among most Canadian Bible schools in its offering of what he calls 'university-type' courses (e.g., logic, sociology, psychology) and in its faculty's possession of university and seminary education (9, 18). But as the oldest continuing Bible school in Canada and one of the largest well into the 1980s, Toronto Bible College should not be ignored in characterizations of North American Bible schools, even if it is noticed as exceptional. Ben Harder's study, for instance, would have been improved by consideration of the work of O'Neil and McKenzie (his notes do not show knowledge of their studies). These studies would have helped him qualify his judgment that the Bible school movement in Canada was 'anti-intellectual' with 'studies which were primarily inspirational and motivational in quality' (30). Consideration of Toronto Bible College's long-time links with the mainline churches would also alter somewhat Harder's judgment that 'the Bible institute/college movement in Canada was also a reaction to institutionalized Christianity as represented by the mainline Protestant denominations' (35). Brereton indicates that most Bible schools in Canada and the United States taught dispensationalism ('Bible Schools and Conservative Higher Education,' 10).

Chapter 4

1 *Catalogue of the Prairie Bible Institute 1950–51*, 17. Citations from Prairie Bible Institute documents come from those at the Institute, Three Hills, Alberta, unless otherwise noted.

2 Ibid., 18. The questions are taken from samples of the second-year course provided in the catalogue to illustrate Prairie's method.

Unfortunately, the *answers* Prairie might have offered to these intriguing questions are not recorded!

3 Gray, 'Miracle at Three Hills,' 54; vertical file, Prairie Bible Institute

4 Mary Slessor (1848–1915), a native of Scotland, served in Nigeria for almost forty years. She helped to end a number of barbaric practices among several major tribes (such as twin-killing), to provide training for Africans in profitable work and medicine, and to establish trade between the coast and the inland areas for their benefit. Slessor was a heroine to many women at Prairie, and she was chosen as a subject for the annual missionary biography night more times (four) than any other. See Meiklejohn, 'Mary Slessor.'

5 *Catalogue 1950–51*, 27

6 *Student Handbook 1975–76*, 51 (emphasis in the original)

7 This story typifies the whole of Maxwell's term of leadership (1922–77). Details would vary from one decade to the next, but this 'generic day' reflects the experience of most of Prairie's students in this half-century. Every important detail of this portrait is drawn either from Prairie documents or the observation of the author during a research visit in 1986. Indeed, it is precisely the detailed nature of Prairie's codes for student life and the similarity of these patterns over the decades here surveyed that allows for this 'composite portrait' to be drawn with a precision and concision that is regrettably impossible to attain for the other institutions in this study.

8 See this rationale, among others, given for not seeking accreditation in Ted S. Rendall, 'The Seventies – Decade of Survival?' Progress Report included with the *Prairie Overcomer* 43 (Feb. 1970): 1–3, 6–8.

9 S.A. Witmer distinguishes between Bible institutes ('more specialized ... with ... three-year diploma courses') and Bible colleges (which are 'degree-conferring' and whose curricula include 'more liberal arts or general education courses'). See his *The Bible College Story*, 37. Basically the same distinction is made by Brereton, 'The Bible Schools and Conservative Evangelical Higher Education, 1880–1940,' 128–30. This distinction has not always been observed by the schools themselves, however, as in the case of PBI itself, which changed its name for the 1987–8 school year to Prairie Bible College without significant changes in its program (Minutes of Board of Directors' Annual Meeting, 29 April 1986). For more on this change see chapter 8.

10 The story of Maxwell's coming to Prairie has been told several times. See Callaway, 'From Small Beginnings'; and Keller, *Expend-*

able! 21–76. A critical sketch of Maxwell is provided in Elliott, 'Studies of Eight Canadian Fundamentalists,' 258–76.

11 *Prospectus for 1923–24*

12 Ibid.

13 Provisions were made in the 1940s for graduates of Prairie's own high school or those with other relevant education to complete a modified form of the four-year course in three years. And a one-year diploma course was introduced at the very end of this era, in 1977.

14 1926–27, p. 10. Part 3 discusses this point and the new quest for accreditation that began in 1990.

15 Indeed, W.C. Stevens was listed as 'honorary president' of Prairie Bible Institute from the very first listing of the board of directors in a school catalogue, 1925–26, p. 7.

16 Ibid.; emphasis in original. This method was followed into the 1980s, albeit supplemented by other materials (see part 3). But Prairie at no time seemed to recognize the basic epistemological contradiction between claiming pure inductivism and having study guided by direct questions. Nor did it seem to allow for the prospect that a student indeed might come up with something truly 'original' – something that might contradict Prairie's own statement of faith. In all of this, of course, Prairie was not exceptional but rather typical of evangelicals. As has been noted, this 'cognitive style' in Canada awaits detailed study; but on this sort of epistemological naiveté in Britain and America, see Bebbington, *Evangelicalism in Modern Britain*, 50–60; Bruce, *Firm in the Faith* 186–93; Boone, *The Bible Tells Them So*; Brereton, 'Bible Schools and Conservative Evangelical Higher Education,' 10–13 and n. 28; Marsden, 'Everyone One's Own Interpreter?' and *Fundamentalism and American Culture*, 55–62, and 212–21; Weber, 'The Two-Edged Sword'; and Noll, *Between Faith and Criticism*.

17 *Prospectus of the Three Hills Bible Institute (Interdenominational) for the Year 1924–25*

18 Ibid.

19 Callaway, 'Prairie Celebrates Jubilee Year.' For a profile of the work of Prairie's missionary graduates in the early 1970s, see Epp, *Into All the World* (with a Foreword by L.E. Maxwell).

20 *Manual* for 1926–7, p. 4

21 By 1972, the school had distributed $3.5 million (Muddle, 'Prairie Missionary Fund Gives Out 3.5 Million').

22 Pentecostalism was not welcome at Prairie, as Maxwell shared the

dispensationalist belief that speaking in tongues was a gift that had passed away with the apostles. See his early statement in 'The Baptism of the Spirit,' *Prairie Pastor* 6 (Oct. 1933): 4–8. The board of directors, almost forty years later, put Prairie on record again: 'While recognizing that there are many born-again believers in its ranks, Prairie Bible Institute is not sympathetic toward the present-day tongues movement, believing its divisive teachings and tendencies are contrary to God's Word. [Presumably the insistence of some charismatics and Pentecostals that the gift of tongues marked an experience superior to that of just 'run-of-the-mill' Christians is in view here.] The Institute, therefore, does not accept or retain as staff members any who participate in the movement' (Minutes of the Board of Directors, 28 June 1971). The issue seems not to have arisen at Prairie again until after Maxwell left the president's office. (The only remarks come in a positive review by Ted Rendall of books that argued against receiving the Holy Spirit after conversion and against the present manifestation of tongues: see *Prairie Overcomer* 45 [July 1972]: 316–17.)

A bibliographic note might be helpful here. Prairie's monthly magazine was originally called the *Prairie Pastor* and was begun in January 1928. In January 1930, a magazine for youth was introduced called the *Prairie Overcomer.* In 1944 these were combined in one publication, and in January 1946 *Prairie Pastor* took the name *Prairie Overcomer* and had a separate children's section. Later, the school introduced *Young Pilot* for youth. Because this history is a little confusing, the full name of the periodical will be given in the notes.

23 Prairie's files do not record the denominational make-up of the student body until the 1968–9 school year, at which time these seven categories were best represented: Baptist, 230; Nondenominational, 75; Interdenominational, 74; Not a member, 67; Evangelical Free Church, 61; Christian and Missionary Alliance, 57; Mennonite, 36. All the rest are in the teens or lower. The largest mainline group (not counting the Baptists) are the Presbyterians at 14, while the Anglican and United churches sent 2 each. This pattern is maintained as a decade later, with Maxwell retiring as president, the numbers are as follows: Baptist, 194; Interdenominational, 79; Nondenominational, 74; Mennonite, 42; Christian and Missionary Alliance, 40; Not members, 39; Evangelical Free Church, 34; Mennonite Brethren, 34 [presumably the others are General Confer-

ence, some other kind of Mennonite, or Mennonite Brethren who did not identify themselves specifically as such]; [Christian] Brethren, 25; and Independent, 20. This year the United Church sent 7, the Presbyterians 5, and the Anglicans 2.

Establishing Prairie's constituency is much harder, then, before the late 1960s. But two kinds of evidence confirm the judgment that the pattern at Prairie, unlike the case of the Toronto Bible College, did not change much through the twentieth century, except for the rise of the Baptist churches over those calling themselves 'inter-' or 'non-denominational.' The most important indication is the one denominational list printed in *Prairie Pastor* (6 [April 1933]: 7). This lists one category called 'undenominational' as sending half of the students, 103; the Baptists sending 55; and the Christian and Missionary Alliance and Presbyterians sending 9 each. The new, small denominations sent similarly small numbers, as did the United and Anglican churches. The other indication is the cumulative record of the travels of Prairie's extension teams. From the 1940s, when their itineraries were printed in *Prairie Overcomer,* it is clear that the teams visited the churches best represented in the later denominational lists outlined above, as well as conference centres (whose denominational affiliation, if any, was not listed) and Youth for Christ meetings — especially in the 1950s. This cumulative evidence may well indicate an 'undenominationalism' among much of Prairie's constituency, a lack of regard for denominations, rather than a 'transdenominationalism,' typical of other evangelical institutions, that recognized the validity of denominations. But PBI as an institution never makes this distinction. (This point owes much to a suggestion made to me by Ian S. Rennie.)

24 O'Neil, 'A Survey of the Bible Schools in Canada,' 41

25 By 1972, 175 Prairie graduates, 10 per cent of a total Prairie missionary force of about 1600 by this time, had gone out with SIM (SIM advertisement in the *Three Hills Capital* [12 April 1972]: 7; vertical file, Prairie Bible Institute). The school regularly published its missionary disbursements in the 1940s and 1950s and the CIM and SIM were always among the top three or four in these lists.

26 The development of Prairie's physical plant, whether new buildings, farmland, or water supply, dominates several later accounts of its history. See especially the *Prairie Pastor* and its successor, the

Prairie Overcomer, throughout PBI's history; but also Davidson, *God's Plan on the Prairies.*

27 *Prospectus 1924–25*

28 'Plumbline,' *Prairie Overcomer* 42 (March 1969): 97

29 See, for example, 'You Need Bible School Training,' *Prairie Pastor* 10 (July–August 1937): 10; and 'Why Bible School First?' *Prairie Overcomer* 31 (May 1958): 183.

30 *Manual* for 1926–27, p. 4

31 Ibid., 9; for the Princeton formulation of the doctrine of Scripture see the relevant selections in Mark A. Noll, ed., *The Princeton Theology 1812–1921*. For the influence of 'Old Princeton' on American fundamentalism, see Sandeen, *The Roots of Fundamentalism*, and Marsden, *Fundamentalism and American Culture*. The influence of Princeton's formulations in Canada has yet to be measured, but an initial inquiry is recorded in Richard W. Vaudry, 'Canadian Presbyterians and Princeton Seminary, 1850–1900' (paper presented to the symposium on 'The Presbyterian Contribution to Canadian Life and Culture,' Presbyterian College, Montreal, 13 Oct. 1988).

32 'It is impossible to estimate the influence that students trained in these Bible schools have had in holding back the flood of Modernism, infidelity, and immorality that has so largely swept away righteousness and faith. No one knows to what depths society, the home and the church life would have sunk but for the Bible schools of the world' ('You Need Bible School Training,' *Prairie Pastor* 10 [July–August 1937]: 9). See also the discussion below of the issues discussed in the Prairie magazines.

33 Ibid.

34 See O'Neil, 'Survey,' 32, for a description of the usual Bible-school statement of faith. Prairie distanced itself from the Holiness movement in the 1933–4 catalogue when it changed the fourth clause to read: 'Salvation, (*not eradication*), etc.' (emphasis added), (p. 12). The Keswick form of spirituality was emphasized instead: see A.T. Pierson, 'The Keswick Movement,' *Prairie Overcomer* 29 (July 1956): 262–6. In the 1934–5 catalogue, however, the following clauses were added: 'The only true and living God, infinite, eternal, unchangeable' (now in first place); 'The virgin birth and essential deity of Jesus Christ our Lord'; 'The physical resurrection of Christ from the dead'; 'The personality and deity of the Holy Spirit, the third Person of the Holy Trinity'; 'The personality of the devil as the enemy of Christ, saints and angels'; 'The fall of man and the universal depravity of

the human race'; 'The guilty and lost condition of all men everywhere outside of Christ'; and 'The physical resurrection of all men – the saints to everlasting joy and bliss, the lost to everlasting conscious torment' (14–15).

35 *Prairie Bible Institute Catalogue 1955–56*, 5. Maxwell, who had belonged to Presbyterian and Baptist churches before his time at Midland, likely learned this emphasis from Stevens, who had taught at the Alliance school at Nyack, New York. Ted Rendall wondered if this change was delayed for the death of the revered instructor D.R. Miller, who maintained these beliefs while Maxwell did no longer (Interview). Certainly Prairie had no truck with 'faith healers': see 'Faith Healing,' *Prairie Overcomer* 28 (Aug. 1955): 288. Later Prairie's leaders restated their position regarding healing: 'While the Institute believes that God does heal and answer the prayer of faith, according to His will, our position precludes any cooperation in healing campaigns conducted by those popularly designated "faith healers" ' (Minutes of the Board of Directors, 28 June 1971). This marked off Prairie from another emphasis of much Pentecostalism and parts of the charismatic movement.

36 Prairie, like most Bible schools (Brereton, 'Bible Schools,' 10), taught dispensational eschatology (for examples of this see *Prairie Pastor* 11 [May–June 1938]: 9, and 'Mideast Miracle,' *Prairie Overcomer* 47 [Sept. 1974]: 407–8). But it was not wholly dispensational. Maxwell, for instance, differed from dispensationalists in his holding of a Reformed understanding of the Old Testament Law as useful in the life of the Christian, while dispensationalists saw the Law to be utterly irrelevant to the dispensation of grace. See Maxwell's *Crowded to Christ* (Grand Rapids, Mich.: Wm. J. Eerdmans 1950; reprint ed., Three Hills, Alta.: Prairie Press 1974). Further, according to Ted Rendall, Maxwell 'often quoted the original *Scofield Reference Bible*'s comments on the giving of the law at Sinai to illustrate what he had concluded was an erroneous approach to the function of law.' This approach, says Rendall, made Moody Press, a dispensational publisher, reject Maxwell's book while Wm. J. Eerdmans, of the Christian Reformed, published it (Ted S. Rendall, 'L.E. Maxwell – His Literary Legacy,' *Prairie Overcomer* 57 [May 1984]: 27).

37 *Prairie Pastor* 11 (Nov.–Dec. 1938): n.p.; *Prairie Pastor* 5 (June 1932): 3

38 Maxwell, 'The Coming School Year,' *Prairie Pastor* 1 (Sept. 1928): 3

39 Their joint position was that men should be in authority in the church and that gifted women could preach under that authority. See D.R. Miller, 'On Women Speaking,' and Maxwell's appendix to this article in *Prairie Pastor* 12 (Dec. 1939): 7–8. Some would see this as ambivalence or even hedging on the issue of the full role of women in the church. Certainly Prairie never wholeheartedly endorsed the full equality of the sexes in terms of leadership in the church.

There is a little evidence as well that Prairie's openness to women preaching and teaching was rooted in the so-called 'missionary exception' among evangelicals: the idea that normally women shouldn't preach, but on the mission field, with the need so great and no men around, they should: 'When so many ministers of the stronger and wiser sex are useless or worse than useless in the work of soul saving, and preach for years without being instrumental in a single conversion, *is there not a cause* for woman's ministry? ... [Yet] had Barak better played the man, Deborah had better played the woman ... Had the disciples tarried longer at the sepulchre, Mary need not have been the first proclaimer of our Lord' (Maxwell, ' "The Weaker Sex," ' *Prairie Overcomer* 39 [April 1966]: 130; emphasis his). On this see L.E. Maxwell, with Ruth C. Dearing, *Women in Ministry* (Wheaton, Ill: Victor Books 1987); and Stackhouse, 'Women in Public Ministry.'

40 For example, see 'Militancy,' *Prairie Overcomer* 46 (Jan. 1973): 24–5. And either Maxwell or, more likely, Rendall, favourably referred to similar restrictions being placed on Royal Canadian Mounted Policemen in regard to social relationships, and especially marriage (see 'Mounties and Marriage,' *Prairie Overcomer* 42 [April 1969]: 168).

41 (Three Hills, Alta.: Prairie Press 1977). See the title article in *Prairie Overcomer* 35 (March 1962): 93–97, 102–3.

42 *Handbook* for 1968–69, pp. 4–5

43 This also would qualify Brereton's judgment that since Bible-school students tended 'to get younger as a school got older,' Bible schools brought in regulations both because the students needed more discipline, since they were now in their teens rather than in their twenties, and because 'Bible schools seem to have begun to admit students who were there simply because their parents thought attendance would do them good' ('Bible School,' 24–5). Prairie always attracted a large number of older students: its 1985–6 school popula-

tion had an average age of over twenty-four years old (registrar's files). It is appropriate to conclude that Prairie, and possibly then other Bible schools as well, had regulations chiefly because of the ethos of the school, however much the aforementioned concerns might also be met thereby. For other brief critiques of the spirituality behind Maxwell's regulations, see Rennie, 'The Doctrine of Man in the Canadian Bible Belt,' and Elliott, 'Eight Canadian Fundamentalists.'

44 This concern surfaced almost immediately at Prairie: see ' "Women's Dress," ' *Prairie Pastor* 1 (Sept. 1928): 1–2, and the discussion of this 'all-important subject' in the catalogue for 1928–9, p. 21.

45 Men's hair length was regulated first in the 1959–60 handbook (25). Facial hair began to be regulated in the handbook for 1970–1, 64.

46 *General Information 1947–48,* 12

47 Ibid. The pages of *Prairie Overcomer* also explained the school's position on this matter. See, for example, Ruth C. Dearing, 'For Women Only,' 45 (April 1972): 186–9.

48 *Handbook 1975–76,* 49. Maxwell's most popular book was entitled *Born Crucified* (Chicago: Moody Press 1945).

49 For the story of the Maxwells' courtship, which involved three years of engagement and separation while Maxwell began the school, see Keller, *Expendable,* 88–94.

50 This reflected Prairie's wide-ranging extension work in the United States. From the beginning, teams travelled not only to Canadian provinces but also to American states, especially those of the Northwest and California. By the 1950s, the number of meetings held across the United States as far east as the seaboard (although not to the southeast) roughly equalled the number of meetings held across Canada. (One sheet of statistics details the number of meetings held in and the number of students received from each state and province for the decade 1947–57: these statistics bear out this summary of the longer period [registrar's records]).

51 The foreign contingent increased during the 1960s: 1966–7 saw the international students make up more than 5 per cent of the student body for the first time, and in most years in the 1970s and 1980s about 10 per cent of the students came from outside Canada or the United States.

52 These numbers probably were increased through the success of the Oscar Lowry radio broadcasts, sponsored by Prairie over Calgary's CFCN in 1938. The story of these broadcasts has been told by W.E.

Mann, *Sect, Cult, and Church in Alberta*, 122–3; and Goertz, 'The Development of a Bible Belt,' 217–19. Goertz quotes Maxwell later saying that Lowry 'came along and put us ... on the map' (interview, no date or location, p. 205). For Prairie's own account see *Prairie Pastor* 11 (Nov.-Dec. 1938): 9, and 12 (Jan. 1939): 1–10. The power of these broadcasts seems exceptional in Prairie's history (Goertz says over one thousand conversions were reported; p. 218). Prairie maintained broadcasts on several Canadian and American stations ever after, but never enjoyed this measure of response to its own programs.

53 I erroneously reported PBI's status as the largest Bible school in the *world* in 'The Protestant Experience in Canada since 1945,' in *The Canadian Protestant Experience 1760–1990*, 205. Moody Bible Institute in Chicago, at least, was always larger than Prairie.

54 As Witmer suggests, 51–2

55 This interpretation originates with Mann's oft-cited study and has been perpetuated in the writings of Ian S. Rennie (see, for example, 'The Western Prairie Revival in Canada').

56 See representative comments regarding 'ecumania' in *Prairie Overcomer* 37 (Dec. 1964): 449; and regarding the One World Church, seen as the goal of the ecumenical movement identified with the Whore of Babylon, in *Prairie Overcomer* 39 (Sept. 1966): 329.

57 See, for example, the early reprint of Louis S. Bauman's article in the American fundamentalist journal *King's Business*, 'Socialism, Communism, Fascism: "Three Unclean Spirits like Frogs," ' *Prairie Pastor* 8 (June–July 1935): 2–6.

58 See below for linkage of Roman Catholicism with communism. For the linkage of Roman Catholicism with ecumenism see Maxwell, 'Ecumenism, or The Woman in the Saddle,' *Prairie Overcomer* 40 (Jan. 1967): 15–20, and (Feb. 1967): 56–9. And for the linkage of ecumenism and communism see idem, 'Perspective: The World Council of Churches,' 45 (Feb. 1972): 72–3; Maxwell wrote here especially of WCC funding of Marxist revolutionaries in Africa. Marsden discovers a similar trio in American fundamentalism, but finds evolution, rather than Roman Catholicism, in the 'big three'; see especially part 4 of his *Fundamentalism and American Culture.* For evolution at Prairie, see below.

59 Here the *Prairie Overcomer* links together Roman Catholicism and communism concisely: 'Communism can flourish best in prepared

soil. The priest-ridden Russians [although the priests here were Eastern Orthodox!] created a perfect soil for Communistic Bolshevism. Poverty-stricken Italy, where Catholicism has dominated for so long, is Western Europe's chief hotbed of Communism. A contemporary well says, "The Papacy breeds Communism." Catholic Quebec is frightened to death of Communism. These two totalitarian powers vie for authority over the masses' ('Communism,' *Prairie Overcomer* 23 [June–July 1950]: 132). On another occasion one short piece on Soviet Communism was entitled, 'Encircling,' and the next piece, on Roman Catholicism, 'Encircled' (*Prairie Overcomer* 28 [Jan. 1955]: 10). And Maxwell treated the quest for world domination by both again in 'Perspective,' *Prairie Overcomer* 50 (Jan. 1977): 31–2.

The hostility towards Roman Catholicism must be understood in the light of the Canadian, and especially the Quebec, experience. Protestant evangelists in Quebec at mid-century were shouted down, threatened, beaten, and occasionally jailed – sometimes at the request of the local priest with the consent of the local government. Prairie's journal records some of these incidents, but the cases were well known across Canada before the 1960s when this degree of hostility ebbed. (For Prairie's perspective on these things, see Louis J. Germain, 'Persecution in Canada,' *Prairie Pastor* 14 [Jan. 1943]: n.p.; 'Inside Quebec,' *Prairie Pastor* 17 [Aug. 1944]: 138–9; 'Persecution,' *Prairie Overcomer* 23 [July 1950]: 131–2; and 'Regrettable,' *Prairie Overcomer* 24 [Oct. 1951]: 290–1).

60 See, among other references, 'Fosdick,' *Prairie Overcomer* 20 (April–May 1947): 102–3; 'Fosdick,' *Prairie Overcomer* 27 (June 1954): 174; 'Fosdick – "That Fox" ' *Prairie Overcomer* 32 (Jan. 1959): 8–9.

61 Maxwell and his associates certainly were not fond of the church they saw to be a hotbed of liberal theology, moral decay, and ecumenism: see, for example, 'Immorality Endorsed' and 'Religion at the U. of A.,' *Prairie Overcomer* 41 (Jan. 1968): 19. The United Church Sunday school curriculum, which offended many evangelicals across denominational lines, came in for criticism from the Institute: see *Prairie Overcomer* 37 (Sept. 1964): 328–31, and the comment that the decline in United Church Sunday school enrolment from 1962–70 was perhaps 'a great mercy that fewer Canadian children and young people are being fed the teachings of that

Church's new curriculum' ('"Path to Oblivion,"' *Prairie Overcomer* 43 [Dec. 1970]: 547).

62 See the delight over the exposure of 'Piltdown Man' expressed in 'Hoax,' *Prairie Overcomer* 27 (Jan. 1954): 4–5. Prairie's antipathy for evolution is reflected in the judgment that 'theistic evolution' was the worst choice of all, compromising both evolution and Christian belief in creation: see 'Evolution versus Creation,' *Prairie Overcomer* 38 (Jan. 1965): 13.

63 E.g., 'Disillusionment,' *Prairie Overcomer* 42 (March 1969): 115

64 See 'Mackenzie King and Spiritualism,' *Prairie Overcomer* 25 (Feb. 1952): 49–56. Prairie's positive appraisal of politicians, rare indeed, tended to be on the same grounds – personal character and spirituality. For instance, when E.C. Manning, Aberhart's successor as Social Credit premier of Alberta, gave his last speech as provincial leader, the *Prairie Overcomer* testified: 'It is no secret that Mr. Manning is an evangelical Christian. Throughout his thirty-three years of government service he has sought to maintain a witness for the Lord Jesus Christ ... The people of Alberta may well be thankful to God for the leadership of such a man for over thirty years' ('Honour to Whom Honour,' 42 [Feb. 1969]: 65).

One rare evaluation of a government's actual record came as the Progressive Conservatives under Peter Lougheed came to power in Alberta in 1971, ending the reign of the Social Credit party: 'We give thanks to God for government that has generally sought to build on principles of justice and righteousness.' But this is the exception that proves the rule (*Prairie Overcomer* 44 [Nov. 1971]: 497).

65 See the Prairie Bible Institute board minutes for 13 June 1932 (? – the year is not given, but this seems the best guess, given what we know of Aberhart) and for 6 March 1934. See also the 'Resolution' from the latter meeting published in *Prairie Pastor* 7 (March–April 1934): 9.

66 '"Let 'Em Starve,"' *Prairie Overcomer* 48 (Aug. 1975): 451–2. Chapter 2 above refers to Prairie's reaction to Aberhart's doctrines and participation in politics rather than preaching. And the editors encouraged their readers to pray about the dangerous proliferation of nuclear arms – this was the most important and powerful thing they could do about this problem (*Prairie Overcomer* 39 [Aug. 1966]: 291–2).

67 The most graphic evidence comes from a survey of the indices for

each year of the *Prairie Pastor* or *Prairie Overcomer*. The entries under the 'Bible' and 'Missions' headings were always numerous: only in one year (1984) – well after Maxwell had given up leadership – did the entries under 'Prophecy' outnumber those in the other categories; normally the articles on prophecy were few.

68 Articles on revival became common as Ted Rendall took on more of the editing responsibilities in 1957. By the mid–1970s, the January issue was devoted to revival. Before this era, however, most of the articles dealt with personal spirituality, and especially Bible study and prayer. And Bible studies-cum-sermons frequently were published throughout the life of the magazine.

69 The magazines reprinted especially five sorts of authors. The first group was nineteenth-century evangelical preachers or devotional writers, both British and American, such as Charles G. Finney, F.B. Meyer, D.L. Moody, George Müller, Andrew Murray, and Charles H. Spurgeon. The second category was nineteenth-century orthodox Protestant theologians, again both British and American, such as J.C. Ryle and three of the Princetonians, Archibald Alexander, Charles Hodge, and B.B. Warfield. The third category included leaders of Canadian, American, and British fundamentalism, such as Dyson Hague, A.C. Dixon, C.I. Scofield, Bob Jones, and Philip Mauro. The fourth type of author was the famous missionary or missionary statesman, whether past or contemporary: Rowland V. Bingham, Jonathan Goforth, A.B. Simpson, and C.T. Studd. Finally, Prairie's magazine frequently excerpted items from the writings of contemporary Canadian, British, and American evangelical preachers and writers, such as H.A. Ironside, D. Martyn Lloyd-Jones, Oswald J. Smith, John R.W. Stott, and A.W. Tozer.

Put negatively, while the Prairie magazine editors drew on a wide range of modern evangelical authors, they – like many evangelicals – seem completely to be cut off from the rest of the church in history. (This selection is reflected in the personal favourites in Maxwell's library: see the list compiled by Ted S. Rendall, 'Authors He Loved,' *Prairie Overcomer* 57 [May 1984]: 12–15.) This lack of conscious connection with the church's heritage of missions is underscored by the fact that in the forty years in which Prairie students presented two biographies of missionaries at an annual 'Biography Night,' only five subjects dated from before the nineteenth century, and of these at least three, Martin Luther, John Bunyan, and John Newton are hardly remembered especially for missionary work! Patrick, Boniface, Cyril and Methodius, Llull, Xavier, Ricci, and a host of other famous missionaries were ignored in favour of such minor figures in recent evangelicalism as Malla Moe, Ramabi Mukti, and Mary Reed.

70 Later in Maxwell's career and beyond, the whole March issue normally was devoted to missions.

71 The editors of the *Prairie Overcomer* state flatly as late as the mid–1970s: 'There is really no alternative to total abstinence' (49 [April 1976]: 208). For comments on the last three, see, respectively, *Prairie Overcomer* 17 (March 1944): 49–50; 24 (Sept. 1951): 258–60; and 29 (Dec. 1956): 445.

72 See, among many other references, 'Proper Child Discipline,' *Prairie Pastor* 17 (Aug. 1944): 161–4; and 'Spank or Not,' *Prairie Overcomer* 20 (Feb. 1947): 34–5.

73 For example, 'Death Penalty,' *Prairie Overcomer* 46 (March 1973): 120–1; and the booklet of radio messages by Maxwell published as *Capital Punishment* (Three Hills, Alta.: Prairie Press 1976).

Chapter 5

1 Interview with Melvin V. Donald, Willowdale, Ontario, December 1986. Donald contributed further information in a telephone interview in April 1987. Donald (at the time of the interviews a pastor with the Fellowship of Evangelical Baptist Churches of Canada) was later president of this early chapter of the Inter-Varsity Christian Fellowship, and, in a record of service sandwiching theological study and a missionary career with the Sudan Interior Mission in Ethiopia (1949–70), worked with Inter-Varsity as associate general director (1941–4), staff worker (1946–7), Ontario divisional director (1977–80), and deputy general director (1980–1). He authored a brief but helpful paper, *History of Canadian Inter-Varsity Christian Fellowship, 1928–1983*, and completed an unpublished history of Inter-Varsity in Canada in 1988 (revised in 1991), 'A Spreading Tree' (a small number of copies were distributed by Donald).

2 C. Stacey Woods, general secretary of the Fellowship from 1934–52, reported that Inter-Varsity's ministry was to 'two types of students – those coming from a fundamental background whose environment has been so restricted to exclusively Christians that they are ill at ease in secular surroundings and the other type who have been

converted from a non-Christian or partly religious environment and who are at home with unchurched students. It is with this latter type that our work has been most blessed' (Minutes of the Board of Directors, 17 May 1945; all citations from Inter-Varsity documents are from those at the National Office, Toronto, unless otherwise noted).

3 This chapter relies on interviews granted by former Chairmen of the Inter-Varsity board of directors Clifford C. Pitt, L. Claude Simmonds, and Richard Vosburgh; then-current Chairman John Irwin; former General Directors H.W. 'Wilber' Sutherland and A. Donald MacLeod; and then-current General Director James E. Berney. All of the interviews were conducted in the Toronto area in December 1986, except for the Vosburgh interview, conducted in Guelph, Ontario, and the Berney interview, conducted by telephone in March 1987.

4 One author enthusiastically traces the impetus back to the English Reformation itself: see Hills, 'How It All Began.'

5 The centennial history of CICCU is Oliver R. Barclay, *Whatever Happened to the Jesus Lane Lot?*

6 For the history of IVF, known since 1974 as the Universities and Colleges Christian Fellowship (Donald's paper mistakenly calls it the Universities and *Community Colleges* Fellowship; p. 1), see Coggan, ed., *Christ and the Colleges*, and Johnson, *Contending for the Faith*. Other helpful background is provided in the large thesis by Phillips, 'The History of the Inter-Varsity Christian Fellowship in Western Canada,' 7–32; in Jones, 'The Inter-Varsity Christian Fellowship in the United States,' 14–57; and in Hunt, *For Christ and the University*.

7 For the SCM in Canada, see Beattie et al., *A Brief History of the Student Christian Movement in Canada 1921–1974*; Kirkey, ' "Building the City of God" '; and McCarville, 'The SCM: A Very Brief History.'

This is as close as the history of Inter-Varsity in Canada seems to get to supporting Phillips's contention that IVCF 'grew out of the Fundamentalistic[sic]-Modernist controversy of the 1920s' (vi). Rather, the roots of Inter-Varsity go back behind the 1920s and overseas to England to differences then and there that have some formal similarities to the so-called Fundamentalist-Modernist controversies on this side of the Atlantic, but few historical connections. Indeed, the clearly identifiable fundamentalists in Canada, T.T. Shields being the most notable, had little to do with Inter-Varsity, and Inter-Varsity's success in representing students from across the denominational board (including the two chief targets of fundamentalist ire, the Baptist Federation of Canada and the United Church) belies this characterization of its roots in what in Canada was a narrow dispute mostly among Baptists and Presbyterians.

8 This is the origin of camping ministry for IVCF, rather than the American revivalist tradition of family 'camp meetings' that later developed permanent sites and camps for children alone as well as for families.

9 This was the term taken over from the British for the chief officer of the group. It was later changed to 'general director.' In the discussion that follows the apposite term is used, but the terms are synonymous.

10 Inter-Varsity Christian Fellowship in Canada is known by several abbreviations: IVCF, I-V, Inter-Varsity, and, occasionally, VCF. Context dictates whether the whole organization or just the university work is meant. Inter-School Christian Fellowship has just one common abbreviation, ISCF.

11 Woods had been raised among the Christian Brethren, but at this time in his life was more closely attached to the Anglican communion. For his account of the early days of Canadian IVCF and the history of the American movement, see his *The Growth of a Work of God*.

12 The statement later was altered slightly as the word 'unique' was inserted before the word 'divine' in article 1, and the word 'vicarious' was changed to 'substitutionary' in article 3 (Minutes of the Board of Directors, 21 Sept. 1938). The latter change aroused at least one American board member to request the record show that 'by this article it was understood that the Lord Jesus Christ died for the sins of the world.' The board decided to say instead that 'the death of Christ was a sufficient sacrifice for the sins of the world' (ibid., 6 Feb. 1942). This seeming Calvinistic response to a seeming Arminian objection did not satisfy the plaintiff, but the board decided that 'nothing further could be done' (ibid., 26 May 1942). This is the only evidence in the minutes, however intriguing, of a Calvinistic majority on the board, and should not be pressed.

13 Letter from Hill to Lawrence Neale Jones, 5 July 1960, quoted in Jones, 'Inter-Varsity Christian Fellowship,' 144–5. Inkster, pastor of Knox Presbyterian Church, was one of the leaders of those Presbyterians who did not join the United Church of Canada in 1925. For

his role, see Clifford, *The Resistance to Church Union in Canada 1904–1939*, passim.

14 Quoted from 'Constitutional Draft,' 1934, by Phillips, 'History,' 105

15 And once again, as in the case of Prairie Bible Institute and especially of Toronto Bible College, a group of evangelicals predominantly premillennial in their eschatology refuses to militantly defend their belief, much less champion dispensational eschatology. This serves to question further the thesis of R.G. Sawatsky that turn-of-the-century Toronto evangelicals were brought together pre-eminently by eschatological concerns, rather than traditional evangelical ones: if this were so, why does this focus play so little part in the formation of evangelical institutions in the very next generation? See Sawatsky, ' "Looking for that Blessed Hope." '

16 Report of the Annual Conference, 18–23 Sept. 1931, quoted in Phillips, 'History,' 85. This was not mere lip-service to the idea of cooperation: as late as 1952 General Secretary Stacey Woods could report on some association with the SCM. Indeed, Woods pointed out to the board of directors that 'Canada was the only English speaking IVCF which continues to associate with the SCM' (Minutes of the Board of Directors, 9 Feb. 1952). And ten years later the board was still having to allay the fears of constituents that IVCF's involvement with some SCM chapters did not mean any straying from evangelical principles (see ibid., 22 Oct. 1963). Phillips details much of the relationship of the IVCF and the SCM in chapter 10 of his thesis, 341–69. And Donald includes some poignant anecdotes regarding the difficulty of cooperation between the two groups in 'A Spreading Tree,' 122, 167, 170.

17 See Kirkey and Beattie for the evolution of the SCM. Indeed, by 1960, at least one IVCF chapter had adopted a radically different view of the SCM: one board member reported to the board that 'during the University of Saskatchewan mission the VCF considered the SCM as a mission field' (Minutes of the Board of Directors, 6 Feb. 1960).

18 'Statement regarding Interdenominational Character of the IVCF of Canada,' Minutes of the Board of Directors, 7 May 1949

19 John Webster Grant links IVCF with only the small, uniformly evangelical denominations in *The Church in the Canadian Era,* 179. This interpretation is echoed in Robert T. Handy, *A History of the Churches in the United States and Canada,* 411, 422. The denominational representation in the leadership, staff, and students connected with Inter-Varsity through this period, however, has not been

established yet. Phillips has broken some ground here, but tends to overplay the undoubted importance of evangelical Anglicans and Christian Brethren in making his case for the English, rather than indigenously Canadian, character of Inter-Varsity. Even by his accounts the movement from its earliest days involved members of Presbyterian and Federation Baptist churches and of many of the smaller, uniformly evangelical denominations. To be sure, the presence of Anglicans and Brethren in the leadership of Inter-Varsity is remarkable: it was not until Samuel Escobar came in 1972 that Inter-Varsity had a general director who was not identified with either the Anglicans or Brethren. But the early and continuing presence of evangelicals of other traditions cautions against overemphasizing this fact.

The one mainline group consistently missing from leadership was the United Church. One sounding, however, a document describing Inter-Varsity composed by General Secretary Wilber Sutherland in 1965, indicates that Inter-Varsity served the United Church as well. This report lists the denominational affiliations of the staff, and the United Church with 5 joins the 'Convention Baptists' (that is, members of the Baptist Convention of Ontario and Quebec, associated with the Baptist Federation of Canada) as having the largest contingents: the Anglicans have 4, the Presbyterians and Associated Gospel churches have 3, and other, smaller denominations are represented by 1 or 2 others (Sutherland, 'Inter-Varsity Christian Fellowship of Canada,' [1965], 1, personal files of H.W. 'Wilber' Sutherland, Toronto [mimeographed paper]; this collection in further references will be abbreviated as 'Sutherland files').

This staff profile is mirrored in the list Sutherland appends to his presentation of the number of Canadian students attending the previous year's Urbana missionary convention. The largest group are the Convention Baptists with 230; then Mennonites with the surprising number of 147 (as we have seen, Mennonites began to join the mainstream of Canadian evangelicalism in the 1950s and 1960s); the United Church is next with 89, then the Anglicans with 64, the Presbyterians with 59, the Christian and Missionary Alliance with 48, and other churches significantly further back. Again, the Plymouth or Christian Brethren deserve notice, however, since the number of students who list themselves as one of 'Brethren,' 'Christian Brethren,' or 'Plymouth

Brethren' is 122, which places them third on the list ('Addendum C,' n.p.). These numbers, admittedly a sample not strong enough to build an entire case upon, yet indicate that Inter-Varsity's declared interest of serving evangelicals across denominational lines was actualized, and that it reached the mainline churches significantly, as well as the uniformly evangelical groups.

There are a few other indications of mainline denominational support for IVCF as well. In 1965, General Director Wilber Sutherland accepted an invitation by the Presbyterian church to sit on its Committee for Higher Learning (Minutes of the Board of Directors, 12 June 1965). Earlier, the Presbyterian church had decided to split its annual grant between SCM and IVCF, an increase for the IVCF at the expense of the SCM (ibid., 15 June 1963). And by 1965 Inter-Varsity was receiving contributions from both the Presbyterian church and the Baptist Federation of Canada (Sutherland, 'Inter-Varsity Christian Fellowship of Canada,' 2).

20 Woods, 'General Secretary's Report, 1936–37'

21 'Report of the Associate General Secretary before Meeting of the Board of Directors, Canada, May 26, 1943,' 3

22 Ibid., 2. Donald reported too that the high-school work in the Maritimes was also 'negligible' (6) and that Teachers Christian Fellowships existed in all provinces except the Maritimes (8), indicating a general lack of support among Maritime Christians for the sort of transdenominational evangelicalism IVCF represented (since the SCM cannot be blamed for the problems in the high schools). Budget and donation records indicate that it was not until the 1960s that Maritimers became full-fledged participants in IVCF, and at the end of Wilber Sutherland's tenure the Atlantic provinces (including Newfoundland, which joined Confederation in 1949 in the middle of this narrative) had but one representative out of twenty-six on the board (see table 3 in Phillips, 'History,' 310).

23 'Resolutions Passed by Inter-Varsity Christian Fellowship Staffs, U.S.A. and Canada, at Staff Conference, September 9–18, 1942, to Be Submitted to the Boards of Directors,' 1

24 'Letters Patent Incorporating ... Inter-Varsity Christian Fellowship of Canada,' 16 Oct. 1944, n.p.

25 See Phillips, 'History,' passim; and Donald, 'A Spreading Tree,' passim.

26 The program of the conference is reproduced in part in Donald,

Inter-Varsity Christian Fellowship, 4. The presence of Maxwell at the conference was a contact between the rural prairie evangelicals and the evangelicals of Canada's cities and universities involved with IVCF that was rare until the 1960s.

27 Phillips, 'History,' 170

28 A pamphlet circulated among Inter-Varsity chapters in Canada and the United States in the 1970s (*Grow a Campus Booktable*) described the first 'evangelistic booktable' as being at the University of California, Berkeley, in 1965. But Stacey Woods described the beginning of the establishment of 'Inter-Varsity book shelves' in each of the Canadian universities, shelves that would supply the students with 'the best in Christian Evidences, Apologetics, and Missionary Endeavour,' in his Report of 1936–7 (2).

29 H.W. 'Wilber' Sutherland, report on Staff Conference, in Minutes of the Board of Directors, 3 June 1950

30 Five years later he joined the faculty of Toronto Bible College.

31 See the general secretary's report to the board of directors in the Minutes of the Board of Directors, 19 May 1947.

32 Donald, *History*, 3; the source for Donald's figure might be extrapolation from the figure of 180 given by Vincent Craven in his report to the board in 1948 (Minutes of the Board of Directors, 8 June 1948).

33 Ibid.

34 So said Sutherland, as he reminisced in his last report to the board in 1970 ('General Director's Report,' 26 June 1970). And Woods himself had indicated that he preferred his successor to be 'a leader who is a Canadian, and an ordained minister of one of the major denominations' – three criteria of which Sutherland met only the first (Woods, 'General Secretary's Report,' Minutes of the Board of Directors, 19 May 1947, 9).

35 Minutes of the Board of Directors, 20 Sept. 1958

36 See Robin W. Winks, *The Blacks in Canada*.

37 For Pentecostalism in Canada see the following: Kulbeck, *What God Hath Wrought*, the only published attempt at a comprehensive history; Hawkes, 'Pentecostalism in Canada'; Kydd, 'The Pentecostal Assemblies of Canada and Society'; Peters, *The Contribution to Education by the Pentecostal Assemblies of Canada*; Riss, *A Survey of Twentieth-Century Revival Movements in North America*, passim; and an editorial, 'Growing Churches in the Sixth Decade 1968–1978,' *Pentecostal Testimony* (Sept. 1978): 4–7. The Canadian

movement of charismatic renewal, which overlapped with but was also distinct from both Pentecostalism and evangelicalism, has only one account: Al Reimers, *God's Country*. Ronald Kydd has looked at 'Pentecostals, Charismatics and the Canadian Denominations.'

38 Quoted by Board Director David Stewart from the minutes of the Central Ontario Regional Executive of 2 March 1965, in the Minutes of the Board of Directors, 12 June 1965

39 Minutes of the Board of Directors, 18 Sept. 1965

40 Minutes of the Special Meeting of the Executive Committee, 27 Nov. 1965; quoted with only minor grammatical corrections

41 Minutes of the Board of Directors, 27 Nov. 1965

42 Minutes of the Executive Committee, 5 Jan. 1967

43 Letter of Sutherland to Herbert Butcher, 4 June 1968; quoted in Phillips, 'History,' 257

44 'Inter-Varsity Christian Fellowship,' 3–4. Since Inter-Varsity as a whole never insisted on formal membership and usually did not keep records of individual chapters, however, it is difficult to know what a word like 'involving' meant and estimates of the numbers of students 'involved' are impossible to verify precisely.

45 Minutes of the Board of Directors, 7 and 8 June 1968. These 'associate staff' were those who had other jobs who none the less devoted a portion of their time to IVCF work.

46 Phillips devotes a chapter to Pioneer Camps, 'History,' 412–46. For the judgment that camping, and in particular the year-round facilities at Sundre Lodge, played a crucial role in Alberta Inter-Varsity, see p. 432; and Donald, 'A Spreading Tree,' 258.

47 Inter-Varsity's work in French-speaking Quebec became known as Groupes Bibliques Universitaires, first mentioned in the Minutes of the Board of Directors, 24 Sept. 1966. Among English-speaking Quebecers Inter-Varsity had grown up since the 1930s, especially at McGill University.

48 Wilber Sutherland explained this decline in 1970: 'This ... decline has been in part a deliberate shrinkage due to the recognition that the staff available to service ISCF clubs could not adequately service according to the demands of the 1960s the number of Clubs they looked after during the 1950s. Changes in the life style and interests of teenagers require far more of the leadership abilities and the time of adults working with them now than formerly. Furthermore, it proved impossible for staff to take the time to explore in depth various new possibilities of evangelistic outreach while struggling to

maintain existing programs on an extensive basis' ('General Director's Report,' 26 June 1970). At least a couple of well-placed observers believed that the decline in the ISCF was also due to poor leadership, even deliberate neglect, on the part of Sutherland who, these critics saw, was preoccupied with the university work (see R.E. Robins's remarks, cited below; this is the view of Melvin Donald also [interview]).

49 To be sure, these changes occurred only towards the end of Sutherland's tenure. As late as 1965 Sutherland could speak of these fellowships as well as those for the high-school students as basically strong (although the critics mentioned above might dispute this) and serving, with the university chapters, a total of at least 20,000 students regularly each week ('Inter-Varsity Christian Fellowship,' 1).

50 One 'similar organization' meant here might have been the Canadian School of Missions and Ecumenical Institute in Toronto, which IVCF joined as an 'observer' in 1965 only after considerable discussion and some disagreement among board members (Minutes of the Board of Directors, 13 March 1965).

51 Minutes of the Board of Directors, 22 Oct. 1963. Cf. the amendment to the minutes carried in the Minutes of 23 Nov. 1963.

52 Inter-Varsity was now entering a period of deficit budgets. Donald links this with the board's decision in 1966 to change IVCF's policy of staff remuneration 'from that of payment on a subsistence scale without guarantee to that of a modest commercial standard to be paid in full in a given year' ('A Spreading Tree,' 209). The first report of financial trouble was in the Minutes of the Board of Directors, 27 Nov. 1965. The Minutes of the Special Meeting of the Board of Directors, 27 May 1969, show that the board continued to discuss the financial crisis. And Sutherland still addressed a 'deficit situation' in his last general director's report in 1970 (26 June 1970, p. 9).

53 See the Minutes of the Board of Directors' Special Meetings, 28 Nov. 1966 and 19 Jan. 1967.

54 Appendix to 'The Objectives and Philosophy of Inter-Varsity Christian Fellowship,' 4 Jan. 1967, p. 9; Sutherland files. Sutherland was moving towards these ideas as early as the late 1950s. In an address to a seminar at Yale Divinity School in 1958, Sutherland anticipated some of his later statements while yet holding back from full-fledged Reformed ideas of cultural influence. He said, for instance, that 'Inter-Varsity then encourages Christians to filter out into the

entire life of the university not only serving as a living, speaking witness to their growing understanding of the truth as it is in Jesus Christ but also acting as the salt of university society. At the same time Inter-Varsity believes that the essential concern of these Christians in their corporate identity within the university is not the reform of the university but the proclamation to it of the gospel ... To attempt ... to face outwards to the university so as to try to make the university a Christian society or "more" Christian would be, in the opinion of Inter-Varsity as an evangelical movement, to accept a false view of the world and of the church.'

These ideas were predicated on Sutherland's view at the time that individuals were to penetrate society with Christian influence while yet maintaining a 'high view of the "separateness" of the Christian life,' an idea Sutherland attributed to Inter-Varsity's 'evangelical heritage.' He believed at the same time that 'the church *qua* church is not essentially called to participate in the life of society but rather to proclaim to it through the life of its individual members ... the Good News of God's salvation' ('The Character and Philosophy of an Evangelical Student Movement,' address given at the Seminar on Current Issues in College Religious Leadership, Yale Divinity School, 23 Oct. 1958, p. 6; Sutherland files [typescript copy]). A decade later Sutherland would not be making these distinctions between individual and corporate missions.

55 It is important to distinguish this evangelical concern for separation from worldly influences from the fundamentalist concern to separate from all ecclesiastical bodies that compromise Christian doctrine. Fundamentalists, to be sure, usually shared the former concern as well, but the two concerns are different. C. Stacey Woods had sounded a similar note of concern about separation a generation before when he suggested that Inter-Varsity was not teaching young campers at Ontario Pioneer the full biblical teaching: 'Once a young person is converted at camp our responsibility toward them is not discharged. They should be made aware of the essential conflict there is between God and the world, and of the definite decision that all Christians must make if they are to go on with God. Recently a Toronto young people's leader in looking back over the apparent failure of a certain enterprise concluded that the reason that so many young [people] who had professed to accept Christ as Savior had drifted away into ineffective worldly living was that they had

not received definite teaching on the sin of worldliness and the necessity of separation' (Annual report on the summer camps and conferences to the members of the camp committee, 1941, p. 5). So Sutherland's critics had reason to believe they were witnessing a change in the character of Inter-Varsity.

56 'A Critique of the Objectives and Philosophy of Inter-Varsity Christian Fellowship as Drafted by the IVCF Steering Committee,' May 1968; Sutherland files (mimeographed paper). D.L. Moody typified this point of view in his famous phrases: 'I look upon this world as a wrecked vessel ... God has given me a lifeboat and said to me, "Moody, save all you can" ' ('The Second Coming of Christ,' *The Best of D. L. Moody*, ed. Wilbur M. Smith [Chicago: n.p., 1971], 193–5, quoted in Marsden, *Fundamentalism and American Culture*, 38).

57 Comment of Robert Jervis, Minutes of Executive Board, 6 June 1968

58 Minutes of the Board of Directors, 7 and 8 June 1968; the capital letters are in the original.

59 Sutherland had spoken of IVCF's third (missionary) purpose in broader vocational terms several years before, describing it as 'fostering of convictions of Christian vocation among students, particularly with respect to the world-wide missionary task of the church' ('Inter-Varsity Christian Fellowship of Canada,' 1). This seems to be the thinking behind the alteration of the 'missionary clause,' rather than Phillips's view that it reflected some dimming of evangelistic zeal: 'This can be understood in light of the increasing lack of interest in religion which was evidenced at the time throughout North America' (Phillips, 'History,' 257).

60 Phillips presents a table of the findings, on p. 259.

61 This is something no one seems to have seen at the time: the board didn't mention it, Sutherland never alluded to it in later reflections on this theme, and the authors of the 'Critique' themselves never discussed it directly. Again one wonders how large a role 'foreign missions' played in Inter-Varsity's self-consciousness.

62 'General Director's Report,' 26 June 1970, p. 7

63 Executive committee members were aware also that it had performed in Toronto parks that summer (Minutes of the Executive Committee, 10 July 1969).

64 See Minutes of the Executive Committee, 18 Sept. 1969, and Minutes of the Board of Directors, 20 Sept. 1969

65 A copy of the letter is appended to the Minutes of the Board of

Directors' Special Meeting, 9 Oct. 1969. Sutherland later recalled a couple of other controversies regarding CREATION 2 and understood why the troupe provoked negative responses in particular cases. He concluded, however, that the rumours of the troupe acting out sexual intercourse – the most sensational of the rumours that swirled around this episode even twenty years later – were utterly unfounded (letter to the author, 8 May 1988). Years later, though, some people in IVCF circles still talked about these issues. For instance, Ken Bresnen, IVCF staff worker in Quebec for some time, blamed a play that Sutherland had brought to Ottawa (almost certainly by CREATION 2) with setting back the work in Quebec because people from Montreal had travelled to see it and were 'quite disillusioned with Wilber' because of 'swearing and cursing' in the play (James E. Berney's report to the executive committee, 23 Sept. 1981, noted in Minutes of the Executive Committee, 26 Sept. 1981).

66 Ibid., and Minutes of the Board of Directors, 22 Nov. 1969

67 This is implicit, for instance, in Donald's 'A Spreading Tree,' 216–21.

Part Three: Introduction

1 For recent Canadian history, see Bothwell, Drummond, and English, *Canada since 1945*; Morton, 'Strains of Affluence (1945–1987)'; and McNaught, *The Penguin History of Canada*.

2 For historical surveys of Canadian religion at this time, see Handy, *A History of the Churches in the United States and Canada*; Grant, *The Church in the Canadian Era*, and Stackhouse, 'The Protestant Experience in Canada since 1945.'

3 Average church attendance among Canadian Christians dropped by one-third between 1956 and 1975 (Canadian Institute of Public Opinion, cited by Bibby, *Fragmented Gods*, 17). In the next fifteen years, it plummeted to an average weekly attendance of just over two in 10 (reported by Reginald W. Bibby in news release no. 11 of 'Project Can90,' 26 March 1991; for a published digest and commentary see the several articles in *ChristianWeek* 5 [16 April 1991]). Between 1961 and 1981, of the four largest Canadian Protestant denominations only the Lutherans – who generally kept themselves out of the mainstream of Canadian culture – reported a gain in membership (of about 21%). The others reported the following declines: United Church 13%, Anglican church 32%, and Presbyterian church 18%

(calculated from figures in Bibby, 14). In 1941, 0.5% of Canadians told census-takers that they had 'no religion'; in 1961, 4% said so; and in 1981, 7% declared that they had 'no religion' (cited by Bibby, *Fragmented Gods,* 47), and indications in early 1992 were that the 1991 census figures would be well over 10% (e.g., Bibby, 'Project Can90'). Allowing for changes in census-taking and social pressures (e.g., what questions are put to people by the census-takers and how free people feel to 'admit' to 'no religion') only, in fact, confirms the sense that Canadian culture was more openly and broadly secular than it had been in generations.

Chapter 6

1 John Webster Grant remarks on the significance of what follows as well in *The Church in the Canadian Era,* 224–5. Indeed, it is this account that first drew my attention to 'Sermons from Science' as a symbol for the evangelicalism examined here.

2 Ibid., 225

3 It is described in the official guidebook as 'a historic step in the forward march of ecumenism' (*Expo67: Official Guide,* 187).

4 The two men were Stanley D. Mackey and Malcolm G. Spankie. Much of the information in this section about the 'Sermons from Science' pavilion comes from an interview conducted with Keith A. Price, former director of the pavilion and of the succeeding organization, Christian Direction, and later minister-at-large with the Evangelical Fellowship of Canada, in Vancouver, November 1986. Further information was provided in a letter from Price received in April 1987. The *interpretation* of this information, however, should not be attributed to Price, but to the present author. Some materials relating to the pavilion are housed in the Montreal offices of Christian Direction, but little was written by Price or the other staff reflecting on the pavilion's history. Price himself is the best source of information, as he was for journalists in the days of the pavilion itself.

5 *Expo67: Official Guide, 196.* On this last point see George M. Marsden, *Fundamentalism and American Culture,* 212–1; and 'Everyone One's Own Interpreter?' In reading Marsden, though, emphasis should be given to the evangelical dependence upon 'everyday' Enlightenment-era common sense, especially in the case of Canadian evangelicals, rather than to formal Scottish Common Sense Realist philosophy per se, whose influence can hardly be

credited with the prevalence of this sort of thinking among these evangelicals. This is a point nicely developed in Michael Gauvreau, *The Evangelical Century*.

6 Donald, 'A Spreading Tree,'

7 Price recalled that 80 per cent of the money came in this form and that less than $50,000 came from foundation grants. (The statistics throughout this section come from the interview with Price.)

8 Over 8000 counsellors were trained for Expo, but only 1600 participated in the pavilion itself during the nine summers the exhibit ran. Many of the rest used the training in various evangelistic projects in their home areas.

9 In this concern, although with even more circumspection, Price stood in the evangelical tradition that included Billy Graham himself. See Stackhouse, 'A Paradigm Case.'

10 The literature on evangelicals, revivals, and communication techniques and technologies has exploded in recent decades. For an introduction, see Blumhofer and Carpenter, eds, *Twentieth-Century Evangelicalism*.

11 See the announcement in the *Evangelical Recorder* 73 (March 1967): 5; the decision to take up this responsibility was made by the TBC board of governors the previous month (see Minutes, 6 Feb. 1967). No further reference, however, is made by Toronto Bible College to its participation in this work.

12 See one counsellor's report in J.M. Murray, 'Fishing at Expo,' *Prairie Overcomer* 40 (Nov. 1967): 402–5; and also the article 'Sermons from Science,' *Prairie Overcomer* 40 (Oct. 1967): 365–6, which praised the pavilion as worthy of the support of Prairie's constituency.

13 The board of directors approved this on 27 Nov. 1965 (see minutes).

14 See Minutes of the Board of Directors, 10 June 1967; for an earlier version of the plan, see the Minutes for 11 March 1967. And for another brief description, see Donald, 225–6.

15 Price remarked that the Roman Catholic church in Quebec all but officially supported the 'Sermons from Science' pavilion. He attributed the substantial Catholic support and attendance – responsible for much of the large number of visitors to the pavilion – to the openness among many Quebec Catholics since Vatican II. The Quiet Revolution in Quebec, furthermore, already almost a decade old, surely contributed as well to the willingness of many Quebeckers to consider something other than traditional Catholicism.

16 On the sometimes uneasy relationship between the sort of Christianity represented by Moody Bible Institute and that of the Billy Graham Evangelistic Association, see Richard Quebedeaux, *The Young Evangelicals*, 25–37.

17 This is a theme addressed in part 4.

Chapter 7

1 This section has been improved by a number of conversations over several years with Ian S. Rennie, dean of Ontario Theological Seminary. I am also grateful for several informal conversations with sometime President and Chancellor William MacRae in the late 1980s, and for a telephone interview with OBC Dean Rod Wilson, 24 Aug. 1992.

2 Originally the school was called the London Bible Institute, and from 1951 to 1962 the London Bible Institute and Theological Seminary. A sketch of Mahood's career can be found in Ian S. Rennie, 'Gratitude for the Past,' *Evangelical Recorder* 90 (Spring 1984): 10–11. Rennie notes that Mahood's work as an evangelist was crowned with the reception of an honorary doctorate in Divinity from the College of the Pacific (10). It apparently is this doctorate that was 'transformed' unwittingly into a degree in medicine by the author of the 1959–62 calendar (for Americans, 'catalog') of LCBM (34; all citations from documents of the London College of Bible and Missions or Ontario Bible College and Theological Seminary come from the records of Ontario Bible College and Theological Seminary, Willowdale, Ontario, unless otherwise noted).

3 'The need for such a school in Canada was impressed upon the late Dr James M. Gray, then president of the Moody Bible Institute, Chicago. He suggested to Dr Mahood, who was at that time on the extension staff of MBI, that he should establish such a work. The shadow of that splendid "school that D.L. Moody founded" has thus been cast over LBI [London Bible Institute, as it was known at the time]. There is no established relationship existing between the schools except in the character of design and, we trust, spirit of ministry. Yet to say that the London Bible Institute is modelled after "The West Point of Christian Service" in purpose and doctrinal position is to speak volumes to multitudes of Bible believers' (LCBM Calendar for 1947–9, p. 5).

4 The original statement of faith of LCBM is much simpler and more

generic than the later nine-point statement that, among other things, set out premillennialism. There is no explicit indication in the calendars of the early years that the school taught premillennialism, but given Mahood's background at Moody it is likely that the later premillennial statement simply articulated teaching that was current in the school from its start. For the early statement, see the calendar for 1938–9, p. 4; for the later one, see the calendar for 1947–9, p. 7.

5 See the graphic representation of this agreement in OBC's symbol, introduced in the *Evangelical Recorder* 74 (Dec. 1968): 12. And see Victor Adrian's restatement of these themes in his 'President's Message to the Ontario Bible College and Theological Seminary Annual Meeting, 4 November 1979,' *Evangelical Recorder* 86 (March 1980): 3–4. (Future references in this section's notes to the *Evangelical Recorder* will show only volume, issue, and page numbers.) LCBM's calendar for 1959–62 says that almost 75 per cent of its graduates were missionaries, pastors (or their wives), or students (35).

6 Stewart L. Boehmer put it concisely in the *Evangelical Recorder*: 'We have here in Ontario two Bible Colleges 125 miles apart, with the same general objectives, seeking to attract the same students, and appealing to the same constituency for help. God's people have been increasingly complaining about what they believe to be this unwise and uneconomical manner of carrying on God's work. "Why cannot two such fine organizations merge to do not only the same job, but a better one?" they ask. We believe the question is valid' ('From the President's Desk,' 74 [March 1968]: 3). See also Boehmer's comments in the Minutes of the Ontario Bible College Corporation, 15 Nov. 1969. Less publicly, the TBC board of governors expressed concern over the chronic cash-flow problems afflicting the school in the mid-1960s, a problem hardly new in the history of TBC (e.g., Minutes of the Board of Governors, 24 Aug. 1966), and in 1968 they heard a report that the projected deficit of $50,000 after the first year of the new Ontario Bible College still would 'not place us in a worse financial position than we expect to encounter at the end of this present school year' (ibid., 29 March 1968). According to TBC Dean Strimple, 'financial factors' therefore were an important consideration in the merger, if not all-important (ibid.).

7 Literature on the history of Ontario Bible College and Ontario Theological Seminary is scarce and journalistic. An account of the early years of OBC and the founding of OTS is provided in William R. Fos-

ter, 'A Decade of Decision: 1966–76,' 90 (Spring 1984): 13–15. A friendly survey of the history of Ontario Bible College and Ontario Theological Seminary is Leslie K. Tarr, 'Bible College Grew from Evening Class.' See also Robert Joseph DeLeebeeck et al., 'Ontario Bible College Policy Report: 1975' (course paper, School of Business Administration at the University of Western Ontario, 1975), Ontario Bible College and Ontario Theological Seminary archives.

8 Cf. the statement of evangelical belief in the calendar of Ontario Theological Seminary, 1986–7, p. 10.

9 In 1967 and 1968, President Boehmer and Chairman of the Board J. William Horsey sponsored an attempt to put *Toronto* Bible College on record as premillennial. This project was abandoned in the face of what Boehmer admitted was 'much adverse criticism' from 'all parts of our constituency' (Minutes of the Board of Governors, 15 Feb. 1968). The debate began with the initial proposal at the board meeting of 16 Nov. 1967; then Boehmer reported the criticism and the board shelved the issue; when the schools joined, they refused to take a premillennial position (see ibid., 29 March 1968). This episode, centring on Boehmer, a Moody Bible Institute graduate and pastor in the Associated Gospel Churches, indicates the presence in TBC in its late years of an element quite congenial to that represented by the London school. The two types would coexist peacefully, for the most part, in the subsequent history of Ontario Bible College by emphasizing their commonalities. (Indeed, this continuing attitude probably reflects an accommodation particularly of the amillennial convictions of some members of the Fellowship of Evangelical Baptist Churches, one of the two largest denominations in OBC's constituency, as well as of many Presbyterians, traditionally among the leading denominations at OBC.) For examples of this refusal to adopt only one view of eschatology for the whole school, see William R. Foster, 'Where We Stand,' 80 (Dec. 1974): 4; Douglas Webster, 'Cutting the Word of God Straight,' 86 (March 1980): 25; and Mariano DiGangi, 'Things to Come,' 89 (March 1983): 18–19.

10 The OBC Doctrinal Statement used the adjective 'inerrant' and several articles in the *Evangelical Recorder* defended this understanding of Scripture: e.g., William R. Foster, 'Where We Stand: Our Authority – The Bible,' 79 (Dec. 1973): 4; several articles in the issue devoted to the subject, 82 (Dec. 1976); Jack Cottrell, 'The Inerrancy of the Bible,' 85 (March 1979): 12–14, and 'Objections to Inerrancy,' 85 (June 1979): 4–6 (both articles reprinted from the author's book

Solid [N.p.: Standard, n.d.], n.p.); Joel Nederhood, 'The Book without Error,' 85 (Dec. 1979): 5–9; William R. Foster, 'Our Commitment: Scripture,' 86 (Dec. 1980): 16–18; and several excerpts from James Montgomery Boice's article, 'Does Inerrancy Matter?' (Oakland, Calif.: 1979 Council on Biblical Inerrancy, n.d.) in volumes 86 and 87. Notice, however, that Ontario Theological Seminary's calendar in 1986–7 did not use 'inerrancy' or its equivalent (10), although it did so by the 1990–91 year (13). This certainly does not imply a significant difference in views of the Bible per se between the two schools, since they shared a common statement of faith, but Dean Rennie (who wrote the copy) was sensitive to the use of the term 'inerrancy' as a shibboleth in some circles and sought to articulate this doctrine in less volatile terms (telephone interview, 24 May 1990). While hardly making the case on its own, this point again indicates, perhaps, something of the accommodation at OBC/OTS of the two types of evangelicalism described throughout this study.

Regarding spirituality, it should be noted that OBC itself experienced at least one revival emerging out of a missionary conference (a pattern noted above in the histories of Toronto Bible College and Prairie Bible Institute): see Douglas C. Percy, 'When the Holy Spirit Took Over the Conference,' 78 (March 1972): 2.

11 90 (Summer 1984): back cover. For a restatement of OBC's view of missions, see Mariano DiGangi, 'Committed to Mission,' 84 (June 1978): 10–11.

12 Photographs of the site can be seen in 82 (March 1976): 13.

13 This decline is manifest in the change of venue for the annual graduation exercises. Formerly, the University of Toronto's Varsity Arena was needed to accommodate the thousands who attended (see part 2). In 1980 the school moved the ceremony to the Coliseum at the Canadian National Exhibition grounds because of problems with the City of Toronto, not because of numbers (see Minutes of the Board of Governors, 21 Sept. 1979). But by 1983 OBC needed only the facilities of the Peoples' Church in Willowdale to house the 2500 who attended that year's graduation (89 [June 1983]: 13). (Ontario Theological Seminary has held all of its graduations at Bayview Glen Church, a large Christian and Missionary Alliance church near the campus.)

14 Ian S. Rennie, 'Focus on Canada, Part III,' 89 (March 1983): 14

15 By 1970, for example, OBC graduates constituted one-third of the

pastors of both the Associated Gospel Churches and the Fellowship of Evangelical Baptist Churches (Charles A. Tipp, 'OBC and Its Pastoral Influence,' 76 [Sept. 1970]: 2).

16 See 'Who Are We?' 74 (Dec. 1968): n.p. Fourteen years later, the denominational profile was similar: the Fellowship and Convention Baptists together dwarfed all other contingents; the Associated Gospel churches, Presbyterian church, Christian and Missionary Alliance, Brethren, and Pentecostal Assemblies made up the other notable cohorts (Victor Adrian, 'President's Address to the Board and Corporation,' 6 Nov. 1982; OBC/OTS archives, FB-HI-OBC-1 [GH] 989-055).

17 Indeed, Adrian eventually left OBC to become executive secretary of the Mennonite Brethren Missions and Services (see Gordon H. Johnson, 'The Significance of Ten Years,' 88 [Sept. 1982]: 17).

18 A sketch of MacRae's career before OBC/OTS can be found in Gordon [H.] Johnson, 'OBC/OTS Appoints New President,' 89 (March 1983): 3.

19 At least three different leaders at OBC addressed the subject in the *Evangelical Recorder* and in each case the OBC teachers repudiated the Pentecostal teaching. See Robert C. Duez (dean of OBC), 'The Ministry of the Holy Spirit,' 77 (Dec. 1971): 3–5; William R. Foster (OBC executive vice-president), 'Where We Stand,' 80 (Sept. 1974): 6; and Robert Little (executive assistant to the president), ' "Be Filled with the Spirit," ' 88 (Sept. 1982): 6–8.

20 OBC recognized this trend in that it offered a concentration in 'Pre-University Studies' for B.Th. students: only a half-dozen or so each year, however, graduated from this course.

21 This is a theme in the study by DeLeebeeck et al.

22 See Ian S. Rennie, 'Theological Education in Canada: Past and Present,' paper presented at Ontario Bible College, January 1974 (photocopy).

23 OTS was awarded 'associate' status by the Association of Theological Schools in 1984 and full status in 1989. It moved into larger quarters in 1992, just after Regent took occupancy of its own new, larger space in Vancouver.

24 Notably Fuller Theological Seminary in Pasadena, California, Dallas Theological Seminary, and Wheaton College Graduate School

25 Another indication of this realignment is the list of missionaries who visited OBC during its missionary conference in 1969. Of the approximately seventy visitors listed, only six were identified with denominational missions: four with Baptist missions and two with

the Canadian Presbyterians. All the rest represented 'faith missions,' transdenominational missionary societies. See 'Thank You for Your Help!' 75 (March 1969): 9.

26 In 1986, the board of governors adopted the term 'multi-denominational' to define the school, but also used 'transdenominational' as a synonym (Minutes of the Board of Governors, 28 Feb. 1986).

27 'OTS Institutes New Two-Year Degree Program,' 84 (June 1978): 15

28 Coincident with the decline in OBC's daytime enrolment was an explosion of interest in the evening program. In 1979–80 OBC enrolled 275 evening students; three years later it enrolled 993, growth attributed by OBC's academic dean to increased publicity and the offering of the degree program through evening study. Satellite programs increased to seven locations beyond Toronto (Robert Duez, 'Unlimited Possibilities,' 90 [Spring 1984]: 18.) (Unless otherwise noted, as here, enrolment statistics come from the files of the registrar, Ontario Bible College.)

29 The offering of this course also reflected the interest of Dean Rennie who had supported this broad vocational interest as a faculty member at Regent College.

30 See the calendar for OTS 1986–7, p. 11; President's Report to the Semi-Annual Meeting of the Corporation, 11 April 1987, 5.

31 Of over 5000 graduates, OBC/OTS had knowledge of 3225 living graduates in 1980. Of this group, more than one-sixth (562) were full-time missionaries while more than one-third (1444) were in pastoral or some other kind of church-related work. The remaining third (1217) were in other vocations (86 [Dec. 1980]: 3). The OBC Self-Study submitted to the American Association of Bible Colleges in 1988 and the OTS Self-Study submitted to the Assocation of Theological Schools record a representative sample of the OBC (standing here for 'OBC/OTS') alumni files and concluded then that about 10% identified themselves as missionaries; just under 20% were in pastoral ministry; and over 15% were in 'parachurch work.' The study allowed, though, that 16% were not identified as to occupation (and some therefore may well have belonged to one of the previous categories), and of the 40% listed as having other occupations 'a significant number of these were listed as "pastor's wife" ' (160). Even a conservative estimate on the basis of the first three categories meant that a little under half of the OBC/OTS alumni were in full-time pastoral work of some sort, and perhaps in fact a slight majority were

so employed. This estimate confirms the idea that fewer OBC/OTS alumni were pursuing traditional pastoral occupations, but the comparison seems too imprecise to press.

32 On abortion, see 'Right to Life Association,' 80 (Sept. 1974): 15; Laurier LaPierre, 'The Slaughter of the Innocents,' 86 (June 1980): 7 (repr. from *Maclean's* [7 Jan. 1980]: n.p.); Robert C. Duez, 'Respect for Life: The Abortion Issue,' 89 (June 1983): 3–4; and Douglas Webster, 'What in the World Is Happening,' 91 (Summer 1985): 8–9. On pornography, see 'We Have a Voice! Let's Use It!' 80 (Dec. 1974): 23. And on the occult, see 'The Sign of the Broken Cross,' 76 (Dec. 1970): 5; several articles in 77 (Sept. 1971); and 'Playing into the Hands of the Occult,' 83 (Sept. 1977): 19.

None the less, the magazine also devoted articles to pollution (see the whole issue, 76 [Dec. 1970]); to nuclear-arms proliferation (Douglas Webster, 'Christ and Peace in the Nuclear Age,' 89 [Sept. 1983]: 4–6); to the Canadian Bill of Rights (see the whole issue, 78 [June 1972]); to feminism and women in society (see several articles in 81 [June 1975] and in 84 [Sept. 1978], plus John D. Beckett, 'The Women's Movement,' 85 [March 1979]: 6–8); and to native Canadians ('Chief Dan George: Profile of a Big Man,' 78 [June 1972]: 6–7). The *Evangelical Recorder* , however, featured articles on contemporary issues only rarely before the 1960s and frequently only since the 1970s, so the conclusions of analysis of this small a sample should not be pushed too far.

33 89 (Dec. 1983): 17. Marshall would return to OTS in a similar capacity and frequently wrote on such subjects for the Evangelical Fellowship of Canada's magazine *Faith Today* and for the biweekly *ChristianWeek.*

34 'I Can Dream, Can't I?' 89 (Sept. 1983): 10–11

35 See, as well as the articles noted below, 'Focus on Canada,' 88 (June 1982): 12. And OBC, for its part, directed students in ministry to minority and ethnic groups in Canada: see, for example, 'Evangelism at OBC,' 84 (Sept. 1978): 15–16.

36 Ian S. Rennie, 'Focus on Canada: Part VI,' 90 (Fall 1984): 18–19. While OBC did not advance as quickly as OTS did in this respect, it signalled its interest in serving Asians in particular when it appointed William Wan as dean in 1989, although Wan later resigned in 1990.

37 Victor Adrian, 'Reaching the Blacks in Toronto,' 88 (June 1982): 22

38 One should note, however, that in the late 1980s OBC did employ

Ebenezer M. Sikakane as coordinator of its missions major – a rare black in Canadian evangelical academe. In this regard of serving non-Anglo-Canadians, OBC also entered into an arrangement with Scott Theological College in Kenya that allowed this school to grant OBC degrees (Minutes of the Board of Governors, 7 March 1987).

39 For a brief account of these developments, see John G. Stackhouse, Jr., 'The Protestant Experience in Canada since 1945,' in Rawlyk, ed., *The Canadian Protestant Experience*, 228–9.

Chapter 8

1 The elder Maxwell died at 86 in 1984 at Three Hills, Alberta. See Richard Hoffman, 'Institute Bids Leader Farewell,' *Calgary Herald* (12 Feb. 1984), vertical file, Prairie Bible Institute; and the memorial issue of the *Prairie Overcomer* 57 (March 1984). Ted S. Rendall, later president of PBI, provided further reflections on Maxwell's career in several articles in the *Prairie Overcomer* 57 (May 1984).

2 Sketches of Rendall's career can be found in 'From Scottish Seaside to Prairie Principal,' *Three Hills Capital* (12 April 1972): 12, vertical file, Prairie Bible Institute, Three Hills, Alberta; and in Ted S. Rendall, 'Salute to LEM,' *Prairie Overcomer* 57 (May 1984): 2. Additional material was provided in an interview with Rendall conducted at PBI in November 1986.

3 See the Minutes of the Board of Directors, 23 June 1977: Rendall was also put forward as a candidate, and there is some evidence that Maxwell was not a unanimous choice. The appointment of Paul Maxwell to the office was announced in the *Prairie Overcomer* 50 (Nov. 1977): 634–5.

4 Maxwell resigned for health reasons. Rendall's was the only name put forward as successor (H. Dolsen, 'Resignation and Election,' *Prairie Overcomer* 59 [June 1986]: 37; see also Minutes of the Board of Directors, 20 March 1986; all citations from Prairie Bible Institute documents are from records at PBI unless otherwise noted).

5 Prairie adopted a new crest in 1983 that illustrated the following commitments: 'We are a Bible Institute that teaches discipleship to the cross of Jesus Christ, His resurrection power as the key to fruitfulness and a disciplined lifestyle that stresses holiness in the Christian walk' (see insert in *Prairie Overcomer* 56 [May 1983]).

6 *Prairie Bible College Catalogue 1989–90*, 7

7 Some change is evident, however. Rendall's opinions were never

more conservative than Maxwell's were and Rendall often was more open to other points of view. For instance, he recognized that authentic Christians have different opinions about evolution, even though he himself maintained belief in a direct act of creation for Adam and Eve (on the former, see 'We Review,' *Prairie Overcomer* 55 [Sept. 1982]: 437; on the latter, see 'The Making of Man,' *Prairie Overcomer* 55 [Sept. 1982]: 399). Rendall spoke also of Christian duties in political life that extended beyond the traditional evangelical actions of praying for and submitting to the ordained rulers: he said Christians ought to participate in the state's affairs, utilize its privileges, and even protest its sins ('Bringing Our Citizenship Down to Earth,' *Prairie Overcomer* 51 [May 1978]: 246–54). But the general emphases were the same; not too much should be made of these relatively small differences, since these issues came up only rarely.

8 See, for example, the whole issues devoted to prayer (58 [Feb. 1985]) and discipleship (57 [Sept. 1984]).

9 The continuity in the magazine is hardly surprising considering that Rendall had edited it throughout the 1970s and participated substantially in the editing since 1957. Every January issue but one from 1977 to 1987 was devoted to revival; similarly, the March issues were devoted to missions.

10 The ratio of Canadian to American students tilted back to the Canadian side in 1975–6, but the extension teams continued to travel as much in the United States as in Canada.

11 See the Supplement to the 1980–1 catalogue.

12 In the annual report for 1984 of the academic dean of the Bible School, Selmer B. Hanson indicated that discussion of a graduate program at least in missions was discussed as early as 1980 (7).

13 Minutes of the Board of Directors' Annual Meeting, 29 April 1986

14 Interview with Rendall. Note that the term 'college' in this context is not congruent with the distinction made by S.A. Witmer and Virginia Lieson Brereton between those schools that offered a relatively large percentage of liberal-arts courses ('Bible colleges') and those, like Prairie, that did not ('Bible institutes'): see Witmer, *The Bible College Story*, 37; and Brereton, 'The Bible Schools and Conservative Evangelical Higher Education, 1880–1940,' 128–30.

15 *In Step* (Dec. 1986): 3

16 Ibid., 4

17 *Bible College Student Handbook 1986–87*, 22

18 Ibid., 21

19 *Prairie Bible College Catalogue 1989–90*, 39–43
20 Interview with Rendall
21 See David Nadeau, 'College Seeks to Upgrade,' *Faith Today* 9 (Jan. 1991): 59–60.
22 One source reports that about 10,000 people spent at least one year at PBI, and out of this total 4000 graduates went into missions (Paul De Groot, 'Bible School Exemplifies Prairie Faith,' *Edmonton Journal* [5 Jan. 1985]; vertical file, PBI). The catalogue for 1989–90 says that 'over 2,100 graduates serve or have served as foreign missionaries in about 80 countries under approximately 75 missionary organizations. Besides these, over 1700 have served or are serving as pastors and Christian workers in denominational, interdenominational and independent works in North America' (6).
23 See, for instance, Maxwell, 'Perspective,' *Prairie Overcomer* 47 (Oct. 1974): 455–6, and 'Social Reform and the Gospel,' 55 (June 1982): 293.
24 'First Things First,' *Prairie Overcomer* 56 (March 1983): 130–1.

Chapter 9

1 The executive published a 'Declaration of Intent' in the autumn of 1970 that set out these priorities. This statement explicitly relegated to a secondary position 'specialized ministries to sectors of society with particular interest (e.g., fine arts, drama),' which reference seems a direct judgment upon some of the work of Wilber Sutherland's later years in IVCF. This committee hereby indicated that it intended to 'correct' at least one aspect of Sutherland's legacy. (The 'Declaration of Intent' was presented to the IVCF board of Directors at its meeting on 19 Sept. 1970; see the minutes for that meeting for the text of the statement. All citations from IVCF documents are from the records at the National Office in Toronto, unless otherwise noted.)
2 Mel Donald notes, however, that certain Canadian students had sent money to support Escobar in Latin America as early as 1958 ('A Spreading Tree,' 192).
3 This judgment and others in this section rely on interviews granted by several Inter-Varsity leaders: former Chairmen of the Board Clifford C. Pitt, Richard E. Vosburgh, and L. Claude Simmonds, former General Director A. Donald MacLeod, former Ontario Divisional Director and Deputy General Director Melvin V. Donald,

then-current Chairman of the Board John Irwin, and then-current General Director James E. Berney. These interviews, again gratefully acknowledged, were conducted in metropolitan Toronto in December 1986 except for the Vosburgh interview, conducted in Guelph, Ontario, at the same time, and the Berney interview, conducted by telephone in March 1987.

4 This resistance to centralization went hand-in-hand with typical Western Canadian resistance to control by Ontario. See Phillips, 'The History of the Inter-Varsity Christian Fellowship in Western Canada,' 302–11. Hints of this sort of trouble appear later in a confidential memo to Ross Bailey and Jim Berney from Morley Less (probably 'Lee'), 22 Sept. 1983. Berney dealt with the tensions in Alberta regarding the national office early in his term.

5 These tensions also bore marks of regional differences: the staff on the prairies and in the Alberta division in particular had little sympathy for many of the Toronto staff's innovations which they saw to depart harmfully from Inter-Varsity's original model. This regionalism should not be overstressed, however, since the Toronto staff received criticism from Ontario associates as well. It was to some extent a manifestation of the 'sectish' sort of evangelicalism challenging the 'churchish' sort.

6 See Minutes of the Board of Directors, 9 and 10 March 1973.

7 See ibid., 22–3 Oct. 1976 and 28–9 Oct. 1977.

8 Several of those interviewed referred specifically to former Ontario Divisional Director Harry Klassen and former Alberta Divisional Director Marjorie Long in this regard, but a number of others were involved as well.

9 'Area committees' were groups of Christians that met regularly to further the work of IVCF by raising funds, praying, and participating in the work of individual chapters.

10 Minutes of the Executive Committee, 10 April 1970

11 Minutes of the Board of Directors, 13–14 May 1977

12 Ibid., 27–8 Jan. 1978. This motion had been anticipated by one at the board meeting on 28–9 Oct. 1977, but was not passed. The later motion was passed with two opposed.

13 An exception that proves the rule here can be seen in the early calendars of Toronto Bible College, which welcomed any student from an evangelical church. This criterion was soon changed to welcome students whose *personal convictions* were evangelical, thus opening the school to those from pluralistic churches which churches' com-

mitments would not always be seen as evangelical from TBC's viewpoint.

14 This pattern has been noted above in the cases of Toronto and Ontario Bible Colleges in relation to Pentecostalism and the charismatic movement.

15 See Minutes of the Board of Directors, 28–9 Oct. 1977; and Donald, 'A Spreading Tree,' 239.

16 See Minutes of the Board of Directors, 12–13 May 1978, 23–4 Nov. 1979, 9–10 May 1980, and 22–3 May 1981. And see Donald, 'A Spreading Tree,' 291.

17 This also included, however, a new relationship with the Christian Reformed church that began in the mid–1970s to second some of its campus chaplains to serve as 'Associate Staff Workers' (see the memo to this effect by Donald MacLeod dated 30 October 1975 in files of IVCF headquarters).

18 And not everyone connected with the movement was happy about some of the changes in it since the 1960s. C. Stacey Woods himself in his reflections on the history of the IVCF in the United States described what he saw to be 'the near disaster of the late 1960s [in IVCF-Canada] with its failure both in legislative and administrative leadership which almost threatened the life of the Canadian movement' (*The Growth of a Work of God*, 21). MacLeod himself earlier had testified to the problem of 'trust' in IVCF among the Canadian evangelical community, a problem manifest in lack of financial support for IVCF in some quarters. (See 'Report of the General Director to the IVCF Board of Directors' in the Minutes of the Board of Directors, 22–3 Oct. 1976.)

But despite MacLeod's indubitable commitment to traditional evangelical concerns, Woods still saw as late as 1979 a straying by the movement from its origins. At a dinner celebrating IVCF's fiftieth anniversary in Canada, Woods urged the Fellowship to return to its earlier, narrower concentration on nurture and evangelism. Clearly he was upset about what he saw to be too much diversity theologically and vocationally in Inter-Varsity. As one account puts it: 'The Former General Director ... urged a return to the fundamentals which characterized the organization at its beginning; a return to a stronger emphasis on the authority of the Word of God; a return to emphasis on the personal Quiet Time, Bible Study for nurture, and prayer for personal growth and evangelism; a renewed commitment to the goals of the organization and its ethical and confessional stance on the part of the staff and all the speakers on all occasions' (Victor Adrian, 'President's Message to the Ontario Bible College and Theological Seminary Annual Meeting: November 4, 1979,' *Evangelical Recorder* 86 [March 1980]: 3). It may be that Woods was reacting to elements still in the movement that pursued goals other than these, although there is little evidence that there were such elements left in IVCF by 1979. It may also be that having served IFES in Switzerland for some decades, he was simply out of touch with the Canadian scene, especially given MacLeod's work of several years before this statement. But perhaps, finally, Woods knew what was going on and simply didn't like the new emphasis on vocation and the willingness to embrace a broader variety of Christian experience and theology than he had been used to thirty years before.

Clearly, however, Woods was not alone in his ambivalence over Inter-Varsity at this time. Victor Adrian, president of OBC/OTS, commented at the end of this summary of Woods's exhortation that 'this resurgence to true Christian spirituality [at IVCF] was most heartening' (ibid.). The word 'resurgence' implies that this commendable sort of spirituality, in Adrian's view, had receded in the recent past. No doubt MacLeod would have received these comments regretfully, as he would have hoped for a stronger endorsement of his attempts to build support among those disturbed by the previous difficulties.

19 See *After Fifty Years: Current University Issues – General Director's Report for 1978* (N.p.: Inter-Varsity Christian Fellowship, n.d.), n.p.

20 See for example his 'Report of the General Director to the IVCF Board of Directors,' in the Minutes of the Board of Directors, 22–3 Oct. 1976.

21 'After Fifty Years,' n.p.

22 Melvin V. Donald, Report on the Ontario Division, in the IVCF Annual Report for 1978–9, p. 15

23 This is the judgment of several of those interviewed, including MacLeod himself.

24 This revised statement of purpose joined several previously approved statements – a pithy 'Focus Statement,' the IFES statement of faith, and a declaration of personal commitment – to constitute the 'Statement of Agreement' approved by the board of

Inter-Varsity in November 1984. This brought to conclusion a decade of discussion on these various aspects of Inter-Varsity's identity and mission.

25 Berney spoke of this matter in an interview granted in Scarborough, Ontario, in July 1989. Terse references to experiences of healing and other graphic manifestations of the Spirit appeared occasionally in his reports: see, for example, the Minutes of the Executive Committee, 16 March 1985; and his report to the board of directors, 15 Nov. 1985, pp. 2–3. Not all of this 'fire,' to be sure, was kept enough in the 'fireplace' to suit IVCF's leaders, as the movement sought to further incorporate emphases that had appeared first only in the 1960s in the form of glossolalia (see concern briefly expressed about the influence of John Wimber and the Vineyard Fellowship movement upon the University of British Columbia chapter in Berney's report to the board of directors, 28 Oct. 1986, p. 3).

26 This included the Groupes Bibliques Universitaires, which became an autonomous movement affilated with IVCF on 23 April 1988.

27 On this latter point see Berney, 'General Director's Report to the Board of Directors,' 12 June 1987, p. 5.

28 See ibid., 'Report to the Review Committee on the General Director's Performance over the Past Five Years,' 7 Feb. 1986, p. 2. (photocopy). The chapter and staff numbers were for the 1986–7 school year and come from a memorandum sent to the author by Berney in April 1987.

Chapter 10

1 Hanson, *On the Raw Edge of Faith*; *The Trinity Story*, passim; and *From Hardship to Harvest*, passim.

2 Enrolment figures are from the registrar's records, Trinity Western University. All citations from Trinity Western University documents are from those at the university unless otherwise noted.

3 The school received considerable opposition in the British Columbia legislature, the press, and universities, generally for requiring faculty and students to subscribe to statements of faith and conduct, a requirement many saw to be incongruous in a university. For accounts see C.B. Hanson, *From Hardship to Harvest*, 183–5; and esp. Guenther, 'A Case Study in Policy Making.'

4 See 'Graduate Performance Attests to Trinity Excellence,' *Trinity Western World* 3 (Special edition, 1979): 12; and 'TWC Students Excel

at UBC,' *Trinity Western World* 3 (Winter 1979): 4. The former article indicates the transfer record.

5 President R. Neil Snider explained this nomenclature in 1979: 'There is a fairly strong argument for [a name change from "College" to "University"] in the Canadian context. In Canada "college" implies only community colleges; "university" is used to describe the post-secondary institutions which have the power to grant degrees. So we would qualify in that sense. But we wouldn't want to be presumptuous ... "university" [also] carries the idea of graduate programs, so probably the best designation for TWC is that of a "university college": we are of university calibre with an undergraduate program leading to a baccalaureate degree' (quoted in 'Historical Perspective: A Christian Alternative,' *Trinity Western World* 3 [Special edition, 1979]: 4). Perhaps because of the addition of a graduate program in theological studies in the later 1980s (described in part 4), or perhaps simply because of common Canadian usage, Trinity Western overcame this initial modesty and changed its name in 1985.

6 Hanson, *On the Raw Edge*, 47. A helpful introduction to the EFCC, especially in regard to British Columbia and the history of TWU, is provided in Robert Kenneth Burkinshaw, 'Strangers and Pilgrims in Lotus Land,' 240–8, 319–23.

7 Burkinshaw, 'Conservative Protestantism,' 98. See also Muriel Hanson, *Fifty Years and Seventy Places*. Indeed, Hanson himself had presided over a Bible institute in Japan, and later president Neil Snider came to Trinity Western from the position of acting President of Winnipeg Bible College and Seminary.

8 Hanson, *On the Raw Edge*, 47

9 This and other sections have been strengthened by material from interviews, here gratefully acknowledged, granted by three Trinity Western University personnel. Deane E.D. Downey, long-time professor of English and acting dean of academic affairs at the time, was interviewed at Trinity Western in November 1986, as was Robert Burkinshaw, assistant professor of history and an authority on British Columbian evangelicalism. Downey was interviewed subsequently by telephone in March 1987, and Burkinshaw provided more information in a follow-up letter (n.d. [1987?]). President Neil Snider shared his perspective on developments in an informal conversation in Winnipeg, Manitoba, 20 March 1992.

10 Hanson, *On the Raw Edge*, 47

11 See ibid., *From Hardship to Harvest*, 149–52

12 Ibid., 153–6
13 Ibid., 144
14 Quoted in Jeffrey James Wiebe, 'Trinity Junior College,' 51–2
15 'Why a School in Canada,' *Beacon*, 23 Feb. 1960, quoted without further reference in Hanson, *On the Raw Edge*, 50. Hanson points out that of the initial administrative team, both the president and the dean had been missionaries and one of the original five full-time faculty members had been a missionary to Guatemala (ibid., 126).
16 In the mid–1970s, the school began to receive a majority of its students from beyond the Evangelical Free churches. After 1983, there were more Baptists than Evangelical Free church students, and almost as many from the Alliance as from the Free Churches. The eighth and ninth clauses of the school's statement of faith set out a 'believers' church' understanding of church membership and the tenth clause affirmed that 'every local church has the right under Christ to decide and govern its own affairs' (*Trinity Western University Calendar 1990–91*, 10).
17 The Christian Reformed churches, largest of the Canadian Reformed groups, sponsored two colleges: Redeemer College, outside Hamilton, Ontario, and The King's College, in Edmonton, Alberta; and New Brunswick was home to the only other four-year, transdenominational, evangelical college in Canada of the time, tiny St Stephen's University.
18 An important exception must be noted here. Academic Dean Kenneth R. Davis presented a broad doctrine of vocation in a chapel address later reprinted in the school magazine (see 'Vocation: A Life of Meaning and Purpose,' *Trinity Western World* 7, no. 1 [1984]: 5). This may have signalled a growing understanding of vocation among the TWU community, or simply an attempt by the TWU leadership to develop this understanding among that community. But it stands none the less as an exception in the general pattern of TWU's public presentation of its mission.
19 The paradigmatic statement here is Holmes, *The Idea of a Christian College*. In this connection see also Carpenter and Shipps, eds, *Making Higher Education Christian*.
20 Olson, quoted in Hanson, *On the Raw Edge*, 50
21 'Our goal is to develop fully the programs we have now, then with a market approach to carefully select majors to meet needs our constituents express. We did that four years ago when we added a business program, which today has our largest number of majors'

(quoted in 'Historical Perspective: A Christian Alternative,' 4 [see n. 5. above]).

22 Olson speaks to the two-year program: 'With these two years of schooling, ... one need not fear so much the influence of schools and teachers who might seek to destroy the faith of our youth' (quoted in Hanson, *On the Raw Edge*, 51).

23 The connection may be only ironic, but the motto of Trinity Western University, translated from the Latin, is, 'A Mighty Fortress Is Our God.'

24 'Historical Perspective: A Christian Alternative,' 4 (ellipsis points in original)

25 'President's Report to the Board of Governors,' 26 Feb. 1980

26 C.B. Hanson, *From Hardship to Harvest*, 184–7. See the calendar for 1990–1 for the statement of faith (10) and the code of conduct (p. 11 and reverse of application form).

27 See Carpenter and Shipps for guides to the American scene. On Canada, see esp. French, 'The Evangelical Creed in Canada'; Gauvreau, *The Evangelical Century*; and Van Die, *An Evangelical Mind*.

28 *1990–91 Calendar*, inside front cover

29 P. 3

30 As Snider's report to the board of governors in 1980, for instance, indicates

31 Ibid., 151

Chapter 11

1 This section relies on interviews granted by Principal Carl E. Armerding and Professor W. Ward Gasque at Vancouver in November 1986; further interviews were conducted by telephone with Armerding and Professor (and former Principal) James M. Houston in March 1987. It also draws from three helpful sketches of Regent's history: Brian P. Sutherland, 'Historical Development,' and James M. Houston, 'The History and Assumptions of Regent College,' papers contributed to the conference 'Openness to the Future: A Prelude to Planning,' held at Regent College, 1974; W. Ward Gasque, 'A History of Regent College,' in 'Report on Institutional Self-Study in Support of Application for Accreditation by the Association of Theological Schools' (Vancouver: Regent College 1984), 1–20 (photocopies); and Regent College Senate Self-Study Committee, 'History of Regent

College 1985–89,' in 'Regent College Self-Study Document' (Vancouver: Regent College 1990), 3–12. All citations from Regent College documents come from those at Regent College unless otherwise noted.

2 On the Brethren, see esp. Coad, *A History of the Brethren Movement*, and McLaren, 'The Triple Tradition.'

3 An introduction to the Brethren in British Columbia, particularly in regard to the history of Regent College, is provided in Robert Kenneth Burkinshaw, 'Strangers and Pilgrims in Lotus Land,' 327–34. Burkinshaw's account is particularly helpful in tracing links between these Brethren and the Vancouver Bible Institute, a school with links to Toronto Bible College, and between the Brethren and IVCF.

4 Houston refers to an article along these lines by T.D. Parks in May 1943, 'Our Attitude toward Higher Education,' *Light and Liberty* (cited without further reference in 'History and Assumptions,' 2 [see n. 1, above]); Sutherland refers to a similar piece by Arthur C. Hill (of IVCF repute) in the Brethren magazine *Letters of Interest* in 1962 (cited without further reference in 'Historical Development,' 2 [see n. 1]).

5 'The Effect of Increased Education – and a Proposal!' *Calling* 7 (Fall 1965): 9–11

6 Cochrane writes: 'The 2- or 3-year course of study would be comparable to that offered by existing graduate schools such as Fuller Seminary in California, but the program would probably be modified to emphasize the training of laymen rather than the development of clergymen' (10). This latter qualification, of course, must be understood in 'Brethren' terms to indicate, none the less, 'a three-year course for those who believe the Lord may be leading them into full-time ministry at home or abroad' (11). This explicit model of an American evangelical seminary as modified by Brethren convictions is important in determining what was in fact the original vision of the college, a matter of some controversy later.

7 See James M. Houston, 'The Inside Story of Regent College,' undated document in the Regent College archives (photocopy).

8 Houston had written several articles in the Brethren magazine *The Witness* and had helped lead the Young Men's Bible Teaching Conference at Oxford for some years: it was thus that his theological interests were known among the Brethren. He was known to the Vancouver people through his preaching at Granville Chapel, the

most important of those assemblies that sponsored Regent, during the summer of 1962 while Houston was visiting the University of Victoria (Houston interview).

9 Houston indicated that Bruce was the committee's first choice for principal, himself their second (interview).

10 Houston explained this concern in 'The Importance of Being on a University Campus?' *Regent College Bulletin* 1 (Spring 1971): n.p.

11 Carl Armerding indicated that he possessed correspondence from that period to demonstrate this discussion (second interview).

12 See Houston's account of the discussion in 'History and Assumptions,' 3 (see n.1). Houston introduced some of the newer ideas in 'A New Venture in Christian Education' and in 'Regent College, Vancouver.' Houston later wrote again of Regent's principles in 'Regent College,' *Crux* 9, no. 1 (1973); repr. as pamphlet, Regent College archives.

13 Gasque, 'History,' 5 (see n. 1)

14 This statement is presented and discussed in part 4. On the World Evangelical Fellowship, see Howard, *The Dream That Would Not Die*.

15 So notes Sutherland, 'Historical Development,' 7 (see n. 1)

16 'The Christian Way of Knowing,' *Regent College Bulletin* 1 (Fall 1971): n.p.). Houston spoke of spirituality eloquently in 'Parameters of Emphasis,' a paper contributed to the conference 'Openness to the Future: A Prelude to Planning,' held at Regent College, 1974, pp. 5–8. And John Ray contributed a paper to the same conference entitled, 'Emphases of the Program: Discipleship.'

17 Houston addressed this aspect in 'Work and Christian Vocation,' *Regent College Bulletin* 4 (Fall 1974): n.p.

18 A critique of the first summer session, raising questions about Regent's claim to be functioning at a graduate level, is Fitch, 'Regent College Challenges Secular Scholarship.'

19 Interviews (although no documents) have indicated that Houston assured the VST that Regent was a lay-training centre only, and would never 'compete' with VST in training pastors. Again, while this could be seen as reflecting a certain Brethren understanding of pastoral ministry – that is, by laypeople rather than by ordained clergy – it more likely represents Houston's personal vision for the school, as discussed below.

20 This is Gasque's judgment; in 'History,' 14 (see n. 1).

21 This reputation was fostered by no one more than Houston: at least as early as 1970 he defined Regent's major emphasis as '[equipping] Christian laymen by academic excellence in the Christian faith' (undated letter to Regent's constituency [Fall 1970?], Regent College archives).

22 Regent generally hired as full-time faculty only those with doctorates earned at universities, especially those of the United Kingdom and United States.

23 Gasque, 'History,' 10

24 Regent's 1984 self-study for the ATS pointed out that Regent sent many graduates especially into work with the Inter-Varsity Christian Fellowship (39).

25 The point was raised in a number of papers at the 1974 planning conference: see especially Carl E. Armerding, 'The Centrality of Biblical Exegesis in Theological Education'; Ian S. Rennie, 'Emphases of the Program: Lay vs. Professional'; and Donald O. Anderson, 'The Conference Summary.' James Houston challenged the idea that the question of Regent's mission could be solved easily by reference to 'origins' in his conference paper, 'Parameters of Emphasis': 'Now those in favour of one or other of the parameters mentioned above can all appeal to the beginnings of Regent College and to its unique character today ... Did Regent begin when the term "theological college" was first used and first mention was made of the three-year course for those entering the ministry? Or did it begin in January 1967 when we laid special emphasis on its character as a new lay-training venture?' (2). Indeed, in one of Houston's own accounts of the history of Regent he tellingly placed his individual conceiving of a Christian institute in 1961 ahead of the story of the Vancouver committee, thus implicitly laying claim to originality ('Inside Story'; see n. 7).

Not too much should be made of this, however: Houston himself recognized that 'we are here now as a result of both events' ('Parameters,' 2). And an indication of the ambivalence among later supporters of Regent's adoption of a Master of Divinity program is Ward Gasque's call at this time for a full-fledged evangelical seminary in Canada that would have all the characteristics of Regent College but with the addition of the applied theology side – yet Gasque suggests that it be located in *Ontario*, 'where the largest number of potential students live'! See Gasque,

'Christian Higher Education in Canada Today.' The important thing to note here is simply that Regent's introduction of the Master of Divinity degree program was rooted in early visions for the school and can judged as an innovation that compromised the lay orientation of the school – as many evangelicals in Canada and elsewhere apparently have seen it – only if Houston's vision is taken as normative and the other disregarded.

26 Indeed, Houston saw these as one and the same, in the sense that he seemed to think that only academic theological study was necessary for religious leaders: 'We hope very soon,' he wrote in 1970, 'to establish a Master of Arts degree in Christian Studies [note: not a Bachelor/Master of Divinity] that will provide such needed professional training' (undated letter sent to Regent constituency [Fall 1970?], Regent College archives). See also Sutherland's account of how the idea of the three-year program was downgraded as early as 1968 ('Historical Development,' 10; see n. 1). And, in 1974, Houston wrote: 'My own conviction was that the development of departments of religious studies replacing the more denominational and professional activities of previous theological education on secular campuses might break up, as it became obvious that such departments lacked adequate coherence and unity. If, then, these were replaced by such more specialized institutes of Jewish, Buddhist, or Islamic studies, we could always assume to be no more than an Institute of Christian Studies' ('History and Assumptions,' 3–4; see n. 1).

27 Houston interview

28 Houston resigned from this office in 1984, officially in order to pursue a worldwide itinerant speaking ministry, but unofficially over some differences with the school's administration. He stayed on as a part-time lecturer until 1986, and then rejoined the full-time staff in 1986 as professor of spiritual theology.

29 The program was introduced to the Regent constituency in Carl E. Armerding, 'The Master of Divinity Program,' *Regent College Bulletin* 9 (Summer 1979): n.p.

30 Enrolment figures here and above come primarily from the records of the Regent College registrar; for a denominational breakdown see the 1985 self-study for the ATS, p. 35. The self-study also notes that in the 1980s, about 60% of the students came from Canada, 30% from the United States, and 10% from elsewhere – from every other inhabited continent (36). The 1990 self-study shows limited change,

with Baptists and Anglicans now leading the list of denominations, and with 80% coming from North America and 15% from Asia and the South Pacific (26).

31 Carl Armerding noted this in 1974; see his 'The Centrality of Biblical Exegesis,' 3.

32 Second interview with Armerding

33 First interview. Armerding expressed concern about this situation, however, at least as early as 1974; see his 'The Centrality of Biblical Exegesis,' 2–3. See also the self-study document for 1990, pp. 18–20.

34 Armerding, second interview

35 Regent presented its goals thus:

'To equip men and women with a firm, well thought-out, biblical faith that will speak with integrity to an increasingly secular society.

'To prepare Christian people from all walks of life to serve Christ within their varied vocations, whether ministerial or lay.

'To advance the church's growth by educating pastors, evangelists, and teachers who will mobilize and train layfolk to take their share in the total, every-member ministry of the Body of Christ.

'To cultivate within our own community qualities of Christian character that will commend the gospel to a skeptical world.

'To model by way of fellowship a worshipping and serving community that demonstrates the reality of God to a broken world.

'To impart attitudes and skills that will break through cultural, social, racial, and linguistic barriers, and thus further the Christian calling to be salt and light inter-racially and internationally' (*Academic Year 1986–87* [Vancouver: Regent College, n.d.]: n.p.).

36 This group also included scholars, of course, since a number of Regent alumni (including some on its own faculty) went on to further degrees. President Walter C. Wright, Jr., formerly an administrator at Fuller Seminary who succeeded Armerding in 1988, spoke to this point in the school catalogue for 1989–90. He identified Regent in terms of the established two tracks of lay and pastoral education, but added to the definition what had been implicit for some time: 'a theological research centre preparing men and women for lives of scholarship' (4).

37 P. 15. For the mission statement and goals, see 15–16.

Chapter 12

1 This section relies on interviews gratefully acknowledged here with Brian C. Stiller, executive director of the EFC, by telephone in March 1987 and in person in July 1989, Markham, Ontario; with Keith A. Price, minister-at-large with the EFC, in Vancouver, November 1986; with A. Donald MacLeod, former president of the EFC, in Toronto, December 1986; and by telephone with J. Harry Faught, founder of the EFC, in October 1989.

2 See the denominational breakdown of the membership in the proposal 'Expansion of the Evangelical Fellowship of Canada,' in Minutes of the Executive Council, [1966]. All citations of EFC documents, unless otherwise noted, are from those housed at the headquarters of the Evangelical Fellowship of Canada, Markham, Ont.

3 Faught had encountered the National Association of Evangelicals (NAE) while a student at Dallas Theological Seminary and had attended its meetings several times since coming to Toronto. He wanted to see if something similar could be started in Canada, and in the early 1960s set up a number of meetings of local pastors and, in a couple of instances, NAE officials as advisers, that ultimately resulted in the founding of EFC (Faught interview).

4 Robert N. Thompson served a term between DiGangi and MacLeod.

5 The prominence of evangelicals from the mainline churches in the EFC's early years is exemplified in the attendance at the 1969 convention. Of the top four denominations represented in the total registration of 749, the first is the Presbyterian, with 202, the third is the Anglican, with 63, and the fourth is the United Church, with 47. In second place is the Baptist, with 123 (Minutes of the General Council, 15 April 1969).

6 This statement is presented and discussed in part 4. On the World Evangelical Fellowship, see David M. Howard, *The Dream That Would Not Die.*

7 Minutes of the Annual Meeting, 21 March 1966

8 Auditor's reports for 1970 and 1976

9 A resolution on the latter subject was reprinted in *Evangelical Recorder* 81 (Sept. 1975): 14.

10 This commitment was set out squarely in William J. Fitch, 'I Am an Evangelical,' *Thrust* 1 (Oct. 1968): 10–11.

11 See the Minutes of the General Council, 8 March 1971; the Fellowship's magazine *Faith Today* (successor to *Thrust* regularly

carried news of this mission. EFC's relations with the NAE were always friendly, and EFC leaders regularly attended the NAE's national conventions. None the less, the EFC was thoroughly independent of the NAE from its beginning.

12 The annual meeting had approved the position of executive secretary pending funding as early as 16 March 1972 (Minutes of the Annual Meeting).

13 *Constitution of the Evangelical Fellowship of Canada*, March 1981 (photocopy). Stiller set out his understanding of the relationship of the evangelical community and Canadian society at large in 'The Tension of Two Kingdoms,' *Faith Today* 4 (March–April 1986): 31–3.

14 Price outlined his commitment to and conception of expository preaching in 'Communicating God's Truth by Expository Preaching,' *Thrust* 12, no. 3 (1980): 6–9.

15 Which briefly later was known as *Faith Alive* before it became *Faith Today*. This should not be confused with the short-lived tabloid *Faith Today* edited by Leslie K. Tarr in the late 1970s. Concern was expressed in the EFC regarding the overlapping of *Thrust* and Tarr's *Faith Today* at least as early as 1979 (see letter from K. Neely encouraging EFC to consider amalgamation of the two magazines reported in the Minutes of the Executive Committee, 11 Sept. 1979). An EFC Communications Commission reported on the issue in May 1980. And Tarr himself then sat on an 'Ad Hoc Committee on Publications' that advised the EFC regarding changes to *Thrust* (see report of 4 Jan. 1982), and helped to edit the new EFC magazine in the 1980s.

16 *National Report*, Evangelical Fellowship of Canada, [1986]

17 One of the conferences dealing with religion and culture was jointly sponsored by the Institute of Christian Studies in Toronto and resulted in VanderVennen, ed., *Church and Canadian Culture.*

18 The resolution presented to the government was reprinted in *Thrust* 13, no. 1 (1981): 2; and in 'Recognition of a Sovereign God,' *Evangelical Recorder* 87 (June 1981): 7–8. Roman Catholic lobbying apparently also was important in this development.

19 See Van Ginkel, ed., *Shaping a Christian Vision for Canada.*

20 Several briefs on homosexuality were prepared, dated 4 March 1986, 13 July 1986, and December 1986. The one including concerns about religious freedom was the brief of 4 March 1986.

21 The 'sabbath' brief was prepared in April 1986. It was anticipated by a discussion at the 1970 EFC convention (Minutes, 5 March 1970).

See also 'Pornography: A Christian Response,' prepared by the EFC's Social Action Commission for presentation to the Government of Canada on the proposed bill C–54 regarding pornography; and Brian C. Stiller, 'Submission to the Fraser Committee on Pornography and Prostitution,' 8 Feb. 1984.

22 Brochures, undated; author's files

23 See, for instance, the account of the EFC debate over whether a clause regarding the 'supremacy of God' ought to be included in the new Constitution: Harold Jantz, 'Proposing Christian Principles for a Country in Turmoil' and 'Let God Be Supreme First in Us,' *ChristianWeek* 6 (26 May 1992): 1, 4, 6. For further reflections on the work of EFC and Canadian public life, see John G. Stackhouse, Jr., 'The National Association of Evangelicals.'

24 An excellent example is Brian Stiller's careful response to the hysterical letter sent out by Progressive Conservative politico Dalton Camp on behalf of the Canadian Civil Liberties Association (both letters on file at EFC; Stiller's reprinted as 'Evangelicals: A Threatening Cloud,' *Faith Today* 7 [Dec. 1985]: 32–5). Another is the series of documents prepared by the Task Force on Canada's Future, in Van Ginkel, ed., *Shaping a Christian Vision for Canada*.

25 *The Evangelical Fellowship of Canada* (N.p.: Evangelical Fellowship of Canada, n.d.), n.p.

26 With Keith A. Price, former director of 'Sermons from Science,' serving with the EFC as minister-at-large and Glenn Smith of Christian Direction on the general council, and with the observation that Prairie Bible Institute was an institutional member of the EFC, the circle of the seven institutions discussed in this study is complete.

27 No data are available in this regard for the period before Stiller's leadership. The lack of support from Quebec is hardly surprising, given its tiny evangelical population. The lack of support from the Atlantic provinces fits a pattern discussed in part 4.

28 The 1983 figure comes from 'The Financial Picture,' part of the promotional publication *It's Time to Break the Silence* (N.p.: Evangelical Fellowship of Canada, n.d.), n.p. The 1988 figure comes from the EFC files. Roughly one-fourth each of the revenue in 1988 was provided by income from *Faith Today*, membership fees, and donations. The other fourth consisted mostly of income from staff support and conferences. In a letter to the author, Stiller mentions that the finances for 1990 were $2,024,024 (10 April 1991).

29 *National Report*

30 *It's Time to Break the Silence*
31 The Christian Reformed tradition was evident in the EFC at least from 1970, particularly in the persons of staff from the Institute for Christian Studies and the Committee on Justice and Liberty / Citizens for Public Justice, and the Canadian Council of Christian Reformed Churches joined the EFC in 1979. Periodically in the 1980s the EFC ran surveys of magazine readers and the following denominations tended to be at the top: Baptist, Pentecostal, Christian and Missionary Alliance, and Mennonite.
32 Seidenspinner was from the Christian and Missionary Alliance (C&MA); Charles Yates was from the Pentecostal Assemblies of Canada; Melvin P. Sylvester was also from the C&MA; and Donald Bastian was from the Free Methodists.
33 This issue was dealt with explicitly by the EFC General Council at least as early as 1970: 'The question was then raised [in terms of the nominating committee] as to whether there was any conflict of interest with a person who sits on both the Canadian Council of Churches and the Evangelical Fellowship of Canada General Council. Can one be an officer of both? Expression of Council after deliberation was 'yes' [to the second question, not to the first!] if the individual is committed to the EFC statement of faith' (Minutes of the EFC General Council, 2 March 1970). Stiller himself was invited to join the Evangelism Commission of the Canadian Council of Churches in 1987 (Minutes of the Executive Committee, 30 Sept. 1987).
34 *National Report*; this explanation, in slightly different words, is bound in with the Minutes of the Executive Committee, 13 June 1986.

Chapter 13

1 Most of these anecdotes are standard fare in church-history textbooks. For the story of the irate blacksmith, see John T. McNeill, *The History and Character of Calvinism*, 264.
2 Barrett, ed., *World Christian Encyclopedia*, 791.
3 See, for example, Rouse and Neill, eds, *A History of the Ecumenical Movement, 1517–1948*; and Rusch, *Ecumenism*.
4 A point similar to the one made here about Canada is made about the United States by Timothy L. Smith in 'A Shared Evangelical Heritage,' *TSF Bulletin* 10 (Nov.–Dec. 1986): 11.

5 See the discussions in Walsh, *The Christian Church in Canada*, and in Grant, *The Church in the Canadian Era.*

6 *The Evangelical Fellowship of Canada* (N.p.: Evangelical Fellowship of Canada [1986]), n.p. On the World Evangelical Fellowship, see Howard, *The Dream That Would Not Die.*

7 See the discussion below on the differences between Trinity Western University and Regent College.

8 Prairie Bible Institute and Trinity Western University had premillennialism in their statements of faith. But considerable evidence suggests that this was not a crucial doctrine among even these evangelicals. The sections on PBI in parts 2 and 3 have demonstrated, for instance, that Prairie's magazines have devoted little attention to this doctrine relative to that afforded concerns common to all evangelicals. And the recognition and support Prairie and Trinity Western gave to other evangelical groups who do not hold to this view also indicates that it was not a crucial conviction for them.

9 See, for example, Weber, 'The Rediscovery of the Laity in the Ecumenical Movement.'

10 Regent College, for one, recognized this pattern, as it introduced its statement of faith in this way: 'We accept wholeheartedly the revelation of God given in the Scriptures of the Old and New Testaments and confess the faith therein set forth and summarized in such historic statements of the Christian Church as the Apostles' Creed and the Nicene Creed. We here explicitly assert doctrines that they regard as crucial to the understanding and proclamation of the Gospel and to practical Christian living' (*1989/90 Catalogue*, 8).

11 See, among others, French, 'The Evangelical Creed in Canada,' and Gauvreau, *The Evangelical Century*, 16–17 and passim.

12 Particularly germane here are the following studies: Masters, *Protestant Church Colleges in Canada* and 'The Rise of Liberalism in Canadian Protestant Churches'; Moir, *A History of Biblical Studies in Canada*; Van Die, *An Evangelical Mind*; and Gauvreau, *The Evangelical Century.*

13 Gauvreau, 112–17

14 This opposition, however, did not keep Prairie from inviting Brian Stiller, an ordained Pentecostal, to speak on campus as a representative of the Evangelical Fellowship of Canada, to which Prairie belonged. (And Briercrest Bible College, heir to Prairie's

mantle as largest in the country, recognized Stiller's work with the Evangelical Fellowship of Canada by awarding him an honorary doctorate.) In fact, by the late 1980s, Prairie was implicitly making room for Pentecostals, while continuing to repudiate their distinctive doctrines: 'There are particular current interpretations of Bible teaching which the College does not endorse. We refer, for example, to the claims that speaking in tongues is the necessary evidence of the fullness of the Spirit and that healing is unqualifiedly available to every believer. The College will not permit students to propagate such view on campus. Persons who intend to make application for admission to Prairie should carefully review the above statement of our position and resolve to honor this position while on campus' (*Prairie Bible College Catalogue 1989–90*, 6).

15 This latter idea is evident, however, in Walsh's book, *The Christian Church in Canada* (chapter XX is entitled 'Persistence of Sect Movements'), in the work of S.D. Clark (for example, a church-sect typology – with evangelicals represented exclusively by sects – underlies his influential *Church and Sect in Canada*, and Hans Mol's later study of religion in Canada (*Faith and Fragility*) speaks of evangelicals only as they are represented by 'new movements' (e.g., Pentecostalism) and does not discuss the crucial category of 'evangelicalism' at all.

16 Semple, 'The Decline of Revival in Nineteenth Century, Central-Canadian Methodism'; Manning, 'Changes in Evangelism within the Methodist Church in Canada'; Buttimer, ' "Great Expectations" '; Chalmers and Grant, 'The United Church of Canada'; H.G. MacLeod, 'The Transformation of the United Church of Canada 1946–1977'; Grant, 'The United Church and Its Heritage in Evangelism'; Clifford, 'The United Church of Canada and Doctrinal Confession'; Van Die, *An Evangelical Mind*; Gauvreau, *The Evangelical Century*; O'Toole et al., 'The United Church in Crisis'; Airhart, *Serving the Present Age*; and Marshall, *Secularizing the Faith*.

17 See Evenson, *Adventuring for Christ*. William E. Hordern writes: 'The Lutheran tradition has had very little influence upon the building of a Canadian ethos. The primary religious traditions have been Calvinist, Anglican, Methodist, Roman Catholic and sectarian ... Canadian Lutherans have tended to remain inward looking. Lutheran churches have been constructed to "serve our

own,'' often with worship services in languages other than English or French. They have been slow to take up an outreach into the total community. Taken as a percentage of the population, Lutherans have been under-represented among politicians and elected officials' ('Interrelation and Interaction between Reformation Principles and the Canadian Context,' 27). A similar assessment, also from within the Lutheran tradition, can be found in Pfrimmer, 'A Lutheran Witness in Canadian Society.'

18 The slowly growing presence of IVCF in Atlantic Canada and the increasing involvement of leaders from Atlantic Baptist College and Acadia Divinity School with the national network of evangelicals, notably with the Evangelical Fellowship of Canada, perhaps betokened a sea change among at least some evangelicals in Atlantic Canada by the 1980s. The refusal of the United Baptist Convention of the Atlantic Provinces in 1989 to join the EFC, however, indicated yet some widespread hesitancy about joining the national transdenominational movement per se. (It should be noted in this respect, however, that the small Atlantic Canada Association of Free Will Baptists *were* members of the EFC.)

19 See the respective sections on both for details. Indeed, a brochure for a 'National Prayer Festival' held at the Peoples Church in Toronto on 4–7 October 1990 listed as participants individuals associated with all seven of the institutions surveyed here: William J. MacRae of OBC/OTS, Ted Rendall of PBI, James Berney and Cathie Nicoll of IVCF, Keith Price of 'Sermons from Science' and EFC, Neil Snider of TWU, Michael Green of Regent, and Brian Stiller of EFC (in author's possession).

20 The presence of notable Pentecostal leaders in the EFC – from J. Harry Faught in the earliest days to Brian Stiller in the 1980s – did not reflect the prominence of Pentecostals themselves in similar evangelical institutions until well into the 1970s. Ontario Bible College and Theological Seminary and Regent College both were notable in their addressing of the needs of both Pentecostal and Asian churches in the 1980s as they offered courses directed specifically to their interests. The latter concern was graphically evident also in the appointment of William K.T. Wan to the deanship of Ontario Bible College and the installation of J.I. Packer in the Sangwoo Youtong Chee Chair of Theology and of Thomas In-Sing Leung as full-time Chinese-studies director at Regent College in 1989.

21 An irony here is that the ecumenical movement itself began out of an international cooperative effort to evangelize the world, starting with the 1910 Edinburgh missions conference. Furthermore, the United Church of Canada began largely out of the practical needs of small towns, especially on the prairies, that could not afford to support several churches of various denominations, rather than simply out of the lofty intentions of denominational leaders; and the later drive towards further church union in Canada (according to one well-placed observer) stalled at least partly because there was too little theological commitment to union for its own sake (so Grant, 'Leading a Horse to Water'). Indeed, the resistance to organic union is less eccentric to Canadian religious history, especially among those who actually *practise* their religion in any systematic sense, than a generation of historians has been accustomed to seeing it. That is, as remarkable as the story of the United Church surely is, it does not provide the dominant paradigm ('church union') for the plot of twentieth-century Canadian religious history, and instead represents only one option among several, which would include also the form of evangelical cooperation discussed here.

22 As Reginald Bibby's research on the 'circulation of the saints' has shown, and as most leaders within the evangelical community already recognized, many evangelicals of this sort are notorious 'church shoppers,' leaving one evangelical congregation for another of a different denomination because of certain key features (preaching, Sunday school for the children, etc.) that usually have nothing to do with denominational distinctives.

23 These comments are prompted especially by the reflections of sociologist Robert Wuthnow on the realignment of American Protestantism along 'conservative' and 'liberal' lines and his wondering about the splitting or withering away of denominations that include both sorts and the rise of 'special interest' voluntary organizations. See his *The Restructuring of American Religion* and *The Struggle for America's Soul.*

24 For an example of the ambivalence of Fellowship Baptists regarding cooperation with other groups, see Tipp, 'Objections to Unity.'

25 See, for example, the editorials to this effect by Ted S. Rendall in the *Prairie Overcomer* 51 (Sept. 1978): 482–3; and 51 (Nov. 1978): 601–2. The difference between the two types of evangelicalism

again is one of tone, of insistence: the common agreement on the absolute authority and trustworthiness of the Scripture must not be minimized.

26 See Stackhouse, 'Respectfully Submitted for American Consideration.'

27 See the several articles regarding Christian higher education in Canada in *ChristianWeek* 5 (21 Jan. 1992); and in *Faith Today* 10 (Jan. 1992). See also Davis, 'New Directions in Bible College Education,' and Stackhouse, 'What *Should* Christians Want from Higher Education?'

28 As in many episodes of this sort, there may well have been other issues at stake here as well. The public record, however, is limited to the following sources.

29 Bystrom referred especially to the work of Fuller Theological Seminary's G.E. Ladd as a model in this regard; see his response to the announcement of his resignation attached to Kenneth R. Davis, Memorandum to TWC Faculty and Staff, 28 April 1981; included in the Minutes of the Board of Governors. Ladd's work was then explicitly repudiated by Davis in 'Some Goals and Methodological Priorities and Parameters for Biblical Studies at TWC,' Appendix B to R. Neil Snider, 'Report to the Board of Governors,' 27 April 1981.

30 Kenneth R. Davis, Memorandum to TWC Faculty, Staff, and Students regarding the Resignation of Ray O. Bystrom, 7 April 1981; Appendix A to Snider, 'Report to the Board of Governors,' 27 April 1981

31 Davis characterized Bystrom's position, which according to Davis Bystrom saw to be fully congruent with belief in inerrancy, as 'limited inerrancy' – and that clearly was not good enough (Minutes of the Religious Studies Evaluating Committee, 5 March 1981).

32 Appendix B to Snider, 'Report to the Board of Governors,' 27 April 1981 (emphasis in original). The controversy was touched off by a letter addressed to President Snider by a pastor of a TWC student from California. The letter was dated 27 January 1981, and the 'Religious Studies question' appears in the minutes of the board of governors frequently until its resolution in April.

33 J.I. Packer was the best-known defender of the doctrine of 'inerrancy' on the Regent faculty. For a sample of his concern both for inerrancy and for evangelical biblical studies that use higher

criticism responsibly, see 'Battling for the Bible,' *Regent College Bulletin* 9 (Fall 1979): n.p. Cf. idem, *'Fundamentalism' and the Word of God.*

34 Acting academic dean Deane E.D. Downey granted a telephone interview on this subject in March 1987.

35 See, for example, the Minutes of the Executive Committee, 19 March 1981.

36 'The Trinity Western Graduate Institute for Christian Ministries: A Proposal for the Board of Governors of Trinity Western College,' in Minutes of the Board of Governors, 29–30 Jan. 1982

37 Pastoral Training Program Meeting Minutes, 21 Jan. 1982

38 Craig Evans and Craig Broyles are examples of the former; John Sutherland and Elmer Dyck are examples of the latter. And in the years following Bystrom's dismissal, several of TWU's professors of biblical studies would go on to make significant marks in biblical scholarship.

39 To select just two examples: Ward Gasque and James Packer, professors together at Regent College in the 1980s, each identified publicly with an evangelical organization at odds with the other one over gender roles in home and church ('Christians for Biblical Equality' and the 'Council for Biblical Manhood and Womanhood' respectively); and (also in the 1980s) Clark Pinnock of McMaster Divinity College and George Rawlyk of Queen's University, both members of the Baptist Convention of Ontario and Quebec and both important evangelical scholars, publicly defended radically different ideologies, with Pinnock on the side of democratic capitalism and Rawlyk democratic socialism.

40 For broad characterizations of twentieth-century evangelicalism in Britain, see esp. Bebbington, *Evangelicalism in Modern Britain*, and Bruce, *Firm in the Faith.* There was an explosion of literature on American evangelicalism in the 1970s and 1980s. Important introductions are the following: Marsden, ed., *Evangelicalism and Modern America*; Quebedeaux, *The Young Evangelicals*; Sweet, 'The Evangelical Tradition in America'; Wells and Woodbridge, eds, *The Evangelicals*; and Woodbridge et al., *The Gospel in America.*

41 A pioneering study that traces British-American connections is Noll, *Between Faith and Criticism.*

42 See the following doctoral theses as examples: Burkinshaw, 'Strangers and Pilgrims in Lotus Land'; McKenzie, 'Fundamental-

ism, Christian Unity, and Premillennialism in the Thought of Rowland Victor Bingham (1872–1942)'; and Sawatsky, '"Looking for that Blessed Hope."'

43 The National Association of Evangelicals, for instance, refused to allow denominations to join that wished to maintain membership also in the National Council of Churches and thus was dominated from the beginning by smaller, uniformly evangelical denominations; the Evangelical Fellowship of Canada had no such proscription and welcomed much more leadership from a wider range of denominations. For a comparison of these two organizations, see Stackhouse, 'The National Association of Evangelicals.'

44 For vivid examples, see Randall Balmer, *Mine Eyes Have Seen the Glory*, and Dayton and Johnston, eds, *The Variety of American Evangelicalism*.

45 Particularly apposite examples of this stance were the establishment in 1991 of a Task Force on Canada's Future by the Evangelical Fellowship of Canada and a set of 'citizens' forums' on the national constitutional debate sponsored across Canada by the Citizens for Public Justice.

46 This argument is sustained at greater length in my account of 'The Protestant Experience in Canada since 1945.'

47 See the several articles devoted to this in *ChristianWeek* 4 (20 Nov. 1990), and esp. the piece by Robert Burkinshaw, 'Flourishing in a Secular Lotus Land,' 8–11.

48 David Bebbington claims that 'it is ... quite mistaken to hold (as it has sometimes been held) that Britain escaped a Fundamentalist controversy.' The remainder of his discussion of the conflicts during the interwar years, however, bears out his judgment that the trauma was much more contained, much less dramatic and significant, than in the United States. 'It seems clear,' he concludes, 'that organised Fundamentalism in Britain was a weak force,' and puts it graphically: 'Fundamentalist controversies did exist in Britain, but they were storms in a teacup when compared with the blizzards of invective that swept contemporary America' (*Evangelicalism in Modern Britain* , 182, 224, 227).

49 This characterization of American fundamentalism relies chiefly upon Marsden, *Fundamentalism and American Culture*. A small gesture symbolizes the distancing of the mainstream of Canadian evangelicalism from fundamentalism. The executive committee

of the Evangelical Fellowship of Canada discussed a proposal for the 'Expansion of [the] Evangelical Fellowship of Canada' in 1966 and deliberately deleted terms like 'campaign,' 'enlist,' and 'militant' from the draft (Minutes of 29 Sept. 1966).

50 Gauvreau, *The Evangelical Century,* 12

51 See Stackhouse, 'Respectfully Submitted.'

52 Bebbington, 249. *Evangelicalism in Modern Britain,* See the chapter following this quotation on 'Evangelical Resurgence in the Later Twentieth Century,' 249–70.

53 For helpful sketches of 'American' and 'British' models, see Marty, *The Modern Schism,* and Guinness, *The Gravedigger File,* 107–39.

54 Reported by Reginald W. Bibby in news release no. 11 of 'Project Can90,' 26 March 1991; for a published digest and commentary see the several articles in *ChristianWeek* 5 [16 April 1991]).

55 *A General Theory of Secularization*

56 Oliver, 'The New Canadian Religious Pluralism'

57 See especially the *oeuvre* on this question of Reginald W. Bibby, summarized in the pertinent sections of his *Fragmented Gods.* A confirming study is Little et al., 'Are the Conservative Churches Reaching Canada?' And see Motz, ed., *Reclaiming a Nation.*

58 Brian Stiller of the Evangelical Fellowship of Canada is an important example here, as several publications of the EFC demonstrate, although writings of his in the early 1990s indicate a shift towards the thesis argued here. For an accessible instance of Stiller's thinking 'in process,' see his 'A Personal Coda,' in VanderVennen, ed., *Church and Canadian Culture,* 193–202. At the scholarly level, see Richard Allen, *The Social Passion,* and Ramsay Cook, *The Regenerators.*

59 This is one of the recurring themes of Gauvreau's *The Evangelical Century.*

60 This questioning owes a debt particularly to the interpretations of John Webster Grant, *A Profusion of Spires,* and William Westfall, *Two Worlds.* See also the pertinent essays in VanderVennen, ed., *Church and Canadian Culture.*

61 So Gauvreau, Westfall, Van Die, and others. For an extreme example, John Webster Grant comments on nineteenth-century Ontario: 'A happy death or resigning oneself to untoward circumstances was the solution to the problems of the poor suggested in tract after tract' (*A Profusion of Spires,* 105).

62 Indeed, a wide range of Canadian Christians became more confrontational as they perceived the cultural climate becoming less hospitable towards Christian ideals: see the explicit remarks to this effect regarding the United Church of Canada, at one end of the 'church and culture' scale, and the Mennonites and Pentecostals, arguably towards the other end, in David Lochhead, 'The United Church and the Conscience of the Nation,' William Janzen, 'Mennonites in Canada: Their Relations with and Effect on the Larger Society,' and Wayne Dawes, 'The Pentecostal Assemblies of Canada,' in VanderVennen, ed., *Church and Canadian Culture,* 25–35, 139–53, and 155–63.

63 Further study, especially of the undeniable proliferation of Canadian voluntary organizations since the 1960s, which has been indicated only briefly in this account, would be necessary to substantiate this proposal. For helpful models on the American scene, however, see Wuthnow, *The Restructuring of American Religion* and *The Struggle for America's Soul*; Hunter, *Culture Wars*; and Blumhofer and Mathisen.

64 This question is put also in Stackhouse, 'Whose Dominion?'

65 The social and economic status of evangelicals through the twentieth century is a virtually unexplored field to date, and a question that obviously would complement those raised in this study.

66 See Bentall, 'The Experience of Women in Canadian Evangelicalism,' and Stackhouse, 'Women in Public Ministry in Twentieth-Century Canadian and American Evangelicalism.'

67 This challenge was recognized in part by Ted S. Rendall of Prairie Bible Institute in 'On the Crest of the Wave,' *Prairie Overcomer* 51 (Sept. 1978): 486–92.

68 Implicit warnings in this regard are raised in terms of late *nineteenth*-century Canadian evangelicals by Cook, *The Regenerators*; by Gauvreau, *The Evangelical Century*; by McKillop, *A Disciplined Intelligence*, esp. 205–32; by Marshall, *Secularizing the Faith*; and by Van Die, *An Evangelical Mind.*

Bibliography

The following list does not contain items drawn from the publications and records of the institutions themselves. The notes for each chapter indicate the nature and locations of such sources. Only if an article in one institution's journal describes another institution is it included here.

Airhart, Phyllis D. 'The Eclipse of Revivalist Spirituality: The Transformation of Canadian Methodist Piety, 1884–1925.' Ph.D. diss., University of Chicago, 1985

– *Serving the Present Age: Revivalism, Progressivism, and the Methodist Tradition in Canada.* Montreal and Kingston, Ont.: McGill-Queen's University Press 1992

Allen, Ralph. 'The Hidden Failure of Our Churches.' *Maclean's Magazine,* 25 February 1961: 11–50

Allen, Richard. *The Social Passion: Religion and Social Reform in Canada 1914–28.* Toronto: University of Toronto Press 1971

Anderson, Owen A. 'The Alberta Social Credit Party: An Empirical Analysis of Membership, Characteristics, Participation and Opinions.' Ph.D. diss., University of Alberta, 1972

Anglin, Gerald. 'The Battling Baptist.' *Maclean's* 62 (15 July 1949): 51

Arnon, Ruth Soulé. 'The Christian College.' *History of Education Quarterly* 14 (1974): 235–49

Atter, Gordon Francis. *The Third Force.* Peterborough, Ont.: College Press 1962

Bailey, T.M. *The Covenant in Canada: Four Hundred Years History of The Presbyterian Church in Canada.* Hamilton, Ont.: MacNab Circle 1975

Balmer, Randall. *Mine Eyes Have Seen the Glory: A Journey into the

Evangelical Subculture in America. New York: Oxford University Press 1989

Barber, Marilyn. 'Nationalism, Nativism and the Social Gospel.' In *The Social Gospel in Canada: Papers of the Inter-Disciplinary Conference on the Social Gospel in Canada, March 21–24 1973, at the University of Regina*, ed. Richard Allen, 186–226. Ottawa: National Museums of Canada 1975

Barclay, Oliver R. *Whatever Happened to the Jesus Lane Lot?* Leicester, Eng.: Inter-Varsity Press 1977

Barr, John. *The Dynasty: The Rise and Fall of Social Credit in Alberta*. Toronto: McClelland and Stewart 1974

Barrett, David B., ed. *World Christian Encyclopedia: A Comparative Study of Churches and Religions in the Modern World AD 1900–2000*. Nairobi, Oxford, and London: Oxford University Press 1982

Bartlett, Billy Vick. *A History of Baptist Separatism*. Springfield, Mo.: Roark & Son 1972

Bass, Clarence B. *Backgrounds to Dispensationalism*. Grand Rapids, Mich.: Eerdmans 1960

Beattie, Margaret, et al. *Brief History of the Student Christian Movement in Canada 1921–1974*. N.p.: Student Christian Movement 1975

Bebbington, D.W. *Evangelicalism in Modern Britain: A History from the 1730's to the 1980's*. London: Unwin Hyman 1989

Bentall, Shirley. 'The Experience of Women in Canadian Evangelicalism.' *Ecumenism* 85 (March 1987): 17–19

Beverley, James A. 'National Survey of Baptist Ministers.' In *Baptists in Canada: Search for Identity amidst Diversity*, ed. Jarold K. Zeman, 267–76. Burlington, Ont.: Welch 1980

Bibby, Reginald W. *Fragmented Gods: The Poverty and Potential of Religion in Canada*. Toronto: Irwin 1987

– 'The Secular in the Sacred: A Study of Evangelism as Reflected in Membership Additions to Calgary Evangelical Churches, 1966–1970.' MA thesis, University of Calgary, 1971

– 'Why Conservative Churches *Really* Are Growing: Kelley Revisited.' *Journal for the Scientific Study of Religion* 17 (1978): 129–37

Bibby, Reginald W., and Merlin B. Brinkerhoff. 'The Circulation of the Saints.' In *Religion in Canadian Society*, ed. Stewart Crysdale and Les Wheatcroft, 346–58. Toronto: Macmillan 1976

Bicha, Karel D. 'Prairie Radicals: A Common Pietism.' *Journal of Church and State* 18 (Winter 1976): 79–94

Blumhofer, Edith L., and Joel A. Carpenter, eds. *Twentieth-Century Evangelicalism: A Guide to the Sources*. New York and London: Garland 1990

Blumhofer, Edith, and James Mathisen. *Evangelicals, Voluntary Organizations, and American Public Life*. Forthcoming

Boda, Rexford A. 'Theological Education in Canada.' *Thrust* 14, no. 2 (1982): 12–13

Boon, Harold Watson. 'The Development of the Bible College or Institute in the United States and Canada since 1880 and Its Relationship to the Field of Theological Education in America.' Ed.D. diss., New York University, 1950

Boone, Kathleen C. *The Bible Tells Them So: The Discourse of Protestant Fundamentalism*. Albany: State University of New York Press 1989

Booth, Rodney M. *The Winds of God: The Canadian Church Faces the 1980s*. Geneva: World Council of Churches; Winfield, BC: Wood Lake Books 1982

Bothwell, Robert, Ian Drummond, and John English. *Canada 1900–1945*. Toronto: University of Toronto Press 1987

– *Canada since 1945: Power, Politics, and Provincialism*. Toronto: University of Toronto Press 1981

Boudreau, Joseph A. *Alberta, Aberhart, and Social Credit*. Toronto: Holt, Rinehart, and Winston of Canada 1975

– 'The Medium and the Message of William Aberhart.' *American Review of Canadian Studies* 8 (Spring 1978): 18–30

Brereton, Virginia Lieson. 'The Bible Schools and Conservative Evangelical Higher Education, 1880–1940.' In *Making Higher Education Christian: The History and Mission of Evangelical Colleges in America*, ed. Joel A. Carpenter and Kenneth W. Shipps, 110–36. Grand Rapids, Mich.: Eerdmans 1987

– 'Protestant Fundamentalist Bible Schools, 1882–1940.' Ph.D. diss., Columbia University 1981

Bromiley, G.W. Introduction to *Zwingli and Bullinger*, ed. G.W. Bromiley, 13–46. Philadelphia: Westminster Press 1953

Brown, Craig, ed. *The Illustrated History of Canada*. Toronto: Lester & Orpen Dennys 1987

Bruce, Steve. *Firm in the Faith*. Aldershot, Eng., and Brookfield, Vt.: Gower 1984

– *The Rise and Fall of the New Christian Right: Conservative Protestant Politics in America 1978–1988*. New York: Oxford University Press 1988

Burgess, Stanley, Gary B. McGee, and Patrick H. Alexander, eds. *Dictionary of Pentecostal and Charismatic Movements*. Grand Rapids, Mich.: Zondervan 1988. S.v. 'Jesus Christ.' by W.G. MacDonald and 'Oneness' by D.A. Reed.

Burkinshaw, Robert. 'Conservative Protestantism.' In *Circle of Voices: A History of the Religious Communities of British Columbia*, ed. Charles P. Anderson, Tirthankar Bose, and Joseph I. Richardson, 79–112. Lantzville, BC: Oolichan Books 1983

– 'Strangers and Pilgrims in Lotus Land: Conservative Protestantism in British Columbia, 1917–1981.' Ph.D diss., University of British Columbia, 1988

A Burning Bush in the West: A 30-Year Historical Review of Berean Bible College Commemorating the 30th Anniversary 1948–1978. N.p., n.d.

Buttimer, Twila F. ' "Great Expectations": The Maritime Methodist Church and Church Union, 1925.' MA thesis, University of New Brunswick, 1980

Calderwood, William. 'Pulpit, Press, and Political Reactions to the Ku Klux Klan in Saskatchewan.' In *Prophecy and Protest: Social Movements in Twentieth-Century Canada*, ed. Samuel D. Clark, J. Paul Grayson, and Linda M. Grayson, 153–78. Toronto: Gage 1975

Callaway, Bernice. 'From Small Beginnings – Fergus Kirk Needed a Teacher.' *Three Hills Capital*, 12 April 1972. Vertical file, Prairie Bible Institute

– 'Prairie Celebrates Jubilee Year.' *The Enquirer*, December 1971. Vertical file, Prairie Bible Institute

Canadian Who's Who, 1952–4 ed. S.v. 'Shields, Rev. Thomas Todhunter.'

Cann, Roger. 'What Is the CCC?' *International Review of Mission* 71 (July 1982): 312–13

Carder, W.G. 'Controversy in the Baptist Convention of Ontario and Quebec, 1908–1929.' BD thesis, McMaster Divinity College, 1950

– 'Controversy in the Baptist Convention of Ontario and Quebec, 1908–1928.' *Foundations* 16 (1973): 355–76

Carpenter, Joel A. 'From Fundamentalism to the New Evangelical Coalition.' In *Evangelicalism and Modern America*, ed. George Marsden, 3–16. Grand Rapids, Mich.: Eerdmans 1984

– 'The Fundamentalist Leaven and the Rise of an Evangelical United Front.' In *The Evangelical Tradition in America*, ed. Leanard I. Sweet, 257–88. Macon, Ga.: Mercer University Press 1984
– ' "A Shelter in a Time of Storm": Fundamentalist Institutions and the Rise of Evangelical Protestantism.' *Church History* 49 (March 1980): 62–75
Carpenter, Joel A., and Kenneth W. Shipps, eds. *Making Higher Education Christian: The History and Mission of Evangelical Colleges in America*. Grand Rapids, Mich.: Eerdmans 1987
Chalmers, Randolph C., and John Webster Grant. 'The United Church of Canada: Its Way of Experiencing and Expressing the Ultimate Reality and Meaning.' *Ultimate Reality and Meaning* 1 (1978): 100–14
Chard, Margaret Joan. 'Literature of the Evangelicals.' MA thesis, Dalhousie University, 1967
Charlton, Warren. 'Dr. John McNichol and Toronto Bible College.' Paper submitted at University of Toronto, n.d.
Clark, S.D. *Church and Sect in Canada*. Toronto: University of Toronto Press 1948
– *The Developing Canadian Community*. 2nd ed. Toronto: University of Toronto Press 1968
Clifford, N. Keith. 'His Dominion: A Vision in Crisis.' In *Religion and Culture in Canada / Religion et Culture au Canada*, ed. Peter Slater, 23–41. Waterloo, Ont.: Wilfrid Laurier University Press for the Canadian Society for the Study of Religion 1977. Originally in *Studies in Religion / Sciences religieuses* 2 (1973): 315–26
– *The Resistance to Church Union in Canada 1904–1939*. Vancouver: University of British Columbia Press 1985
– 'The United Church of Canada and Doctrinal Confession.' *Touchstone* 2 (May 1984): 6–21
Coad, F. Roy. *A History of the Brethren Movement*. Greenwood, SC: Attic; Exeter, Eng.: Paternoster 1976
Cochrane, John. 'The Effect of Increased Education – and a Proposal!' *Calling* 7 (Fall 1965): 9–11
Coggan, F.D., ed. *Christ and the Colleges: A History of the Inter-Varsity Fellowship of Evangelical Unions*. London: Inter-Varsity Fellowship of Evangelical Unions 1934
Cook, Ramsay. *The Regenerators: Social Criticism in Late Victorian English Canada*. Toronto: University of Toronto Press 1985

Cook, Ramsay, D.G. Creighton, and W.L. Morton, eds. *The Canadian Centenary Series*. Toronto: McClelland and Stewart 1963–88

Cronmiller, Carl Raymond. *A History of the Lutheran Church in Canada*. N.p.: Evangelical Lutheran Synod of Canada 1961

Cross, F.L., and E.A. Livingstone, eds. *The Oxford Dictionary of the Christian Church*. 2nd ed. Oxford: Oxford University Press 1974 S.v. 'Evangelicalism'

Crysdale, Stewart, and Les Wheatcroft, eds. *Religion in Canadian Society*. Toronto: Maclean-Hunter for Macmillan 1976

Davidson, Roy L. *God's Plan on the Prairies*. Three Hills, Alta.: By the author, 1986

Davies, Robertson. 'Keeping Faith.' *Saturday Night* 102 (January 1987): 187–92

Davis, Kenneth R. 'New Directions in Bible College Education.' *Thrust* 12, no. 3 (1980): 10–11

Dayton, Donald W., and Robert K. Johnston, eds. *The Variety of American Evangelicalism*. Knoxville: University of Tennessee Press; Downers Grove, Ill.: InterVarsity Press 1991

De Groot, Paul. 'Bible School Exemplifies Prairie Faith.' *Edmonton Journal*, 5 January 1985. Vertical file, Prairie Bible Institute

Dollar, George W. *The Fight for Fundamentalism: American Fundamentalism, 1973–1983*. Sarasota, Fla.: By the author, 1983

– *A History of Fundamentalism in America*. Greenville, SC: Bob Jones University Press 1973

Donald, Melvin V. *History of Canadian Inter-Varsity Christian Fellowship, 1928–1983*. Toronto: Inter-Varsity Christian Fellowship of Canada 1983. Photocopy

– 'A Spreading Tree: A History of Inter-Varsity Christian Fellowship of Canada 1928–29 to 1988–89.' Unpublished ms. 1991.

Dozois, John Donald Egide. 'Dr. Thomas Todhunter Shields (1873–1955) in the Stream of Fundamentalism.' BD thesis, McMaster Unversity, 1963

Elliot, David Raymond.'The Dispensational Theology and Political Ideology of William Aberhart.' MA thesis, University of Calgary, 1975

– 'Studies of Eight Canadian Fundamentalists.' Ph.D. diss., University of British Columbia, 1989

Elliott, David R., and Iris Miller. *Bible Bill: A Biography of William Aberhart*. Edmonton: Reidmore Books 1987

Ellis, Walter E. 'Baptists and Radical Politics in Western Canada (1920–1950).' In *Baptists in Canada: Search for Identity amidst*

Diversity, ed. Jarold K. Zeman, 161–82. Burlington, Ont.: Welch 1980
- *Can the God of the Desert Grow Grapes?: A Study of Toronto Baptists*. N.p., n.d.
- 'Gilboa to Ichabod: Social and Religious Factors in the Fundamentalist-Modernist Schisms among Canadian Baptists, 1895–1934.' *Foundations* 20 (1977): 109–26
- 'Social and Religious Factors in the Fundamentalist-Modernist Schisms among Baptists in North America, 1895–1934.' Ph.D. diss., University of Pittsburgh, 1974
- 'What the Times Demand: Brandon College and Baptist Higher Education in Western Canada.' In *Canadian Baptists and Christian Higher Education*, ed. G.A. Rawlyk, 63–87. Kingston and Montreal: McGill-Queen's University Press 1988

Elwell, Walter A., ed. *Evangelical Dictionary of Theology*. Grand Rapids, Mich.: Baker 1984

Encyclopedia of the Social Sciences, 1938 ed. S.v. 'Fundamentalism' by H. Richard Niebuhr

Epp, Margaret. *Into All the World: The Story of the Missionary Outreach of Prairie Bible Institute*. Foreword by L.E. Maxwell. Three Hills, Alta.: Prairie Press 1973

Estep, William R. *The Anabaptist Story*. Rev. ed. Grand Rapids, Mich.: Eerdmans 1975

Evenson, George O. *Adventuring for Christ: The Story of the Evangelical Lutheran Church of Canada*. Calgary: Foothills Lutheran Press 1974

Expo67: Official Guide. Toronto: Maclean-Hunter 1967

'*Faith Today* 1992 Christian Higher Education Guide.' *Faith Today* 10 (January 1992): 33–50

Falwell, Jerry, et al. *The Fundamentalist Phenomenon: The Resurgence of Conservative Christianity*. Garden City, NY: Doubleday 1981

Ferguson, Sinclair B., et al., eds. *New Dictionary of Theology*. Downers Grove, Ill.; Leicester, Eng.: InterVarsity Press 1988

Fitch, William J. 'Canada's Fragmented Evangelicals.' *Prairie Overcomer* 41 (February 1968): 53–5
- 'Regent College Challenges Secular Scholarship.' *Thrust* 2 (October 1969): 9–14

Flanagan, Thomas E. 'Social Credit in Alberta: A Canadian "Cargo Cult"?' *Archives de Sociologie des Religions* 34 (1972): 39–48

Foster, Charles Melvin. 'Protestant Evangelism in French Canada.' BD thesis, McMaster University, 1950
Foster, Franklin Lloyd. 'The 1921 Alberta Provincial Election: A Consideration of Factors Involved with Particular Attention to Overtones of Millennialism within the U.F.A. and Other Reform Movements of the Period.' MA thesis, Queen's University at Kingston, 1977
Fowler, Robert Booth. *A New Engagement: Evangelical Political Thought 1966–1976*. Grand Rapids, Mich.: Eerdmans 1982
French, Goldwin. 'The Evangelical Creed in Canada.' In *The Shield of Achilles: Aspects of Canada in the Victorian Age*, ed. W.L. Morton, 15–35. Toronto and Montreal: McClelland and Stewart 1968
Gasque, W. Ward. 'Christian Higher Education in Canada.' *Thrust* 6 (July 1974): 14–15
Gauvreau, Michael. 'Beyond the Half-Way House: Evangelicalism and the Shaping of English Canadian Culture.' *Acadiensis* 20 (1991): 158–77
– *The Evangelical Century: College and Creed in English Canada from the Great Revival to the Great Depression*. Kingston and Montreal: McGill-Queen's University Press 1991
– 'History and Faith: A Study of Aspects of Presbyterian and Methodist Thought in Canada, 1820–1940.' Ph.D. diss., University of Toronto, 1985
– 'Protestantism Transformed: Personal Piety and the Evangelical Social Vision, 1815–1867.' In *The Canadian Protestant Experience 1760–1990*, ed. George A. Rawlyk, 48–97. Burlington, Ont.: Welch 1990
– 'The Taming of History: Reflections on the Methodist Encounter with Biblical Criticism, 1830–1890.' *Canadian Methodist Historical Society Papers* 3 (1983): 1–38
– 'War, Culture, and the Problem of Religious Certainty: Methodist and Presbyterian Church Colleges, 1914–1930.' *Journal of the Canadian Church Historical Society* 29 (April 1987): 12–31
Gerbrandt, H.J. 'The Conference of Mennonities in Canada.' In *Call to Faithfulness: Essays in Canadian Mennonite Studies*, ed. Henry Poettcker and Rudy A. Regehr, 81–91. Winnipeg: Canadian Mennonite Bible College 1972
Goertz, Donald Aaron. 'The Development of a Bible Belt: The Socio-Religious Interaction in Alberta between 1925 and 1938.' MCS thesis, Regent College, Vancouver, 1980

Grant, John Webster. *The Church in the Canadian Era*. Rev. ed. Burlington, Ont.: Welch 1988
- 'The Churches in Canadian Space and Time.' *Mid-Stream* 22 (July/October 1983): 354–62
- 'Leading a Horse to Water: Reflections on Church Union Conversations in Canada.' In *Studies of the Church in History*, ed. Horton Davies, 165–81. Allison Park, Pa.: Pickwick 1983
- *A Profusion of Spires: Religion in Nineteenth-Century Ontario*. Toronto: University of Toronto Press 1988
- 'The United Church and Its Heritage in Evangelism.' *Touchstone* 1 (October 1983): 6–13

Gray, James H. 'Miracle at Three Hills.' *Maclean's Magazine*, 15 December 1947: 16–56

Grow a Campus Booktable. Downers Grove, Ill.: InterVarsity Press, n.d.

'Growing Churches in the Sixth Decade 1968–1978.' *The Pentecostal Testimony*, September 1978: 4–7

Guenther, Victor J. 'A Case Study in Policy Making: The Trinity College Act (1977, 1979).' Doctoral paper, University of British Columbia, 1984. Photocopy

Guinness, Os. *The Gravedigger File: Papers on the Subversion of the Modern Church*. Downers Grove, Ill.: InterVarsity Press 1983

Hamm, Peter M. *Continuity and Change among Canadian Mennonite Brethren*. Waterloo, Ont.: Wilfrid Laurier University Press 1987

Handy, Robert T. 'Fundamentalism and Modernism in Perspective.' *Religion in Life* 24 (Summer 1955): 381–4
- *A History of the Churches in the United States and Canada*. Oxford: Oxford University Press 1976
- 'The Influence of Canadians on Baptist Theological Education in the United States.' *Foundations* 23 (1980): 42–56

Hanson, Calvin B. *From Hardship to Harvest*. Edmonton: Evangelical Free Church of Canada 1984
- *On the Raw Edge of Faith*. N.p., n.d.
- *The Trinity Story*. Minneapolis: Free Church Press 1983

Hanson, Muriel. *Fifty Years and Seventy Places: The Story of the Evangelical Free Church in Canada*. Minneapolis: Free Church Publications 1967

Harder, Ben. 'The Bible Institute-College Movement in Canada.' *Journal of the Canadian Church Historical Society* 19 (April 1980): 29–45

Harris, J.E. *The Baptist Union of Western Canada: A Centennial History, 1873–1973.* Saint John, NB: Lingley Printing, n.d.

Harrop, G. Gerald. 'The Era of the "Great Preacher" among Canadian Baptists.' *Foundations* 23 (1980): 57–70

Harshaw, Josephine Perfect. *When Women Work Together: A History of the Young Women's Christian Association in Canada.* Toronto: Ryerson 1966

Hassey, Janette. *No Time for Silence: Evangelical Women in Public Ministry around the Turn of the Century.* Grand Rapids, Mich.: Zondervan 1986

Hawkes, Paul. 'Pentecostalism in Canada: A History with Implications for the Future.' D.Min. diss., San Francisco Theological Seminary 1982

Hayes, John F. *The Challenge of Change: 50 Years, 1912–1962.* Toronto: The Downtown Churchworkers' Association [1963]

Hill, Mary Bulmer Reid. 'From Sect to Denomination in the Baptist Church in Canada.' Ph.D. diss., State University of New York at Buffalo 1971

Hiller, Harry H. 'Continentalism and the Third Force in Religion.' *Canadian Journal of Sociology* 3 (Spring 1978): 183–207

Hills, James W.L. 'How It All Began: The Birth and Growth of Inter-Varsity.' *His* 40 (April 1980): 29–31

Hoffman, Richard. 'Institute Bids Leader Farewell.' *Calgary Herald,* 12 February 1984. Vertical file, Prairie Bible Institute

Holmes, Arthur F. *The Idea of a Christian College.* Rev. ed. Grand Rapids, Mich.: Eerdmans 1987

Hordern, William E. 'Interrelation and Interaction between Reformation Principles and the Canadian Context.' In *In Search of Identity: A Look at Lutheran Identity in Canada,* ed. Norman J. Threinen, 19–32. Winnipeg: Lutheran Council in Canada 1977

Houston, James M. 'A New Venture in Christian Education.' *Calling* 9 (Fall 1967): 16–18

– 'Regent College, Vancouver: A New Venture in Christian Scholarship.' *Thrust* 1 (January 1969): 2–8

Howard, David M. *The Dream That Would Not Die: The Birth and Growth of the World Evangelical Fellowship 1846–1986.* Exeter, Eng.: Paternoster 1986

Hudson, Winthrop S. 'The Interrelationships of Baptists in Canada and the United States.' *Foundations* 23 (1980): 22–41

Hunt, Keith and Gladys. *For Christ and the University: The Story of*

InterVarsity Christian Fellowship of the U.S.A. 1940–1990. Downers Grove, Ill.: InterVarsity Press 1991

Hunter, James Davison. *Culture Wars: The Struggle to Define America.* New York: Basic Books 1991

'Huntley Street Covers the Continent.' *Faith Today* 4 (November–December 1986): 58

Hutchison, William R. *The Modernist Impulse in American Protestantism.* New York: Oxford University Press 1976

Hylson-Smith, Kenneth. *Evangelicals in the Church of England 1734–1984.* Edinburgh: T. & T. Clark 1988

Irving, John A. 'The Evolution of the Social Credit Movement.' *Canadian Journal of Economics and Political Science* 14 (1948): 321–41. Repr. in *Prophecy and Protest: Social Movements in Twentieth-Century Canada,* ed. Samuel D. Clark, J. Paul Grayson, and Linda M. Grayson, 130–52. Toronto: Gage Educational Publishing 1975

– *The Social Credit Movement in Alberta.* Toronto: University of Toronto Press 1959

Ivison, Stuart. 'Is There a Canadian Baptist Tradition?' In *The Churches and the Canadian Experience: A Faith and Order Study of the Christian Tradition,* ed. John Webster Grant, 53–68. Toronto: Ryerson Press 1963

Jacquet, Constant H., ed. *Yearbook of American and Canadian Churches 1986.* Nashville, Tenn.: Abingdon Press 1986

Jantz, Harold. 'Let God Be Supreme First in Us.' *Christian Week* 6 (26 May 1992): 6

– 'Proposing Christian Principles for a Country in Turmoil.' *ChristianWeek* 6 (26 May 1992): 1, 4

Johnson, Douglas. *Contending for the Faith: A History of the Evangelical Movement in the Universities and Colleges.* Leicester, Eng.: Inter-Varsity Press 1979

Jones, Lawrence Neale. 'The Inter-Varsity Christian Fellowship in the United States: A Study of Its History, Theology, and Relations with Other Groups.' Ph.D. diss., Yale University, 1961

Kehler, Larry. 'Inter-Church Relationships.' In *Call to Faithfulness: Essays in Canadian Mennonite Studies,* ed. Henry Poettcker and Rudy A. Regehr, 117–28. Winnipeg: Canadian Mennonite Bible College 1972

Keller, W. Phillip. *Expendable!: With God on the Prairies, the Ministry of Prairie Bible Institute, Three Hills, Alberta, Canada.* Three Hills, Alta.: Prairie Press 1966

Kirkey, Donald L. '"Building the City of God": The Founding of the Student Christian Movement of Canada.' MA thesis, McMaster University 1983

Klassen, William. 'Mennonites in Canada: Taking Their Place in Society.' *International Review of Mission* 71 (July 1982): 315–19

Kleinsteuber, R. Wayne. *More than a Memory: The Renewal of Methodism in Canada.* N.p.: Light and Life Press Canada 1984

Kulbeck, Gloria G. *What God Hath Wrought: A History of the Pentecostal Assemblies of Canada.* Ed. Walter E. McAlister and George R. Upton. Foreword by A.G. Ward. Toronto: Pentecostal Assemblies of Canada 1958

Kydd, Ronald A.N. 'The Pentecostal Assemblies of Canada and Society.' *Canadian Society of Church History Papers* (1972–3): 1–15 and i–viii.

– 'Pentecostals, Charismatics and the Canadian Denoninations.' *Eglise et Théologie* 13 (1982): 211–31

Laverty, Susan M. 'The Jesus Movement: A Critical Assessment.' M.Div. thesis, Acadia Divinity College, 1975

Levy, George E. *The Baptists of the Maritime Provinces: 1753–1946.* Saint John, NB: Barnes-Hopkins 1946

Levy, I. Judson. 'Canadian Baptist Ecumenical Relationships.' *Foundations* 23 (1980): 84–96

Liebman, Robert C., and Robert Wuthnow, eds. *The New Christian Right: Mobilization and Legitimation.* New York: Aldine 1983

Little, Ken, et al. 'Are the Conservative Churches Reaching Canada?' *His Dominion* 4 (Spring 1977): 12–13

McCarville, Des. 'The SCM: A Very Brief History.' Paper presented to the Central Regional Conference of the Student Christian Movement of Canada, 28–29 January 1978. Photocopy

McGovern, Marcia A. 'The Woman's Christian Temperance Union Movement in Saskatchewan, 1886–1930: A Regional Perspective of [sic] the International White Ribbon Movement.' MA thesis, University of Regina, 1977

McKenzie, Brian A. 'A History of the Toronto Bible College (1984–1968): A Study in Canadian Fundamentalism.' Doctoral paper, University of Toronto, June 1982

– 'Fundamentalism, Christian Unity, and Premillennialism in the Thought of Rowland Victor Bingham (1872–1942): A Study of Anti-Modernism in Canada.' Ph.D. diss., University of Toronto, 1985

Mackey, Lloyd. 'Canadian Churches Gain Independence from Their US Counterparts.' *Christianity Today* 28 (14 December 1984): 70–1

McKillop, A.B. *A Disciplined Intelligence: Critical Inquiry and Canadian Thought in the Victorian Era.* Montreal: McGill-Queen's University Press 1979

McLaren, Ross H. 'The Triple Tradition: The Origins of the Open Brethren in North America.' MA thesis, Vanderbilt University, 1982

MacLeod, A. Donald. 'Inter-Varsity in Canada: The First Fifty Years.' *His* 39 (January 1979): 24–6

Macleod, Henry Gordon. 'The Transformation of the United Church of Canada, 1946–1977: A Study in the Sociology of the Denomination.' Ph.D. diss., University of Toronto, 1980

McLoughlin, William G., ed. *The American Evangelicals: 1800–1900.* New York: Torchbooks 1968

McNaught, Kenneth. *The Penguin History of Canada.* Rev. ed. London: Penguin 1988

McNeill, John T. *The History and Character of Calvinism.* Oxford: Oxford University Press 1954

Macpherson, Crawford B. *Democracy in Alberta: Social Credit and the Party System.* Toronto: University of Toronto Press 1962

MacRae, Arthur. 'A History of the Evangelical Movement in the Canadas, 1840–1880: With Special Emphasis on Evangelical Principles in Anglican Theological Education.' STM thesis, McGill University, 1961

Mainse, David, with David Manuel. *God Keep Our Land: A Salute to Canada.* Toronto: Mainroads Productions 1981

Mallish, H.L. 'A Socio-Historical Study of the Legislature of Alberta, 1905–1967.' Ph.D. diss., University of Alberta, 1970

Mann, W.E. *Sect, Cult, and Church in Alberta.* Toronto: University of Toronto Press 1955

Manning, Harry. 'Changes in Evangelism within the Methodist Church in Canada during the Time of Carman and Chown, 1884–1925: A Study of The Causes for the Shifts in Evangelism.' Th.M. thesis, Toronto School of Theology, 1975

Marsden, George M. 'The Evangelical Denomination.' In *Evangelicalism and Modern America*, ed. George M. Mardsen, vii–xix. Grand Rapids, Mich.: Eerdmans 1984

– 'Everyone One's Own Interpreter?: The Bible, Science, and Authority in Mid-Nineteenth Century America.' In *The Bible in America:*

Essays in Cultural History, ed. Nathan O. Hatch and Mark A. Noll, 79–100. New York and Oxford: Oxford University Press 1982

– *Fundamentalism and American Culture: The Shaping of Twentieth Century Evangelicalism 1870–1925*. New York and Oxford: Oxford University Press 1980

– *Understanding Fundamentalism and Evangelicalism*. Grand Rapids, Mich.: Eerdmans 1991

– ed. *Evangelicalism and Modern America*. Grand Rapids, Mich.: Eerdmans 1984

Marshall, David B. *Secularizing the Faith: Canadian Protestant Clergy and the Crisis of Belief, 1850–1940*. Toronto: University of Toronto Press 1992

Martens, Hildegard M. 'Accommodation and Withdrawal: The Response of Mennonites in Canada to World War II.' *Social History* 7 (1974): 306–27

Martin, David. *A General Theory of Secularization*. New York: Harper & Row 1978

Marty, Martin E. *The Modern Schism: Three Paths to the Secular*. New York and Evanston, Ill.: Harper & Row 1969

– *A Nation of Behavers*. Chicago and London: University of Chicago Press 1976

– *Religious Crises in Modern America*. Waco, Tex.: Baylor University Press 1981

Marty, Martin E., and Scott Appleby. 'The Fundamentalism Project: A User's Guide.' In *Fundamentalisms Observed*, ed. Martin E. Marty and Scott Appleby, vii–xiii. Chicago: University of Chicago Press 1991

Masters, D.C. *Protestant Church Colleges in Canada*. Toronto: University of Toronto Press 1966

– 'The Rise of Liberalism in Canadian Protestant Churches.' Canadian Catholic Historical Association *Study Sessions* (1969): 27–39

May, George S. 'Des Moines University and Dr. T.T. Shields.' *Iowa Journal of History* 54 (July 1956): 193–232

Meiklejohn, J.W. 'Mary Slessor.' In *The New International Dictionary of the Christian Church*, rev. ed., ed. J.D. Douglas, 908. Grand Rapids, Mich.: Zondervan 1978

Merton, Robert K. *Social Theory and Social Structure*. Enlarged ed. New York: Free Press; London: Collier-Macmillan 1968

Moir, John S. *Enduring Witness: A History of the Presbyterian Church in Canada*. Special ed. N.p., [1974]

– *A History of Biblical Studies in Canada: A Sense of Proportion.* Society of Biblical Literature series on *Biblical Scholarship in North America*, no. 7. Chico, Calif.: Scholars Press 1982
– 'Sectarian Tradition in Canada.' In *The Churches and the Canadian Experience*, ed. John Webster Grant, 119–32. Toronto: Ryerson 1963
– 'The Smouldering Bush: The Presbyterian Church in Canada Faces Its Second Century.' *Chelsea Journal* 2 (March–April 1976): 97–9
Mol, Hans [J.]. *Faith and Fragility: Religion and Identity in Canada.* Burlington, Ont.: Trinity 1985
Moore, R. Laurence. *Religious Outsiders and the Making of Americans.* New York: Oxford University Press 1986
Morrison, Charles Clayton. 'The Fundamentalist Fiasco.' *Christian Century* 46 (22 May 1929): 672–4
Morton, Desmond. 'Strains of Affluence (1945–1987).' In *The Illustrated History of Canada*, ed. Craig Brown, 467–543. Toronto: Lester & Orpen Dennys 1987
Motz, Arnell, ed. *Reclaiming a Nation: The Challenge of Re-Evangelizing Canada by the Year 2000.* Richmond, BC: Church Leadership Library 1990
Moyles, R.G. *The Blood and Fire in Canada: A History of the Salvation Army in the Dominion 1882–1976.* Toronto: Peter Martin Associates 1977
Muddle, A.H. 'Prairie Missionary Fund Gives Out 3.5 Million.' *Three Hills Capital*, 12 April 1972: 14. Vertical file, Prairie Bible Institute
Murray, Iain H. *David Martyn Lloyd-Jones: The First Forty Years 1899–1939.* Edinburgh, Scot.; Carlisle, Pa.: Banner of Truth Trust 1982
Murray, J.M. 'Fishing at Expo.' *Prairie Overcomer* 40 (November 1967): 402–5
Nadeau, David. 'College Seeks to Upgrade.' *Faith Today* 9 (January 1991): 59–60
Neuhaus, Richard John, ed. *The Bible, Politics, and Democracy.* Encounter Series no. 5. Grand Rapids, Mich.: Eerdmans 1987
Neuhaus, Richard John, and Michael Cromartie, eds. *Piety and Politics: Evangelicals and Fundamentalists Confront the World.* Washington: Ethics and Public Policy Center 1987
Noll, Mark A. *Between Faith and Criticism: Evangelicals, Scholarship, and the Bible in America.* San Francisco: Harper & Row 1986
– ed. *The Princeton Theology 1812–1921: Scripture, Science, and*

Theological Method from Archibald Alexander to Benjamin Breckinridge Warfield. Grand Rapids, Mich.: Baker Book House 1983

Oliver, Dennis Mackintosh. 'The New Canadian Religious Pluralism.' Paper delivered to the Canadian Society of Church History, Saskatoon, Sask., 1 June 1979

'101 Reasons to Prepare for Life and Ministry in Canada.' *Faith Alive* 3 (November 1985): 36–54

O'Neil, Leonard F. 'A Survey of the Bible Schools in Canada.' BD thesis, McMaster University, Hamilton, Ont., 1949

O'Toole, Roger, et al. 'The United Church in Crisis: A Sociological Perspective on the Dilemmas of a Mainstream Denomination.' *Studies in Religion / Sciences religieuses* 20 (Spring 1991): 151–63

Packer, J.I. *'Fundamentalism' and the Word of God: Some Evangelical Principles*. London: Inter-Varsity Press 1958

Parent, Mark. 'The Christology of T.T. Shields: The Irony of Fundamentalism.' Ph.D. diss., McGill University, 1991

Paul, Gerald Walton. 'The Board of Evangelism and Social Service of the United Church of Canada: An Historical Analysis of the Enterprises of the Board from 1925 to 1968.' M.Th. thesis, Vancouver School of Theology, 1974

Perkin, James R.C. 'Many Confessions, One Creed.' *Foundations* 23 (1980): 71–83

Peters, Erna Alma. *The Contribution to Education by the Pentecostal Assemblies of Canada*. Altona, Man.: By the author, 1971

Pfrimmer, David. 'A Lutheran Witness in Canadian Society.' In *Church and Canadian Culture*, ed. Robert E. VanderVennen, 125–37. Lanham, Md.: University Press of America 1991

Phillips, David. 'The History of the Inter-Varsity Christian Fellowship in Western Canada.' MCS thesis, Regent College, Vancouver, 1976

Pinnock, Clark H. 'The Modernist Impulse at McMaster University, 1887–1927.' In *Baptists in Canada: Search for Identity amidst Diversity*, ed. Jarold K. Zeman, 193–207. Burlington, Ont.: Welch 1980

Pousett, Gordon H. 'A History of the Convention of Baptist Churches of British Columbia.' M.Th. thesis, Vancouver School of Theology, 1982

– 'The History of the Regular Baptists of British Columbia.' BD thesis, McMaster University, 1956

Prang, Margaret. '"The Girl God Would Have Me Be": The CGIT, 1915–39.' *Canadian Historical Review* 66 (June 1985): 154–84

Quebedeaux, Richard. *The Young Evangelicals: Revolution in Orthodoxy.* New York: Harper & Row 1974

Rawlyk, George A. 'A L. McCrimmon, H.P. Whidden, T.T. Shields, Christian Higher Education, and McMaster University.' In *Canadian Baptists and Christian Higher Education*, ed. G.A. Rawlyk, 31–62. Kingston and Montreal: McGill-Queen's University Press 1988

– ed. *The Canadian Protestant Experience 1760–1990.* Burlington, Ont.: Welch 1990

– 'The Champions of the Oppressed? Canadian Baptists and Social, Political and Economic Realities.' In *Church and Canadian Culture*, ed. Robert E. VanderVennen, 105–23. Lanham, Md.: University Press of America 1991

– *Champions of the Truth: Fundamentalism, Modernism, and the Maritime Baptists.* Montreal and Kingston: McGill-Queen's University Press 1990

Rawlyk, George, and Kevin Quinn. *The Redeemed of the Lord Say So: A History of Queen's Theological College, 1912–72.* Kingston, Ont.: Queen's Theological College 1980

Reed, Joseph W., and William Klempa. 'An Enduring Witness: The Work and Outreach of the Presbyterian Church in Canada.' *International Review of Mission* 71 (July 1982): 287–94

Regehr, Rudy A. 'A Century of Private Schools.' In *Call to Faithfulness: Essays in Canadian Mennonite Studies*, ed. Henry Poettcker and Rudy A. Regehr, 103–15. Winnipeg: Canadian Mennonite Bible College 1972

Regehr, T.D. 'Mennonites and the New Jerusalem in Western Canada.' In *Visions of the New Jerusalem: Religious Settlement on the Prairies*, ed. Benjamin G. Smillie, 109–20. Edmonton: NeWest Press 1983

Reid, Daniel G., et al., eds. *Dictionary of Christianity in America.* Downer Grove, Ill.: InterVarsity Press 1990

Reid, W. Stanford. 'Calvin's Influence in Canada.' In *John Calvin: His Influence in the Western World*, ed. W. Stanford Reid, 309–21. Grand Rapids, Mich.: Zondervan 1982

Reimers, Al. *God's Country: Charismatic Renewal.* Toronto: Welch 1979

Rendall, Ted S. 'On the Crest of the Wave.' *Prairie Overcomer* 51 (September 1978): 486–92

Rennie, Ian S. 'Conservatism in the Presbyterian Church in Canada in 1925 and Beyond: An Introductory Exploration.' *Canadian Society of Presbyterian Church History Papers*, 1982, n.p.
– 'The Doctrine of Man in the Canadian Bible Belt.' N.p., 1973. Photocopy
– 'Gratitude for the Past.' *Evangelical Recorder* 90 (Spring 1984): 6–11
– 'Theological Education in Canada: Past and Present.' Paper presented at Ontario Bible College, Toronto, 1974. Photocopy
– 'The Western Prairie Revival in Canada: During the Depression and World War II.' N.p., n.d. Photocopy
Richards, John B. *Baptists in British Columbia: A Struggle to Maintain 'Sectarianism.'* Vancouver: Northwest Baptist Theological College and Seminary 1977
Riss, Richard Michael. 'The Latter Rain Movement of 1948 and the Mid-Twentieth Century Evangelical Awakening.' MCS thesis, Regent College, Vancouver, 1979
– *A Survey of Twentieth-Century Revival Movements in North America*. Peabody, Mass.: Hendrickson 1988
Ross, John Arthur. 'Regionalism, Nationalism and Social Gospel Support in the Ecumenical Movement of Canadian Presbyterianism.' Ph.D. diss., McMaster University, 1973
Rouse, Ruth, and Stephen Charles Neill, eds. *A History of the Ecumenical Movement, 1517–1948*. 2nd rev. ed. Philadelphia: Westminster Press 1967
Rusch, William G. *Ecumenism: A Movement toward Church Unity*. Philadelphia: Fortress Press 1985
Russell, C. Allyn. 'Thomas Todhunter Shields, Canadian Fundamentalist.' *Ontario History* 70 (1978): 263–80
Sandeen, Ernest R. 'The Fundamentals: The Last Flowering of the Millenarian-Conservative Alliance.' *Journal of Presbyterian History* 47 (March 1969): 55–73
– *The Roots of Fundamentalism: British and American Millenarianism, 1800–1930*. Chicago: University of Chicago Press 1970; reprint ed., Grand Rapids, Mich.: Baker Book House 1978
Sawatsky, Ronald G. 'The Bible School/College Movement in Canada: Fundamental Christian Training.' *Canadian Society of Church History Papers* (1986): 1–15
– ' "Looking for That Blessed Hope": The Roots of Fundamentalism in Canada, 1878–1914.' Ph.D. diss., University of Toronto, 1985

Schultz, Harold J. 'Portrait of a Premier: William Aberhart.' *Canadian Historical Review* 45 (September 1964): 185–211
– 'William Aberhart and the Social Credit Party: A Political Biography.' Ph.D. diss., Duke University, 1959
Scott, Randolph Bruce. 'A History of Church Union Conversations between the Anglican Church of Canada and the United Church of Canada.' M.Th. thesis, Toronto Graduate School of Theological Studies, 1966
Semple, Neil. 'The Decline of Revival in Nineteenth Century, Central-Canadian Methodism: The Extraordinary Means of Grace.' *Canadian Methodist Historical Society Papers* 2 (N.d.)
'Sermons from Science.' *Prairie Overcomer* 40 (October 1967): 365–6
Sherwin, William Webster. 'The Church and Penal Reform in Canada.' M.Th. thesis, Victoria University, 1963
Shields, T.T. *The Inside of the Cup*. Toronto: Jarvis Street Baptist Church 1921
– *The Plot That Failed*. Toronto: The Gospel Witness 1937
Sinclair-Faulkner, Tom. 'Theory Divided from Practice: The Introduction of the Higher Criticism into Canadian Protestant Seminaries.' *Studies in Religion / Sciences religieuses* 10 (1981): 321–43
Smillie, Benjamin G. 'The Social Gospel in Canada: A Theological Critique.' In *The Social Gospel in Canada: Papers of the Inter-Disciplinary Conference on the Social Gospel in Canada, March 21–24, 1973, at the University of Regina*, ed. Richard Allen, 317–42. Ottawa: National Museums of Canada 1975
Smith, Timothy L. 'A Shared Evangelical Heritage.' *TSF Bulletin* 10 (November–December 1986): 10–16
Stackhouse, John G., Jr. 'The National Association of Evangelicals, the Evangelical Fellowship of Canada, and the Limits of Evangelical Cooperation.' In *Evangelicals, Voluntary Associations, and American Public Life*, ed. Edith Blumhofer and James Mathisen. Forthcoming
– 'A Paradigm Case: Billy Graham and the Nature of Conversion.' *Studies in Religion / Sciences religieuses* 21 (1992): 337–50
– 'The Protestant Experience in Canada since 1945.' In *The Canadian Protestant Experience 1760–1990*, ed. George A. Rawlyk, 198–252. Burlington, Ont.: Welch 1990
– 'Respectfully Submitted for American Consideration: Canadian Options in Christian Higher Education.' *Faculty Dialogue* no. 17 (1992): 51–71

– 'Thomas Todhunter Shields.' In *Twentieth-Century Shapers of American Popular Religion*, ed. Charles H. Lippy, 393–402. Westport, Conn.: Greenwood Press 1989
– 'What *Should* Christians Want from Higher Education?' *Christian-Week* 5 (18 February 1992): 14
– 'Whose Dominion?: Christianity and Canadian Culture Historically Considered.' *Crux* 28 (June 1992): 29–35
– 'William Aberhart.' In *Twentieth-Century Shapers of American Popular Religion*, ed. Charles H. Lippy, 1–9. Westport, Conn.: Greenwood Press 1989
– 'Women in Public Ministry in Twentieth-Century Canadian and American Evangelicalism: Five Models.' *Studies in Religion / Sciences religieuses* 17 (Fall 1988): 471–85
Stewart, Gordon, and George Rawlyk. *A People Highly Favoured of God: The Nova Scotia Yankees and the American Revolution*. Toronto: Macmillan 1972
Stiller, Brian C., et al. 'Canadian Evangelicals: A Changing Face.' *Faith Alive* 3 (September 1985): 10–17
Stone, C.G., and F. Joan Garnett. *Brandon College: A History, 1899–1967*. Brandon, Man.: Brandon University 1969
Sturm, Harvey. 'Prophet of Righteousness.' *Alberta History* 23 (1975): 21–7
Sweet, Leonard I. 'The Evangelical Tradition in America.' In *The Evangelical Tradition in America*, ed. Leonard I. Sweet, 1–86. Macon, Ga.: Mercer University Press 1984
Tarr, Leslie K. 'Another Perspective on T.T. Shields and Fundamentalism.' In *Baptists in Canada: Search for Identity amidst Diversity*, ed. Jarold K. Zeman, 209–24. Burlington, Ont.: Welch 1980
– 'Bible College Grew from Evening Class.' *Toronto Star*, 3 November 1984: L12
– 'Conservative Churches Grow, but Not by Witnessing, Canadian Researchers Find.' *Christianity Today* 26 (12 November 1982): 95
– *Shields of Canada*. Grand Rapids, Mich.: Baker Book House 1967
– *This Dominion His Dominion: The Story of Evangelical Baptist Endeavour in Canada*. Willowdale, Ont.: Fellowship of Evangelical Baptist Churches in Canada 1968
Thomas, Theodore Elia. 'The Protestant Churches and the Religious Issue in Ontario's Public Schools: A Study in Church and State.' Ph.D. diss., Columbia University, 1972

Thompson, John H. 'The Prohibition Question in Manitoba, 1892–1928.' MA thesis, University of Manitoba, 1969

Thompson, Margaret E. *The Baptist Story in Western Canada.* Calgary: Baptist Union of Western Canada [1974]

Thompson, Retta L.B. *A Goodly Heritage: A Synoptic View of the History of the Woman's Christian Temperance Union of Saskatchewan, Canada 1913–1973.* 3rd ed. Saskatoon, Sask.: Early Mailing Service 1975

Threinen, Norman J. 'The American and European Influences on the Canadian Lutheran Churches.' In *In Search of Identity: A Look at Lutheran Identity in Canada,* ed. Norman J. Threinen, 1–17. Winnipeg: Lutheran Council in Canada 1977

– 'The Churches, the Councils and Campus Ministry.' *Consensus* 5 (April 1979): 22–6

Tipp, Charles A. 'Objections to Unity.' In *One Church, Two Nations?* ed. Philip LeBlanc and Arnold Edinborough, 54–68. Don Mills, Ont.: Longmans 1968

Tonks, A. Ronald. 'The History of the Christian and Missionary Alliance with a Brief Summary of the Work in Canada.' BD thesis, McMaster University, 1958

Toon, Peter. 'Puritans; Puritanism.' In *The New International Dictionary of the Christian Church,* rev. ed., ed. J.D. Douglas, 815. Grand Rapids, Mich.: Zondervan 1978

Trinier, Harold U. *A Century of Service: Story of* The Canadian Baptist, *1854–1954.* N.p.: Board of Publication of the Baptist Convention of Ontario and Quebec, n.d.

VanderVennen, Robert E., ed. *Church and Canadian Culture.* Lanham, Md.: University Press of America 1991

Van Die, Marguerite. *An Evangelical Mind: Nathanael Burwash and the Methodist Tradition in Canada, 1839–1918.* Kingston and Montreal: McGill-Queen's University Press 1989

Van Ginkel, Aileen, ed. *Shaping a Christian Vision for Canada: Discussion Papers on Canada's Future.* Markham, Ont.: Faith Today Publications 1992

Vanoene, W.W.J. *Inheritance Preserved: The Canadian Reformed Churches in Historical Perspective.* Winnipeg: Premier Printing 1975

Walsh, H.H. *The Christian Church in Canada.* Toronto: Ryerson 1956

Warkentin, Henry. 'A History of the Protestant Church in Quebec.'

BD thesis, Waterloo Lutheran Seminary, Waterloo, Ont., 1963

Weber, Hans-Ruedi. 'The Rediscovery of the Laity in the Ecumenical Movement.' In *The Layman in Christian History*, ed. Stephen [C.] Neill and Hans-Reudi Weber, 377–94. London: SCM Press 1963

Weber, Timothy P. *Living in the Shadow of the Second Coming: American Premillennialism*. New York and Oxford: Oxford University Press 1979. Enlarged ed., *Living in the Shadow of the Second Coming: American Premillennialism 1875–1982*. Grand Rapids, Mich.: Zondervan 1983

– 'The Two-Edged Sword: The Fundamentalist Use of the Bible.' In *The Bible in America: Essays in Cultural History*, ed. Nathan O. Hatch and Mark A. Noll, 101–20. New York and Oxford: Oxford University Press 1982

Wells, David F., and John D. Woodbridge, eds. *The Evangelicals: What They Believe, Who They Are, Where They Are Changing*. Rev. ed. Grand Rapids, Mich.: Baker 1977

Westfall, William. *Two Worlds: The Protestant Culture of Nineteenth-Century Ontario*. Kingston and Montreal: McGill-Queen's University Press 1989

Whan, R. Lloyd. 'Premillennialism in Canadian Baptist History.' BD thesis, McMaster University, 1945

Wicks, Donald A. 'T.T. Shields and the Canadian Protestant League, 1941–1950.' MA thesis, University of Guelph, 1971

Wiebe, Jeffrey James. 'Trinity Junior College: Its History, Development and Institutional Mission.' Ph.D. diss., University of North Dakota, 1970

Winks, Robin W. *The Blacks in Canada: A History*. New Haven: Yale University Press 1971

Witmer, S.A. *The Bible College Story: Education with Dimension*. Manhasset, NY: Channel 1962

Woodbridge, John D., Mark A. Noll, and Nathan O. Hatch. *The Gospel in America: Themes in the Story of America's Evangelicals*. Grand Rapids, Mich.: Zondervan 1979

Woods, Bruce A. 'Theological Directions and Cooperation among Baptists in Canada.' In *Canadian Baptist History and Polity: The McMaster Conference*, ed. Murray J.S. Ford, 178–85. Hamilton, Ont.: McMaster University Divinity College, n.d.

Woods, C. Stacey. *The Growth of a Work of God*. Downers Grove, Ill.: InterVarsity Press 1978

Wright, Robert A. 'Breaking Out of the Neo-Liberal Consensus: Historians and Canadian Protestantism in the 1920s and 1930s.' Department of History, Queen's University, Kingston, Ont., June 1986. Photocopy

– 'The Canadian Protestant Tradition 1914–1945.' In *The Canadian Protestant Experience 1760–1990*, ed. George A. Rawlyk, 139–97. Burlington, Ont.: Welch 1990

– *A World Mission: Canadian Protestantism and the Quest for a New International Order 1918–1939*. Montreal and Kingston: McGill-Queen's University Press 1991

Wuthnow, Robert. *The Restructuring of American Religion: Society and Faith since World War II*. Princeton: Princeton University Press 1988

– *The Struggle for America's Soul: Evangelicals, Liberals, and Secularism*. Grand Rapids, Mich.: Eerdmans 1989

Zeman, Jarold K. 'Canada.' In *Baptist Relations with Other Christians*, ed. James Leo Garrett, 105–19. Valley Forge, Pa.: Judson Press 1974

Index

Christian and Missionary Alliance [not to be confused with the Overseas Missionary Fellowship, the new name of the CIM].

An evangelical, evangelistic, and missionary movement, organized by Rev. A.B. Simpson, in New York, in 1887. It stresses "the deeper Christian life and consecration to the Lord's service."

H/Q – New York. Publication Alliance Witness.